Seattle Children's Theatre

SIX PLAYS
FOR
YOUNG AUDIENCES

Smith and Kraus *Books For Actors*
YOUNG ACTORS SERIES

If you require pre-publication information about upcoming Smith and Kraus books, you may receive our semi-annual catalogue, free of charge, by sending your name and address to *Smith and Kraus Catalogue, P.O. Box 127, One Main Street, Lyme, NH 03768.* Or call us at (800) 895-4331, fax (603) 795-4427.

Seattle Children's Theatre

SIX PLAYS
FOR
YOUNG AUDIENCES

MARISA SMITH, EDITOR

Young Actors Series

SK

A Smith and Kraus Book

A Smith and Kraus Book
Published by Smith and Kraus, Inc.
One Main Street, PO Box 127, Lyme, NH 03768

Manufactured in the United States of America
Cover and Text Design by Julia Hill
Cover Photo by Chris Bennion

First Edition: January 1997
10 9 8 7 6 5 4 3 2 1

Library of Congress Cataloging-in-Publication Data

Seattle Children's Theatre: six plays for young audiences /
Marisa Smith, editor. —1st ed.
p. cm. —(Young actors series)
includes bibliographical references
Summary: A collection of plays dealing with family, friendship,
freedom, and courage.
ISBN 1-57525-008-X
1. Children's plays, American—Washington (State)—Seattle.
2. American drama—20th century. [1. Plays—Collections.]
I. Smith, Marisa. II. Series.
PS625.5.S43 1996
812'.540809282—dc20 96-18740
CIP
AC

CONTENTS

PREFACE

Guided by the belief that children deserve professional theatre of the highest quality, Seattle Children's Theatre commissions and develops new plays for young audiences with appeal to people of all ages. This anthology is the first collection of our plays, representing over two decades of world premieres. Our hope in selecting this broad range of work is to showcase some of the infinite ways in which theatre for young people can be defined and made.

At SCT, we strive to develop and produce plays that are aesthetically and culturally diverse. Our repertoire includes adaptations of classic and contemporary literature, as well as original plays for the stage. In this volume, there are portraits of many Americas, spanning numerous decades to reveal the wide variety of faces that define us. From a Depression-era rural township to today's affluent suburbia, these plays deal with family, friendship, freedom and courage.

Despite their individuality, there is a common thread strongly woven through each play. Each has at its core a young person attempting to define who he is and where he fits in the world. Whether she is an orphan on a farm, a Native American taken from her family, or a new kid on the block, the young people in these plays use humor, strength, imagination, and resilience to find what we all want—some place on this earth where we can be comfortable, that feels like home.

It would be impossible to fulfill our commitment to bringing children the sophisticated theatrical experiences they so richly deserve without the playwrights who generate the work that is interpreted, directed, designed, and produced. It has been our goal to work both with playwrights who write primarily for young audiences, and at the same time, to introduce new writers to this demanding and rewarding audience.

Seattle Children's Theatre has produced over sixty new plays, with some seasons consisting entirely of premieres. There is no greater theatrical thrill than seeing a play grow from the seedling of a one sentence idea to the living thing called a full production. One of our greatest hopes, however, is to have these plays continue to have a life long after the curtain comes down on SCT's final performance of them. We hope that this collection is a step in strengthening the body of stage literature that is available for young and family audiences, and that you may one day enjoy sharing these plays with your audience as much as we enjoyed sharing them with ours.

To the playwrights...to the plays...and most of all, to the young people who inspire our work.

Linda Hartzell   Deborah Frockt
Artistic Director   *Dramaturg*

INTRODUCTION

Some years back, I was invited to sit in on rehearsals of a couple new productions that Peter Brook was preparing. In each case, at some vital crossroads in the rehearsal period, he would invite an audience of children to see the work. The point of the exercise was clear: If the work and his actors couldn't hold the attention of children, he didn't believe it had the resonance needed to hold an adult audience.

Those of us who have spent most of our careers playing mostly to adults know that reading audience responses can be a bit like reading tea leaves. Into the slightest shifts and sighs, coughs and fidgets we read the most dire of consequences. That's because most adult audiences know what's expected of *them* when they come to the theater. They're often polite to a fault.

That's one of the reasons playing to young audiences can be so exhilarating. They have few preconceptions as to what a theater event should be. They're open to anything and impatient only with what is boring. Boring because it's pretentious or precious or because it panders.

Enter Seattle Children's Theatre. One of the reasons this anthology of plays from Seattle Children's Theatre is so welcome is that these scripts brim with life and invention. They've all seen "active duty," and I can personally testify as to how gripping they are for audiences young and old. They meet, in short, the Peter Brook test.

Even though this volume tells us these plays are "for young audiences," my experience is that they are really meeting places for children and adults. Linda Hartzell and her partners at Seattle Children's Theatre are passionate in their belief that great writing creates great theater. That's why these plays have been commissioned from some of our finest writers. Hartzell has lured many of our top playwrights to the world of children's theater and gotten them hooked (in this volume, that would be Dietz and York) while commissioning exciting new works from leading writers for young people (here represented by Sachar, Sandberg, and Zeder). The results are triumphs of dramatic imagination and, at the same time, they're thoughtful and literate. In other words, they're a joy to *read* as well as to view.

One day I slipped into rehearsals of *The Rememberer,* the first work in this anthology. For playwright Dietz, it was his first work for young audiences. The actors were rehearsing a most moving passage when a devastating wave of influenza has hit, causing many deaths. Actors were slowly crumpling to the floor as the disease hit them. At this moment, Steven leaned over to me, a twinkle in his eyes, and whispered, "So, John, how do you like my kiddie show?" The point, I think, is that young audiences can absorb challenging material if the people preparing it care about that material as the five writers represented here so clearly do. That, in turn, brings us back to the theme of what's involving for young audiences. The world can be a scary place and theater that tries to deny that doesn't really help, anymore than entertainments that flow with mindless violence do. Yes, there are frightening things out there but watching young people on stage working through them, learning how to cope with them through love, courage, and honesty can only help prepare our new generations for the world we're leaving them. And these five savvy playwrights know that these journeys can be lots of fun, too.

The distinction between literature for children and literature for adults is a fairly recent one. A century ago, Robert Louis Stevenson's works were best-sellers alongside those of Tolstoy. Now that children's literature is more ghettoized, I sometimes encounter colleagues who view theater for young people as a lesser creature in the dramatic hierarchy. These plays should prove them wrong again.

Much of this is due to the pioneering work of Linda Hartzell. She's insisted on creating a new model for a theater whose primary focus is young people, one that's free of cuddly creatures and empty diversions. The result has been to thrust her troupe into the forefront of theaters nationwide as an innovator and home to some of the most exciting stage work to be seen anywhere. Each of these plays bears the imprint of her passion for theater that can make a difference in the lives of young people and create a place where young and old can both enjoy great theater.

I think my favorite play in this collection is Dietz' *The Rememberer*. It takes the audience on a journey across time to a fascinating world whose very existence is imperiled. But the struggle of its central character, the Squaxin Indian girl Joyce, to keep her Native American culture intact, to "remember" it as a way to keep it alive is a lesson to us all. Our spiritual legacy, no matter where we come from, is a fragile thing and ultimately it's the young that must carry it forward.

No, wait. I think I have to change my mind here. Louis Sachar's *There's a Boy in the Girls' Bathroom* is just too much fun not to be my favorite in this collection. Was there ever a more heartbreakingly sweet bully as Bradley Chalkers? What a joy to have Sachar bring his wildly popular tale to the stage.

Of course, the carrot-topped and freckled orphan Anne Shirley has been a favorite of generations of readers since she first came vividly alive in L.M. Montgomery's charming *Anne of Green Gables*. So, R.N. Sandberg's witty adaptation which brings turn-of-the-century Prince Edward Island to life is hard to deny as the best in this volume. How can you deny the precocious and wild-spirited Anne's request: "I'll try to do and be anything you want, if only you'll keep me?"

On the other hand, Y York's haunting *Afternoon of the Elves* is easily a candidate for the best work in this ambitious anthology. York's adaptation of Janet Taylor Lisle's Newbery Award-winning book will touch your heart as two young girls from very different backgrounds befriend each other and discover a secret world in the process.

But York has a terrific follow-up punch with *the Portrait the Wind the Chair*. It takes an exuberant look at a vexing modern problem, "latchkey" children. Two sisters, home alone, create an amazing kingdom of imagination and in the process meet one of the most original theater characters I've encountered, the "ChairMan," a fellow well-stuffed for his sit-down part.

Or perhaps my favorite is Suzan Zeder's instant classic *Mother Hicks*. There's witchcraft in the air as a young and homeless girl in the darkest years of the Depression meets the indomitable title character and her friend, an eloquent deaf man named Tuc.

I guess I'll just have to go back and read these plays again to see if I can figure out if I do have a favorite after all. I'll get back to you if I can make up my mind. Until then, you're on your own.

Happy reading.

John Dillon

The Rememberer
by Steven Dietz

"Your ancestors are looking through your eyes when you are carving."
— Al Charles, canoe carver,
Lower Elwha Reservation, 1993.

AUTHOR'S NOTE

Joyce Simmons was born at Mud Bay near Olympia, Washington, on January 31, 1901. She was the third of seven children of Julian Sam Simmons and John D. Simmons.

Lacking a written language, knowledge among these Indian peoples was passed on from one generation to the next through the stories and recollections of a chosen member of the tribe – the "Rememberer." Early in life, Joyce was chosen to succeed her grandfather as the Rememberer among her people.

In 1964, Joyce Simmons Cheeka began to tell her stories to educator and child drama advocate Werdna Phillips Finley. Over the next five years, Ms. Finley taped hundreds of hours of Joyce's memories of growing up as a Squaxin Indian girl in lower Puget Sound. These reminiscences were edited down to a 270 page manuscript titled "As My Sun Now Sets."

Chapter Four of the manuscript deals with Joyce being forcibly taken from her home and placed in the Tulalip Training School, a government run boarding school under the jurisdiction of the Bureau of Indian Affairs.

That is where this play begins.

ORIGINAL PRODUCTION

The Rememberer was originally produced by Seattle Children's Theatre on March 18, 1994. It was directed by Linda Hartzell with the following cast:

RICHARD	Tony Adams
SHERIFF MULLIN/MR. CONRAD	Mark Chamberlin
LONGHOUSE/TWIN RIVER	Cecil P. Cheeka
HENRY/DARIN LONGFEATHER/PITCH WOMAN	Stefan Enriquez
SARAH	Rachel Hobart
DR. BUCHANAN	Craig D. Huisenga
ADULT JOYCE	Jane Lind
LUCAS	Ian LaFontaine
SUPERINTENDENT/MISS BRENNAN	Sharva Maynard
LILLIAN	Danielle J. Moore
DANCER	Rosetta Pintado
MUD BAY SAM	Richard H. Restoule
CHARLES	David Rice
EMILY SAM/AUNT SOPHIE/PITCH WOMAN	Maria Antionette Rogers
YOUNG JOYCE	Christine Pilar Salvador
NURSE WARNER/PITCH WOMAN	Laura Saunders
FRANCES	Ah-Bead-Soot
OTIS	Frank Yaska
ELEANOR	Kimberly Yaska
VOICE OF CHIEF SEATTLE	Stefano LoVerso

CHARACTERS

(5 men, 4 women, 8 children, dancers, musicians)

JOYCE, a twelve-year-old Squaxin Indian girl

ADULT JOYCE, Joyce as a forty-year-old woman

{ EMILY SAM, Joyce's grandmother
  SQUAXIN WOMAN, a distant relative of Joyce's family
  AUNT SOPHIE, a deceased relative of Joyce's
  PITCH WOMAN, a mythical old woman

MUD BAY SAM, Emily Sam's husband, the tribal Rememberer

{ HENRY, Joyce's cousin, twenties
  DARIN LONGFEATHER, a student, seventeen

{ TWIN RIVER, Kwakiutl Indian, employed by the B.I.A
  LONGHOUSE, Henry's father
  CHIEF SEATTLE, a Duwamish Chieftain

{ MULLIN, the county sheriff
  MR. CONRAD, a teacher at the Tulalip Training School

{ SUPERINTENDENT, head of the U.S. Indian Schools, forties
  MISS BRENNAN, a teacher at the school

NURSE WARNER, a nurse at the school, thirties

DR. BUCHANAN, head of the Tulalip Training School

OTIS, a student, six years old

GIRL ONE, student, fifteen

GIRL TWO, student, twelve

YOUNG GIRL, student, eight

BOY ONE, student, thirteen

BOY TWO, student, twelve

YOUNG BOY, student, eight

(Note: pairings indicate suggested actor doubling.)

TIME AND PLACE

1911, and the present. The Squaxin Indian reservation in southern Puget Sound, Washington; and the Tulalip Training School, near Marysville, Washington.

SETTING

A darkly colored, open playing space which will be transformed into a variety of locales. This transformation will be done primarily through lighting, as well as through the use of a few set pieces, as noted. The ability to move quickly from scene to scene, without blackouts, should be the defining principle of the design.

Upstage, a cyclorama envelopes the stage. When lit from the front, the cyclorama features a huge image of Mount Rainier. When actors are lit from behind it, the cyclorama becomes filled with their huge shadows.

The musicians are in plain view, to the side of the stage.

All costumes, masks and props are true both to the era of the play, and to the specific tribe or tribes from which they come.

THE REMEMBERER

ACT ONE

Silence. The stage is bare, except for a large screen which is hanging fully to the floor at center. The drummers/singers enter and take their positions to the side of the stage. A crash of drums – sudden darkness. Another crash of drums – a shaft of light on Joyce Cheeka ["Adult Joyce" in this text], 40 years old, dressed in a simple skirt, blouse and sweater. Around her neck hangs a small, woven pouch. A flute plays, under the following.

ADULT JOYCE: My name is Joyce Simmons Cheeka. I am from the Squaxin tribe, in the southern reaches of Puget Sound.

This area has been known as Washington State for over a hundred years. This continent has been home to the United States of America for over two hundred years.

My family has lived and worked here for seven hundred and fifty years. (*She smiles.*) There is a lot to remember.

(*Crash of drums – on the screen a film begins: the famous Edward S. Curtis footage of the arrival of the long canoes from "In the Land of the War Canoes," circa 1914.*)

ADULT JOYCE: Think about your parents and grandparents and great-grandparents. Think about how they lived, many years ago, when they were young, like you. You may know about them because of movies you've seen.

Now, imagine you have no movies.

(*She claps her hands – the film goes to black.*)

ADULT JOYCE: You may know about them because of photographs you've seen.

(*Crash of drums – on the screen a series of photographs is projected: the faces of Salish women and children, taken by Curtis, circa 1915.*)

ADULT JOYCE: Your parents may have shown you pictures and said "That is your great-uncle, that is your great-great-grandmother." You looked at them and tried to imagine their lives.

Now, imagine you have no photographs.

(*She claps her hands – the photographs go to black.*)

ADULT JOYCE: So, instead, you read about them.

(*Crash of drums – on the screen a series of slides is projected: pictures of numerous books about the Indian people, past and present.*)

ADULT JOYCE: And, as you read, you thought about the past. You thought about what you would have done if you had lived long ago.

Now, imagine your language has never been written down. That means you have no books.

(*She claps her hands – the slides go black.*)

ADULT JOYCE: Without movies, without pictures, without books – how will your history be remembered? How will you learn the story of your family, your tribe, your people?

(*Crash of drums – as the screen flies away, revealing…A canoe, suspended roughly three feet above the ground on a pivoting pedestal. Deep blue sidelights flood the stage floor, providing a vast expanse of water around the canoe.*

We hear the sound of waves lapping against the canoe. A man paddles the canoe toward us. This is Mud Bay Sam. Drumming continues, under, as does the flute. Upstage, looming over the scene, is Mount Rainier. Adult Joyce remains in a shaft of light, watching.)

ADULT JOYCE: Among my family, and among my people, the past was brought to you in the form of stories. And the stories were brought to you by a chosen member of your tribe. That person was known as The Rememberer.

(*Note: All speeches typed in **Bold** will be spoken in the Lushootseed language – the language of Joyce's people.*)

MUD BAY SAM: Wake up, Joyce. Wake up, **little one.**

(*A young Joyce Cheeka ["Joyce" in this text], age 12, sits up in the canoe.*)

MUD BAY SAM: The Mountain is out. It's telling us to get home before the storm.

JOYCE: How do you know it will storm?

MUD BAY SAM: The clouds are sitting on the west side of the mountain. That means rain.

JOYCE: But, Grandfather, how do you know?

MUD BAY SAM: I know because my father knew, and his father, and his. The mountain always tells us when a storm is coming.

(*Lighting and thunder – as Joyce ducks down again, and Mud Bay Sam paddles through the water.*)

ADULT JOYCE: His name was Mud Bay Sam. He knew about the mountain. He knew the story of the Great Flood. It seemed like he knew about everything. In our tribe, he was known as The Rememberer.

MUD BAY SAM: Don't be frightened, **little one.** We'll be home soon.

JOYCE: (*Peeking back up.*) I'm not frightened.

    (*Lightning and thunder – as Joyce screams and ducks down again, quickly. Mud Bay Sam smiles.*)

MUD BAY SAM: Not even a little?

JOYCE: No.

MUD BAY SAM: The sparrow is frightened of the crow, the crow is frightened of the hawk. Sometimes, the Great Spirit gives us fear to protect us.

JOYCE: I'm not frightened of anything.

MUD BAY SAM: I knew a little girl just like you. She said she wasn't afraid of the night.

JOYCE: I'm not, either.

MUD BAY SAM: So, she disobeyed her father and went walking. But, one night, this little girl met up with the Pitch Woman.

JOYCE: Who's that?

ADULT JOYCE: And that's when he told me.

    (*Lightning and thunder – as the Pitch Woman, covered in black rags, runs around the floating canoe, and enacts/dances the following as it is described. Bursts of drumming accompany her movements.*)

MUD BAY SAM: The Pitch Woman lives far away.

ADULT JOYCE: She is very big and covered in pitch, black as night.

MUD BAY SAM: At twilight time, the Pitch Woman throws her basket over her back –

ADULT JOYCE: Takes a handful of pitch –

MUD BAY SAM: And goes forth into the night, looking for –

ADULT JOYCE: Looking for –

JOYCE: Looking for what?

MUD BAY SAM: *Disobedient children.*

    (*Thunder. Joyce screams, frightened. Mud Bay Sam smiles. The Pitch Woman unveils a small wooden figure who will represent the "child."*)

JOYCE: What happens if she finds one?

MUD BAY SAM: The Pitch Woman sneaks up behind the child –

ADULT JOYCE: Quiet as can be –

MUD BAY SAM: And then *grabs her* –

ADULT JOYCE: Before she can make a sound –

MUD BAY SAM: And puts a gob of pitch over each of her eyes –

ADULT JOYCE: Tosses the little girl in her basket –

MUD BAY SAM: And disappears into the night.

    (*The Pitch Woman – having tossed the "girl" into the basket on her back – disappears into the darkness. The drumming fades away.*)

JOYCE: What happens to the little girl?

MUD BAY SAM: She belongs to the black night now. She will never be seen again.

(*Thunder, Joyce grabs hold of Mud Bay Sam, and hangs onto him as he paddles.*)

ADULT JOYCE: I was taught to remember the story of the Pitch Woman.

MUD BAY SAM: You're a brave girl, Joyce. And bravery is a great teacher. But we must learn from our fears, as well. (*He touches her face, tenderly.*) Come on, **little one.** It's time to go home.

ADULT JOYCE: It was an honor to ride in Mud Bay Sam's canoe. He loved that canoe more than anything in the world. He had carved it himself from a twenty foot cedar tree. He was fond of saying:

MUD BAY SAM: When I go to the next world, I will carve a new canoe and paddle it across time.

(*The canoe turns – pivoting on its pedestal – and now paddles away, facing upstage. Light on the canoe fades.*)

ADULT JOYCE: The year was 1911. I was living with my grandparents in Mud Bay. My father knew they'd teach me the ways of our people.

(*The yard in Mud Bay. Emily Sam enters and kneels near a campfire. She is making "ashes" bread. Adult Joyce moves toward her, watching. Mount Rainier remains prominent, upstage.*)

ADULT JOYCE: In the fall, we'd travel to pick berries. In the spring, the salmon would run. And Emily Sam, my grandmother, would teach me how to make "ashes" bread.

(*Joyce enters, holding a doll carved of cedar. She kneels down next to Emily Sam.*)

EMILY SAM: Dig a hole near the campfire, Joyce, and line it with hot coals. Wait till the coals have burned down to nothing but embers –

(*She reaches out her hands. Joyce sets down her doll and hands her an unbaked loaf of bread which is next to them.*)

EMILY SAM: – then put the bread inside. Make sure it's covered with lots of flour, or –

(*She makes a bad face and pretends to spit. Joyce laughs. Emily Sam smiles.*)

EMILY SAM: Then…fill the hole with hot ashes.

(*They cover the bread with ashes during the following.*)

ADULT JOYCE: The bread baked in the ground just like in a real oven. There was no difference…(*Smiles.*)…except I remember the "ashes" bread tasted better.

EMILY SAM: Learn to accomplish one thing, Joyce. Even if it's a small thing. A loaf of bread, a whistle made of alder, a small carved stone. Accomplishing even *one small thing* will build strength into your character. And you will have that accomplishment with you for life.

(*The bread is covered. Joyce is holding her doll.*)

EMILY SAM: We'll need a lot of bread for the potlach. **Do you want to bake some on your own?**

(*Joyce understands what she's said, but slowly shakes her head "No" – not knowing if she knows how.*)

EMILY SAM: **Why don't you try? Just one loaf.** Just one little loaf.

(*Joyce stares at her. Emily Sam smiles.*)

EMILY SAM: If it's bad, we'll feed it to the ducks.

(*Joyce smiles. Then, she nods. She hands Emily Sam her doll.*)

EMILY SAM: That's my girl. I'll meet you inside.

(*Joyce runs off, excitedly. Emily Sam looks at the doll, as Adult Joyce stands near her.*)

ADULT JOYCE: And, so I baked my first loaf of "ashes" bread – and, lucky for the ducks, at least it floated. (*She smiles.*)

(*Singing and drumming begin.*)

ADULT JOYCE: The day of feasting and celebrating arrived…the "potlach" had begun.

(*A flurry of activity: The kids run on from all directions, playing a game of hide-and-seek with Joyce. Longhouse and other adult guests are playing the "bone game," in which two teams try to amass twenty-one sticks by guessing whether a "bone" held by the other team is marked or unmarked. Emily Sam is preparing food. Henry – Joyce's cousin – stands at a conspicuous distance from the others. He reads from a book. He watches the festivities. Unlike the others, Henry wears a suit, with a white shirt and tie. Shiny black shoes. A carved and painted house post is featured prominently, rising fifteen feet into the air. Mud Bay Sam joins the others at the "bone game." Joyce is "tagged" by Boy Two.*)

BOY TWO: **C'mon, Joyce. You've got to sing while we hide!**

JOYCE: **What are we playing?**

GIRL ONE: **Hoo-hoo-hoo.**

BOY TWO: **I tagged you!**

YOUNG BOY: **You've got to sing!**

GIRL TWO: (*Points across the stage at Henry.*) **Joyce, go tag Henry!**

(*Joyce looks across the stage at Henry. He is reading a book. She approaches him, as the others run off. She "tags" him.*)

JOYCE: **You're it.**

HENRY: What?

JOYCE: (*In English now.*) You're it. You've got to sing while we hide.

HENRY: Do you remember me?

JOYCE: You're Henry, my cousin.

HENRY: You were just a baby last time I saw you.

JOYCE: Who made you wear that?

HENRY: It's my new suit. What do you think?

JOYCE: I think you look stupid.

HENRY: I've been away at school, Joyce. I've –

JOYCE: Do they make you wear *shoes,* too?

>   (*Before Henry can respond – *)

KIDS: (*Calling from their hiding places.*) **You're it!**

>   C'mon, Henry!

>   **Sing, Henry!**

>   Hoo-hoo-hoo! Hoo-hoo-hoo! (*Etc.*)

HENRY: Joyce, I don't –

JOYCE: C'mon. Sing "Hoo-hoo-hoo!" while we go hide. Then come find us.

HENRY: Have you ever read a book, Joyce?

>   (*She grabs the book from him and tosses it to one of the kids, who runs off with it.*)

JOYCE: Close your eyes and sing.

KIDS: (*As before.*) Henry, c'mon!

>   **Come find us, Henry!**

>   Hoo-hoo-hoo! Hoo-hoo-hoo!

>   **Close your eyes!** (*Etc.*)

>   (*Henry looks at her. He looks at the others. Then, he covers his eyes and begins to sing, as Joyce runs off and joins the other kids, hiding.*)

HENRY: "Hoo-hoo-hoo

>   Ha lay-ay-ay

>   Hoo-hoo-hoo

>   Ha lay-ay-ay…"

BOY TWO: Louder, Henry!

>   (*Mud Bay Sam walks up very close to Henry, and inspects his clothes – as Henry keeps singing, louder now, his eyes still covered with his hands.*)

HENRY: "Hoo-hoo-hoo

>   Ha lay-ay-ay

>   Hoo-hoo-hoo

>   Ha lay-ay-ay…"

>   (*When Henry uncovers his eyes, Mud Bay Sam is standing right in front of him, startling him.*)

MUD BAY SAM: The boy who went away to school! How are you, Henry?

HENRY: I'm fine, Sam. You frightened me.

MUD BAY SAM: And you frightened me, Henry. **Look at yourself.** You've joined the Sears & Roebuck tribe. How can you fish in those clothes?

HENRY: I'm not a fisherman, Sam. I'm going to be a teacher.

MUD BAY SAM: We have guests coming, Henry. Today, I need you to be a fisherman.

JOYCE AND OTHERS: (*Offstage.*) Henry!
    Come find us! (*Etc.*)
    (*Longhouse – Henry's father – joins them, carrying a fishing net and spear.*)

MUD BAY SAM: Come help your father.

LONGHOUSE: **Do as he says, son.** We're catching fish for the potlach.

MUD BAY SAM: I saw a school of porpoises out on the water. They are our cousins. They'll give us some fresh fish if we ask them.

HENRY: Oh, not the story about our "cousins" again. I thought I'd heard the last of that.

JOYCE AND OTHERS: (*Offstage.*) **Henry, come find us!**
    Henry! (*Etc.*)

LONGHOUSE: (*Firmly.*) They are our cousins. After the Great Flood, many of our ancestors came back to this world as porpoises. **They are our cousins.**

HENRY: Why do you talk so crazy?

MUD BAY SAM: They will help us find food for the potlach.

HENRY: It's superstition, nothing else.

LONGHOUSE: Henry, you must respect the teachings of –

HENRY: *No one believes that old nonsense, anymore.*
    (*Silence. Longhouse turns away. Joyce rushes on.*)

JOYCE: Henry, you have to come find us!
    (*Henry looks at her, then looks at his father.*)

HENRY: Joyce, I want you to have something.
    (*Henry takes a pouch – the one we saw Adult Joyce wearing earlier – from around his neck. He puts it around Joyce's neck.*)

HENRY: This pouch was my father's.
    (*Joyce admires the small pouch.*)

HENRY: He believes it holds a spirit that will protect me. I want you to have it now.
    (*Longhouse stares at Henry, hard.*)

JOYCE: Will this protect me from the Pitch Woman?

HENRY: (*To Mud Bay Sam.*) Are you still scaring kids with stories of the Pitch Woman?

JOYCE: She finds little children and she –

HENRY: Joyce. There is no Pitch Woman. It's a foolish old myth.

MUD BAY SAM: Henry, don't *ever* do that to your old people. (*Pause.*) You've been away, you've learned things from your white teachers. It's all right to learn those things, but you must also honor your elders. They know things that you don't.

HENRY: *I* know those porpoises are not going to bring us gifts!

(*Silence. Longhouse stands very close to Henry, speaks firmly.*)

LONGHOUSE: **You left here my son, and you return as a stranger.**

HENRY: What are you saying?!

LONGHOUSE: I'm speaking our language. Have you forgotten that, too?

HENRY: Father, I don't –

LONGHOUSE: You say you'll be a teacher – but what will you teach? You've turned your back on everything we've taught you.

HENRY: Father –

LONGHOUSE: You've given the **little one** the pouch I made for you.

HENRY: Those are your beliefs, Father. Not mine.

ADULT JOYCE: Henry and his father looked each other in the eye for a long time. I had never seen two men do that.

MUD BAY SAM: Henry is going out on the water, **little one.** Would you like to go with him?

HENRY: I'm not going out on –

LONGHOUSE: **It's the only way that you'll learn, son.**

MUD BAY SAM: (*To Joyce.*) Take him out on the water and be very still.

JOYCE: (*Nods.*) **I will.**

MUD BAY SAM: And Joyce.

JOYCE: Yes?

MUD BAY SAM: Remember what you are about to see.

(*Mud Bay Sam begins to chant. Emily Sam, Longhouse and the other guests, join in the chanting. Joyce hands her doll to Emily Sam. Joyce grabs Henry's hand, and they get in the canoe. Lights shift – the canoe floats in the blue-lit water, as before. As Joyce paddles, the canoe pivots until it is facing the audience. Then, she and Henry sit in the canoe in silence, keeping very still. The drums join in with the chanting.*)

MUD BAY SAM AND OTHERS: (*Chanting, repeat as needed.*) **Oh, our great cousins, We are traveling. We have traveled far. We are tired. We are camping here and have not much meat. Would you honor us by sharing with us the fruits of the sea?**

(*The four cousins – four dancers wearing wooden hand-carved porpoise masks – move in a pattern around the canoe. They respond and react to both the chants from the shore, and the canoe in their midst. Chanting and drumming continues. One by one, each cousin comes very near the canoe. Henry and/or Joyce touches each cousin's head – taking hold of a small fish which is attached there. Then, as each cousin moves away, a brightly colored string of fish and other sea animals – depicted in the style of the porpoise masks – unfurls from inside the cousin's costume. After each cousin's string of fish has been unfurled, they stand at the four corners of the stage, still attached to Henry and Joyce via the string. They then begin to circle the canoe, wrapping Henry and Joyce in the fish and sea animals, filling the canoe. Then, as a group, the cousins leave. Henry and Joyce are smiling, amazed, their canoe and their arms filled with the fish and sea animals. The chanting and drumming fade. Lights shift to the yard – the canoe is now ashore. Everyone helps carry the fish and sea animals up to the house for cooking. Joyce, Henry, Emily Sam, Mud Bay Sam and Longhouse remain behind. Emily Sam hands Joyce her doll.*)*

JOYCE: What do you think of our cousins now, Henry?

HENRY: (*His arms full of fish.*) I think they're very kind –

JOYCE: It's enough to feed the whole potlach!

HENRY: But there are other things to learn, Joyce. Things your grandfather can't teach you.

(*A Squaxin Woman appears at the side of the stage.*)

SQUAXIN WOMAN: Mud Bay Sam –

(*Mud Bay Sam sees her and goes to her.*)

MUD BAY SAM: **Hello, friend, How are you?**

SQUAXIN WOMAN: **I have something to ask you**…(*She continues to talk to him, softly.*)

ADULT JOYCE: Often, people from all over the area would come to ask the Rememberer questions. To learn about their ancestors.

(*Mud Bay Sam turns and calls to Joyce.*)

MUD BAY SAM: **Little one,** our friend wants to know the name of Klook-kwa-kay's father. (*Pause, he smiles a bit, a challenge.*) Do you remember?

(*Joyce looks at him. He nods. Joyce looks around, then steps forward, and begins talking – softly at first, then with increasing confidence.*)

JOYCE: Deeaht was succeeded by his brother, Odiee. (*Pause.*) His descendants were Kat'hi-che-da, then Wa-wa-tsoo-pa, then Wat-lai-waih-kose, Klatch-tis-sub, How-e-sub, Ko-shah-sit –

(*Henry and Longhouse look on, amazed. Mud Bay Sam and Emily Sam, proudly. The others look on, as well.*)

JOYCE: And, then Tai-is-sub…who was the father of Klook-kwa-kay.

(*Very pleased, the woman looks at Joyce, takes her hand.*)

SQUAXIN WOMAN: **Thank you. You are a fine young girl.**

JOYCE: Thank you. Now, go hide, Henry!

(*The old woman leaves. Emily Sam exits with her.*)

HENRY: Joyce, how did you know all that?

MUD BAY SAM: She listens to her elders.

LONGHOUSE: Go hide, now. She'll find you.

HENRY: Father, I –

LONGHOUSE: Go.

(*Henry looks at Joyce, who smiles a bit. He looks back to his father, then runs off to hide. Longhouse exits, opposite. Several kids rush on, calling to Joyce – then run off.*)

KIDS: **Sing hoo-hoo-hoo!**

Hurry, Joyce!

Come find us! (*Etc.*)

(*Joyce covers her eyes. The yard has emptied. Just as she is about to begin singing, Mud Bay Sam approaches her.*)

MUD BAY SAM: Joyce, I have something for you.

(*She uncovers her eyes and looks at him. He holds a small oyster shell in his hand.*)

MUD BAY SAM: Put this shell in the pouch Henry gave you. Keep it with you. (*He hands her the shell.*) The oyster's shell protects him, just as the Great Spirit protects us. And remember that all things, even the smallest things, are worthy of protection.

JOYCE: Thank you, **grandfather**. (*She puts the shell in her pouch.*)

MUD BAY SAM: The time will come, **little one**, when you will take my place.

(*She looks up at him, curious.*)

MUD BAY SAM: You will hold our history and our stories in your mind. And you will pass them on.

JOYCE: But, how do I learn them?

MUD BAY SAM: You watch. You listen. And no matter what happens to you, or to your family, or to your people – you *remember*. (*He puts his arm around her.*) It's a great responsibility, **little one**. But, you've been chosen. And we are never chosen for something that we don't have the power to do.

(*Mud Bay Sam leaves. Joyce watches him go. Then, slowly, she covers her eyes and begins to sing, to herself.*)

JOYCE: "Hoo-hoo-hoo

Ha lay-ay-ay

Hoo-hoo-hoo
Ha lay-ay-ay…"
(*Behind her, we see the huge shadows of two men on the upstage wall.*)

JOYCE: Hide yourself good, Henry, or I'll find you! (*Returns to singing.*)

"Hoo-hoo-hoo
Ha lay-ay-ay
Hoo-hoo-hoo
Ha lay-ay-ay…"

(*During the following, the men enter the stage, quietly, approaching Joyce from behind. She does not see or hear them. The men are: Mullin, a United States Marshall; and Twin River, a Klickitat Indian, employed by the Bureau of Indian Affairs.*)

(*Note: Twin River speaks the Sahaptin language, not spoken or understood by Joyce or her family. This language will be indicated by **Bold Italics.***)

JOYCE: I'm almost there, Henry! Get ready! (*Returns to singing.*)

"Hoo-hoo-hoo
Ha lay-ay-ay
Hoo-hoo – "

MULLIN: Joyce Cheeka, come with us.

TWIN RIVER: ***Do as he says, little girl.***

(*Joyce turns and sees them. She is frozen with fear. Her doll drops to the ground. Drumming and wailing begin to pierce the following scene at random intervals. The men approach her, slowly.*)

(*Simultaneously.*)

MULLIN: Be a good girl now –

TWIN RIVER: ***We have spoken with your father –***

JOYCE: *Grandfather!*

(*Simultaneously.*)

MULLIN: It won't help to call –

TWIN RIVER: ***Just do as we say to do –***

JOYCE: *Emily Sam!*

(*The men grab her and carry her away. She kicks and screams.*)

MULLIN: You're coming with us.

JOYCE: (*A hideous scream.*) *Nooooooooo!*

(*The drumming and wailing crescendo. Joyce is carried away by the men – as lights shift abruptly to the upstage wall: A huge shadow of the Pitch Woman dances, wildly. The drumming, wailing and Joyce's screaming continue for a few moments – then, suddenly stop. Lights snap out on the shadow – as lights rise on Adult Joyce, at center stage. She slowly picks up the abandoned doll and holds it. The sound of wind, as well as the sound of horses hooves is heard under the following.*)

ADULT JOYCE: The men put me in a wagon and drove away.

(*The rear of a horse-drawn, uncovered wagon is visible at one side of the stage. Joyce is inside, tethered to the wagon with a rope. The wagon shakes Joyce about as it travels. Two other Indian children – a Young Boy and a Young Girl – are with her, also tethered to the wagon as it travels.*)

ADULT JOYCE: We rode for several days, but they never told us where we were going. Sometimes we stopped, and the men got out and grabbed more children.

(*The wagon stops shaking. Joyce looks into the distance.*)

ADULT JOYCE: I remember I saw a little boy playing in his yard. I saw the men approaching him –

JOYCE: **Run, little boy!**

ADULT JOYCE: The little boy looked up when he heard me –

JOYCE: **Run back in your house!**

ADULT JOYCE: The men reached out to grab him –

JOYCE: **RUN BEFORE THEY CATCH YOU!**

ADULT JOYCE: The men took the little boy from his yard. I heard him scream for his mother.

OTIS: (*Offstage.*) **Mother!**

ADULT JOYCE: They brought the little boy to our wagon.

(*Otis, an Indian boy from a neighboring tribe, is brought to the wagon, and set down in the back, next to Joyce, by Mullin and Twin River. Otis is crying and very frightened.*)

ADULT JOYCE: I had to hold onto him so he wouldn't fall out as we drove.

(*Mullin and Twin River exit to the unseen front of the wagon. Otis looks at Joyce, the Young Boy and the Young Girl, saying nothing. The wagon begins to shake as they begin to travel again. Gradually, the image of Mount Rainier fades away and is gone. Joyce puts her arms around Otis and holds him, protecting him. He holds onto her tightly. Long silence. Then…*)

OTIS: (*Quietly.*) Were we bad?

JOYCE: No.

OTIS: Then why are they taking us away?

(*Joyce stares at Otis. She takes the shell out of the pouch around her neck. A flute begins to play, melancholy and distant.*)

JOYCE: My Grandfather gave me this shell. He said it would keep me safe.

(*She hands him the shell and he looks at it.*)

JOYCE: The oyster's shell protects him, just as the Great Spirit protects us.

(*Long silence as the wagon travels. Otis gives her back the shell, then looks away, sadly.*)

JOYCE: What's your name? (*Pause.*) My name's Joyce. (*Pause.*) If I don't know your name, I can't be your friend.

OTIS: (*Pause, then quietly.*) I'm Otis.

JOYCE: (*Smiles a bit.*) **Say you'll be my friend, Otis.**

OTIS: (*Pause, then speaks tentatively.*) **I'll be your friend.**

(*A crash of drums, as lights shift to – The Superintendent of Indian Schools, a woman in her forties, holding a book and a Bible.*)

SUPERINTENDENT: "In our efforts to humanize, Christianize and educate the Indian, we should endeavor to divorce him from his primitive habits and customs. He should be induced to emulate the white man in all things that conduce to his happiness and comfort."

(*During the following, we see Joyce and the Young Girl sitting on small stools – lit by a lone shaft of harsh sidelight. Nurse Warner stands behind them. She is cutting off the girls' long black hair with scissors. She tosses the cut off clumps of hair onto the ground near their feet. Random drumming, under.*)

ADULT JOYCE: The government started with the children, stating they needed to be taken from their homes at an early age – before their parents could instill in them the principles of Indian life.

With the girls, one of the first things they did was cut off our hair. We had been raised to be very careful with our hair, to let it grow and take care of it – because our hair has a connection to our life, and mistreatment of it could bring harm to us.

And, if someone in your family died, you would cut your hair as a way of mourning, and to show honor to the dead.

But, none of us said anything about that. We just sat there. And none of us cried until we were alone in our rooms.

(*Nurse Warner leaves. The girls sit on the stools, hair cut short, staring front, motionless. The drumming fades away and is gone.*)

SUPERINTENDENT: "Experience has shown that it is possible to do a great deal for the Indian; that it is possible to educate them; and that it is possible to prepare them to take their places along with us as citizens in this great Republic."

(*A trumpet plays "Reveille," loudly. Lights shift to the schoolyard. Several students in uniforms enter and walk past Joyce, Otis, the Young Boy and Young Girl – laughing and pointing at the new arrivals.*)

ADULT JOYCE: And so we were given our uniforms. And shoes for our feet. And we were marched inside to meet the other students.

They still hadn't told us where we were, or why we'd been brought there. What I remember most about that first day is the buildings. Brick and mortar, rising far into the sky. They were the biggest buildings I'd ever seen.

(*The house post is quickly and efficiently "walked down" onto its side by two boys in school uniforms. The boys carry the house post away – revealing, in its place, a tall flagpole. Two girls in school uniforms hoist an American flag up the flagpole as the music continues. "Reveille" concludes – as Dr. Buchanan enters and addresses the four new arrivals.*)

DR. BUCHANAN: Welcome to the Tulalip Training School. I'm Dr. Buchanan.

(*Silence, Joyce and the others just stare at him.*)

DR. BUCHANAN: Good. Well, let me show you around. The Tulalip School was, until recently, an abandoned Catholic mission. We have converted the buildings into – (*He points into the distance, showing them.*) A schoolhouse. A shop. A hospital. An office. A sawmill. A laundry. The headmaster's house (that's where I live). And two Dormitories. One for boys. One for girls.

You'll spend your mornings in the classroom, learning to read and write and do basic arithmetic. And you'll spend your afternoons on work detail. The boys will learn carpentry, farming and general upkeep. The girls will learn weaving, sewing, cooking – and a few girls will be selected to learn nurse's training.

We also will put together a marching band and a drill team.

(*Otis has walked up and tugged on Dr. Buchanan's coat.*)

DR. BUCHANAN: Young man, the first thing you'll have to learn is how to raise your hand. If you have something to say, you must raise your hand.

(*Otis looks up at him, blankly.*)

DR. BUCHANAN: Do you have something to say?

(*Otis looks at him for a moment, then walks back and stands in the line.*)

DR. BUCHANAN: Very well. Now, first of all –

(*Otis raises his hand.*)

DR. BUCHANAN: Yes, young man. What is your question?

OTIS: (*Simply.*) Can I go home now?

(*Dr. Buchanan stares at him. Silence. He walks over to Otis.*)

DR. BUCHANAN: You know I've asked myself that question a lot, over the past few years. I'm away from home, too. What's your name, young man?

OTIS: I'm Otis.

DR. BUCHANAN: What tribe are you from Otis?

(*Otis just stares at him. Then, Otis looks to Joyce. She also stares at Dr. Buchanan. Awkward silence.*)

DR. BUCHANAN: Well, what about the rest of you? Don't be shy.

(*Silence. The students all stare at him.*)

DR. BUCHANAN: I'd like to know who your people are, what tribes you're from.

(*More silence. Nurse Warner and Mr. Conrad enter and join the others.*)

DR. BUCHANAN: Well. This is Nurse Warner, our head nurse.

NURSE WARNER: Welcome.

DR. BUCHANAN: She'll show the girls to their rooms. And Mr. Conrad, our history teacher –

(*Mr. Conrad nods.*)

DR. BUCHANAN: – will show the boys to theirs. I'll see you all bright and early tomorrow morning.

And remember, listen for the bells. (*Dr. Buchanan turns and leaves.*)

NURSE WARNER: Well, ladies, shall we go.

(*Joyce and the Young Girl look at her, then nod.*)

NURSE WARNER: Follow me.

(*Nurse Warner turns and starts off, Joyce and the Young Girl follow. Mr. Conrad turns to Otis and the Young Boy.*)

MR. CONRAD: Off we go, gentlemen.

(*Mr. Conrad turns and starts off. The Young Boy follows him. Otis follows for two steps – then turns and runs after Joyce.*)

OTIS: **Joyce, don't go –**

MR. CONRAD: Young man, get back here.

(*Otis grabs Joyce before she leaves, holding onto her tightly.*)

MR. CONRAD: Get back here this instant.

(*Otis just holds onto Joyce, terrified.*)

JOYCE: Otis, it's all right.

NURSE WARNER: (*To Otis.*) You'll see her soon, don't worry.

MR. CONRAD: Young man, something you will learn is that orders are meant to be followed. Now, let go of her and stand up straight.

JOYCE: He wants to see his Mom. He wants to –

MR. CONRAD: I'm not talking to you, girl. Follow Nurse Warner to your room. (*To Otis.*) *Let go of her and look at me.*

(*Otis slowly lets go of Joyce, and looks up at Mr. Conrad.*)

MR. CONRAD: Your Mother is not here, son. From now, until you are a grown and civilized young man, this is your home. We are your family. And when we tell you to do something, you do it.

Now. Are you ready to go?

(*Otis looks at Joyce. Then, he nods, sadly.*)

MR. CONRAD: Good day, ladies.

(*Mr. Conrad starts off. The Young Boy follows him. Otis, too, follows him. Unseen to Mr. Conrad, Joyce follows Otis for a few steps. As she does, she takes the small pouch from around her neck and places it around Otis' neck. Otis turns and starts to say something to her. She gestures: "Ssshhh." She gestures: "Now, go on." He holds the pouch tightly and follows Mr. Conrad off. Joyce turns back and looks at Nurse Warner. Nurse Warner turns and exits, followed by the Young Girl and Joyce. A flute plays.*)

ADULT JOYCE: They took us to what was called "the Girls' home." Our rooms were on the second floor.

At night, they made us take off our shoes and leave them in the basement. (This was done to soften our footsteps. They were very concerned with "quiet.") In the morning, we had to walk down barefoot to get our shoes. The basement was always the coldest place of all. In the winter, this made for a very cold walk.

There were many of us in one room. But, my bed was at the end of the room, near a window, away from the other girls.

(*Lights rise on Joyce's room. A small, tin box is on the bed. Also on the bed is the bundle of Joyce's own, Indian clothing. Girl One and Girl Two enter, looking around.*)

GIRL ONE: What's her name?

GIRL TWO: I think it's Joyce.

(*Girl One has found something underneath Joyce's pillow.*)

GIRL ONE: Look…(*She pulls a large piece of Joyce's hair out from under the pillow.*) It's her hair. She kept it after they cut it off.

GIRL TWO: Let me see.

GIRL ONE: She *saved* it.

(*A bell rings, loudly – the sound is made by what today we'd call a "triangle" – struck with a piece of metal. The girls quickly put the hair back under the pillow, as – Joyce enters, wearing a school uniform.*)

JOYCE: What's that noise?

GIRL ONE: (*Urgent, frightened.*) Hurry up!

JOYCE: Where are you going?

GIRL TWO: Grab your box and come!

(*The Young Girl joins them.*)

JOYCE: My what?

GIRL ONE: Hurry!

(*The bell rings, again. Joyce looks around, grabs her tin box and follows the other girls, as lights shift to – the washroom, indicated by a long board which represents the counter and the sinks. The girls enter, marching in a line, holding their identical tin boxes in front of them.)*

ADULT JOYCE: (*During the above action.*) Everything happened by bells. Every night, we'd be marched into the washroom just before bedtime.

(*Sound of military drumming. The girls turn, in unison, and face their individual mirrors and sinks. In unison, they set their tin boxes on the counter in front of them. Then, they take their toothbrushes out of the box, and hold them in their right hands, at the ready. Nurse Warner enters, holding a container of tooth powder. She stops, looking at the girls. In unison, the girls all extend their left hands in front of them, palms up. Nurse Warner walks down the line of girls, putting a small amount of tooth powder in the each girl's left palm. Then, she stops, stands nearby, and observes. A bell rings. The girls all avidly brush their teeth in an identical pattern.*)

ADULT JOYCE: The school was very strict about grooming. They thought we didn't know any better. This was funny to us, because our families were always very concerned with daily bathing, and having good, clean teeth.

(*In unison, they all spit. A bell rings. The girls put their toothbrushes back inside their tin boxes, and remove their hairbrushes. In unison, they brush their hair.*)

ADULT JOYCE: We had been taught by our parents to watch the animals, and to care for ourselves as well as they do.

(*In unison, the girls put their hairbrushes in their tin boxes. Then, they turn and face Nurse Warner, smiling. Nurse Warner walks down the line and quickly inspects each girl for cleanliness.*)

ADULT JOYCE: Of course, the teachers didn't know any of this. Their job was to "clean us up" – and we did our best to help them along.

(*Another bell rings. Still in unison, the girls pick up their tin boxes, turn, and march past Nurse Warner in a line, leaving the washroom. Nurse Warner then follows them out, as lights shift back to – Joyce's room. Joyce enters, sets her tin box on the chair. She goes to the window and looks out. Then, she goes to her "own" clothes, picks them up and holds them tightly. She carries them to the bed with her, and sits. She rocks back and forth, holding her clothes in her arms. The military drumming fades out, as – a flute plays, melancholy and distant. During the following, Nurse Warner enters. She takes Joyce's "own" clothes from her. She hands Joyce a "store-bought" doll. She leaves. Joyce looks at the doll…then lets it fall to the ground. She curls up on her bed, crying.*)

ADULT JOYCE: I'd never been so far from home. We asked how long we'd be gone...and they said nothing. For all we knew, and for all our families knew, we were gone for good.

(*Loud drumming – as the room goes suddenly dark, except for a shaft of moonlight streaming through the window and onto Joyce's face. Singing – in Salish – is heard, distantly, at first. This song will come to be known as "Joyce's song":*

"Hoo lad chad sthloo la ha ha ob

Hoo lad chad sthloo la ha ha ob

Ha woo, ha woo, ha woo, ha woo..."

Upstage, against the back wall, the shadow of a woman dances. The woman wears a long dress, a fringed shawl, moccasins, and a kerchief on her head. She carries, and dances with, a "khawa" – a shoulder-high staff, or walking stick.)

JOYCE: (*Looking around, fearfully.*) Who is it? Who's there?

(*The singing and drumming continues. The shadow of a woman continues to dance, upstage.*)

JOYCE: **Who are you? What do you want?**

(*Singing grows louder. Drumming continues. The woman's dancing continues, growing wilder.*)

JOYCE: Nurse Warner! Nurse Warner, someone's here! (*Joyce jumps into her bed, and pulls the covers over her head, hiding herself.*)

(*The shadow of the woman grows larger and larger, upstage – as the singing and drumming reach a crescendo. Suddenly, the shadow vanishes...and the woman herself pops up directly behind Joyce's bed. The singing and drumming stops, abruptly. Though Joyce doesn't know it, yet, this is her Aunt Sophie. Aunt Sophie stares down at the still-covered Joyce. Hearing the silence, Joyce gets curious. Slowly, she pulls the covers back from her head. When she uncovers her eyes, she is looking directly up into the face of Aunt Sophie – Joyce screams and covers her head again. Aunt Sophie laughs. Aunt Sophie sings, while she does her dance in Joyce's room. After a moment, Joyce is more curious than afraid. She uncovers her head, slowly and listens to the song. She watches Aunt Sophie dance.*)

JOYCE: **Who are you?**

(*No response.*)

JOYCE: What do you want?

(*Again, no response.*)

JOYCE: Are you the Pitch Woman? My Grandfather told me about you. You take a handful of pitch and you –

(*Suddenly, Aunt Sophie stops singing, turns, and looks directly at Joyce. Aunt Sophie walks slowly, threateningly, toward Joyce. Joyce, still in bed, cowers with fear. When she is very near Joyce, Aunt Sophie slowly shakes her head "no." Silence. Then, Joyce speaks.*)

JOYCE: You're *not* the Pitch Woman?

(*Aunt Sophie shakes her head "no," again.*)

JOYCE: You're not here to hurt me?

(*Aunt Sophie again shakes her head "no."*)

JOYCE: Then why *are* you here? Why don't any of the other kids see you, except me?

(*Aunt Sophie smiles. Then, quietly and beautifully, she sings one final, brief phrase of the song, looking directly at Joyce. On the last note of the song, Aunt Sophie points to the upstage wall with her walking stick. Joyce looks – and sees the shadows of Mud Bay Sam, Longhouse and Henry. Drumming is heard, under. Facing upstage, Joyce speaks, amazed.*)

JOYCE: It's Mud Bay Sam. And Henry. (*Joyce turns back to the room, saying – *) **It's my family.**

(*Aunt Sophie is gone. Joyce looks all around, under the bed, out the window.*)

JOYCE: Hello? Hello!? Where'd you go? (*Joyce sits down on her bed.*) Tell me who you are!

(*A crash of drums – then, silence. Joyce sits for a while, then lies back on her bed.*)

ADULT JOYCE: I lay awake all night that first night. Wondering what I'd seen. Wondering if it was only my imagination.

(*"Reveille" sounds, loudly – followed by military drumming. Joyce sits up, quickly. Then, she rushes into the washroom and joins the other girls, once again, at the counter. Nurse Warner joins them, as before. The girls and Nurse repeat the entire teeth and hair brushing routine from before – except, this time, they do it at double the speed.*)

ADULT JOYCE: And, at five in the morning, we had to get all cleaned up again – even though we hadn't done anything except *sleep!*

(*A bell rings, as lights shift to – the schoolyard. Dawn. Mr. Conrad blows his whistle – and begins to lead all the boys and girls in calisthenics. Adult Joyce speaks, while watching the calisthenics.*)

ADULT JOYCE: The school knew that, living with our families, all of us were used to a great deal of exercise – hiking, swimming, hunting, fishing. But they were determined to direct our energies into what were called "useful channels."

(*Another whistle, a new exercise. As before, a shaft of light rises on the Superintendent.*)

SUPERINTENDENT: "The Indian is splendidly equipped for *manual labor.* However, in a literary or professional sense he is apt to be deficient."

(*A whistle, a new exercise.*)

SUPERINTENDENT: "Therefore, rather than requiring an Indian boy to solve hypothetical equations or study the geography of countries he will never visit, we believe *industrial training* should have the foremost place in Indian education."

(*A whistle, a new exercise.*)

SUPERINTENDENT: "So, too, Indian girls should study and practice the 'domestic sciences' – since culture can be obtained as readily from baking a pumpkin pie as through studying Greek mythology."

(*A whistle, a new exercise.*)

ADULT JOYCE: Be gentle in your judgments. These men and women were the social reformers of their day. And they had inherited, from the government which had displaced the Indian people, the task of "righting a great national wrong."

(*A whistle, a new exercise. Lights snap out on the Superintendent.*)

ADULT JOYCE: But, even though they may have had the best of intentions, to this day I don't think Mr. Conrad knew the *slightest thing* about calisthenics.

(*Led by Mr. Conrad, the boys and girls are now engaged in a particularly weird, uncomfortable, seemingly pointless exercise. The students, however, give it their best. Dr. Buchanan enters and observes.*)

DR. BUCHANAN: What do you call this one, Mr. Conrad?

MR. CONRAD: (*From his very awkward position.*) I call this one the "Hackensack High-Topper."

DR. BUCHANAN: Fascinating.

(*A bell rings. Mr. Conrad stands.*)

MR. CONRAD: Up and at 'em, now. Flag drill at noon. Marching at three. Good day. (*Mr. Conrad exits.*)

(*The students stop their exercise, and stand in one line, facing Dr. Buchanan.*)

DR. BUCHANAN: Good morning, troops. Those of you who are new here have discovered this morning that we like to spend as much time in the open air as possible –

(*Otis raises his hand.*)

DR. BUCHANAN: Yes, young man. What is it?

OTIS: My leg hurts.

DR. BUCHANAN: I'm not surprised. I'll talk to Mr. Conrad about his exercises. In the meantime, to rest your leg, let's all have a seat.

(*Dr. Buchanan sits on the ground. The students, surprised at first, follow his lead and sit, in a line facing him.*)

DR. BUCHANAN: Now, Thanksgiving is just around the corner and I'm planning to –

(*Otis raises his hand, again.*)

DR. BUCHANAN: Yes, Otis, What is it now?

OTIS: Duwamish.

(*Silence.*)

DR. BUCHANAN: I'm sorry, what?

OTIS: My tribe.

DR. BUCHANAN: Your –

GIRL TWO: Wynoochie.

(*Dr. Buchanan looks at her. Then, one by one – and not "down the line" – the other students state the names of their tribes.*)

YOUNG GIRL: Nisqually.

BOY ONE: Skagit.

GIRL ONE: Chehalis.

BOY TWO: Kikiallus.

YOUNG BOY: Makah.

JOYCE: Squaxin.

(*Silence. Dr. Buchanan looks at them all for a long moment.*)

DR. BUCHANAN: I had no idea there were so many tribes represented here. No idea at all.

OTIS: What about you?

DR. BUCHANAN: Pardon?

OTIS: What's your tribe?

DR. BUCHANAN: (*Pause.*) Well…I guess I come from a tribe called Philadelphia.

ADULT JOYCE: I liked Dr. Buchanan.

(*A bell rings. During the following, the boys exit one direction, and the girls exit the other. Dr. Buchanan exits, also.*)

ADULT JOYCE: But, sometimes at Tulalip, the more they taught me, the more I missed my family, and the way things were done at home.

(*A classroom. Miss Brennan enters, carrying a small quilt. The girls each hold small blocks of fabric and a sewing needle.*)

MISS BRENNAN: Joyce, are you stitching?

(*Joyce moves to the classroom.*)

MISS BRENNAN: This is called the log cabin quilt. Each square is sewn individually, then added to the rest. (*Hands the quilt to the girls.*) There are many kinds of quilts you can make, and each kind tells a story.

(*Adult Joyce moves and stands behind Emily Sam, who is sewing a quilt. Joyce, also, is looking at Emily Sam.*)

ADULT JOYCE: My Mother and Grandmother made blankets using designs inspired by stories of the raven, the eagle, the whale and the salmon. Stories that went back to days of the Great Flood, and before.

MISS BRENNAN: Joyce, did you hear me?

(*Joyce turns and watches Miss Brennan.*)

MISS BRENNAN: Now, this quilt comes from the pioneer women, women who came west with their families. Who can tell me the story of those women's journey?

(*Girl One raises her hand.*)

MISS BRENNAN: Lillian?

GIRL ONE: The gold rush in California in 1849, and in Colorado in 1859 brought hundreds of families to the West in covered wagons.

MISS BRENNAN: Good. Perhaps our next quilt can be a covered wagon design.

JOYCE: I want to make a salmon quilt.

MISS BRENNAN: What's that?

JOYCE: I want to tell the story of my family, how they travel in the spring to catch salmon.

MISS BRENNAN: That's not what you're here to learn, Joyce.

JOYCE: I want to make a salmon quilt.

MISS BRENNAN: Someday you will. But first you must learn this log cabin design and –

JOYCE: **I think your quilts are stupid.**

(*The girls laugh for a moment, startled. Then, silence. Miss Brennan does not understand what Joyce has said.*)

MISS BRENNAN: Joyce, you know you're to speak English, and English *only* at this school. You know that, don't you?

JOYCE: Yes.

MISS BRENNAN: Now, what did you say? (*Silence.*) Joyce?

(*Joyce stares at Miss Brennan, who then turns to Girl One.*)

MISS BRENNAN: Lillian, tell me what Joyce just said.

GIRL ONE: (*After an apologetic look to Joyce.*) She said your quilts are stupid.

MISS BRENNAN: (*To Joyce.*) Is that true?

(*Joyce nods.*)

MISS BRENNAN: You must learn to sew, Joyce. You –

JOYCE: I know how to sew. My Grandmother taught me.

MISS BRENNAN: But you must learn to sew *this way*. This is the way quilts are made now. You'll be able to make them for your family, but you'll also be able to sell them, to make a living with them. Wouldn't you like that?

(*Joyce holds up a corner of the quilt.*)

JOYCE: But, this is your story, not mine. I want to remember my stories. Mud Bay Sam told me to remem –

MISS BRENNAN: But, don't you want to learn new stories?

JOYCE: Yes, but I –

MISS BRENNAN: That's all I'm asking you to do. To learn new stories, in addition to your own. That's why you're here. So you'll have the skills to live as well as you can when you leave here.

JOYCE: But, when I leave here, I'm going home.

MISS BRENNAN: Home to the reservation?

JOYCE: Home to my *home.* To my family, at Oyster Bay.

(*Silence.*)

ADULT JOYCE: And Miss Brennan just looked at me. I don't think she'd ever thought about what I'd just said – that maybe they were preparing me for a world I would never enter.

MISS BRENNAN: Girls, let's finish up for the day. We'll continue tomorrow.

(*Miss Brennan takes the quilt and exits. The girls exit, opposite. Joyce stands alone.*)

ADULT JOYCE: I remember wanting to stay in my room and not go to class.

(*As Emily Sam leaves the stage, she stops and puts her arms around Joyce.*)

EMILY SAM: Each day is a gift from the Great Spirit. To waste one of your days is inexcusable. You must account for yourself and your time on Earth. You must learn to be *useful.*

ADULT JOYCE: So…I started a quilt of my own.

(*Joyce's room. Night. A flute plays. Joyce and the other girls sit on the floor in the darkened room, their faces lit only by a few candles in their midst. Joyce is sewing the first few squares of her quilt. Girl Two has a small knife, and is carving a small toy out of cedar. Girl One is painting a toy she has carved. The Young Girl is weaving a small bracelet.*)

GIRL ONE: **What kind of quilt will it be?**

JOYCE: A salmon quilt.

GIRL TWO: Where'd you get the cloth?

JOYCE: Where'd you get that knife?

GIRL TWO: (*Smiles.*) **Secret.**

JOYCE: (*Smiles.*) **Secret.**

(*They shake hands.*)

GIRL ONE: I'm hungry.

GIRL TWO: Potatoes, stewed in fish oil.

GIRL ONE: (*Nods.*) And berries for dessert.

JOYCE: And Emily Sam's "ashes" bread.

>*(They make hungry moans and groans, playfully. Except for the Young Girl, who begins to cry, quietly.)*

YOUNG GIRL: I want to go home.

>*(The other girls look at her.)*

GIRL ONE: It's all right, Sarah.

>*(Girl One holds the Young Girl. Then, Girl One looks up at Joyce.)*

GIRL TWO: Joyce…tell her a story.

>*(Joyce begins to tell a story. As the story progresses, the girls lift a sheet off the bed and drape it up behind the candles. They then use the props in the scene [brush, knife, fabric, bracelet, piece of cedar, etc.] to "act out" a tiny shadow play in the candlelight.)*

JOYCE: A long time ago, before the time of the Great Flood, there were two brothers who lived with their grandparents.

One was very dark.

The other was very white.

They fought all the time.

This made their grandparents very angry.

One day, the grandparents said to them:

GIRL TWO: "Now that you have grown into young men, it is time for you to leave."

JOYCE: To the dark brother, they said: "You must go toward where the sun sets and grow with the land. Make a good life. Be useful."

Then, to the white brother, they said:

GIRL ONE: "You must go toward where the sun rises. Far from your dark brother. Make your life there."

JOYCE: Then, to both brothers they said:

GIRL TWO: "Because of your fighting, you will never in your lifetime come together again."

JOYCE: "But, someday, many years from now, your *children* – "

GIRL ONE: "And your *children's children* – "

GIRL TWO: "May find a way to come together."

JOYCE: "And, on that day, and not before…

>*(Joyce looks at the Young Girl, who has wiped away her tears.)*

YOUNG GIRL: "…They may live together in peace."

JOYCE: (*Nods.*) "The peace which you never found."

>*(The lights snap on in the room. Flute stops, abruptly. The girls leap up – the*

candle is blown out, the quilt, knife and carving are hidden. Miss Brennan enters.)

MISS BRENNAN: You should be asleep, girls. But…since you're up…I have a present for all of you. It's an anonymous gift to the school that came in the mail today.

(Miss Brennan reveals four gold crosses on chains. She puts a cross around each girl's neck, as – the singing of a hymn is heard from offstage: a youthful choir's rendition of "Onward Christian Soldiers" – slowly, deliberately, beautifully. Miss Brennan leaves. The girls look at their crosses. They look at each other, as lights shift to – the schoolyard. Day. A young Indian man, Darin Longfeather, is pushed onstage. He falls to the ground, hard. His arms are tied behind his back with rope. His clothes are torn and dirty. There is blood on his neck and face. Mullin, the County Sheriff, enters, carrying a rifle. He grabs Darin by his hair and pulls him to his feet. Joyce watches all of this, from a distance. They do not see her.)

MULLIN: This is your new school, boy. And this one's not so easy to run away from as the last one. But, I hope you try. I really do. Because, when you do, I'll be waiting for you. *(Yanks his hair, hard.)* Got me?

(Darin nods. Mullin sees Joyce.)

MULLIN: Girl.

JOYCE: *(Quietly.)* Yes, sir?

MULLIN: Where's the headmaster's house?

(Joyce points. Mullin shoves Darin off in that direction, following behind him. Joyce watches, frightened, confused. The hymn concludes. Lights shift to – another part of the schoolyard. Morning. Dr. Buchanan enters, his good clothes covered by a 'work apron' of some kind, his sleeves rolled up. He carries a burlap sack and a small shovel. He is planting tulips. Joyce stands near him, staring at him. After a moment, Dr. Buchanan looks up at her. The hymn ends.)

DR. BUCHANAN: Shouldn't you be in class, Joyce?

(Joyce nods.)

DR. BUCHANAN: Did you need to ask me something?

(Joyce nods.)

DR. BUCHANAN: Well, what is it?

JOYCE: Why did they beat that boy? He was all bloody. Why did they do that?

(Dr. Buchanan looks at Joyce…then slowly stands, facing her.)

DR. BUCHANAN: I'm sorry you had to see that.

JOYCE: Did you tell them to beat him?

(Silence. He moves closer to her, looks in her eyes.)

DR. BUCHANAN: (*Soft, firm.*) No, Joyce. I didn't.

JOYCE: But what did he do wrong?

(*Silence.*)

DR. BUCHANAN: (*This is the truth.*) I don't know.

(*She puts her head against his chest, wiping away tears, frightened. He puts an arm around her, tentatively. Speaks softly.*)

DR. BUCHANAN: You should be in class, Joyce.

(*She nods, still holding onto him.*)

DR. BUCHANAN: Well…would you like to help me plant some tulips?

(*She nods, slightly. During the following, he releases her, hands her a sack of tulip bulbs, kneels and resumes his work. She joins him.*)

DR. BUCHANAN: Did you know the world "tulip" can be traced back to the Turkish word *tulbend* – meaning "gauze" – which is also the root of the word "turban."

JOYCE: (*Referring to the bulbs.*) Like this?

DR. BUCHANAN: Give 'em just a little more room.

(*She does, as – the Superintendent enters, unseen, holding a small briefcase of some kind. She stands upstage, watching them plant.*)

DR. BUCHANAN: There you go. The people of the Ottoman empire believed the tulip resembled a turban in the way its petals wrapped around one another. There are literally hundreds of varieties to choose from. The important thing is to plant them in the fall –

JOYCE: (*Busy working.*) – **Before the first frost.**

(*These words slipped out. She quickly covers her mouth, fearful. Dr. Buchanan looks at her.*)

DR. BUCHANAN: What have you said?

(*She looks away.*)

DR. BUCHANAN: Joyce. Tell me.

JOYCE: (*Pause.*) **Before the first frost.**

DR. BUCHANAN: (*Firm.*) In *English,* Joyce.

JOYCE: Before the first frost. (*Pause.*) Isn't that right?

SUPERINTENDENT: Dr. Buchanan.

DR. BUCHANAN: (*Turns to her and stands, startled.*) Superintendent Lang. Hello. We weren't expecting you till next week.

SUPERINTENDENT: There was a change in my schedule.

DR. BUCHANAN: Well, we're thrilled you're here. Joyce, this is Mrs. Lang, the Superintendent of Indian Schools, visiting from Washington, D.C.

SUPERINTENDENT: I see we've added horticulture to our list of classes.

DR. BUCHANAN: Oh, I was just –

SUPERINTENDENT: Who authorized that purchase, Dr. Buchanan?

DR. BUCHANAN: Well, you did, Mrs. Lang. In your most recent report.

SUPERINTENDENT: I authorized the cultivation of local trees and plants, *not* tulips from Holland.

DR. BUCHANAN: I'll be glad to cover the cost myself, Mrs. Lang –

SUPERINTENDENT: The *cost* is only part of the issue. The use of student time to plant flowers seems a willful extravagance. Why isn't this girl in class with the others?

DR. BUCHANAN: With all due respect, I don't feel that beauty is an *extravagance*. I feel these students have a right to live in a schoolyard which is as rich in beauty as the homes we took them from.

SUPERINTENDENT: (*Sharp.*) And are you a position to *grant them rights?* Such as the right to speak their native language.

DR. BUCHANAN: I wanted to know what she said. Surely we can –

SUPERINTENDENT: Dr. Buchanan, the Indian language is not only discouraged, it is *forbidden.* (*Puts her arm around Joyce, speaks with compassion.*) The way to care for this girl, Dr. Buchanan, is to give her useful knowledge, and help her forget the pagan superstitions of her people.

(*A bell rings. The other girls and boys enter in a line, followed by Mr. Conrad. They carry large baskets filled with berries.*)

MR. CONRAD: What have I told you, Richard? No cutting in line. Cutting in line will not be tolerated here.

(*They stop when they see the Superintendent.*)

SUPERINTENDENT: Well, hello. What do we have here?

DR. BUCHANAN: Children, this is Superintendent Lang. Can you say hello?

STUDENTS: Hello.

MR. CONRAD: We've been out picking fall berries. Care for a taste?

SUPERINTENDENT: Certainly. (*The Superintendent takes a few berries in her hand and eats them, dropping a leaf or two to the ground in the process.*)

MR. CONRAD: Well?

SUPERINTENDENT: They're delicious. Thank you. I'd like a photograph of all of you, on the front steps of the school, for our files in Washington.

MR. CONRAD: We'll be waiting for you there. (*To the students.*) Let's go now. And remember, Richard, no cutting in line.

(*Mr. Conrad leaves, followed in a line by the other girls and boys, taking their baskets of berries with them. Nurse Warner enters and stands nearby.*)

SUPERINTENDENT: Dr. Buchanan, have I made myself clear on these issues?

DR. BUCHANAN: Yes.

SUPERINTENDENT: Good. (*Holds out her berry-stained fingers.*) I should wash up before our photo. The berries are delicious, but they do stain the skin.

(*Joyce kneels, picking up one of the dropped berry leaves. She hands it to the Superintendent.*)

SUPERINTENDENT: What is this?

JOYCE: It's the leaf of that berry. It'll remove the stain.

SUPERINTENDENT: (*Starting off.*) I've learned to rely on soap and water.

DR. BUCHANAN: I'd do as she says. It's the best way we've found.

(*The Superintendent stops and stares at Dr. Buchanan.*)

JOYCE: Lick it with your tongue, then rub it on your fingers in a circle, slowly.

(*The flute is heard, distant and soft. The Superintendent looks at Joyce. Then, she uses the leaf as Joyce suggested. The stains disappear. She looks back up at Joyce.*)

DR. BUCHANAN: Amazing, isn't it? Her grandfather taught her that. We've also learned that Madrona leaf tea is good for ulcers; and as for high-blood pressure, the leaf of the Huckleberry bush can –

SUPERINTENDENT: (*Firmly.*) Let's take that photo, shall we?

(*The Superintendent leaves. After a look at Joyce, Dr. Buchanan follows her.*)

NURSE WARNER: Joyce, I've been asked to pick one of the girls to be my nurse's aid. We'll tend to cuts and scrapes. And we'll learn about treating illness and preventing disease. Are you afraid of blood?

JOYCE: No.

NURSE WARNER: Good. Because I've chosen you, Joyce.

JOYCE: But, I've already been taught those things. My grandfather told me about remedies for fevers and illness –

NURSE WARNER: I know that. That's why I've chosen you. The things you learned at home will help us put the students at ease here.

(*Joyce stares at her.*)

NURSE WARNER: Now, why don't you tell me the Squaxin word for "doctor."

JOYCE: But we're not supposed to speak our language.

NURSE WARNER: I asked you something, Joyce.

(*Joyce looks around to make sure no one's listening, then speaks, softly.*)

JOYCE: (*Saying the word in her language.*) **Doctor.**

NURSE WARNER: (*Awkwardly, trying to say it.*) **Do-ct-or.** Close?

JOYCE: (*A bit of a smile.*) Sort of.

NURSE WARNER: What about "medicine."

JOYCE: (*Again, in her language.*) **Medicine.**

NURSE WARNER: (*Trying it.*) **Me-di-cine.**

(*Joyce shakes her head "no." Nurse Warner tries again.*)

NURSE WARNER: **M-edi-cin-e.**

(*Joyce nods.*)

NURSE WARNER: Okay. One more. How about "remedy." What is your word for "remedy."

(*Joyce stares at her, then looks away. Flue begins, quietly, distantly.*)

NURSE WARNER: Joyce?

(*Joyce keeps looking away.*)

NURSE WARNER: Well, maybe there isn't one. Not all languages have words for the same things we do.

(*Joyce looks back at Nurse Warner.*)

ADULT JOYCE: But, there *was* a word for it. But, no matter how long I stood there, I couldn't think of it. I couldn't *remember* it.

NURSE WARNER: Don't worry, Joyce. You're going to be a fine nurse's aid. And here. A letter came for you. It's from home.

(*Nurse Warner gives Joyce the letter and goes, leaving Joyce alone. Joyce watches her go. Then, she looks down at the letter in her hands. During the following, Joyce opens and reads the letter, silently. Behind her, all the students, the Superintendent, Dr. Buchanan, Mr. Conrad and Nurse Warner gather and pose for a group photo. The flag flies behind them. The flute is joined by distant drumming.*)

ADULT JOYCE: I'd never gotten a letter before. I knew it must be from Henry, since he knew how to write. It was a short letter.

(*A shaft of light on Henry, opposite.*)

HENRY: Dear Joyce, I have news from home. Your grandfather has passed on to the next world.

(*Behind those gathered for the photo, the shadow of Mud Bay Sam paddling his canoe is seen on the upstage wall.*)

DR. BUCHANAN: Joyce, we're waiting for you.

(*Joyce moves and takes her place amidst the others, facing the camera. She still holds the letter. The shadow of Mud Bay Sam remains.*)

HENRY: He loved nothing more than carving his cedar canoes. He spoke of one day paddling a new canoe across time.

SUPERINTENDENT: Look at the camera everyone.

HENRY: We know in our hearts that he is doing just that, and that he will meet all of our cherished ancestors on his journey.

MR. CONRAD: Say "Cheese."

ALL [EXCEPT JOYCE]: Cheese.

(*A crash of drums and a flash of brilliant white light as the picture is taken…When the light recedes, a shaft of light illuminates only Joyce, standing in the midst of the others, who are now in darkness. The shadow of Mud Bay Sam is gone.)*

HENRY: And we know his thoughts are with you, Joyce. Because your day has come. You are The Rememberer now.

(Lights fade on Henry and Adult Joyce, as the flute concludes its song. Then, a crash of drums – as lights snap out on Joyce.)

END ACT ONE

ACT TWO

As the audience gathers for Act Two – drumming, singing and dancing have already begun. This is a "Greeting Dance," led by Adult Joyce, which includes all of the native cast members – including Joyce, and the other boys and girls. Each wears the decorative clothing of their particular tribe. [The children wear blankets over their school clothes.] As the dance continues, the boys and girls gradually exit, leaving the adults to continue the dance. The group of adults moves downstage and parts…revealing Miss Brennan and Mr. Conrad in their midst. They are teaching the boys and girls to waltz. They count "one-two-three, one-two-three" as the boys and girls emerge in their school clothes, paired off in groups of two, learning the dance. Drumming, singing and dancing continue, as the adults dance offstage in one direction…and the boys and girls waltz offstage, opposite. Adult Joyce is left alone at one side of the stage. Joyce is left alone, opposite, holding a small, partially completed quilt.

ADULT JOYCE: It was winter now. I hadn't seen my family in six months. But, I kept working on my salmon quilt – stitching it together in my room at night, when no one was around.

(A trumpet plays "Reveille." Morning. Lights reveal the washroom, again – as Joyce enters in line behind the other three girls. They bring their tin boxes with them, as before. Nurse Warner, as before, walks down the line and gives them their tooth powder. They begin to brush their teeth, identically, as before. Nurse Warner leaves. The girls are alone. They immediately turn and start talking to each other – now brushing any way they want to.)

GIRL TWO: **You were laughing, I saw you!**

JOYCE: **You were laughing louder!**

YOUNG GIRL: **Laughing at what?**

GIRL TWO: **At the fish oil!**

(*Joyce and Girl Two laugh, as – Girl One quiets them, quickly.*)

GIRL ONE: (*An urgent whisper.*) **Quiet. She's here –**

(*The girls straighten up and brush their teeth very formally, as – Miss Brennan looks in on them.*)

MISS BRENNAN: No Indian words, girls. You know better.

(*Miss Brennan checks her hair in their mirror, quickly. She also gives the perfume on her wrist a quick sniff. She smiles.*)

MISS BRENNAN: I'll see you in class.

(*Miss Brennan goes, the girls relax.*)

GIRL ONE: You did not!

GIRL TWO: Yes, I did!

YOUNG GIRL: What? Did what?

GIRL ONE: Who saw you?

GIRL TWO: Joyce saw me.

YOUNG GIRL: What? Saw what?

GIRL TWO: Tell her.

JOYCE: Yeah, I saw her.

GIRL ONE: Really?

JOYCE: Yeah.

YOUNG GIRL: What? Saw her do what?

GIRL TWO: Tell her, Joyce.

JOYCE: She found a bottle of Miss Brennan's perfume.

GIRL ONE: So?

JOYCE: And she dumped out the perfume and filled it with fish oil.

YOUNG GIRL: Really?

GIRL ONE: (*To Girl Two.*) Did she get mad?

JOYCE: She hasn't noticed!

(*The girls laugh, heartily.*)

YOUNG GIRL: When did you do this?

GIRL TWO: Two weeks ago!

(*The girls laugh even louder. They finish brushing their teeth and hair during the following.*)

GIRL ONE: Darin Longfeather showed me the scars on his back.

(*The girls laugh a bit.*)

JOYCE: What scars?

GIRL ONE: It's not funny. The scars from his other school. Where they whipped him with a belt.

(*The girls are more serious, now.*)

JOYCE: Why'd they do that?

GIRL ONE: I don't know. But, they did. I *saw*. That's why he ran away.

JOYCE: They caught him and sent him here.

GIRL TWO: I bet he runs away again.

GIRL ONE: The Sheriff'll kill him if he does. Darin said so.

JOYCE: Dr. Buchanan wouldn't let them hurt him.

GIRL TWO: They can do whatever they want, Joyce. It doesn't matter what the teachers say.

GIRL ONE: Darin said there's no way he'll get caught.

JOYCE: What do you mean?

GIRL ONE: He says he knows a trail. A secret trail that will get him home.

(*A bell rings. The girls file out in a line – as the shadow of the Pitch Woman is seen upstage, briefly. She is wielding her walking stick as a weapon, swinging it around over her head. Joyce stops and looks at the shadow. The shadow of the Pitch Woman's movements are accompanied by quick bursts of drumming and wailing. After a moment, the shadow vanishes, the drumming and wailing fades, as lights shift to – a classroom. Mr. Conrad stands in front of all of the gathered boys and girls, holding a history book. In groups of twos, the boys and girls are sharing history books and listening to Mr. Conrad. One of the boys is Darin Longfeather. Joyce shares her book with Otis – who still wears the pouch around his neck.*)

MR. CONRAD: Now, this period of history was preceded by what we call the Great Flood. Joyce, I believe its your turn to read to us.

(*Joyce stands, holding her book.*)

MR. CONRAD: Why don't you begin with "God commanded Noah to build an ark…"

JOYCE: (*Reading.*) "God commanded Noah to build an ark…"

(*Otis raises his hand.*)

MR. CONRAD: Yes, Otis?

OTIS: What's an ark?

GIRL ONE: A boat.

MR. CONRAD: A very large boat. You'll see. Continue, Joyce.

JOYCE: "And God told Noah to fill the ark with two of every sp – , (*Trying to pronounce the word.*) every spec –

MR. CONRAD: *Species.*

JOYCE: "With two of every *species* of animal on the earth."

MR. CONRAD: Good. Keep going.

JOYCE: "Having done this, Noah and his – " (*She stops.*)

MR. CONRAD: Go on, Joyce. "Noah and his family gathered with the animals on the ark."

JOYCE: But there aren't any animals, yet.

MR. CONRAD: Sure there are. God created them on the sixth day. Noah has saved them, prior to the flood. He has brought them to the ark two by two. Now –

JOYCE: There are no animals until *after* the Great Flood.

MR. CONRAD: What did you say?

(*Joyce hands the book to Otis and continues.*)

JOYCE: During the Great Flood, some of the Indians made it safely to the top of a high mountain on rafts they had built of cedar logs. When the Flood was over, some of the Indians were selected by the Great Spirits to carry on as people. Others were –

MR. CONRAD: Joyce, I won't have you telling those stories in this class.

JOYCE: It's not a story, it's the way the animals –

MR. CONRAD: This is history class, not story hour. There is no place here for your native superstitions. Now, please sit down.

JOYCE: But you asked me to tell about the –

MR. CONRAD: *Sit. Down.* Otis, perhaps you can continue where Joyce left off.
(*Mr. Conrad looks at Otis. Joyce looks at Otis. The others look at Otis. Otis stands, holding the book. He looks at Joyce. Then, he faces Mr. Conrad.*)

MR. CONRAD: Well?

OTIS: (*Reads, slowly, clearly.*) "Having done this, Noah and his family gathered on the ark."

MR. CONRAD: Good. Keep going.

OTIS: (*Reads.*) "The rains came and flooded the earth."
(*He looks at Joyce, then continues, not reading from the book.*)

OTIS: And then the Great Spirit chose *some* of the Indians to carry on as people –

JOYCE: (*Standing next to Otis.*) – And he made some of the other people into animals.

MR. CONRAD: That's enough –

JOYCE: (*Bolder now.*) The Great Spirit said to one young man:

BOY ONE: "You are fleet of foot, but you are overly vain – "

GIRL TWO: (*Stands.*) "So you shall be called 'Deer' and forever depend on your fleetness of foot to survive."

MR. CONRAD: Now, look here, I will not have –

GIRL ONE: (*Stands.*) And to one cross old woman, the Great Spirit said: "You are a grumpy woman so you shall be known as 'Bear' –

BOY TWO: (*Stands.*) "And you will have to walk around forever on all-fours – "

YOUNG BOY: (*Stands, smiling.*) "And scratch around for your food."

MR. CONRAD: Sit down, all of you –

JOYCE: And that is why, to this day, our parents will say –

YOUNG GIRL: (*Stands, proudly.*) "Be nice to bears in the woods – "

OTIS: "Because one of them might be your grandmother!"

(*The students laugh, enjoying themselves.*)

MR. CONRAD: Sit down this instant!

(*They remain standing. The only student who is not standing is Darin Longfeather.*)

JOYCE: And the Great Spirit said: "Always respect the animals – for they once were your brothers and sisters, your aunts and uncles, your mothers and your fathers."

(*Silence. Mr. Conrad stares at Joyce.*)

MR. CONRAD: As you can see, Darin Longfeather did not stand up. That's because he knew better. Now, you're about to learn the same lesson he did.

(*He slams his book shut with anger – causing everyone except Joyce to sit. Mr. Conrad and Joyce stare at one another.*)

MR. CONRAD: Follow me.

(*Lights shift – as Joyce follows Mr. Conrad across the stage. A flute plays.*)

ADULT JOYCE: As we walked across the schoolyard, I thought of the words of my father's grandfather. A Duwamish chief who has come to be called Chief Seattle.

(*Chief Seattle is seen, in silhouette upstage. His voice is amplified, on tape.*)

VOICE OF CHIEF SEATTLE: Your religion was written on tablets of stone by the iron finger of an angry god.

Our religion is the tradition of our ancestors, the dreams of our old men, given to them in the solemn hours of night by the Great Spirit.

And, it is written in the hearts of our people.

(*Dr. Buchanan's office. It is designated by a high-backed leather chair and a small, wooden chair. Dr. Buchanan sits in the leather chair. Joyce enters and sits in the wooden chair – followed by Mr. Conrad, who stands. Joyce is between the two men as they talk. Adult Joyce stands nearby, watching. The flute fades away…as does the image of Chief Seattle.*)

DR. BUCHANAN: Joyce, Mr. Conrad has told me what happened in class today.

JOYCE: He's asking me to learn things that never happened!

MR. CONRAD: I will not stand for this impudence and –

DR. BUCHANAN: Enough, enough. (*To Joyce, calmly but firmly.*) Joyce, I expect you to respect your instructors here.

JOYCE: But I was –

(*Dr. Buchanan raises his hand, and she stops, immediately.*)

DR. BUCHANAN: This nation is currently governed on Christian principles. Those principles have found their way into the lessons which Mr. Conrad is hired to teach. There are, naturally, *differences* between our teaching and the teaching of your elders. But, I require you to respect the difficult task which Mr. Conrad has been given. (*Pause.*) Is that clear?

JOYCE: (*Softly.*) Yes.

MR. CONRAD: Thank you, Dr. Buchanan. Joyce, I'll see you in class. (*Mr. Conrad starts out.*)

DR. BUCHANAN: Just a moment, Mr. Conrad. I'm not finished with you.
(*Mr. Conrad stops.*)

DR. BUCHANAN: I have filed a request with the Superintendent. That request asks that our students be allowed one hour a day in which to tell the stories of their culture. In this way, as we prepare them for the future, their lineage with the past will not be severed. (*Pause.*) I want your assurance that you will support my request.

MR. CONRAD: I most certainly will not.

DR. BUCHANAN: And why is that?

MR. CONRAD: We can't be expected to instill Christian and patriotic principles in these children, while at the same time allowing them to retreat to their savage heritage.

DR. BUCHANAN: We are charged with giving them a humane, moral outlook.

MR. CONRAD: But we must not make them *self-consciously moral* – giving us only the answers they know we want to hear. We must, instead, make them *unconsciously, automatically moral.*

DR. BUCHANAN: And how do you propose to do *that*, Mr. Conrad?

MR. CONRAD: In the words of our Superintendent: "*We must kill the Indian to save the man.*" (*Silence. Standoff.*) So, *no*, Dr. Buchanan. I cannot support your request. It flies in the face of our mission here. If this gives you grounds to dismiss me, so be it. I have made my position clear.
(*Mr. Conrad leaves. Dr. Buchanan watches him go, then returns to his chair and sits. Silence. Joyce does not move.*)

DR. BUCHANAN: (*Simply.*) It's time for your next class, Joyce. Don't be late.
(*Joyce stands and looks at him. Dr. Buchanan has picked up some work and is writing with a pen. Joyce takes a few steps away. Then, Joyce stops, staring at the ground.*)

ADULT JOYCE: We don't always have the words when we're young. There were so many things I wanted to say. I wanted to say I was sorry. But I also wanted to tell him that I was now The Rememberer, I was now the protector of the past. I wanted to tell him I was afraid I'd fail. Both in his eyes – and in the eyes of my tribe, my family.

I looked up at him.

(*Joyce does. Dr. Buchanan looks up from his work, meeting her eye. Silence.*)

ADULT JOYCE: But, no words came.

(*Joyce leaves, as lights shift to – the schoolyard. As Joyce walks, she is passed by Darin Longfeather, who is pushing a wheelbarrow filled with large feed sacks. Joyce stops, as Darin goes past her. When he is nearly gone, she says…*)

JOYCE: Darin.

(*He stops, but does not turn to her. She looks around, then approaches him, cautiously.*)

JOYCE: I'm Joyce.

(*He does not respond.*)

JOYCE: I've never talked to you.

(*He does not respond.*)

JOYCE: Lillian said at your old school they beat you.

(*He turns and looks at her. Long silence.*)

JOYCE: Why?

DARIN LONGFEATHER: (*Softly.*) What did you say?

JOYCE: Why? (*Pause.*) What did you do?

DARIN LONGFEATHER: You're a stupid girl.

(*He grabs the handle of the wheelbarrow and prepares to leave –*)

JOYCE: (*Angry.*) You must have deserved it.

(*He immediately lets go of the wheelbarrow and walks up to Joyce. Stands very close to her, frightening her.*)

DARIN LONGFEATHER: Do you want to know what I did? *Do you?* (*Pause, softer now.*) I said my Mother's name. At night, *in my sleep,* I said my Mother's name. And they heard me. *"No Indian names"* they said, *"No Indian names."* So, the next night, they made me sleep on the wood floor, without a blanket. And they watched me. And, I closed my eyes and I tried with all my heart to *forget my Mother's name.* But, in my sleep, I said it again. So, the next night they took me to the barn. And they stuffed cloth in my mouth. And, they all stood around me while I slept. I tried to stay awake. I tried not to think about her, or her face, or her voice. *I tried to pretend my Mother was dead.* But, in the middle of the night, they woke me up and tied my hands to a post. They told me I'd said her name again in my sleep. And I swore I'd never do it again – but they said it was too late. That I would have to be taught a lesson. (*Pause.*) They took off my shirt. (*Pause.*) One of the men took off his belt. (*Pause.*) And he started hitting me.

(*Pause. Very distant sound of leather striking flesh.*)

DARIN LONGFEATHER: And I didn't cry. Because I could hear my Mother's voice, saying: **You'll be home soon, my beautiful boy.** (*Pause, softly.*) You'll be home soon.

(*The sound of the whipping stops. Darin stares at Joyce. She says nothing. He walks back to the wheelbarrow. Lifts it.*)

JOYCE: They say you know a secret trail.

(*Darin looks back at her, as – Mr. Conrad enters.*)

MR. CONRAD: C'mon, Darin. We're waiting.

(*Darin looks at Joyce for another moment, then pushes the wheelbarrow past Mr. Conrad.*)

MR. CONRAD: Where are you supposed to be, Joyce? Do you know?

(*Joyce is looking off into the distance. She nods.*)

MR. CONRAD: Then, go.

(*Mr. Conrad leaves, as lights shift to – Joyce's room. Joyce arrives and sits on the bed. She takes out her quilt and begins sewing, concentrating hard on her work. As she does, she speaks to the empty room…*)

JOYCE: (*Repeat and continue until noted…*) Deeht was succeeded by this brother, Odiee. His descendants were Kat'hl-che-da, then Wa-wa-tsoo-pa, then Wat-lai-waih-kose, Klatch-tis-sub, How-e-sub, Ko-shah-sit, and then…and then…(*Repeat until noted.*)

(*Drumming begins, distantly. The lights shift to night during the following – a shaft of moonlight coming through the window and illuminating Joyce. The following cacophony of taped voices begins softly, then builds to a deafening crescendo. The voices overlap one another, forming a rush of language, distorted, echoing, filing the theater.*)

MR. CONRAD: (*Amplified/distorted.*) Kill the Indian to save the man –

DR. BUCHANAN: (*Amplified/distorted.*) Joyce, I expect you to respect your instructors here –

EMILY SAM:: (*Amplified/distorted.*) Learn to accomplish one thing, Joyce –

DARIN LONGFEATHER: (*Amplified/distorted.*) I tried to forget my Mother's name –

(*Joyce stops sewing and holds the quilt to her, tightly. She looks in the direction of the window, still repeating the family names. Drumming grows very loud, during the following. It is joined, at random intervals, by the sound of wailing.*)

MUD BAY SAM: (*Amplified/distorted.*) At twilight time, the Pitch Woman throws her basket over her back –

SUPERINTENDENT: (*Amplified/distorted.*) The Indian language is not only discouraged, it is *forbidden* –

GIRL ONE: (*Amplified/distorted.*) He says he knows a trail –

MUD BAY SAM: (*Amplified/distorted.*) And goes forth looking for disobedient children –

EMILY SAM: (*Amplified/distorted.*) You must account for yourself and your time on Earth –

NURSE WARNER: (*Amplified/distorted.*) How about "remedy?" What is your word for "remedy?" –

DARIN LONGFEATHER: (*Amplified/distorted.*) *"No Indian names"* –

MUD BAY SAM: (*Amplified/distorted.*) She is part of the black night now –

GIRL ONE: (*Amplified/distorted.*) A secret trail that will get him home –

(*Joyce sets the quilt down. She moves to the window and looks out.*)

DARIN LONGFEATHER: (*Amplified/distorted.*) I tried to pretend my Mother was dead –

MR. CONRAD: (*Amplified/distorted.*) Kill the Indian to save the man –

EMILY SAM: (*Amplified/distorted.*) You must learn to be useful –

MUD BAY SAM: (*Amplified/distorted.*) She will never be seen again –

(*Henry's voice is heard, also amplified and distorted, singing the "Hoo-hoo-hoo" song, from Act One. This joins the ongoing drumming and wailing. Joyce turns from the window. She looks at her quilt one more time…then hurries across the room to her chair. She picks up the chair and brings it across the room, setting it just below the window. She climbs up on the chair.*)

MUD BAY SAM: (*Amplified/distorted.*) The time will come, **little one,** when you will take my place –

SUPERINTENDENT: (*Amplified/distorted.*) The way to care for this girl is to give her useful knowledge –

DARIN LONGFEATHER: (*Amplified/distorted.*) *"No Indian names"* –

LONGHOUSE: (*Amplified/distorted.*) **It's the only way that you'll learn, son** –

SUPERINTENDENT: (*Amplified/distorted.*) And help her forget the pagan superstitions of her people –

(*Joyce opens the window and climbs onto the sill, looking out. Drumming, wailing and Henry's singing reach a crescendo.*)

MUD BAY SAM: (*Amplified/distorted.*) You will hold our history and our stories in your mind –

DARIN LONGFEATHER: (*Amplified/distorted.*) *"No Indian names"* –

MR. CONRAD: (*Amplified/distorted.*) Kill the Indian to save the man –

GIRL ONE: (*Amplified/distorted.*) A secret trail that will get him home –

MUD BAY SAM: (*Amplified/distorted.*) And you will pass them on –

(*Joyce jumps out the window, and instantly there is – Silence, darkness. Joyce's room is gone. We are now in – the woods. It begins to rain. The sound of rain is joined by occasional bursts of thunder. As Joyce fearfully navigates through this darkness – a branch snaps. Joyce stops, moves in the other direction. But, then, seemingly in front of her – another branch snaps. She changes directions, as – still another branch snaps. And another. And another. She does not know which way to turn, when suddenly – a loud crack of thunder, as – Joyce is enveloped in a black shawl and "disappears." She screams. A shaft of moonlight slowly rises on…Aunt Sophie, who has thrown her shawl over Joyce.*)

AUNT SOPHIE: Quiet, **little one.** It's a cold night. I'm just trying to keep you warm. What are you doing out here?

JOYCE: (*Terrified, shaking.*) Who are you?

AUNT SOPHIE: You'll come to know me.

JOYCE: You're the Pitch Woman! I knew it!

(*Joyce tries to run, but Aunt Sophie easily restrains her.*)

JOYCE: Let me go! I want to go home.

AUNT SOPHIE: I know you want to go home, Joyce. That's why I'm here.

JOYCE: Let go of me!

AUNT SOPHIE: Is that what you want me to do?

JOYCE: Yes.

AUNT SOPHIE: Are you sure?

JOYCE: Yes.

AUNT SOPHIE: Then, I will. **Find your way now, Joyce. Find your way home.**

(*Aunt Sophie lets go of Joyce. Joyce turns to run, as – suddenly, there is another loud crack of thunder. Instantly, the stage goes black, except for a tight shaft of downlight on Joyce. She is frozen with fear, staring front. The moonlight is mysteriously gone. The sound of rain grows louder. Drumming joins the rain, randomly, under. Aunt Sophie stands a distance, watching.*)

AUNT SOPHIE: Why don't you go? There's no one to stop you.

JOYCE: The moon is gone. I can't see. (*Looks around more.*) I can't see anything at all. (*Joyce stares front in the tight shaft of downlight – as the rain continues to fall.*)

AUNT SOPHIE: Did your grandmother tell you about "Taman'us"?

JOYCE: Yes.

AUNT SOPHIE: What did she say?

JOYCE: She said when I got old enough, I would go into the woods, and pray to the Great Spirit – and I would be given power.

AUNT SOPHIE: You would be given "Taman'us."

JOYCE: Yes.

AUNT SOPHIE: How?

JOYCE: She said I would be given my song. And my song would give me direction.

(*As the rain continues to fall, Aunt Sophie approaches Joyce, slowly, singing "Joyce's song" to her. Joyce watches and listens, carefully. After a moment, Joyce says –*)

JOYCE: Who are you?

AUNT SOPHIE: Sing with me.

(*Aunt Sophie sings the song, and, gradually, Joyce joins in and sings with her…*)

JOYCE AND AUNT SOPHIE: "Hoo la chad sthloo la ha ha ob

Hoo la chad sthloo la ha ha ob

Ha woo, ha woo, ha woo, ha woo…"

(*As they sing, the shadows of Joyce's family are seen, upstage. They, too, join in the singing of "Joyce's song." When the song has been learned, Aunt Sophie steps away from Joyce. The shadows of the family continue singing, softly.*)

AUNT SOPHIE: This is your song now. It's the voice of your ancestors speaking to you across time. And, as you sing it, you will find direction.

JOYCE: But, I'm lost. I don't know which way to –

AUNT SOPHIE: Close your eyes, Joyce. And sing your song.

JOYCE: Will it show me the way home?

AUNT SOPHIE: It will show you where you are *most needed*. It will show you how best to use your gift of life.

(*Aunt Sophie looks at Joyce. Joyce turns front, closes her eyes, and begins to sing her song. The sound of rain continues. After a moment, Joyce turns to speak to Aunt Sophie…*)

JOYCE: But what is your name – ?

(*Aunt Sophie is gone. The shadows of Joyce's family are gone, also. Joyce stands, alone. Then, she begins once again to sing her song. And she begins to walk…*)

ADULT JOYCE: I still didn't know where I was. But I sang my song…and I kept walking. I walked all night through the woods. And every time I got frightened, I sang louder. And as the sun rose. I hadn't found my way home. I had found myself…

(*Distantly…"Reveille" is heard.*)

ADULT JOYCE:…Back at the school. I still didn't know the name of that woman, but I remembered what she told me: that my song would lead me to where I was most needed.

(A bell rings. Lights reveal the washroom. The girls enter in a line, as before, but this time there are only three of them: Joyce, Girl Two and the Young Girl. Girl One is not with them, though her tin box is sitting on the counter, unopened. As the girls talk their language, Nurse Warner enters and stands behind them, listening. They do not see her.)

GIRL TWO: One of the boys says it's a curse.

JOYCE: What are you talking about?

GIRL TWO: It's a curse on all of us here.

YOUNG GIRL: Why? What have we done?

GIRL TWO: We've forgotten our people, so we're being punished.

(Nurse Warner steps forward. Seeing her, the girls stop talking and ready their toothbrushes. Nurse Warner walks down the line with the tooth powder, as before.)

JOYCE: Nurse Warner?

NURSE WARNER: Yes, Joyce.

JOYCE: Where's Lillian?

(The other girls stop brushing, and look at Joyce. Nurse Warner looks at Joyce for a moment, then turns to the other girls.)

NURSE WARNER: Girls, finish up now.

(Girl Two and the Young Girl finish brushing and exit, taking their tin boxes with them.)

NURSE WARNER: Joyce, you're my nurse's aid. And I'm going to need your help. Many of the children are getting sick. We need to quarantine them – keep them away from the others – and we've got to help them get better.
(Joyce nods.)

NURSE WARNER: It's called "influenza." We'll do everything we can to fight it.
(Joyce is looking at Girl One's abandoned tin box.)

NURSE WARNER: Lillian got very sick. And she died.
(Nurse Warner gently puts her arm around Joyce.)

NURSE WARNER: Have you known anyone who died, Joyce?

ADULT JOYCE: And I thought about Mud Bay Sam. I remembered how he told us not to speak the name of someone who had died for one year after their death – for fear we'd call them back to this world when they should be moving on to the next.

NURSE WARNER: Can I count on you to help me?

(Joyce nods. Joyce and Nurse Warner exit, as the lights shift to – a hospital room. Nurse Warner and Joyce move into the room, putting white masks on to cover their nose and mouth. They encounter – Dr. Buchanan and Miss Brennan, each wearing heavy coats and pieces of fabric covering their noses

and mouths. They are carrying a stretcher. On the stretcher is the Young Boy. He is dead.)

ADULT JOYCE: This was the epidemic that would kill millions of people, world-wide. It moved across the land like a plague. And we at Tulalip were not exempt.

NURSE WARNER: Who is it, Dr. Buchanan?

DR. BUCHANAN: (*Quietly.*) It's Lucas.

(*Nurse Warner kneels down, looking at the Young Boy. Then she makes a notation on her clipboard. Joyce covers the Young Boy's head with a sheet.*)

NURSE WARNER: When will the burial detail be here?

DR. BUCHANAN: They said Friday.

NURSE WARNER: We need them sooner. The disease is spreading. If we don't get the bodies buried, those still living won't stand a chance.

DR. BUCHANAN: I know that. I told them. (*Silence.*)

NURSE WARNER: Take him to the basement with the others.

(*Dr. Buchanan and Miss Brennan lift the stretcher and carry it off. During the following, Nurse Warner and Joyce take their positions behind a small cart which holds the medicinal drinks, as – Boy One, Boy Two, Darin Longfeather, Girl Two, the Young Girl and Otis enter in a line, waiting to receive their medicine. Everyone in line is wrapped in blankets or heavy coats.*)

ADULT JOYCE: I remember thinking how strange it was that we were staying in the same building where death had been. At home, when there was a death, often the building would be torn down, or left empty for a year until the spirit of death had passed.

But that year, at Tulalip, there was nowhere to go.

Death was in all the buildings.

(*Mr. Conrad enters, coughing, bundled in a blanket, very sick. He stands at a distance from the line of students.*)

NURSE WARNER: It's important that you abide by the quarantine. All of you. You must only leave your rooms to report here for your liquids and vitamins.

BOY TWO: Mr. Conrad.

(*Mr. Conrad looks up. Boy Two speaks, gently.*)

BOY TWO: You can cut in line.

(*Mr. Conrad stares at him.*)

BOY TWO: Right here. In front of me.

(*Mr. Conrad moves and takes his place in line in front of Boy Two.*)

MR. CONRAD: (*Quietly.*) Thank you.

(*The line begins to move. Joyce hands out the medicinal drinks, one by one. Nurse Warner makes notes on a clipboard.*)

JOYCE: Here you are. (*To the next in line.*) Here you are. Make sure you drink all of it.

(*The next person in line is Mr. Conrad.*)

JOYCE: Hello, Mr. Conrad. How are you feeling?

(*Mr. Conrad shakes his head "no." Joyce hands him a drink.*)

JOYCE: Drink this. It'll help you feel better.

(*Mr. Conrad takes the medicine and drinks, then moves on. Boy One hesitates as he approaches Joyce. She offers him the drink. He shakes his head "No."*)

JOYCE: It won't hurt you.

(*Again, he shakes his head "No" and steps out of the line. Joyce moves close to him, speaks softly in her language.*)

JOYCE: **It will give us strength. The strength to go home.**

(*He looks at her. Then, he drinks the medicine. Looks at her.*)

BOY ONE: **Thank you.**

(*When the others have gone, Otis – the last student in line – is handed his medicine by Joyce.*)

JOYCE: Drink it all up, Otis.

(*Otis drinks, winces, and coughs a bit.*)

JOYCE: Are you scared?

OTIS: No.

(*Otis shows Joyce the pouch he still wears around his neck.*)

OTIS: You said this pouch will protect me.

JOYCE: And it will.

(*Nurse Warner feels Otis' forehead.*)

NURSE WARNER: Do you feel all right, Otis?

(*Otis nods, bravely, then walks off.*)

JOYCE: (*Looking in the direction of Otis.*) How is he?

NURSE WARNER: Not good. He's got a bad fever. We'll have to watch him.

(*Nurse Warner makes a note on her clipboard.*)

JOYCE: Nurse Warner?

NURSE WARNER: Yes, Joyce?

JOYCE: How many is it now?

(*Nurse Warner lowers her clipboard and looks at Joyce, but she can't find the words. She turns away, and pushes the small cart offstage. Joyce is left alone.*)

ADULT JOYCE: The epidemic was taking several children a day. Many teachers had died, also. Nurse Warner carried her clipboard with her everywhere, keeping a record of the epidemic.

(A bell rings. Lights reveal the washroom, as before. A flute begins to play, distant and melancholy. As Adult Joyce speaks, Joyce enters and stands in front of her tin box. She is alone. The boxes of the other girls sit on the counter, unopened. The sound of drumming, echoing quietly in the distance. Joyce takes out her hair brush, and holds it in front of her. She does not brush her hair. She just stares front. Alone.)

ADULT JOYCE: These were the coldest days of winter. And, as the school waited for a military burial detail to arrive – the school had only one place to store the bodies of the dead. In the freezing cold basement of the schoolhouse.

And, as the winter wore on, the basement filled up with bodies.

(The hospital room, lit only by a few lamps. Dr. Buchanan and Darin Longfeather enter, carrying an empty stretcher. They wear cloth masks over their nose and mouth. Flute and drumming continue, under. Joyce moves into the room. Dr. Buchanan removes his mask.)

DR. BUCHANAN: Joyce, Nurse Warner has taken ill. She's been quarantined with the others. She needs your help.

(Joyce nods.)

DR. BUCHANAN: The burial detail arrives tomorrow. We need to have an accurate count before the bodies are taken away. Nurse Warner needs you to find her clipboard and bring it to her. Right away.

JOYCE: I'll look in her office.

DR. BUCHANAN: Don't be late, Joyce. We all need our rest. We've got to keep each other strong.

(Dr. Buchanan starts off. Darin follows, then turns back to Joyce.)

DARIN LONGFEATHER: I think I saw her clipboard tonight.

JOYCE: Where?

DARIN LONGFEATHER: At the schoolhouse. Downstairs.

JOYCE: In the basement?

DARIN LONGFEATHER: Yes.

(Darin leaves – as Joyce takes her lamp and leaves, opposite. Joyce descends a small staircase into a dark, cold, musty room – the basement of the schoolhouse. The floor of the room is covered with bodies, most wrapped in dirty grey sheets or blankets. The bodies are only dimly visible in the foreboding darkness. The sound of water dripping. Joyce wears a heavy coat, and a hospital mask over her nose and mouth. She carries the small lamp. She stops at the foot of the stairs and looks, horrified and motionless, at the bodies. She coughs, wipes her eyes…and then begins to walk amidst the bodies, slowly, looking for the clipboard. When she is surrounded by the bodies, Joyce

stops. She has seen something. She bends down toward an [unseen] body in the midst of the pile. She covers her eyes with her hands, crying. She reaches toward the body with her hand. She lifts something away from the body and holds it to the light of her lamp. It is the small, leather pouch. She holds it to her chest, crying. She stands. She looks, again, back down at the [unseen] body. She wipes tears from her eyes. She continues on, moving through the bodies, looking for the clipboard. Then, a very soft, frightened voice...)

VOICE: **Where am I?**

(Joyce stops. She turns and looks in the direction of the voice – which is coming from the pile of bodies.)

VOICE: **Hello?**

(Joyce looks around the room, too frightened to speak. Suddenly, a little boy's head rises out of the pile of bodies. It is Otis.)

OTIS: *(Very quietly, frightened.)* Where am I?

(Joyce sees him.)

JOYCE: Otis! *(She rushes to him and holds him, lifting him out of the pile of bodies.)*

(He throws his arms around her and holds on tightly, crying.)

OTIS: **Don't go. I'm scared. Don't go.**

JOYCE: It's okay. I'm right here.

(They hold each other for a long time. Then, Joyce puts the pouch around Otis' neck.)

OTIS: I wore my pouch. Just like you said.

JOYCE: **Come on, Otis. Let's go.**

(They leave the basement – as lights shift to Adult Joyce.)

ADULT JOYCE: He had been unconscious, with a bad fever – but they'd thought he was dead. They had mistakenly brought him to the basement with the others. I found him one hour before the burial detail arrived.

He survived the epidemic and is alive to this day.

(The schoolyard slowly fills with warm light. A flute plays, softly, beautifully. The flag flies at half-mast. Dr. Buchanan enters, walking slowly to his flower box. He discovers several beautiful tulips. He kneels and views them quietly, joyously. Joyce enters and stands near Dr. Buchanan, looking at the tulips.)

DR. BUCHANAN: *(Quietly.)* Have you seen them, Joyce?

(Joyce nods, he speaks very quietly.)

DR. BUCHANAN: Spring is here. And nature, once again, has healed the world.

(A bell rings. The students enter and stand in a line, facing upstage, looking at Dr. Buchanan. Their backs are to the audience. Joyce joins them in line.

Mr. Conrad and Miss Brennan walk behind them, placing small bundles in a row, downstage. The students do not see them. The flute fades away.)

ADULT JOYCE: And then one day, without warning, they told us what we'd been waiting to hear.

DR. BUCHANAN: Have a safe trip home. I'll see you in the fall.

(Dr. Buchanan exits. Mr. Conrad and Miss Brennan exit, opposite. The students – still in line – turn and face downstage. They see the bundles on the ground…their clothes. Their own clothes. A lost moment: They look at each other. Then, some of the students rush to their clothes, put on a shirt, etc. Others stand, staring at the clothes, frightened. They look at each other. Some of them hug. Some of them walk off in groups. Some alone. Joyce stands, looking down at her clothes. Otis stands next to her, doing the same. Otis turns to Joyce. He takes the pouch from around his neck. He puts it around Joyce's neck. They embrace. Otis smiles, grabs his clothes, and runs off. As Joyce bends down to pick up her clothes, she feels a tap on her shoulder. She turns and sees – Aunt Sophie, holding a small suitcase. Joyce screams and jumps back.)

AUNT SOPHIE: Did you miss me?

JOYCE: What do you want now?

AUNT SOPHIE: I came to say goodbye. My work is done. *(Pause, a tender smile.)* Joyce, I've been with you since you were given your name. *(Pause.)* You're a young girl. You don't have to understand it all, yet – but in time you will. *(A flute begins to play "Joyce's song," under the following.)*

AUNT SOPHIE: You're frightened about going home, aren't you?

(Joyce nods.)

AUNT SOPHIE: Remember your grandfather's words: We are never chosen for something that we don't have the power to do. *(Aunt Sophie goes to Joyce and nearly touches her face.)* You have your song now, Joyce. It will give you strength. Never forget that.

(Joyce looks at the suitcase. Then, she quickly kneels and puts her "own" clothes in the suitcase. Aunt Sophie smiles. Joyce stands and says –)

JOYCE: But, I don't know your name –

(Aunt Sophie is gone. Joyce finds herself in the midst of – the yard in Mud Bay. Mount Rainier, once again, looms in the distance. The housepost is raised back up, in place of the flagpole. A potlach is in full swing: Loud singing and drumming, as a procession of guests – young and old – enter. They carry a long wooden plank, decorated with cedar boughs. In the midst of the cedar boughs, lies the first salmon of the year. Joyce stands at the edge of the celebration, unseen. She still wears her school uniform. She holds her small

suitcase. Adult Joyce stands, opposite, watching. After parading the salmon around the schoolyard, the guests place it downstage and gather around it. Emily Sam looks up and is the first to see Joyce. Singing and drumming stop, abruptly. Everyone stands, motionless – staring at Joyce. After a long silence, Emily Sam says quietly, simple…)

EMILY SAM: **My girl. You're home.**

(Emily Sam walks to Joyce…looks in her eyes…looks at her clothes…touches her now-short hair…then…embraces her. They hold each other tightly. Silently. Still no one else moves. When the embrace is over…Longhouse, standing at the head of the board containing the first salmon, speaks.)

LONGHOUSE: Joyce, we've caught the first salmon. *(Pause.)* Will you help us honor it?

(Joyce stares at Longhouse, and at the others. Joyce looks at Emily Sam…who nods. Joyce walks…very slowly…through the guests…as they greet her, embrace her, welcome her. Finally, she arrives in their midst, at the place of prominence. When she is in place, Longhouse looks at the others – the singing and drumming start up again.)

ADULT JOYCE: My people believe we must treat the first salmon with great respect and kindness – so the remaining salmon will continue to travel our way.

(Two of the guests conduct the ritual as it is described by Adult Joyce. The others look on. Music and drumming continues, under.)

JOYCE: The Earth is a shrine.

ADULT JOYCE: We would lift the salmon from his bed of cedar boughs.

JOYCE: But it is a *borrowed* shrine.

ADULT JOYCE: We would take a cloth and wash the salmon's face.

JOYCE: It is loaned to us by the Great Spirit.

ADULT JOYCE: We would sing a song thanking the salmon for providing us with food today, and in years gone by.

JOYCE: We must use the gifts of the Earth wisely, for they are sacred.

ADULT JOYCE: The salmon would be carried away and cooked.

JOYCE: *(With a look at Emily Sam.)* We must account for ourselves and our time on earth.

ADULT JOYCE: It's skeleton would be carefully preserved and returned to the water where it was caught.

JOYCE: We must learn to be useful.

(Emily Sam smiles. The guests carry off the first salmon – the singing and drumming fading into the distance. A flute begins to play "Joyce's song." Henry walks up to Joyce. He looks at her clothing. Smiles.)

HENRY: Well, look at you.

(*They embrace.*)

JOYCE: I have something for you.

(*She opens her suitcase and hands him a book. He smiles.*)

HENRY: Welcome home, Joyce. (*He follows the others off.*)

(*Emily Sam has remained behind. Joyce removes her small, completed quilt from the suitcase. It is a "Salmon" pattern. Emily Sam looks at it, impressed.*)

EMILY SAM: It's beautiful.

JOYCE: **It's for you.**

(*Joyce wraps the quilt around Emily Sam's shoulders. They embrace.*)

JOYCE: I learned the stitching from Miss Brennan and Nurse Warner. And, I learned the design from you.

EMILY SAM: **Thank you.**

JOYCE: Emily Sam, can I ask you something?

EMILY SAM: (*Nods.*) **Of course.**

(*Adult Joyce gradually joins them, standing alongside Joyce.*)

JOYCE: At the school, I met an old woman. She wore a long dress covered with a shawl, and a kerchief on her head.

EMILY SAM: Did she carry a walking stick?

JOYCE: Yes.

(*Emily Sam looks at Joyce, then laughs a bit.*)

JOYCE: What's so funny?

EMILY SAM: That woman is your Aunt Sophie. She's an ancestor of ours who died many years ago. She came back to be my helping spirit when I was a young girl. You must have inherited her from me.

JOYCE: She gave me a song.

EMILY SAM: (*Smiles.*) I was hoping she would. (*Pause.*) Joyce, your grandfather left something for you.

(*Emily Sam holds out a beautifully carved canoe paddle. Joyce looks at it. Adult Joyce reaches out her hand and takes hold of it.*)

EMILY SAM: His spirit is still upon the waters.

(*Emily Sam leaves, as – Joyce and Adult Joyce look at one another for a long time. Upstage, as before, the silhouette of Chief Seattle. During the following, Joyce takes the pouch from around her own neck…and puts it around Adult Joyce's neck. They look each other in the eye. Adult Joyce hands Joyce the canoe paddle. Joyce takes it from her…turns…and goes. Flute continues.*)

VOICE OF CHIEF SEATTLE: There was a time when our people covered the land as the waves of a wind-ruffled sea covers its shell-paved floor. That time has passed away.

But, when your children's children think themselves alone in the fields, the store, the shop, upon the highway or in the silence of the pathless woods, they will not be alone.

At night when the streets of your villages and cities are silent, and you think them deserted, they will throng with the returning hosts that once filled them...and that still love this beautiful land.

(*The light on Chief Seattle fades to black. The flute continues. Adult Joyce turns to the audience.*)

ADULT JOYCE: I went to the Tulalip School for several years, coming home each summer to visit my family.

Years later, when I was married and raising children of my own, I passed onto them things I'd learned at the school.

(*Lights rise on Joyce, paddling the canoe toward us, in the blue-lit water. Mount Rainier looms behind.*)

ADULT JOYCE: And, I passed something else onto them, as well: the teachings of Mud Bay Sam.

The history, the humor, the legends. The stories of our people.

(*Adult Joyce watches Joyce paddle the canoe, then turns back to the audience. She smiles.*)

ADULT JOYCE: There is a lot to remember.

(*Light fades slowly to black on Adult Joyce – as the flute continues to play. After a moment, light fades slowly on Joyce, paddling the canoe into the distance. The song ends as the stage goes to black.*)

END OF PLAY

There's a Boy in
the Girls' Bathroom

by Louis Sachar

AUTHOR'S NOTE

The play was written so that it could be performed by eleven actors, four adults and seven kids.

Mrs. Chalkers and Mrs. Nathan can be played by the same person. That person can also operate the Turtle.

Mr. Chalkers and Mr. Verigold can be played by the same person. That person can operate Bartholomew the Bear.

Mrs. Ebbel and Mrs. Verigold can be played by the same person. That person can also operate the Goose.

The person who plays Carla can operate Ronnie the Rabbit.

(Note: I don't mean to suggest that they appear to be the same person to the audience. The actors would need to wear wigs and otherwise disguise their voices and appearances to avoid confusion.)

In addition, the cast can be enlarged, with more students in the classroom scenes, and more boys playing basketball with Brian and Robbie. If other children are added to the classroom, it would be better if Colleen, Lori and Melinda weren't in the class. Their lines can be given to others.

There is an optional birthday party scene which was omitted during the original performance. If an enlarged cast is being used, more girls can appear in this scene, but not boys.

The story takes place in contemporary America. The kids are in the fifth grade. Carla is young and pretty. She dresses in funky, hip clothes.

Mr. and Mrs. Chalkers are middle-class parents.

Mr. and Mrs. Verigold appear more urbane. They possibly speak with New York or Boston accents.

ORIGINAL PRODUCTION

There's a Boy in the Girls' Bathroom was originally produced by Seattle Children's Theatre on April 26, 1991. It was directed by Linda Hartzell with the following cast:

MR. CHALKERS, MR. VERIGOLD, AND BARTHOLOMEW THE BEAR......Geoffrey Alm
LORI WESTIN ....Ina Daniels
MRS. CHALKERS, MRS. NATHAN, AND THE TURTLE ....Caren Graham
MELINDA BIRCH....................................Jean Michele Gregory
BRIAN ....Max Moore
COLLEEN VERIGOLD.............................Gretchen V. O'Connell
MRS. EBBEL, MRS. VERIGOLD, AND THE GOOSE ....Peggy O'Connell
JEFF FISHKIN ....Ryan O'Connor
BRADLEY CHALKERS.......................................Dan Spiegelman

ROBBIE ....Rob van Wyk/T. George Yasutake
CARLA DAVIS AND RONNIE THE RABBIT ....Sarah Welsh

CHARACTERS
Kids:

BRADLEY CHALKERS	JEFF FISHKIN
ROBBIE	BRIAN
COLLEEN VERIGOLD	LORI WESTIN
MELINDA BIRCH	

Adults:

MRS. EBBEL, Bradley's teacher	CARLA DAVIS, the counselor
MRS. CHALKERS, Bradley's mother	MR. CHALKERS, Bradley's father
MRS. NATHAN, the school principal	MR. VERIGOLD, Colleen's father
MRS. VERIGOLD, Colleen's mother	

Puppets:

RONNIE THE RABBIT	BARTHOLOMEW THE BEAR
A GOOSE	A TURTLE

THE SETS

Though there are many scene changes, it is best if this can be done fluidly, with someone always on stage and without blackouts. Snippets of music can be played between scenes.

For the original performance three sets were on stage at all times. Each set had a floor and two half-walls. These sets were on locking rollers, so that when they weren't in use, their backs faced the audience. The sets were revolved around as needed. (When using the sets it was not necessary that the actors stayed on the set's floor. The sets suggested a larger area.)

When all three sets had their backs to the audience, they fit together forming what appeared to be a solid jagged wall, on which a mural was painted. Most of the time however, the sets were staggered, so that the spaces between the sets suggested hallways and doors.

These three sets were from right to left: (1) Bradley's bedroom, (2) the counselor's office, and (3) the girls'/boys' bathroom. The sets were fairly minimal.

(1) BRADLEY'S BEDROOM: This included a bed upon which the four puppets sat. The bed served as a stage for the puppets. The wall behind the bed was, in fact, not a solid wall, but rather part of it consisted of a cloth flap. The puppeteers could not be seen as they controlled the puppets from behind the flap. Their voices were amplified by microphones.

The set also included a nightstand with drawers, where Bradley put away his socks.

(2) THE COUNSELOR'S OFFICE: This included simply a round table, with two chairs and a stool. The walls were covered with bulletin boards.

(3) THE GIRLS'/BOYS' BATHROOM: The girls' bathroom consisted of a sink with a mirror above it, a working paper towel dispenser, and a stall. (The door to the stall should be low enough so the audience cannot see if there is a person behind it.) For the boys' bathroom the stall was removed, revealing a urinal behind it.

For the hallway and/or outdoor scenes, the back of each set faced the audience. A basketball hoop could swing into place.

The only other set needed was the classroom. This was done with seven desks in one row. Four were attached together and three were attached together. They slid out from each side of the stage and met in the middle. There was also a portable blackboard.

THERE'S A BOY IN THE GIRLS' BATHROOM

ACT ONE
Scene 1

> *A classroom. Seven desks are in a row. They are, from front to back respectively, the desks of Colleen, Lori, Melinda, Robbie, Brian, Jeff, and Bradley. Bradley's desk is a mess. When the scene opens, all the children except Jeff are on stage. They are seen briefly horsing around before class. Bradley is not a part of the horseplay. He is a loner. If he interacts at all with the other kids, it is as a bully. Mrs. Ebbel enters, and everyone knocks off the horseplay.*

MRS. EBBEL: Good morning everyone. Please sit down.
> *(Everyone takes their seats, except Bradley. He makes a point of waiting just a second too long as Mrs. Ebbel stares at him. When he does sit down, he plops in his desk, and slouches with his legs sticking out to the side.)*

MRS. EBBEL: Your morning work is on the board. Make sure your pencils are sharpened. If you have any questions, raise your hand. Okay, get started.
> *(All the other students start working carefully on their notebooks. Bradley looks through the junk in his desk, finds a pencil, then takes it to the front of the room where he noisily sharpens his pencil. No one can work while he uses the pencil sharpener. He stops sharpening, then looks at his pencil, and sharpens some more. On his way back to his seat he bumps into Colleen's desk, causing her to mess up what she's writing.)*

COLLEEN: Quit it, Bradley.

BRADLEY: (*Innocently.*) Sorry. It was an accident.
> *(As he continues to his desk, he pulls Lori's hair, flicks Melinda's pencil, pushes Robbie's arm, and knocks Brian's book to the floor. He sits back down and scribbles in his notebook. Sometimes his pencil wanders off the notebook and he scribbles on his desk. He grunts and laughs to himself the whole time. The other children occasionally glance back at him, obviously disturbed by him.)*

MRS. EBBEL: Bradley.

(She starts towards him, and doesn't see Jeff awkwardly enter. Jeff is holding a note.)

COLLEEN: *(Upon seeing Jeff.)* Uh, Mrs. Ebbel.

(Mrs. Ebbel stops, turns and sees Jeff.)

MRS. EBBEL: *(To Jeff.)* Yes?

(Jeff holds out the note to her. She takes it and reads it.)

MRS. EBBEL: *(Brightly.)* Everybody. I would like you all to meet Jeff Fishkin. Jeff has just moved here from Washington, D.C., which, as you know, is our nation's capital.

(Everyone except Bradley sits up and stares at Jeff. Jeff fidgets nervously. He is awkward and shy, and all the more so because he is standing at the front of the room with everyone staring at him.)

MRS. EBBEL: Why don't you tell the class a little bit about yourself, Jeff?

JEFF: Um, well, my name is Jeff Fishkin, um, I'm not related to fish!

(Mrs. Ebbel laughs at his joke. No one else does. Jeff looks at her and she stops laughing.)

MRS. EBBEL: Go on.

JEFF: Well, uh…

MRS. EBBEL: *(Enthusiastically.)* Have you ever been to the White House, Jeff? I'm sure the class would be very interested to hear about that.

(Jeff looks at the class, then shrugs and shakes his head.)

MRS. EBBEL: Or the Washington Monument?

JEFF: *(He doesn't want to talk in front of the class.)* No I've never been there!

MRS. EBBEL: *(Smiles sympathetically at Jeff.)* Well I guess we better find you a place to sit. *(She puts her hand on Jeff's shoulder.)* Hmmm…I don't see any place except, I suppose you can there, toward the back.

(She points to the empty desk in front of Bradley. Everyone else turns around and looks at the desk.)

LORI: Yuck. Not in front of Bradley!

MELINDA: *(To Lori.)* At least it's better than next to Bradley.

MRS. EBBEL: I'm sorry, Jeff, but there are no other empty desks.

JEFF: I don't mind where I sit.

MRS. EBBEL: Well, nobody likes sitting…there.

BRADLEY: That's right! Nobody likes sitting next to me!

(He smiles, a forced, unnatural smile, stretching his mouth out as wide as possible. He slowly turns his head, aiming his smile at Jeff who slowly and awkwardly sits down.)

MRS. EBBEL: Lori. Would you please hand these back to the class.

(Mrs. Ebbel hands Lori a stack of graded tests. Lori checks each name as she

hands them back to members of the class. When she hands back Bradley's test she stands as far away from him as possible, and gives it to him as someone may give meat to a wild animal. Lori and Bradley make faces at each other. Lori looks at Jeff like he's some kind of geek, but of course doesn't have a test for him. She returns to her seat.)

MRS. EBBEL: I must say I was very pleased. There were fourteen A's and the rest B's. Of course there was one F, but…

(Everyone turns and looks at Bradley. Bradley proudly waves his test in the air.)

MRS. EBBEL: *(Speaking to everyone in the class.)* Please have a parent sign your test and bring it back tomorrow.

(Bradley takes out a pair of scissors and begins to cut up his test paper.)

BRIAN: *(Raises his hand, but doesn't wait to be called on before speaking. He is somewhat snotty, happy to correct a teacher.)* But we won't be here tomorrow. It's Parent Conference Day.

MRS. EBBEL: *(Annoyed.)* Well then the day after tomorrow. Bradley! *(Goes to Bradley.)*

BRADLEY: *(Stands up.)* Huh? I didn't do anything wrong.

MRS. EBBEL: Did you ever give my note to your mother?

BRADLEY: Huh? What note? You never gave me a note.

MRS. EBBEL: *(Patiently.)* Yes, I did, Bradley. In fact, I gave you two notes because you said the first one was stolen.

(The other children all turn around to watch. Mrs. Ebbel gestures with a flick of the wrist while snapping her fingers, and the children return to their work.)

BRADLEY: Oh yeah, now I remember. I gave it to her a long time ago.

MRS. EBBEL: Bradley, I think it's very important for your mother to come for Parent Conference Day tomorrow.

BRADLEY: *(Nonchalantly.)* Okay.

MRS. EBBEL: She was supposed to make an appointment.

BRADLEY: Oh, she can't come. She's sick.

MRS. EBBEL: *(Sighs.)* You never gave her the note, did you?

BRADLEY: Call her doctor if you don't believe me.

(The bell rings. Colleen, Lori, Melinda, Robbie and Brian exit. Jeff remains, waiting.)

MRS. EBBEL: The school has just hired a new counselor and I think it's very important for your mother to meet her.

BRADLEY: Oh, they already met. They go bowling together.

MRS. EBBEL: I'm trying to help you, Bradley.

BRADLEY: Call the bowling alley if you don't believe me!

MRS. EBBEL: Okay, Bradley. (*She lets the matter drop.*)
    (*Bradley, smiling over his victory, starts to walk away.*)
JEFF: Hey, Bradley, wait up!
    (*Startled, Bradley turns around.*)
JEFF: (*Timidly.*) Hi.
    (*Bradley stares at him.*)
JEFF: I don't mind sitting by you. (*Smiles.*) Really. I like it.
    (*Bradley doesn't answer.*)
JEFF: I have been to the White House. Lots of times. If you want I can tell you about it.
BRADLEY: Give me a dollar or I'll spit on you!
    (*Jeff fumbles in his pocket for a dollar then gives it to Bradley.*)

END SCENE 1
Note: During the scene change, Jeff can remain on stage, feeling hopeless and dejected. He exits just before the next scene begins.

Scene 2

    Bradley's bedroom. There is a bed with the four stuffed animals on it, Ronnie the Rabbit, Bartholomew the Bear, a goose and a turtle. These are actually puppets who move and talk. The bed serves as their stage. The actors cannot be seen as they control the puppets from behind a false wall. Their voices are amplified by microphones. Mrs. Chalkers is sweeping the room. A door slams offstage.

MRS. CHALKERS: Hi, Sugar-Dumpling.
    (*Beat, then Bradley enters.*)
MRS. CHALKERS: No homework?
BRADLEY: Finished it all at school. Call Mrs. Ebbel if you don't believe me.
    (*Mrs. Chalkers stares at her son. She doesn't believe him, but it's easier to pretend she does.*)
MRS. CHALKERS: Well, good. See? You do your work at school, and you have plenty of time to play. Not like last year, right? (*She asks hopefully.*)
BRADLEY: That's right!
    (*He stares at his mother, waiting for her to leave. She exits.*)
BRADLEY: Hi everybody.
    (*The stuffed animals come to life.*)
GOOSE: Hey everybody, Bradley's home!

OTHER STUFFED ANIMALS: Hi Bradley. Hi Bradley. (*Etc.*)

> (*Bradley pats and hugs his animals.*)

BRADLEY: Look, I brought you some food! (*He takes his cut-up test paper out of his pocket and drops the pieces on the bed.*)

> (*The animals all move to the food. The turtle is the slowest.*)

TURTLE: Not so fast.

BRADLEY: There's plenty for everybody.

RONNIE: Thank you, Bradley. It's delicious!

BARTHOLOMEW: Yeah, it's real good.

TURTLE: Hooray for Bradley! Hip...Hip...

ALL THE OTHER ANIMALS: Hooray!

GOOSE: Let's play a game.

RONNIE: What do you want to play?

BARTHOLOMEW: Anything but basketball! I hate basketball.

RONNIE: Basketball's a stupid game.

TURTLE: It's the worst game in the world!

GOOSE: Why would anybody want to play *basketball?* Ha. Ha. Ha.

> (*All the other animals laugh, too.*)

RONNIE: Let's go swimming in the pond. (*Singing.*) Doo de-doo de-doo.

> (*Bradley takes Ronnie and moves her off the bed to the floor. Note: Bradley works Ronnie's mouth as she continues to talk, while the actor behind the bed says the words.*)

RONNIE: Help! I have a cramp!

BRADLEY: (*Motherly.*) You shouldn't have gone swimming right after eating.

RONNIE: Help! I'm drowning!

> (*Mr. Chalkers enters carrying a basketball. Bradley guiltily moves away from Ronnie as all the animals become inanimate.*)

BRADLEY: I wonder how that got there.

MR. CHALKERS: I wouldn't know.

BRADLEY: I wasn't playing with it!

MR. CHALKERS: I'm sure you weren't.

BRADLEY: I don't even like it. Babies play with stuffed animals.

MR. CHALKERS: (*Baiting Bradley.*) Guess we might as well just give them all away, huh?

BRADLEY: Might as well. Oh, I just remembered! I need them for a school project. Call Mrs. Ebbel if you don't believe me.

MR. CHALKERS: Don't worry. I'm not going to get rid of them. I just wish...(*Shakes his head.*) I was thinking. Since I have the afternoon off, how about us putting up the basketball hoop over the garage. Then maybe your friends can come here for a change, instead of you going to their house all the time.

BRADLEY: No. They don't like coming here.

MR. CHALKERS: Well, maybe they would if –

BRADLEY: They're allergic. Jeff Fishkin. He's my best friend. But every time he comes here, he gets warts all over his face. So he doesn't come anymore.

MR. CHALKERS: I see. (*Starts to exit.*)

BRADLEY: Call him up if you don't believe me.

(*The phone rings off stage, startling them both.*)

BRADLEY: That's probably Jeff calling me, now. I wonder what he wants this time.

(*It rings again, then is answered.*)

BRADLEY: Probably wants help with his homework.

MR. CHALKERS: I'll tell you one thing. If Jeff is your friend, you better hope he doesn't find out you still play with stuffed animals. (*Exits.*)

(*Beat.*)

BRADLEY: (*Calls after his father.*) Jeff plays with dolls! Girl dolls! He likes to take off their clothes.

RONNIE: Who's Jeff?

BRADLEY: Oh, he's this new stupid kid. He said he liked sitting next to me.

(*Bradley says the last line as if it was a nerdy thing for Jeff to say.*)

BARTHOLOMEW: What a nerd-ball.

GOOSE: Sounds like a real jerk.

TURTLE: He's a weirdo…

ALL THE ANIMALS:…if you ask me.

BRADLEY: (*Thoughtfully this time.*) He said he liked sitting next to me.

(*Mrs. Chalkers enters.*)

BRADLEY: (*Nastily.*) What do *you* want?

MRS. CHALKERS: Is everything all right in school? Is there something I should know about?

BRADLEY: Um. We're having class elections. I think I'm going to run for president.

MRS. CHALKERS: Your grades are okay?

BRADLEY: Yes. Mrs. Ebbel handed back a language test today and I got another A. In fact, it was an A plus.

MRS. CHALKERS: Oh, may I see it?

BRADLEY: Mrs. Ebbel hung it on the wall, next to all my other A tests. Call her up if –

MRS. CHALKERS: Mrs. Ebbel just called. (*Pause.*) Why didn't you tell me that tomorrow was Parents Conference Day?

BRADLEY: (*Innocently.*) Didn't I tell you? I told you. You said you couldn't go. You must have forgot.

MRS. CHALKERS: Mrs. Ebbel said that your school has hired a counselor. She thinks a counselor can help you. What does a counselor do?

BRADLEY: Just stupid stuff.

MRS. CHALKERS: (*Almost apologetically.*) Well anyway. Mrs. Ebbel feels very strongly that I should come tomorrow.

BRADLEY: Oh, that's just her job. The more parents she sees, the more money she makes.

MRS. CHALKERS: So I made an appointment with her for eleven o'clock tomorrow morning.

BRADLEY: (*Horrified.*) No!

MRS. CHALKERS: I'm sorry –

BRADLEY: You can't go! (*Stamps his foot.*) It's not fair!

MRS. CHALKERS: Bradley, what –

BRADLEY: It's not fair! It's not fair! (*He turns his back on his mother.*)

MRS. CHALKERS: What's not fair?

BRADLEY: It's not fair! You promised!

MRS. CHALKERS: What did I promise? Bradley? What did I promise?
(*Bradley hugs Ronnie.*)

MRS. CHALKERS: Bradley?

MR. CHALKERS: (*Entering.*) What's going on in here? Why are you shouting at your mother?

MRS. CHALKERS: (*Trying to protect Bradley.*) Oh, we were just having a little –

BRADLEY: (*Turns to face his parents.*) She promised she'd take me to the zoo tomorrow, and now she won't!

MRS. CHALKERS: The zoo? I never said I'd –

BRADLEY: She did too! Since there is no school tomorrow, she said she'd take me to the zoo.

MRS. CHALKERS: (*To Bradley, again almost apologizing.*) I didn't even know there was no school until your teacher just called me.

BRADLEY: You promised!

MR. CHALKERS: His teacher called?

MRS. CHALKERS: (*To her husband.*) It was really nothing. She just called to remind us that tomorrow was Parent Conference Day. It's for every child in her class, not just Bradley.

MR. CHALKERS: Somehow I don't think Bradley's teacher calls every parent on the telephone.

BRADLEY: You said you'd take me to the zoo! You promised!

MRS. CHALKERS: (*Apologetically.*) I never said I'd take you to the zoo.

BRADLEY: You did! And we have to go in the morning. We have to be at the zoo at eleven o'clock!

MR. CHALKERS: (*In a voice that indicates he really doesn't want to hear the answer to his question.*) Why do you have to be at the zoo at eleven o'clock?

BRADLEY: Because that's when they feed the lions.

(*His father puts his hand over his eyes and shakes his head.*)

BRADLEY: She promised she'd take me to see them feed the lions at eleven o'clock.

MRS. CHALKERS: I – I don't even know when they feed the lions!

BRADLEY: Eleven o'clock.

MR. CHALKERS: Don't lie to your mother.

BRADLEY: Really. They feed the lions at eleven o'clock.

MR. CHALKERS: I don't tolerate lying.

BRADLEY: Call the zoo if you don't believe me.

MR. CHALKERS: Your mother said she never promised to take you to the zoo.

BRADLEY: She's lying.

(*He regrets that remark as soon as he says it. Mr. Chalkers is about to explode. Mr. Chalkers raises his hand as if to strike Bradley. Bradley runs to the other side of his room.*)

MR. CHALKERS: Don't *ever* call your mother a liar!

MRS. CHALKERS: Maybe I did tell him I'd take him to the zoo.

BRADLEY: See!

MR. CHALKERS: Keep it up, Bradley. Just keep it up.

BRADLEY: Call the zoo!

MR. CHALKERS: Just keep it up. (*He exits.*)

(*Mrs. Chalkers looks helplessly at Bradley.*)

BRADLEY: (*Calmly.*) Call the zoo.

(*Mrs. Chalkers exits. Bradley sits on his bed, holding his head in his hands. Ronnie snuggles up next to him.*)

RONNIE: Don't worry Bradley. You'll think of something. You're the smartest kid in the whole world.

END SCENE 2

Note: Even before the bedroom rolls away, Jeff can enter the other half of the stage to begin Scene 3. He looks lost.

Scene 3

Note: This scene begins in the hallway at school, moves to the girls' bathroom, then back through the hall to the counselor's office. The hallway is suggested by the backs of the three movable sets, staggered on stage. As Jeff moves from one location to the other, that set revolves to greet him.

Jeff enters hallway, lost. He starts one direction, then turns around and starts to go back the way he came. He is about to exit, then suddenly stops as if he sees something that has scared him. He quickly backs away towards center stage. What Jeff had seen was Bradley who now enters.

BRADLEY: Jeff!

JEFF: (*Jeff looks around for a teacher or someone to save him. He's scared of Bradley but tries to sound brave.*) Just leave me alone, Bradley. I don't have any more money and even if I did I wouldn't give it to you.

BRADLEY: Where you goin'?

JEFF: I'm trying to find the counselor's office. And I'm already late.

BRADLEY: Ooh, she's going to be mad. She's real mean. And ugly.

JEFF: Have you already seen her?

BRADLEY: Me? Why would I have to see a counselor? I didn't do anything wrong!

JEFF: Uh, I just thought Mrs. Ebbel – Well I have to see her. She's supposed to help me "adjust to my new environment." (*Short laugh.*)

BRADLEY: That's stupid.

(*Jeff starts to leave.*)

BRADLEY: Jeff.

(*Jeff stops.*)

BRADLEY: I'll give you a dollar, if you'll be my friend.

(*Jeff is too stunned to answer. Bradley reaches in his pocket and holds out a dollar. Jeff stares at it a moment then reaches out and takes it.*)

JEFF: (*Looks at the dollar in his hand.*) If you want, I can help you with your homework sometime. I know I'm new here, but I'm pretty smart, and we learned the same stuff at my old school. (*He shrugs modestly.*)

BRADLEY: (*Looking at Jeff like he was crazy.*) I don't need any help. I'm the smartest kid in class. Ask anyone. (*Exits.*)

(*Jeff puts dollar in pocket. Sighs and rubs his face. Mrs. Ebbel enters carrying a stack of papers.*)

JEFF: (*Frantic, yet polite.*) Excuse me, Mrs. Ebbel. Can you tell me where the counselor's office is please.

MRS. EBBEL: The counselor's office...Let's see. Go down this hall to the end. Turn right, and it's the third door on your left.

JEFF: Thank you very much. (*He starts to go as he talks to himself.*) Right, third door.

MRS. EBBEL: No wait. That's not right. She's in the new office in the other wing. Turn around and go back the way you came, go right, then turn left at the end of the hall and it's the door immediately to your right.

JEFF: Thank you.

(*Mrs. Ebbel exits. Jeff turns around and moves across the stage talking to himself.*)

JEFF: Turn right. Third door on left. (*Enters girls' bathroom.*) I'm sorry I'm late.

(*Colleen is buttoning her pants as she steps out of a stall.*)

COLLEEN: What are you doing in here?

JEFF: (*It hasn't yet registered yet where he is.*) Huh?

COLLEEN: Get out of here! This is the girls' bathroom!

(*Jeff stands frozen a moment then exits, running.*)

COLLEEN: (*After Jeff has already left.*) THERE'S A BOY IN THE GIRLS' BATHROOM! (*She shouts it one or two more times as the set revolves away, taking her with it. Jeff moves through the hall and backs into the counselor's office. The office is a mess, cluttered with boxes and papers. The walls are blank bulletin boards. There is a round table with two chairs. There is also a stool. Carla is putting something up on bulletin board, but stops to greet Jeff who has his back to her.*)

CARLA: You must be Jeff.

(*Startled, Jeff turns to face her.*)

CARLA: I'm Carla Davis.

(*She holds out her hand. Jeff numbly shakes it.*)

CARLA: Come in.

(*Carla indicates for Jeff to have a seat and they both sit down around the round table.*)

CARLA: You'll have to excuse the mess. I'm still getting moved in.

(*Jeff stares blankly at her.*)

CARLA: So how do you like Red Hill School so far?

(*Jeff is numb and dumb.*)

CARLA: I imagine it must seem a little scary. I think it's scary. It seems so big! Anytime I try to go anywhere, I get lost.

(*Jeff smiles weakly – if she only knew.*)

CARLA: It's hard for me because I'm new here. I don't know anybody. Nobody knows me. The other teachers all look at me strangely. I think some of them don't understand what a counselor does. It's hard for me to make friends with them. They already have their own friends.

(*Jeff nods along.*)

CARLA: Maybe you can help me?

JEFF: Me? How can *I* help *you*. You're supposed to help me.

CARLA: Maybe we can help each other. What do you think about that?

(*Jeff smiles and shrugs.*)

CARLA: We're the two new kids at school. We can share our experiences and learn from each other.

JEFF: Okay, Miss Davis.

CARLA: Jeff, if we're going to be friends, I want you to call me Carla, not Miss Davis.

(*Jeff laughs.*)

CARLA: Do you think Carla is a funny name?

JEFF: Oh, no! I just never called a teacher by her first name, that's all.

CARLA: But we're friends. Friends don't call each other Miss Davis and Mr. Fishkin, do they?

JEFF: (*Laughs again.*) The kids in my class all call me Fishface.

CARLA: Have you made any friends?

JEFF: One. But I don't like him.

CARLA: How can he be your friend if you don't like him?

JEFF: Nobody likes him. At first I felt sorry for him because nobody even wants to sit near him. Even Mrs. Ebbel said so.

CARLA: It must have hurt his feelings.

JEFF: No, he just smiled.

CARLA: He may have been smiling on the outside, but do you think he really was smiling on the inside?

JEFF: I don't know. I guess not. I guess that's why I tried to be friends with him. I told him I didn't mind sitting by him. But then he said, "Give me a dollar or I'll spit on you!"

CARLA: What'd you do?

JEFF: (*Obviously, as if he had no choice.*) I gave him a dollar. I didn't want to get spit on. But then, today, he said, "I'll give you a dollar if you'll be my friend."

CARLA: What'd you do?

JEFF: (*Obviously.*) I took it. (*Pause.*) So does that mean I have to be his friend, even though I just broke even?

CARLA: What do you think friendship is?

JEFF: I don't know. I mean I know what it is, but I can't explain it.

CARLA: Is it something you can buy and sell? Can you go to the store and get a quart of milk, a dozen eggs, and a friend?

JEFF: (*Laughing.*) No. So does that mean I don't have to be his friend? I don't even know if Bradley wants to be friends.

CARLA: I think you'll find that if you're nice to Bradley, he'll be nice to you. It's just like with the dollar. You always break even.

(*Mrs. Nathan, the principal, enters quietly and stands off to the side. She is trying to be inconspicuous, but that is impossible.*)

CARLA: (*To the principal.*) Mrs. Nathan.

MRS. NATHAN: Please continue, Miss Davis. Just pretend I'm not here.

CARLA: (*Looks at Jeff. Starts to say something, then stops, and claps her hands together.*) Well, I think we're just about finished for the day, aren't we Jeff. (*She rises, then so does Jeff.*) I'll see you next week, okay Jeff.

(*She holds out her hand, and he shakes it.*)

JEFF: Yes, Miss Davis.

CARLA: Jeff. Call me Carla.

JEFF: (*Looks at the principal, then quietly with his head down.*) Carla. (*Exits.*)

MRS. NATHAN: (*Mrs. Nathan looks around in a manner which suggests she disapproves of the room's messy condition.*) So how's it going so far?

CARLA: Fine. They're neat kids.

MRS. NATHAN: They are. I wish I had more time with them, but I'm just too busy. (*Sits down at the round table.*)

CARLA: Is there something I can –

MRS. NATHAN: I just came by to observe.

CARLA: (*Unsure.*) Okay. (*Sits down. Takes out a file, but doesn't look at it. Tries to be tactful.*) Mrs. Nathan, when I'm with a student, I try to build a trust between the student and myself. It would be difficult to do that with the principal in the room.

MRS. NATHAN: The students trust me.

CARLA: I didn't mean they didn't. It's just –

MRS. NATHAN: And more important, they *respect* me.

CARLA: I'm sure –

MRS. NATHAN: You know, Carla, it is very important for the students to respect their teachers. (*Pointedly.*) That's why we have a policy against students calling teachers by their first names.

CARLA: Yes. But for my purposes, I'm trying –

MRS. NATHAN: It's a sign of respect. It's the same with the way one dresses. If you wear a knit suit, or at least a skirt, you generate an aura of respect.

Respect. That's the key. And if you want others to respect you, you have to respect yourself. The way you keep your room.

CARLA: I'm just getting settled in.

MRS. NATHAN: You know, Carla, there are a lot of people who don't see the need for an elementary school counselor. We've never had a counselor here. Several parents have already raised questions. They don't like things that are…unconventional. It makes it all the more important that you carry yourself with a certain…(*Tries to find the right word.*)

CARLA: Respect?

MRS. NATHAN: (*Points a finger at Carla.*) Exactly! (*Doesn't realize that in a way Carla is making fun of her. Rather she viewed Carla's last line as very perceptive.*) So, who do you see next?

CARLA: (*Looks at the file.*) Uh, Bradley Chalkers.

MRS. NATHAN: (*Laughs.*) Good luck.

CARLA: Mrs. Ebbel seems to think I can help him.

MRS. NATHAN: I think Mrs. Ebbel just wants him out of her hair once a week. Well if you need anything remember, I'm on your side.

CARLA: Thank you.

(*Mrs. Nathan exits, stepping around boxes on her way out. Carla sits at the round table and returns to the file.*)

CARLA: Bradley Chalkers…(*She reads something in the file that makes her laugh.*)

BRADLEY: (*Entering.*) I'm here, whadda ya' want?

CARLA: (*Stands and smiles warmly at him.*) Hello Bradley. I'm Carla Davis. It's a pleasure to see you today. (*She holds out her hand for him to shake.*) I've been looking forward to meeting you.

(*Bradley just stares at her.*)

CARLA: Aren't you going to shake my hand?

BRADLEY: Nah, you're too ugly.

(*He walks past her and sits down at the round table. Carla sits across from him.*)

CARLA: I appreciate your coming to see me.

BRADLEY: I had to come. Mrs. Ebbel made me.

CARLA: For whatever reason, I'm glad you came.

BRADLEY: I meant to go to the library. I came here by accident.

CARLA: Oh, I don't believe in accidents.

BRADLEY: (*Looks at her funny.*) What about when you spill your milk?

CARLA: Do you like milk?

BRADLEY: No, I hate it!

CARLA: So maybe you spill it on purpose. You just think it's an accident.

BRADLEY: (*Stares angrily down at the table. He feels like she tricked him.*) I don't drink milk. I drink coffee. (*Beat.*) I didn't do anything wrong!

CARLA: Nobody said you did.

BRADLEY: Then how come I have to be here?

CARLA: I was hoping you'd like it here. I was hoping we could be friends. Do you think we can?

BRADLEY: (*Without anger.*) No.

CARLA: Why not?

BRADLEY: (*Matter of fact.*) Because I don't like you.

CARLA: I can like you, can't I? You don't have to like me.
(*Bradley squirms.*)

CARLA: I was hoping you'd be able to teach me some things.

BRADLEY: You're the teacher, not me.

CARLA: That doesn't matter. A teacher can often learn a lot more from a student than a student can learn from a teacher.

BRADLEY: (*Nodding.*) I've taught Mrs. Ebbel a lot.

CARLA: What do you want to teach me?

BRADLEY: What do you want to know?

CARLA: You tell me. What's the most important thing you can teach me?

BRADLEY: (*Ponders a moment.*) The elephant's the biggest animal in the world. But it's afraid of mice.

CARLA: I wonder why that is.

BRADLEY: (*Eagerly.*) Because, if a mouse ran up an elephant's trunk, it would get stuck, and then the elephant wouldn't be able to breathe, and so it would die. That's how most elephants die, you know.

CARLA: I see. Thank you. You're a very good teacher. What else would you like to teach me?

BRADLEY: Nothing. (*Snidely.*) You're not supposed to talk in school.

CARLA: Why not?

BRADLEY: It's a *rule*. Like no sticking gum in the water fountains.

CARLA: Well, in this room, there are no rules. In here, everyone thinks for himself. No one tells you what to do.

BRADLEY: You mean I can stick gum in the water fountain?

CARLA: You could, except I don't have a water fountain.

BRADLEY: Can I break something?

CARLA: Certainly.

BRADLEY: (*Gets up and walks around the room, looking for something to break, then looks back at Carla unsure.*) I'm not in the mood.

CARLA: Okay. But if you're ever in the mood, there are lots of things you can break – things I like very much and things other children use.

BRADLEY: I will! (*Sits back down.*) I know karate. (*Raises his hand over the table as if ready to give it a karate chop.*) I can break this table with my bare hand.

CARLA: Ooh. Won't that hurt?

BRADLEY: Nothing ever hurts me. I've broken every table in my house. Call my mother if you don't believe me!

CARLA: I believe you.

BRADLEY: (*Looks at her, surprised that she believes him.*) So now what am I supposed to do?

CARLA: Would you like to draw a picture? I've got a whole box of crayons.
(*She gives Bradley a sheet of paper and the box of crayons. Bradley chooses a black crayon and stays with it the whole time.*)

BRADLEY: (*While scribbling.*) My parents only feed me dog food.

CARLA: How does it taste?

BRADLEY: (*Stops coloring and looks up at her, surprised by her reaction.*) Delicious! Meaty and sweet.

CARLA: I've always wanted to try it.

BRADLEY: (*After scribbling some more.*) The president called me on the phone last night.

CARLA: How exciting! What'd you talk about.

BRADLEY: (*Still scribbling.*) Hats.

CARLA: What about hats?

BRADLEY: I asked him why he didn't wear a hat like Abraham Lincoln.

CARLA: And what did the president say.

BRADLEY: I'm not allowed to tell you. It's top secret. (*Scribbles some more.*) Done! (*Holds up his picture.*)

CARLA: That's very nice.

BRADLEY: It's a picture of night time.

CARLA: Oh, I thought it was the floor of a barber shop, after someone with black curly hair got his hair cut.

BRADLEY: That's what it is! That's what I meant.

CARLA: It's very good. May I have it?

BRADLEY: (*Suspiciously.*) What for?

CARLA: I'd like to hang it up on my wall.

BRADLEY: (*Stares at her in amazement.*) No, it's mine!

CARLA: I was hoping you'd let me.

BRADLEY: It costs a dollar.

CARLA: I'm sure it's worth it.

(*Bradley shakes his head.*)

CARLA: Okay. But, if you ever change your mind…

BRADLEY: You can make me give it to you.

CARLA: No, I can't do that.

BRADLEY: Sure you can! Teachers make kids do things all the time.

CARLA: Not in here. (*She holds out her hand for him to shake.*) I've enjoyed your visit very much. Thank you for sharing so much with me.

(*Bradley, taking his picture, backs away from her without shaking her hand. He walks out of her office, then rips up his picture and drops it on the ground.*)

END SCENE 3

Scene 4

Recess. A basketball hoop is up. Jeff is standing by himself as Brian and Robbie enter bouncing a basketball and throwing it back and forth.

JEFF: Can I play?

BRIAN: Sorry. Game's locked.

(*Jeff moves off to one side of the stage. Robbie and Brian shoot baskets. Bradley enters and walks right through Robbie's and Brian's game, to Jeff, although Bradley doesn't acknowledge Jeff's presence.*)

JEFF: Hi, Bradley.

(*Bradley looks at him, but doesn't answer.*)

JEFF: So what do you want to do?

BRADLEY: Nothing with you.

(*For a moment neither boy says anything, then Jeff tries again.*)

JEFF: So, I guess you went and saw Carla.

BRADLEY: Yeah, Mrs. Ebbel made me.

JEFF: She's nice, isn't she?

BRADLEY: Who?

JEFF: Carla.

BRADLEY: She's we-ird! She says she wants to eat dog food!

JEFF: She said that?

BRADLEY: I hate her.

(*The basketball rolls away from the game toward Bradley and Jeff.*)

ROBBIE: Somebody get the ball!

(*The ball is closer to Bradley but he makes no effort to pick it up. Jeff walks around Bradley and picks it up.*)

ROBBIE: Fishface. Over here!

BRADLEY: Kick it over the fence.

(*Jeff dribbles a couple of time for Robbie's benefit, then throws it to him.*)

ROBBIE: Good throw, Fishface.

JEFF: (*To Bradley.*) Wanna see if they'll play some two on two?

BRADLEY: With those Bozos? No way!

(*Bradley and Jeff remain, hanging out but doing nothing, on one side of the stage as Melinda, Lori and Colleen enter on the other side.*)

COLLEEN: I was washing my hands and he just walked right in.

MELINDA: Who was it?

COLLEEN: You know, that new kid.

LORI: Jeff Fishnose. He's kind of weird isn't he?

COLLEEN: I don't know. I think he's kind of cute.

(*Colleen's two friends, look at her surprised.*)

MELINDA: Ooooh!

(*All three giggle. Then Melinda spots Jeff and hurries to him, with Lori right behind her. Colleen timidly follows.*)

MELINDA: Hi, Jeff.

JEFF: Hi.

LORI: (*In a teasing kind of voice.*) Hello, Jeff.

JEFF: Hello.

(*Lori laughs.*)

COLLEEN: (*Shyly.*) Hi, Jeff.

JEFF: Hi.

(*All three girls giggle.*)

BRADLEY: Get outta here or I'll punch your faces in.

LORI: Euuuu! Bradley Chalkers!

BRADLEY: Lori Loudmouth! The ugliest girl in the school!

MELINDA: Grow up, Bradley.

BRADLEY: Make me!

(*He shakes his fist at the girls, and they back away. They start to exit, but Lori suddenly stops and turns.*)

LORI: (*Teasingly.*) Hey, Jeff. What were you doing in the girls' bathroom?

(*The three girls exit, laughing, as Jeff covers his face.*)

BRADLEY: (*Suddenly impressed.*) You went into the girls' bathroom?

JEFF: It wasn't – I mean –

BRADLEY: Me too! I go all the time. I like to make them scream.

(*Bradley now fully accepts Jeff as a friend. Jeff is still not fully recovered from his humiliation.*)

BRADLEY: Stupid girls!

JEFF: (*Quietly.*) Stupid girls. (*Saying it makes him feel better.*)

BRADLEY: Stupid girls!

JEFF: (*Boldly.*) Stupid girls!

BRADLEY: Wait a minute. Why'd you say hello to them?

JEFF: I don't know. They said hello to me first.

BRADLEY: So?

JEFF: Whenever anybody says hello to me, I always say hello back.

BRADLEY: (*Genuinely curious.*) Why?

JEFF: I don't know. I can't help it. Its like when someone says 'thank you.' Don't you automatically say 'you're welcome'?

BRADLEY: No.

JEFF: I do. It's like a reflex. Like when you go to the doctor and he taps your knee. You have to kick. You can't help it. It's the same thing. Whenever someone says hello to me, I always say hello back.

BRADLEY: (*Thinks it over.*) I know! The next time one of those stupid girls says hello to you – kick her!

END SCENE 4

Note: Jeff exits. Bradley remains on stage as his bedroom revolves around. He sits on his bed as Scene 5 begins.

Scene 5

Bradley is sitting on his bed, surrounded by his animals.

BRADLEY: Jeff and I are a lot alike. We're both smart. We both hate girls. And we both like to sneak into the girls' bathroom.

BARTHOLOMEW: Jeff went into the girls' bathroom? Cool!

RONNIE: And he's really your friend?

BRADLEY: He has to be. I gave him a dollar. Actually, I've never been in a girls' bathroom – but I always wanted to go.

BARTHOLOMEW: Maybe Jeff will go with you.

THE GOOSE: Ooh, and maybe there'll be a bunch of girls in there!

RONNIE: Jeff sounds pretty neat.

BRADLEY: Yeah. Except you want to hear something weird? (*The animals move closer to him.*) Anytime someone says hello to him, he always says hello back. Even if it's a girl he hates. He still says hello.

ALL THE ANIMALS: (*A beat as the animals look at each other, then.*) That *is* weird.

BRADLEY: He does all his homework, too. He already has two gold stars next to his name.

RONNIE: How many gold stars do you have?

BRADLEY: None.

THE TURTLE: Gold stars are stupid.

RONNIE: Maybe if you did your homework, you'd get a gold star too.

BRADLEY: Maybe.

(*Mr. Chalkers enters with a basket of laundry. The animals become inanimate.*)

BRADLEY: I wasn't doing anything.

MR. CHALKERS: That's the problem. I wish you would. (*Gives Bradley some laundry to put away.*)

MR. CHALKERS: Is there anything you'd like to talk about?

BRADLEY: No.

MR. CHALKERS: Well, I tried.

(*Starts to exit, but Mrs. Chalkers enters.*)

MRS. CHALKERS: I'm making fudge brownies if you want to lick the spoon. (*Notices her husband.*) Oh.

MR. CHALKERS: You never told me. How'd the conference go with Bradley's teacher?

MRS. CHALKERS: (*Pause.*). Fine. Bradley is doing very well.

MR. CHALKERS: Good. Glad to hear it. (*Exits.*)

MRS. CHALKERS: (*Waits to make sure her husband is gone.*) How did it go today? Did you like the counselor?

BRADLEY: No. She's mean. If you accidentally spill your milk, even if it wasn't your fault, she still gets mad at you like you did it on purpose.

MRS. CHALKERS: Maybe if you explained to her –

BRADLEY: She asked me why the president doesn't wear a hat. Now, how am I supposed to know something like that?

MRS. CHALKERS: I don't know.

BRADLEY: Well, I'm never going to see her again.

MRS. CHALKERS: Please, Bradley. I wish you'd give her a chance.

BRADLEY: I hate her.

MRS. CHALKERS: I think she can help you, Bradley. If you'll let her.

BRADLEY: I don't need any help. You said I was doing very well. I heard you!

MRS. CHALKERS: Did you want me to tell your father the truth? He already thinks you can't do anything right.

BRADLEY: You should have taken me to the zoo. (*Hugs Ronnie and holds her until the scene is over.*)

MRS. CHALKERS: (*Sadly looks at Bradley. Starts to exit, then stops.*) Think about it. (*Bradley turns his back on her. She exits.*)

BARTHOLOMEW: The reason the president doesn't wear a hat is because his head is too big.

THE GOOSE: No, his head's too *small.* The hat keeps falling down over his face, and then he can't see where he's going and he bumps into things. (*As the sets are being moved.*)

RONNIE: His head isn't too big or too small. Hats come in all sizes. The reason he doesn't wear a hat is because he doesn't want to mess up his hairdo.

TURTLE: I got it. Hats make his ears sweat.

ALL THE ANIMALS: Yeah. That's it. Yeah, that's a good one. Yeah.

END SCENE 5

Scene 6

> *The counselor's office. The room is no longer messy, although there is still some healthy clutter. The bulletin boards are covered with children's art. Carla is in her office when Colleen timidly enters.*

COLLEEN: Are you Miss Davis?

CARLA: Yes, but I prefer to be called Carla.

COLLEEN: Do I have to tell you my name?

CARLA: No, not if you don't want to.

COLLEEN: Colleen Verigold. (*She sits at the round table.*) I don't know whom to invite to my birthday party. See, there's this boy I want to invite. Do I have to tell you his name?

CARLA: No.

COLLEEN: Jeff Fishkin. (*Carla smiles.*) But if I invite Jeff, then I'll have to invite another boy, because I can't invite seven girls and only one boy, can I? Except Jeff has only one friend and he's the most horrible, rotten, monster in the school! I can't invite Bradley Chalkers to my birthday party! I just can't! So what should I do? (*Eagerly looks at Carla as if she'll have a magic answer to her dilemma.*)

CARLA: You want me to tell you whom to invite to your birthday party? (*Colleen nods.*)

CARLA: Well, actually, Colleen, I'm not really allowed to talk to you without your parents' permission.

COLLEEN: That's dumb.

CARLA: No it isn't. There are some parents who object to my being here. They don't want other people counseling their children.

COLLEEN: My parents won't care. They said I can invite anybody I want to my party.

CARLA: That's not the point. I'll give you a form for your parents to sign. Then, when you come back, I'll help *you* figure out who *you* want to invite. Okay?

COLLEEN: Okay.

(*Takes the form from Carla, and goes from the counselor's office to the hall, where Lori and Melinda enter to meet her.*)

MELINDA: So who are you going to invite? Are you going to invite Bradley?

LORI: (*Dramatically.*) No. Please no. *Please* not Bradley.

MELINDA: If you invite Jeff, don't you have to invite Bradley?

COLLEEN: I don't know yet. She won't tell me until my parents sign this stupid form.

(*Bradley enters, walking past the girls towards the counselor's office. He's wearing a light jacket.*)

LORI: Oh, yuck, it's Bradley Chalkers. I think I'm going to throw up.

BRADLEY: You look like you threw up.

LORI: That's because I looked at you.

(*Bradley shakes his fist at her. Lori shrieks and backs off. She obviously enjoys teasing Bradley. The girls exit. Bradley enters the counselor's office.*)

BRADLEY: The reason the president doesn't wear a hat is because the doorways are too low. He used to wear one, but every time he walked through a door, he hit his hat and it would fall off.

CARLA: (*Almost laughs.*) That makes sense. But, (*Looks around, then whispers.*) I thought it was top secret.

BRADLEY: The president says he trusts you.

CARLA: Thank you, Bradley. I'm glad you trust me.

BRADLEY: (*Stares at her a moment. That wasn't what he said, but he chooses not make an issue of it.*) Jeff trusts you too.

CARLA: I understand you two have become good friends.

BRADLEY: He's my best friend.

CARLA: That's very nice. I'm sure Jeff appreciates having you as a friend.

BRADLEY: I'm his only friend.

CARLA: But even if he had other friends –

BRADLEY: He won't. I'm his only friend.

CARLA: But suppose he makes new friends.

BRADLEY: I don't want him to.

CARLA: But if he made new friends, then his new friends could be your friends too.

BRADLEY: He won't.

CARLA: Let me ask you something, Bradley. What do you think friendship is? When you say you have a friend, does that mean you own him? I have a book. I have a bicycle. I have a friend. Or is friendship something you share between the two of you?

(*Bradley stares at her like she's crazy.*)

CARLA: Just because you and Jeff are friends, does that mean he can't be friends with other kids, too?

BRADLEY: Yes!

CARLA: Why?

BRADLEY: (*Proudly.*) Because. So long as Jeff is friends with me, nobody else will like him!

END SCENE 6

Note: Bradley remains on stage as the counselor's office revolves away taking Carla with it. Jeff enters holding a school book. Bradley moves to join him, ready to begin Scene 7.

Scene 7

Outside, after school. (Note: In the scene, Bradley will fall into a mud puddle, getting his pants wet. It is not necessary to have an actual puddle on stage. It can be suggested by lights and the actions of the characters. It has been done with Bradley having a plastic bag of water inside his pants, which he opens by a trigger system after he falls.) Jeff is on stage, wearing a jacket and holding a school book. Bradley joins him.

BRADLEY: So you want to go sneak into the girls' bathroom?

JEFF: Uhhh…now? Now's not a good time.

BRADLEY: Why not?

JEFF: Uhhh…There won't be any girls there now. They all go home to use their own bathrooms.

BRADLEY: You're right. Good thinking. We'll do it tomorrow during recess.

(*Colleen, Lori and Melinda enter and walk towards them. They're wearing jackets and some or all have umbrellas but they close their umbrellas because it has stopped raining.*)

LORI: (*Teasingly.*) Hello, Jeff.

COLLEEN: Hi, Jeff.

MELINDA: Hello, Jeff.

JEFF: Hello, Hi, Hello.

> (*The girls laugh as they walk to the far end of the stage, careful to avoid the puddle. They talk and laugh together, quietly.*)

JEFF: (*Turns to Bradley.*) Sorry, I can't help it.

BRADLEY: I know. Whenever anyone says hello to you, you have to say hello back. (*Thinks a moment.*) I just got a great idea!

JEFF: What?

BRADLEY: Let's go beat them up. Then they won't say hello to you anymore. (*Starts toward the girls.*)

JEFF: Wait.

> (*Bradley stops and looks at him.*)

JEFF: I've got to go home and do my homework. (*Taps his book.*)

BRADLEY: How come you're always doing *homework.*

> (*Jeff shrugs.*)

BRADLEY: Do you like it?

JEFF: It's okay.

BRADLEY: Maybe I should try it sometime.

JEFF: Why don't you come over to my house. We can do it together.

BRADLEY: Now?

JEFF: Sure. I can help y – (*Uses psychology.*) You can help me with the stuff I don't understand.

> (*Bradley thinks it over.*)

JEFF: Then maybe we can shoot some hoops or something.

BRADLEY: All right, I'll do it!

JEFF: Good!

BRADLEY: After we beat up those girls. (*Again, starts towards the girls.*)

JEFF: (*Trying to stop Bradley.*) I think the homework might take a long time. We should probably get started right away.

BRADLEY: (*Stops.*) It won't take long. You just have to hit them once, then they cry and run away. (*Again starts towards the girls.*)

JEFF: But it's so wet and muddy. It'll probably start raining again.

BRADLEY: (*Stops.*) Good! We can push them in the mud. Girls hate it when their clothes get dirty.

JEFF: I don't know. We really should get started on our homework.

BRADLEY: Girls kick. They don't know how to punch, so they try to kick you.

> (*Bradley walks over to the girls, carefully avoiding the mud puddle. Jeff lags a little behind.*)

MELINDA: What do you want, Bradley?

BRADLEY: Nothing you got, Melinda. (*Looks at Jeff and laughs.*)

COLLEEN: (*Shyly.*) Hello, Jeff.

JEFF: Hello, Colleen.

BRADLEY: Quit saying hello to him!

LORI: It's a free country. We can say hello.

BRADLEY: Not to us!

LORI: We didn't say hello to *you*. Just him. Hello, Jeff.

JEFF: Hello.

> (*Lori laughs.*)

MELINDA: Why don't you just leave us alone, Bradley.

BRADLEY: No. You leave us alone first!

> (*Bradley pushes Melinda. She pushes him back. He stumbles backwards and falls on his rear end into the mud puddle. Lori laughs. Bradley climbs out of the mud, madder than ever.*)

BRADLEY: You got my clothes dirty!

LORI: (*Teasingly, in a sing-song voice.*) Bradley wet his pants!

BRADLEY: Shut up!

MELINDA: (*Nervously.*) You started it.

BRADLEY: (*Shaking his fist.*) I'll punch your face in, Melinda!

> (*Melinda fearfully raises her fists. She doesn't think she knows how to box. Bradley comes at her and kicks her. Frightened, Melinda slugs him hard in the eye with everything she's got. She surprises herself by how hard she hit him, and covers her mouth with her hands. Bradley stumbles back, holding his eye, but doesn't fall.*)

BRADLEY: No fair! Four against one!

> (*Bradley runs to the other end of the stage, where Mrs. Chalkers enters to meet him. Meanwhile Jeff is confused. Melinda is in shock. Lori is elated. Colleen looks from one to the other. The three girls exit. Jeff glances after Bradley, then also exits.*)

MRS. CHALKERS: (*Hugging Bradley.*) My poor baby.

BRADLEY: (*Sobbing, and pretending he hurts all over, not just his eye. He flinches at wherever his mother touches him.*) They beat me up and threw me in the mud. Then they ripped up my homework.

MRS. CHALKERS: Who were they? I want to know their names.

BRADLEY: (*Hesitatingly. He can't tell her he got beat up by a girl.*) Uh…I don't know all their names.

MRS. CHALKERS: Don't be afraid. I'll make sure they don't hurt you anymore.

BRADLEY: Jeff Fishkin! He was the leader of the gang.

MRS. CHALKERS: I'll call the school. We won't let Jeff Fishkin get away with this.

BRADLEY: Good! I hope he gets expelled!

END SCENE 7

Scene 8

The schoolyard. The basketball hoop is up. Jeff walks across stage, confused as usual. Robbie and Brian enter. Brian holds a basketball.

ROBBIE: Jeff.

BRIAN: Hey, Jeff.

JEFF: Me?

ROBBIE: Hi, Jeff.

JEFF: Hi.

BRIAN: So, how's it goin Jeff?

JEFF: Fine?

ROBBIE: All right!

BRIAN: So what did the principal say? Did you get in trouble?

JEFF: No.

ROBBIE: (*Laughing.*) Probably gave him a medal!

BRIAN: Man, I've been waiting all year for somebody to teach Chalkers a lesson. (*He holds the basketball under his arm, and punches it with his fist as if it's Bradley's head.*)

ROBBIE: Yeah. I would have done it myself, but, uh…you know how it is.

BRIAN: Yeah, I know how it is. (*Still friendly.*) You're chicken.

ROBBIE: Well I didn't exactly see you taking on Chalkers either.

BRIAN: Yeah, well, Jeff's here now. So, Jeff. You want to play some b-ball.

JEFF: Uhh…Sure!

(*They all head towards the basket.*)

ROBBIE: All right. Jeff's on my team.

BRIAN: No, he's on mine. (*Throws the basketball to Jeff who dribbles and shoots.*)

ROBBIE: All right, Jeff.

BRIAN: Nice shot, Jeff.

END SCENE 8

Scene 9

The counselor's office. Carla is sitting on the floor of her office when Colleen enters.

CARLA: Hello, Colleen.

COLLEEN: I just came to tell you I can't talk to you.

CARLA: Your parents didn't sign the form?

COLLEEN: No, and they won't either! (*Sits next to Carla.*) You know what they said? They said it was a waste of money for the school to hire you! They heard you were (*Making a face.*) strange. They said you should get married and have your own children before you start telling other parents how they should raise theirs. And they said if I have a problem, I should talk to them.

CARLA: That's their choice.

COLLEEN: But then when I try to talk to them, they don't even listen. Anyway it doesn't matter. At least I don't have to invite Bradley Chalkers to my birthday party. Jeff has other friends now.

Anyway I couldn't invite Bradley even if I wanted to, because Melinda is my best friend, except for Lori, and she beat up Bradley. (*Colleen quickly covers her mouth with her hand, then slowly takes it away. Sheepishly.*) That was supposed to be a secret. Melinda doesn't want anybody to know.

CARLA: I won't tell.

COLLEEN: Good. Melinda would kill me.

CARLA: So have you asked Jeff to your party?

COLLEEN: No, not yet. But I will! I know he likes me because he says hello to me whenever I say hello to him. But then I always get so scared. I never know what to say next. I wish you could help me. Why did my parents say such bad things about you? They don't even know you.

CARLA: I'm sure they're just trying to do what's best for you. A lot of people think counselors don't belong at schools. (*In a highly affected, humorously scary voice.*) I guess they're afraid I might fill your head with all kind of crazy ideas.

(*Colleen exits and Jeff enters. This can be done very stylistically, either through blocking, or with a quick blackout. The point is that Jeff has taken Colleen's place.*)

JEFF: I don't need any help anymore. I have lots of friends now. We play basketball and I'm the best. Everyone says so.

CARLA: Good for you Jeff. I'm very proud of you.

JEFF: And I'm not friends with Bradley anymore.

CARLA: Oh, I'm sorry to hear that.

JEFF: Why? I'm not. I hate him. In fact…(*Looks around the room*)…I beat him up.

CARLA: What happened?

JEFF: Oh, he wouldn't stop bothering me. I never liked him. No one does. So then he tried to hit me (*Jeff pantomimes his fight with Bradley.*) but I ducked and then smashed him right in the face. He came at me again, but I blocked with my left, a right to the gut, and then pow! (*Shrugs.*) I didn't want to have to do it, but I had no choice. (*Pause.*) So, I don't think I need to see a counselor anymore, since I have normal friends.

CARLA: Okay, Jeff. If that's how you feel.

JEFF: They might think I'm weird or something. None of them see a counselor.

CARLA: Okay.

JEFF: Does that mean I can go?

CARLA: (*Nods.*) But anytime you want to talk again, please feel free to come and see me. Even if you just feel like getting out of class for a while. (*She holds out her hand for him to shake.*)

(*Jeff is replaced by Bradley who doesn't shake her hand. Bradley has a black eye.*)

BRADLEY: I beat myself up. No one else can beat me up.

(*He sits at the table. Carla joins him.*)

BRADLEY: I wanted to hit somebody. But if I hit another kid, I would have gotten in trouble, so I hit myself.

CARLA: Why'd you want to hit somebody?

BRADLEY: Because I hate him.

CARLA: Who?

BRADLEY: Everybody.

CARLA: Is that why you hit yourself? Do you hate yourself? (*Bradley looks at her like she's crazy.*) Do you like yourself? Maybe the reason you say you don't like anybody else is because you really don't like yourself.

BRADLEY: I like myself. (*Without anger.*) You're the one I don't like.

CARLA: Tell me some things about yourself that you like. I like you. I think you have lots of good qualities. But I want you to tell me something you like about yourself.

BRADLEY: I can't talk anymore.

CARLA: Why not?

BRADLEY: I'm sick. The more I talk, the sicker I get. Call the doctor if –

CARLA: That sounds serious.

BRADLEY: It is! I've probably said too much already, and it's your fault. I'll probably throw up.

CARLA: Shh. Don't say another word. Let's just sit together in silence. Sometimes people can learn a lot about each other by just sitting together in silence. (*She zips her mouth shut.*)

BRADLEY: You're weird!

CARLA: (*Unzips her mouth.*) A lot of people tell me that. (*Zips it back up, and puts her finger to her lips.*)

(*They sit in silence, glancing at each other out of the corners of their eyes. Bradley squirms a lot. He finds it very unsettling.*)

BRADLEY: I can probably talk a little bit.

CARLA: Oh no, I don't want you to get sick. I like you too much.

BRADLEY: The doctor says I'm supposed to talk a little. Just not a lot.

CARLA: (*Hesitatingly.*) All right. Shall we talk about school?

BRADLEY: No! The doctor said if I talk about school, I'll die.

CARLA: Oh, that's a problem. See as part of my job, I'm supposed to help you do better in school. But how can I help you if we can't talk about it?

BRADLEY: (*Rubs his chin as he tries to figure out a solution to Carla's problem.*) I know! Tell them that you tried to help me, but I wouldn't let you. Tell them that I was too mean and nasty. That's it. Tell them I said I'd spit on you.

CARLA: Oh, I could never say that about you. You're too nice.

BRADLEY: They'll believe you. I'm not usually this nice.

CARLA: I just wish I knew why a bright kid like you keeps failing.

BRADLEY: Because Mrs. Ebbel doesn't like me.

CARLA: Ssh! Don't talk about it.

BRADLEY: Well, I can probably talk about school a little bit without dying.

CARLA: (*Sounding unsure.*) O-kay. But as soon you feel even a little bit like dying, let me know and we'll stop.

BRADLEY: Okay.

CARLA: Okay. Well, I have one suggestion. Usually the same questions that are on your tests, are also on your homework assignments. So if you did your homework, the tests might be easier for you.

BRADLEY: The tests *are* easy. I could get a hundred if I wanted. I answer all the problems wrong on purpose.

CARLA: You want to know what I think? I think you would like to get good grades but you're afraid that even if you tried, you'd still fail.

BRADLEY: I'm not afraid of anything.

CARLA: I think you're afraid of yourself. But you shouldn't be. I have lots of confidence in you, Bradley Chalkers.

BRADLEY: I'm starting to feel a little bit like I'm going to die.

CARLA: Okay. Thank you for talking about it as much as you did. You are very brave. Maybe for next week you can write down a list of safe topics for us to discuss. (*She hands Bradley a pad of paper and a pencil.*)

BRADLEY: (*He looks at it, unsure.*) Is that homework?

CARLA: No. You don't even have to put your name on the top of the paper.

BRADLEY: Good.

CARLA: (*Stands up.*) Thank you for sharing so much with me today. I enjoyed your visit very much. (*She holds out her hand. Bradley takes the pad and paper and walks out of her office without shaking her hand.*)

END SCENE 9

Note: Bradley remains on stage, working on his list, as the counselor's office revolves away, taking Carla with it.
Lori comes running on stage screaming, beginning scene 10.

Scene 10

The scene begins in a neutral area and moves to Bradley's bedroom. Bradley is working on his list as Lori enters running. She screams, trying to bait Bradley.

LORI: AAAAAAAAAAAAAHHHHHHHHHHHHH! It's a monster!
(*Bradley looks up at Lori, then returns to his list.*)

LORI: You're not even human! You're a monster from outer space! (*She runs, expecting Bradley to chase her, but he doesn't, so she stops and again tries to entice him into chasing her. Sing-song.*) Mon-ster. Mon-ster from outer space!
(*He continues working on his list. She throws up her hands in disgust. She looks at him one last time like she thinks he's weirder than ever, then she exits.*)

BRADLEY: (*To himself as he writes on the pad of paper.*) Monster from outer space. (*Thinks a while then writes some more.*) Girls with big mouths.
(*Robbie, Brian and Jeff enter. They stride down the middle of the stage, forcing Bradley out of their way. Throughout this encounter, Robbie and Brian talk tough, while Jeff is unsure and feels a little bit guilty.*)

ROBBIE: Hey. Out of our way, Chalkers!

BRIAN: Yeah, Chalkers.

(*Bradley looks to Jeff for sympathy.*)

JEFF: (*A little bit timid.*) Yeah, Chalkers.

BRIAN: Not so tough anymore, are you?

ROBBIE: Not since Jeff came along.

BRIAN: (*Patting Jeff on the back.*) Jeff is top-gun now.

ROBBIE: Chalkers is just a big chicken. When he goes to a barber shop he doesn't get his hair cut. He gets his feathers plucked.

(*They continue past Bradley, but he can still hear them talking.*)

BRIAN: (*To Jeff, but making sure Bradley can hear.*) I can't believe you used to hang out with *Chicken Chalkers!*

ROBBIE: (*Patting Jeff on the back.*) I guess it just took a while to find out who your real friends are.

(*Jeff, Brian, and Robbie exit.*)

BRADLEY: (*Writing, as his bedroom revolves around to meet him.*) Basketball …Real friends…Are…chickens…really…afraid?

(*Bradley continues studying the list as he enters his room.*)

RONNIE: Whatcha doin', Bradley?

BRADLEY: (*Sits on bed.*) I'm trying to make a list of topics to talk about with my counselor.

BARTHOLOMEW: Whatcha got so far?

BRADLEY: (*Reading aloud from his list.*) Trees that lose their leaves

Gold stars

Chalk

Why people laugh

What does it feel like to be shot

Pencils

Pencil sharpeners

Accidents

Coffee

Military school…

RONNIE: (*Interrupting Bradley's reading.*) That's a lot of topics. How many do you have?

BRADLEY: Uh, (*Turning the page.*) eighty-one. See, I write down all the stuff I see or hear at school, or anything I think about. Carla will be so surprised. She probably thinks I'll have like five or six topics. She'll say, what do you want to talk about today, Bradley? Then I'll hand her this list! (*Laughs and shows list to Ronnie and Bartholomew.*)

RONNIE: She won't believe it!

BRADLEY: Let's see…

BARTHOLOMEW: Have you got bears?

BRADLEY: Oh, that's a good one. (*Writing.*) Eighty-two…bears.

RONNIE: How about rabbits?

BRADLEY: Good! (*Writing.*) Eighty-three rabbits.

GOOSE: Let me see that list. (*He shows it to the Goose.*) It's not in alphabetical order! It's supposed to be in alphabetical order.

TURTLE: Oh, put a sock in it! Carla doesn't care about the order.

GOOSE: What about spelling?

TURTLE: She doesn't care about spelling either.

RONNIE: She just cares about Bradley.

> (*Bradley suddenly stops, as Mr. Chalkers enters. Bradley sits on the list.*)

MR. CHALKERS: What's that?

BRADLEY: Nothin'

MR. CHALKERS: It's not nothing. What is it?

BRADLEY: Just something for school.

> (*Mr. Chalkers gestures, indicating for Bradley to show it to him. Bradley does so.*)

MR. CHALKERS: This is how you treat your homework.

BRADLEY: It's not homework. See my name's not even at the top.

MR. CHALKERS: (*Quickly skims the list.*) What is this?

BRADLEY: Just stuff for me and my counselor to talk about.

MR. CHALKERS: Oh, your counselor. This is what you talk about? (*Reads randomly from the list. Bradley sits head down feeling ashamed during the reading.*) Hopscotch

Dodgeball

Four square

One potato

Two potato

Three potato

Four

Five potato

Six potato

Seven potato

More

Less

Nothing at all

What's it like to be in jail?

Have you ever been to the White House?

What's it like inside the girls' bathroom? (*Stops reading.*) Do you mean the girls' bathroom in the White House?

(*Bradley shrugs. Mr. Chalkers continues reading.*)

MR. CHALKERS: When will I be able to grow a beard?

Things that smell bad

Things you like about yourself

Things you don't like about yourself

Things nobody likes about yourself

Things you don't like about anybody else

Gold stars

Does my head look like a chili bowl?

(*Looks at Bradley. Bradley points to his head. Mr. Chalkers nods, then continues to read.*)

MR. CHALKERS: I wish I could fly.

Kids with glasses

Glasses you drink from

What happens when you grow old?

What happens when you die?

What if you were never born?

Can someone else be you?

Can you be someone else?

If I was someone else I wouldn't make fun of me.

Monsters from outer space

Girls with big mouths (*Abruptly stops reading.*) I don't think these are the kind of things you and your counselor are supposed to be talking about. At least I wouldn't think so.

BRADLEY: You don't know. She'll talk about anything I want to talk about. She listens to me. She likes me.

MR. CHALKERS: That's her job. (*Beat.*) I don't see how any of this is going to help you, but I guess she's the expert, not me. (*He gives the list back to Bradley and exits.*)

BRADLEY: (*Studies the list, then writes:.*) Eighty-four...Jobs. (*He studies the list a moment more, then rips it to pieces.*)

END OF ACT ONE

ACT TWO
Scene 1

> *The counselor's office. Carla is doing paperwork, and doesn't notice Mrs. Ebbel enter.*

MRS. EBBEL: Carla? You asked to see me.

CARLA: Thanks for coming. I wanted to talk to you about Bradley.

MRS. EBBEL: (*Sits at the round table.*) I should have guessed. What's he done now? There's only so much I can do. I tried taking away his recess privileges. Believe me, it doesn't do any good.

CARLA: Bradley hasn't done anything. He's a delightful and charming young man.

MRS. EBBEL: Are you sure we're talking about the same Bradley?

CARLA: He has a little problem with self esteem. I thought maybe there might be some special project he can do around the classroom.

MRS. EBBEL: (*Somewhat suspicious and resentful of Carla telling her how to run her classroom.*) Like what?

CARLA: I don't know – clean the erasers.

MRS. EBBEL: You want me to tell Bradley to clean the erasers. Fine, I'll tell him to clean the erasers.

CARLA: Don't tell him. Ask him. As a favor.

> (*Mrs. Ebbel looks at Carla like she thinks she's crazy. Mrs. Nathan barges in, a little angry.*)

MRS. NATHAN: (*While entering.*) Did you tell Chad Lakeland that it was Good To Fail?

CARLA: What?

MRS. NATHAN: I just got off the phone with Chad's mother. She said you told Chad that grades don't matter, and that it was good to fail.

CARLA: I never told him it was good to fail.

MRS. NATHAN: Exactly what did you tell him.

CARLA: His parents put so much pressure on him. They expect him to – I don't know. He could do a lot better if he didn't worry so much about his grades, and just relaxed and enjoyed school.

MRS. NATHAN: That is all well and good, but let's keep our priorities straight, shall we? A child goes to school to learn.

MRS. EBBEL: Not to have A Good Time.

CARLA: He would learn more, if he enjoyed learning.

MRS. EBBEL: Maybe Chad's teacher should ask him to clean the erasers.

MRS. NATHAN: What? I just spent the last twenty minutes having my ear taken off by Mrs. Lakeland. Do me a favor. In the future, do not tell any child that sometimes it is better to fail than to get good grades.

CARLA: When I see him –

MRS. NATHAN: You're not going to see him. (*Mrs. Ebbel exits. Mrs. Nathan starts to exit, then stops.*) Didn't we talk about the proper way to dress?

CARLA: (*Calmly, yet defiant.*) Yes I believe we did.

(*They look at each other a moment, then Mrs. Nathan exits. Bradley enters. Carla holds out her hand.*)

CARLA: It's a pleasure to see you today. I appreciate your coming to see me.

(*Bradley walks past her without shaking her hand and sits down at the round table.*)

CARLA: Did you make a list of topics for us to discuss?

BRADLEY: (*Gloomily.*) No, you're the teacher. (*He picks up a crayon and starts to color on a piece of paper.*)

CARLA: (*Tries to hide her disappointment.*) So?

BRADLEY: So you're the one who has to say what we talk about, not me. That's your job.

CARLA: Okay, well, let me think. Are you sure you can't think of anything? I thought you would have come up with at least three or four interesting and exciting topics.

BRADLEY: Nope.

CARLA: Well, then, let's talk about school. Shall we start with homework?

BRADLEY: (*After a long pause.*) Monsters from outer space.

CARLA: Pardon?

BRADLEY: You said I can pick the topic. I want to talk about monsters from outer space.

CARLA: What a wonderful topic!

BRADLEY: The only way to kill them is with a ray gun. Regular guns or even hand grenades won't kill them. (*He stands up and pretends to shoot a ray gun, making an appropriate noise.*)

CARLA: (*Putting up her hands.*) Don't shoot me.

BRADLEY: You're a monster from outer space.

CARLA: No I'm not. I'm a counselor.

BRADLEY: Do you believe in monsters from outer space?

CARLA: No. I don't believe in monsters. I believe there are many other types of creatures living in our universe. Some are probably quite primitive, others smarter than you and me. But out of all those creatures, I don't believe there is even one monster.

BRADLEY: I do.

CARLA: I think everyone has good inside him. Sometimes people think someone's a monster. But that's only because they can't see the 'good.' And then you know what they do?

BRADLEY: They kill him?

CARLA: Worse. (*Dramatically.*) They call him a monster! And they all treat him like a monster. And then, after a while, he starts believing it himself! He thinks he's a monster. So he acts like one. But he really isn't a monster. He still has a lot of good, buried deep inside him.

BRADLEY: But what if he's real ugly? What if he has green skin, and three arms, and a big black eye in the middle of his face?

CARLA: You and I might think that is ugly, but maybe, on that planet, that might be considered beautiful. You may have just described a handsome movie star. (*Bradley laughs.*) On that planet, they would probably think I was ugly because I have two eyes and my skin isn't green.

BRADLEY: No one would ever think you were ugly.

CARLA: (*Truly astonished.*) Why Bradley. That's the nicest thing you ever said to me. Thank you.

BRADLEY: (*Looking down.*) I don't want to talk about monsters anymore.

CARLA: Okay, I think we had a very good conversation. You picked a great topic.

BRADLEY: (*Colors awhile.*) Carla?

CARLA: Yes.

BRADLEY: Can *you* see inside monsters. Can you see the good?

CARLA: That's all I see.

BRADLEY: Well, how does a monster stop being a monster? I mean, if everyone keeps treating him like a monster?

CARLA: It isn't easy. I think first he has to realize for himself that he isn't a monster. That I think is the first step. Until he knows he isn't a monster, how is anybody else supposed to know?

(*Bradley colors a while longer then holds up his finished drawing. It's a three armed green monster with a big black eye. It also has a large red heart, to show the "good" inside him.*)

BRADLEY: He's a movie star on his planet. Everybody loves him.

CARLA: He's very handsome.

BRADLEY: You want it? I mean, I don't want it anyway, so you can have it.

CARLA: I'd love it! Thank you.

(*Bradley watches Carla tack his picture to the wall. The picture will be prominently displayed in all the remaining scenes in the counselor's office.*)

CARLA: I'm looking forward to seeing you next week. I can hardly wait to hear what wonderful topics you come up with for us to discuss.

(*Bradley starts to go, then stops and turns around.*)

CARLA: Yes?

(*Bradley stares at her, hands on hips.*)

CARLA: Did you forget something?

(*Bradley stands and waits. Carla suddenly realizes what he wants. She holds out her hand.*)

CARLA: I enjoyed your visit very much. Thank you for sharing so much with me.

(*Bradley exits without shaking her hand.*)

END SCENE 1

Scene 2

Outside. Colleen, Lori, and Melinda are on one side of the stage. They are hanging out, or perhaps playing a game like jump rope.

LORI: Oh look, here he comes! Don't be a chicken.

COLLEEN: Maybe I should wait til tomorrow.

(*Lori and Melinda grab Colleen and don't let her get away. Jeff enters.*)

LORI: Jeff!

COLLEEN: (*To Lori.*) No.

(*Lori and Melinda hurry to Jeff. Colleen hurries after them.*)

LORI: (*Teasingly.*) Hello, Jeff.

MELINDA: Hi, Jeff.

JEFF: Hello, hi.

(*Lori laughs.*)

MELINDA: C'mon, Colleen. Ask him.

(*Colleen looks away.*)

LORI: Colleen has something she wants to ask you.

COLLEEN: Well, see, um, okay, well –

JEFF: (*Annoyed but not angry.*) Quit bothering me.

LORI: We're not bothering you. Colleen just wants to ask you –

MELINDA: (*Stopping her.*) Let Colleen ask him.

COLLEEN: Well, see...Okay. (*She takes a breath.*) I'm –

JEFF: I don't want her asking me anything! And quit saying hello to me.

MELINDA: We can say hello if we want. It's a free country.

JEFF: I don't want you saying it to me.

COLLEEN: (*Insulted.*) Don't worry! I won't!

LORI: I will. Hello, hello, hello, hello, hello.

JEFF: Shut up!

LORI: Hello, Jeff, hello, Jeff, Jello, Jeff. (*She laughs.*) Jello, Jeff. Hello Jello. (*She laughs some more.*)

JEFF: And quit laughing!

COLLEEN: She can laugh. You can't tell her she can't laugh.

LORI: Hello-hello-hello-hello-hello

JEFF: (*Shouts.*) Shut up!

MELINDA: You shut up.

JEFF: I'm not afraid of you, Melinda.

MELINDA: I'm not afraid of you either.

(*They both raise their fists. Melinda is much more confident than the last time. Lori is very excited.*)

JEFF: Okay, hit me.

MELINDA: You hit me first.

JEFF: No, you hit me first.

LORI: Somebody hit somebody!

(*Jeff lightly taps Melinda's shoulder with his fist, not really wanting to fight. She wails into him, hitting him over and over again in the face and body, finally knocking him down. She climbs on top of him, her knees on his chest, and pins him. Lori, like a referee, kneels down and slaps the ground as she counts.*)

LORI: One...two...three...four...five...six...seven...eight...nine-ten!

(*Melinda gets up. Lori, continuing to imitate a referee, holds Melinda's hand up in the air.*)

LORI: The winner and still champion of the world – Marvelous Melinda!

(*Colleen claps her hands. The three girls walk away as Jeff lays there. Colleen turns and looks scornfully at him, then the girls exit.*)

END SCENE 2

*Note: Jeff remains sitting on stage, while Bradley's bedroom
revolves into place for Scene 3, then Jeff exits.*

Scene 3

Bradley's Bedroom. Bradley is sitting on the bed with his animals.

RONNIE: (*Hopping across the bed, singing.*) Doo de-doo de-doo. (*Talking.*) Oh, I don't feel too good. I think I'm sick.

BRADLEY: What's wrong?

RONNIE: I'm sick. I think I'm going to throw up. I need a doctor.

(*Goose and Turtle close in on Ronnie.*)

BARTHOLOMEW: (*Suddenly remembers.*) I'm a doctor. Back up. Give her air.

(*Goose and Turtle back away.*)

BARTHOLOMEW: Let me have a look. (*Looks at Ronnie from all angles.*) It's your heart. You need a heart transplant. (*Looks around and shouts.*) Anybody got a heart they don't want?

TURTLE: Sorry, you can't have mine.

GOOSE: You can't have mine.

BRADLEY: Here, you can have mine. (*Pretends to give his heart to Ronnie.*)

RONNIE: Thank you, Bradley. That was such a good thing to do.

BARTHOLOMEW: That was. It was very good.

BRADLEY: I'm going to be good all the time now. Even at school. And then, when everybody sees how good I am, they'll know I'm not a monster.

RONNIE: And Mrs. Ebbel will give you a gold star.

TURTLE: You even look different.

BRADLEY: I do?

GOOSE: Yeah, Bradley. You look like a *good* kid.

BARTHOLOMEW: It's obvious.

TURTLE: Mrs. Ebbel will notice for sure. Teachers can tell if you're good or bad just by looking at you.

BARTHOLOMEW: Just remember, don't talk in class.

BRADLEY: I won't.

RONNIE: And don't spit on anybody.

BRADLEY: I won't.

TURTLE: And raise your hand if you have to go to the bathroom.

BRADLEY: I will.

RONNIE: But don't go in the girls' bathroom.

GOOSE: Cheese it! Here comes the big guy!

(*Mr. Chalkers enters.*)

MR. CHALKERS: Bradley. Your breakfast is ready.

BRADLEY: (*Overdoing it.*) Good morning, father.

MR. CHALKERS: (*Taken aback.*) And a good morning to you too, son.

BRADLEY: How are you feeling today?

MR. CHALKERS: (*Finding Bradley's behavior a little bit odd.*) Fine thank you. And you?

BRADLEY: Good. Very good.

MR. CHALKERS: Is there something special happening at school today?

BRADLEY: No. Yes. I just think it's going to be a good day.

MR. CHALKERS: Well, I hope you're right. I think it will be a good day too. The sun is out. The sky is blue. What more can we ask for?

(*Mrs. Chalkers enters, with a lunch box. Note: A banana is inside the lunchbox.*)

MRS. CHALKERS: (*While entering.*) Bradley, breakfast is ready. I made oatmeal.

BRADLEY: I hate oatmeal.

MRS. CHALKERS: Oh, I thought you liked it. Well, I suppose I can eat it. What would you like?

MR. CHALKERS: He'll eat oatmeal.

BRADLEY: I mean I like oatmeal. Yum, delicious!

MRS. CHALKERS: (*She hands the lunch box to Bradley.*) Really, you don't have to eat it. I can make something else.

MR. CHALKERS: He'll eat oatmeal. This isn't a restaurant.

BRADLEY: I love oatmeal. You are a wonderful cook, mother. No one can make oatmeal as good as you.

MRS. CHALKERS: I'll just make something else. It's no big deal.

BRADLEY: No! I want oatmeal!

MR. CHALKERS: Don't yell at your mother.

BRADLEY: I would like some oatmeal please.

MRS. CHALKERS: The oatmeal is probably cold.

BRADLEY: That's the way I like it. Cold and lumpy.

MRS. CHALKERS: How about a waffle?

MR. CHALKERS: You made oatmeal. He'll eat oatmeal.

MRS. CHALKERS: Really, it's no trouble. I just have to take it out of the freezer and pop it in the toaster. How about a waffle, Bradley?

BRADLEY: (*Sighs.*) Okay, I'll have a waffle. Thank you, mother.

MRS. CHALKERS: Good. (*She exits.*)

MR. CHALKERS: The way you treat your mother. I never would have gotten away with that kind of behavior when I was your age. (*He exits.*)

RONNIE: Wow, Bradley. You were so good.

GOOSE: You said "please" and "thank you."

BRADLEY: (*Sits on bed.*) If someone says "thank you" to me today, you know what I'm going to say?"

RONNIE: What?

BRADLEY: You're welcome!

RONNIE: Oh, that's so good.

BRADLEY: I shouldn't have said I hated oatmeal.

TURTLE: But then you said you liked it.

GOOSE: Cold and lumpy.

RONNIE: So you were still good.

BRADLEY: I guess. I don't know why I said I hated it. It just came out. I like oatmeal. (*Pause.*) I hate waffles.

END SCENE 3

Note: Bradley gets off bed and remains on stage with his lunch box
as his bedroom revolves away, ready for Scene 4.

Scene 4

School hallways.

Note: Bradley will go from the hallway to the girls' bathroom, back to the hallway, then to the counselor's office. Bradley, lunch box in hand, is walking across the hall when Melinda enters, crossing the other way.

BRADLEY: (*Eagerly.*) Hello, Melinda!

(*Melinda looks at him funny as she keeps walking, and exits. Mrs. Ebbel enters. Mrs. Ebbel is occupied with papers, and doesn't' notice at first that it is Bradley who greets her.*)

BRADLEY: Good morning, Mrs. Ebbel.

MRS. EBBEL: Good mor – (*Stops when she realizes it's Bradley.*) Bradley, don't start. It's too early in morning for me to put up with any of your nonsense.

BRADLEY: I'm not –

MRS. EBBEL: Just don't give me any trouble right now.

(*Bradley turns to talk to Mrs. Ebbel who's walking away from him, thus Bradley is walking backwards, and doesn't see Colleen enter behind him. Colleen is holding a notebook.*)

BRADLEY: I'm not going to cause any trouble. I'm going to be good.

(*He backs into Colleen knocking her books from her hand.*)

COLLEEN: Unh. Hey cut it out, Bradley.

MRS. EBBEL: (*Turns to see the commotion.*) Bradley what did I just say?

BRADLEY: (*To Mrs. Ebbel.*) I'm sorry. (*To Colleen.*) I'm sorry, Colleen. (*Bradley tries to help Colleen pick up her books. They each grab the same book at the same time and pull on it.*)

COLLEEN: Leave me alone, Bradley.

MRS. EBBEL: Bradley, leave her alone!

(*Bradley jerks the book from Colleen then hands it to her.*)

BRADLEY: Here you go, Colleen.

(*Colleen takes the book, then she and Mrs. Ebbel exit, both miffed at Bradley.*)

BRADLEY: I'm sorry. It was an…accident.…I think.

(*Brian and Robbie enter.*)

ROBBIE: Hey Chalkers. What's the big idea?

BRADLEY: Huh?

(*As Brian pushes him.*)

BRIAN: Jeff told us what you did.

BRIAN AND ROBBIE TOGETHER: (*Calling.*) Jeff! We found him.

(*Jeff enters. He has a black eye.*)

BRADLEY: You – ?

JEFF: (*Quickly.*) You hit me in the eye when I wasn't looking! And anyway, I was holding a bag full of groceries.

ROBBIE: He didn't want the eggs to break.

JEFF: That's right. I didn't want the eggs to break.

(*The three other boys crowd in on Bradley.*)

BRIAN: (*Pushing Bradley towards Robbie.*) Not so brave now, are you?

ROBBIE: (*Pushing Bradley towards Brian.*) Now that it's a fair fight.

(*Bradley fakes one way, then runs the other.*)

BRIAN: Get him!

(*The boys chase Bradley. They run in and out of the staggered sets. This can be done in a slapstick manner, as the characters pop in and out between the sets.*)

ROBBIE: Where'd he go?

BRIAN: Over there!

(*Robbie and Brian exit. Bradley enters. He is alone on stage having momentarily eluded his pursuers. He looks around, then covers his eyes and ducks into the girls' bathroom. He uncovers his eyes and looks around. He breathes a sigh of relief, thinking he is alone, but in fact, Lori is in the stall. Bradley walks around the girls' bathroom not knowing what to do with himself. Finally, he opens his lunch box and removes a banana, which he proceeds to peel. He takes one bite out of the banana, when the toilet flushes, then Lori steps out of the stall, buttoning her pants. Lori and Bradley look at each other in horror. They both open their mouths as if to scream, but neither does.*)

LORI: (*Remarkably calm.*) Why are you eating a banana in the girls' bathroom?

BRADLEY: Uh…

LORI: How long have you been in here?

BRADLEY: Not too long. Really. See, I just had one bite.

(*Jeff, Robbie and Brian enter, outside the bathroom.*)

BRIAN: Where'd he go?

ROBBIE: He's gotta be around here somewhere.

(*Lori gets what's happening. Bradley puts his finger to his lips.*)

BRADLEY: (*Whispers.*) Sh.

LORI: (*Whispers.*) You know what they'll do if they find you in here?

(*Bradley shrugs.*)

LORI: They'll stick your head in the toilet.

(*She wiggles her finger, indicating for him to come closer. As he approaches, she puts her hand to her mouth, like she wants to whisper something to him. Robbie, Brian, and Jeff exit just as Bradley brings his ear to Lori's mouth. She screams loud and long. She is still screaming as Bradley drops the banana back into the lunch box and runs out of the girls' bathroom. Robbie, Brian, and Jeff, responding to Lori's scream, come running back, see Bradley, and chase after him. They all exit then Bradley returns, this time to the counselor's office.*)

CARLA: Bradley? What a pleasant surprise?

BRADLEY: (*Out of breath.*) Hello, Carla. (*He holds out his hand.*) It's a pleasure to see you today.

CARLA: (*Shakes Bradley's hand.*) The pleasure is mine.

(*Robbie, Brian and Jeff enter, see Bradley with Carla, then turn around and exit. Bradley and Carla sit at the round table.*)

BRADLEY: Do you know where I just was? (*Slams his fist on the table.*) The girls' bathroom!

See, they all wanted to beat me up, so I went in there to hide. At first I thought it was empty, right? So I started eating a banana. (*He opens his lunch box and shows her the banana with a bite out of it.*) Only it wasn't empty. Lori Westin was, uh…you know. Well, then she flushed the toilet, so that's how I knew she was doing what she was doing, with me right there!

CARLA: I heard her scream.

BRADLEY: (*Flatly, without malice.*) She's got the biggest mouth in the whole school. Jeff has a black eye, just like me! They all think I beat him up.

CARLA: Did you?

BRADLEY: *No.* I mean, how can I hit him in the *eye* when he's not looking? (*Carla shrugs.*) Besides, I can't even beat up a girl. Melinda Birch beat me up. Do you know her?

CARLA: No.

BRADLEY: Oh. You'd like her. She's nice.

(*Carla just stares at him. Her face is a mixture of warmth and amazement.*)

BRADLEY: I'm trying to be good. I really am! But nobody notices. Everyone still thinks I'm a monster. Maybe they're right.

CARLA: Just give them time. I know something good you can do, that Mrs. Ebbel will notice.

BRADLEY: What?

CARLA: Your homework.

BRADLEY: No, I can't.

CARLA: Sure you can.

BRADLEY: (*Covers his head.*) I can't. I can't.

CARLA: Sure you can. You can do anything you want to do, Bradley Chalkers. I have a lot of confidence in you.

BRADLEY: I can't! I can't!

CARLA: Bradley, it's not that difficult. You're making a big deal out of something that is really quite simple.

BRADLEY: I can't!

CARLA: Why, Bradley? Why can't you?

BRADLEY: (*Meekly.*) I don't know what page we're on.

(*Carla moves around the table and kisses Bradley's cheek. He is embarrassed, but in heaven.*)

END SCENE 4

Scene 5

Bradley's bedroom. Bradley is lying on his stomach on his bed, with his head propped up by one hand. His other hand holds a pencil. His open math book and paper lay in front of him.

BRADLEY: (*To himself.*) What is three fourths of two thirds?

THE GOOSE: Hey, Bradley, whatcha doin'?

BRADLEY: Homework.

THE GOOSE: What's homework?

BRADLEY: Work you do at home.

THE GOOSE: Is that supposed to be funny.

BRADLEY: No, really. That's what they do at school. They give you work to do at home, and they call it homework.

TURTLE: You've never done it before.

BRADLEY: I'm doing it for Carla. Now leave me alone so I can concentrate. (*Sighs.*) What is three fourths of two thirds?

RONNIE: Why are you doing it for Carla?

BRADLEY: (*Looks around, then whispers.*) Okay, I'll tell you, but you can't tell anyone.

ALL THE ANIMALS TOGETHER: We promise.

BRADLEY: We're in love.

TURTLE: Really? How do you know?

BRADLEY: She kissed me.

RONNIE: Oooh, that means she loves you!

GOOSE: Are you going to marry her?

BRADLEY: Maybe when I'm older. First I have to do my homework.

RONNIE: I'm going to marry Bartholomew.

BRADLEY: I know. Now let me do my homework. Question one. What is three-fourths of two-thirds?

BARTHOLOMEW THE BEAR: So how's it going so far?

RONNIE: Leave him alone. He's trying to do his homework. He can't concentrate when you're talking to him.

BARTHOLOMEW: Maybe I can help. What's the first problem?

BRADLEY: What is three fourths of two thirds?

BARTHOLOMEW: Three fourths of two thirds. That's a tough problem all right. Three fourths of two thirds. Let's see. You divide four into – no, you multiply two times, no…

RONNIE: Of means divide. Like if you take half of something, it means you divide by two. You divide three by two, and four by three.
(*Bradley starts to write that down. As his stuffed animals continue to give him mathematical advice, Bradley keeps writing and erasing on his piece of paper.*)

THE TURTLE: No. Of means times. You have to multiply everything.

GOOSE: First you have to reverse the nominators.

THE TURTLE: You don't reverse. You inverse.

RONNIE: I think you have to find a common denumerator.

BARTHOLOMEW: Not for multiplication. That's only for addition.

RONNIE: No, that would make multiplication easier than addition. That's impossible.

THE TURTLE: Multiplication is the same thing as addition. Only faster.

THE GOOSE: You cancel out the threes. You always cancel out threes.

THE TURTLE: You multiply the threes.

BRADLEY: Three times three equals nine.

RONNIE: The answer can't be nine. If you start with fractions you have to end up with fractions. That's called the identity property.

BRADLEY: (*Slams the book shut and shouts.*) None of you know what you're talking about!

MR. CHALKERS: (*Steps in.*) What?

BRADLEY: Nothing. I was just talking to…Uh

MR. CHALKERS: (*Looks at the animals.*) I see.

BRADLEY: I mean I was doing my homework.

MR. CHALKERS: (*Puts up his hands.*) I'm in no mood. (*Starts to exit.*)

BRADLEY: Dad?

(*His father stops.*)

BRADLEY: Will you help me?

(*Mr. Chalkers stares at Bradley.*)

BRADLEY: Please.

MR. CHALKERS: Oh. All right. (*Sits next to Bradley.*)

BRADLEY: (*Hands his Father the book.*) Page forty-three.

MR. CHALKERS: (*Opens book and thumbs through to the correct page.*) Okay. First thing we need to do is start with a clean sheet of paper.

(*Bradley tears a new piece out of his notebook.*)

MR. CHALKERS: (*Reading.*) Problem one. What is three fourths of two thirds? (*Puzzled.*) What is three fourths of two thirds? (*Pause.*) How did your teacher tell you to go about solving these?

BRADLEY: (*Bitterly.*) Oh she never tells us anything. She just says – (*Stops, and changes his tone.*) I guess I wasn't paying attention.

MR. CHALKERS: Well, it's been awhile but let's see. Okay, the first thing you want to do is write the equation.

(*Bradley stares blankly at him.*)

MR. CHALKERS: Of means you multiply. So you write "three fourths times two thirds equals – You understand so far?

BRADLEY: Of means times.

MR. CHALKERS: Okay now you multiply. Three times two.

BRADLEY: Six.

MR. CHALKERS: And four times three.

(*Mrs. Chalkers enters, and stands back and watches, delighted.*)

BRADLEY: Twelve.

MR. CHALKERS: So you have six over twelve, or six twelfths, or one-half.

BRADLEY: One half? That's the answer?

MR. CHALKERS: Yes.

BRADLEY: Three fourths of two thirds is one half. That's amazing!

MR. CHALKERS: (*Laughs.*) Yes, it is amazing.

(*Lights begin to fade.*)

MR. CHALKERS: All right, problem two...

END SCENE 5

Scene 6

> *Outside. A basketball hoop is off to the back. Bradley is studying his homework as Colleen walks by.*

BRADLEY: (*Still trying to be good.*) Hello Colleen. It's a pleasure to see you today.

> (*Colleen screws up her face and looks at him like he's the weirdest kid in the world. Before she can respond, Robbie, Brian and Jeff enter. Brian holds a basketball.*)

ROBBIE: Chalkers!

> (*Bradley is backed into a corner. Colleen remains near the action.*)

BRIAN: What's the matter, Bradley. No place to run. (*Threatens Bradley with basketball.*)

ROBBIE: Hey, Bradley, what you got there?

BRADLEY: Homework.

ROBBIE: (*Feigning friendliness.*) Oh yeah, let me see it.

> (*Bradley clutches it to his chest.*)

ROBBIE: Aw, c'mon Bradley. I just want to see it.

> (*Robbie smiles at Jeff and Brian then steps towards Bradley. Bradley holds the homework in his left hand. He raises his right fist. ready to defend it.*)

ROBBIE: Ooh, he wants to fight. (*Robbie backs off.*) Jeff.

> (*Jeff approaches Bradley, fists raised. Bradley puts his homework in his back pocket, then raises both fists ready to meet Jeff.*)

BRIAN: C'mon Jeff, teach him a lesson.

ROBBIE: Give him another black eye.

> (*Bradley and Jeff face each other, then Bradley lowers his hands as he gets an idea.*)

BRADLEY: Hello, Jeff.

> (*Robbie and Brian snicker.*)

JEFF: (*Looks down and answers in spite of himself.*) Hello.

> (*Robbie and Brian look at Jeff, surprised.*)

ROBBIE: C'mon, Jeff. Let him have it!

> (*Jeff moves closer to Bradley.*)

BRADLEY: It's a pleasure to see you today. (*Holds out his hand.*)

JEFF: You gave me a black eye.

BRADLEY: (*Still with his hand out.*) I have a black eye.

JEFF: But I still owe you one.

BRADLEY: Why?

JEFF: Because…(*Looks back at Robbie and Brian.*) Okay, see I was holding a bag of groceries, (*Looks at Colleen, then back at Bradley.*) with eggs and…I don't know. (*Shakes Bradley's hand.*) I guess we're even.

(*Bradley can't believe it.*)

ROBBIE: (*Disgusted.*) Sheesh! (*Robbie walks away, but remains on stage, his back to everyone.*)

(*For a long moment everyone else stands around unsure of each other, and themselves.*)

JEFF: So, Bradley. Do you like to play basketball?

BRADLEY: (*After he gets over the shock.*) I'm not very good.

BRIAN: So? (*Bounces ball to Bradley.*) None of us are.

(*Bradley fumbles the pass, then picks up the ball. He dribbles with both hands together, and even then the ball bounces away from him to Colleen. Meanwhile Robbie has turned around, and laughs at the way Bradley dribbles. Colleen, unsure, gives the ball back to Bradley.*)

BRADLEY: Thank you, Colleen.

(*Bradley dribbles with both hands to the basket, then stops.*)

JEFF: Shoot, Bradley.

BRIAN: Shoot it.

ROBBIE: Go ahead, Bradley. Shoot.

(*Everyone's quiet as Bradley puts all his concentration into it. He throws the basketball clear over the backstop.*)

END SCENE 6

Scene 7

The scene begins in the boys' bathroom then will move to the counselor's office. The boys' bathroom is the same set as the girls' except the stall has been removed revealing a urinal. Bradley and Jeff are in the boys' bathroom, wiping their faces with paper towels.

BRADLEY: I told you I wasn't very good.

JEFF: Aw, you weren't that bad. You just have to learn how to shoot. And dribble. And Pass.

BRADLEY: So, how did you get the black eye?

JEFF: (*Smiles.*) Melinda.

BRADLEY: She's pretty strong, huh?

JEFF: Whew, I think she's ready to fight Mike Tyson.

(*They both laugh.*)

JEFF: It's weird when you think about it. (*Somewhat confused as he tries to sort it out.*) I mean, the only reason they wanted to be friends with me, was because they thought I beat you up. And now they think we're even because you beat me up. But really, Melinda beat us both up.

BRADLEY: So we are even. We should thank Melinda.

JEFF: (*Laughs.*) So you really did your homework?

(*Bradley smiles. He takes his homework out of his pocket.*)

JEFF: Why didn't you turn it in this morning?

BRADLEY: I'm waiting to show it to Carla.

JEFF: But you're supposed to – (*Shrugs.*) well. I should talk to Carla again.

BRADLEY: You should. (*Starts to leave, then awkwardly.*) Well, I'll see you in Mrs. Ebbel's.

JEFF: See you later, Bradley.

BRADLEY: See you later, Jeff.

(*Bradley exits. Jeff combs his hair.*)

JEFF: (*To the mirror.*) Life's weird.

(*Colleen enters. She holds a notebook. Jeff looks at her. Colleen looks at Jeff.*)

COLLEEN: I just. Um. (*She runs out.*)

(*Jeff stares with his mouth open, as the bathroom revolves away, taking Jeff with it. The counselor's office revolves around. Carla is seated reading 'Raise High The Roofbeam, Carpenters' by J.D. Salinger. Colleen bursts in.*)

COLLEEN: I have to see you, Carla! It's an emergency! You won't believe what I just did!

(*Colleen sits at the table. Carla waits for her to catch her breath. Jeff enters and stands at what would be the door to the counselor's office.*)

JEFF: Carla.

(*Carla stands up and goes to Jeff, as Colleen holds her notebook in front of her face, so Jeff can't see her.*)

CARLA: Jeff?

JEFF: Hello, Carla. You said I could come talk to you, even if I just felt like getting out of class.

CARLA: Well, I'm with someone right now but – (*She steps back to Colleen, still behind her notebook.*) Do you mind if Jeff joins us?

(*The notebook moves back and forth as Colleen shakes her head.*)

CARLA: (*Back to Jeff.*) Come in.

(*Jeff sits next to Colleen who comes out from behind her notebook. Carla sits on her stool behind them.*)

COLLEEN: (*To Jeff.*) You better not tell anybody!

JEFF: Don't worry, I won't.

CARLA: Tell anybody what?

JEFF: Oh, she went into the boys' bathroom.

COLLEEN: Jeff! You just promised you wouldn't tell.

JEFF: Oops. It was just Carla.

COLLEEN: That's okay. (*To Carla.*) It was an accident. I didn't go in on purpose.

CARLA: Oh, I don't believe in accidents.

COLLEEN: (*Gapes at her.*) How'd you know?

CARLA: What?

COLLEEN: (*To Jeff.*) I went in on purpose. I saw you go in, so I went in after you. You've been acting so weird. I thought maybe it was because you went into the girls' bathroom. So I figured if I went into the boys' bathroom, we'd be even, and you wouldn't be so weird anymore. I mean, I thought you liked me. You always said hello to me, after I said hello to you.

JEFF: I always do that. I can't help it. Whenever anybody says hello to me, I always have to say hello back. (*He notices the picture of the monster on the wall.*) If a one-eye green monster said, "hello Jeff," I'd probably say "hello" back to it, too.
(*Colleen laughs.*)

CARLA: So, what's wrong with that? If a monster says hello to you, you should say hello back. Otherwise I have to wonder, which one of you is really the monster.
(*Colleen puts her hand to her mouth. She suddenly remembers something as she stares at the picture of the monster.*)

JEFF: You can say hello to me anytime. I don't mind.

COLLEEN: (*Smiles.*) Hello, Jeff.

JEFF: Hello, Colleen.

CARLA: I was just reading…(*She thumbs through her book.*) Here it is. (*Reads.*) "In certain Zen monasteries, it's a cardinal rule…that when one Monk calls out 'Hi' to another Monk, the latter must call back 'Hi' without thinking."

COLLEEN: Jeff should be a Zen monk!

JEFF: (*Laughs.*) I already say hello to anybody who says hello to me.

COLLEEN: Can girls be Zen monks too?

CARLA: Why not?

COLLEEN: (*Laughs with delight.*) Jeff, do you want to come to my birthday party?

JEFF: Yes. That's the second most important rule about being a Zen monk. Whenever another Zen monk invites you to a birthday party, you have to say yes.

COLLEEN: (*Laughs.*) You're the only boy so far. I'll invite one more, but only one. I can't invite too many boys.

(*Colleen looks at the picture of the monster. Colleen and Jeff exit the counselor's office, but remain on stage. The lights dim on the counselor's office. Mr. Verigold, Mrs. Verigold, and Mrs. Nathan enter and stand directly behind Jeff and Colleen. Two additional chairs are brought into the counselor's office. Colleen and Jeff exit. Mrs. Verigold, Mr. Verigold, and Mrs. Nathan stride into the counselor's office and all sit down at the round table with Carla.*)

MR. VERIGOLD: Kids have enough counseling. What they need is more discipline. If they're bad, they should be punished.

MRS. VERIGOLD: We need to get Back To Basics. Reading, writing, and arithmetic. And of course, computers. (*Nudges her husband.*)

MR. VERIGOLD: (*Hands chart to Mrs. Nathan.*) This chart shows that if the counselor was fired, it would save the school enough money to put a computer in every classroom.

MRS. NATHAN: No one is being fired. If you don't want your child to see the counselor, that's fine. We have a strict rule. Miss Davis doesn't see any child without the parents' permission.

MRS. VERIGOLD: But we didn't give our permission. Colleen came home with one of those forms for us to sign, and we refused to sign it. We try to give her all the counseling she needs at home.

MR. VERIGOLD: But then we find out the *counselor* has been talking to her anyway.

(*Mrs. Nathan turns to Carla.*)

CARLA: Colleen came into my office this afternoon very upset and said she had to talk to me. She said it was an emergency.

PRINCIPAL: What kind of emergency?

CARLA: It was personal.

PRINCIPAL: These are her parents.

CARLA: I'm sorry I never repeat anything a child tells me.

MRS. NATHAN: You're not supposed to see a child without the parents' permission. Now, if it's an emergency, then you might have been justified. But we have to know the nature of the emergency.

CARLA: I'm sorry.

MRS. VERIGOLD: If there was an emergency, don't you think I should know about it?

CARLA: Ask Colleen. If she wants to tell you, she will. I can't break my promise to her.

MR. VERIGOLD: Colleen's a child. You don't have to keep promises to children.

CARLA: I do.

MR. VERIGOLD: (*To Mrs. Nathan.*) See. See what I mean.

MRS. VERIGOLD: It wasn't any emergency. She's been trying to make our daughter change religions. Colleen came home from school and announced she didn't want to be Christian anymore. She wants to be a Zen monk!

(*Carla laughs, then quickly covers her mouth.*)

MRS. VERIGOLD: I thought you weren't allowed to teach religion in public school.

CARLA: I wasn't teaching religion. I read a passage from a book, *Raise High the Roof Beam, Carpenters* by J.D. Salinger.

MRS. NATHAN: Salinger! You read Salinger to an elementary school student. They just banned one of his books at the high school. (*Controls herself.*) Okay, why don't you explain for yourself, just what it is you try to do when you meet with a child.

CARLA: (*To Colleen's parents.*) Mainly, I talk to them. I listen to their problems, but I never tell them what to do. I try to help them learn how to think for themselves.

MRS. VERIGOLD: Colleen is in the fifth grade. How do you expect her –

MR. VERIGOLD: But what if she did something bad? Wouldn't you tell her that it's wrong?

CARLA: No. I think it's better if she can figure that out for herself.

MRS. VERIGOLD: She's in the fifth grade.

MR. VERIGOLD: Okay. What if there was a boy who bit his teacher?

CARLA: What?

MR. VERIGOLD: Wouldn't you tell him not to bite her?

CARLA: No, I'd talk to him about it and try to find out why he bit her, but –

MR. VERIGOLD: What if he keeps biting her? What if, every day, he sneaks up behind her and bites her on the backside. Then what would you do?

CARLA: This is getting ridiculous.

PRINCIPAL: Tell him what you'd do.

CARLA: (*Sighs.*) I'd try to help the boy understand the reason he wants to bite his teacher, and then help him reach the conclusion that he shouldn't do it. (*Throughout the rest of the scene, Carla looks at Colleen's parents as if they're bonkers.*)

MR. VERIGOLD: But what if he still keeps biting her. She could get seriously hurt.

MRS. VERIGOLD: She could die. How would you feel then? What if the boy had rabies?

MR. VERIGOLD: I bet you'd feel differently if he bit your behind.

MRS. VERIGOLD: What if he bit you?

MR. VERIGOLD: It's easy to sit back and be so *understanding*, so long as it's not your butt he's biting.

MRS. VERIGOLD: What if he bit you?

MR. VERIGOLD: You'd punish him then, wouldn't you. Then you wouldn't wait for him to think for himself.

MRS. VERIGOLD: Not if he bit you!

END SCENE 7

Note: The counselor's office can remain on stage, unlit, for the beginning of the next scene.

Scene 8

The scene will move from the outside, to the counselor's office, to the boys' bathroom. Bradley is practicing dribbling. He's getting a little better at it. Colleen enters. He doesn't notice her. She watches him a while then looks up at the sky, summoning her courage, then back to Bradley. She speaks very quickly, like someone removing a band aid. It hurts less if you do it quickly.

COLLEEN: Hello, Bradley. Would you like to come to my birthday party Saturday?

(*Bradley looks up. The basketball rolls away off stage.*)

COLLEEN: Jeff will be there. He's the only boy.

(*Bradley tries to speak, but can't.*)

COLLEEN: Everyone else will be girls.

BRADLEY: Yes!

COLLEEN: (*Makes a face.*) Good. (*Moves toward side of stage where Melinda and Lori enter to meet her.*)

BRADLEY: You're welcome. I mean thank you.

(*Bradley enters counselor's office, but area remains dark while the girls speak.*)

MELINDA: Is he coming?

COLLEEN: Yes.

(*Lori sticks out her tongue and screams.*)

MELINDA: Oh, it'll be fun. Bradley's not like he used to be. He's changed.

COLLEEN: Oh, you can't come anymore, Melinda.

MELINDA: (*Hurt.*) What? Why not?

COLLEEN: (*Looks at Melinda, surprised Melinda has to ask.*) Because, Bradley and Jeff are coming. And you beat them both up!

MELINDA: (*For a moment too flabbergasted to speak.*) They started it.

(*Colleen and Melinda stare at each other, each thinking the other is being unreasonable.*)

MELINDA: I thought I was your best friend.

COLLEEN: You are. But they're *Boys!* (*Sighs.*) Oh, okay. You can come. But you better not cause anymore trouble.

(*Colleen and Melinda exit.*)

LORI: (*Following Colleen and Melinda.*) I thought I was your best friend. (*She exits.*)

(*Lights come up on the counselor's office. Bradley and Carla are in the middle of a talk, seated around the round table.*)

BRADLEY: (*In anguish.*) I've never been to a birthday party!

CARLA: Never?

BRADLEY: A long time ago, in third grade, I went to one. But they made me go home because I sat on the cake.

CARLA: Well, you're not in third grade anymore.

BRADLEY: But I don't know what to do! Maybe I just shouldn't go.

(*He waits for Carla to say something, but she just looks at him.*)

BRADLEY: Do I have to bring my own chair?

CARLA: Why would you have to bring your own chair?

BRADLEY: For musical chairs! That's why I sat on the cake. I got mad because there was no other place to sit. And what about pin the tail on the donkey?

CARLA: You don't have to bring your own donkey.

BRADLEY: But what if I pin it in a bad place. They put a blindfold over you so you can't see what you're doing. What if I pin it on Colleen?

CARLA: You want to know what I think? I think you're a little overwhelmed by all that has happened to you. You think you are Cinderella.

BRADLEY: Cinderella?! (*Laughs.*)

CARLA: You're Cinderella and you've just been invited to the ball, and you're afraid that right in the middle of Colleen's birthday party, you'll suddenly turn into a pumpkin.

(*Bradley laughs.*)

BRADLEY: Do I have to bring a present?

CARLA: You don't *have* to do anything. But it's a nice thing to do, don't you think?

BRADLEY: What should I get her? Should I get her perfume? Is that what girls like?

CARLA: (*Shrugs in response to Bradley's last question.*) Give her something you like. If you like it, then she probably will too. Give her a gift from the heart.

BRADLEY: (*Pulls his homework out of his pocket.*) I did my homework!

CARLA: (*Smiles.*) I'm so proud of you!

BRADLEY: I was supposed to turn it in yesterday. I don't know why I didn't. I got scared.

CARLA: What were you afraid of?

BRADLEY: I don't know. I know I got all the answers right. I checked them over twice. And my Dad checked them too. I guess I could turn it in today, except I don't even know if it counts anymore.

CARLA: It counts with me. (*Beams at him.*) You're making friends. You're going to a girl's birthday party. You're doing your homework. I'm really proud of you, Bradley. Especially since –

BRADLEY: What? What's wrong?

CARLA: (*Calmly.*) Nothing's wrong. There's just something I need to tell you.

BRADLEY: (*Fearfully.*) What?

CARLA: I'm going to be leaving Red Hill School. But I know you can continue to do your work and make friends without me.

BRADLEY: You're leaving?

(*Carla nods.*)

CARLA: Yes.

BRADLEY: No, you can't go. It's not fair! (*Gets up, angry, but then controls his anger as he gets an idea.*) What if I don't do my homework? Then you'll have to stay and make me want to do it again!

(*Carla smiles at him.*)

BRADLEY: No, it's not fair! You tricked me!

(*Carla gets up and goes toward him, presumably to hug him. Bradley stops her as he slowly rips up his homework.*)

BRADLEY: I hate you!

(*Bradley runs out of her office and into the boys' bathroom. He throws his homework in the sink. Carla comes after him. She stops briefly outside the bathroom, then takes one step inside. He has his back to her but can see her in the mirror. He keeps his back to her for the remainder of the scene. Carla will slowly move towards him.*)

CARLA: Bradley? Are you going to be all right?

BRADLEY: (*Astonished she came into the boys' bathroom.*) Go away! I hate you!

CARLA: I know you don't mean that.

BRADLEY: You're not allowed in here.

CARLA: I think it's important we talk. That's how friends handle their problems, by talking about them. That's why we've become such good friends.

BRADLEY: I'm not your friend. Why would I want to be friends with you?

CARLA: I want to thank you, Bradley. You've made my short time here very special. I feel very lucky I got to know you.

BRADLEY: I'm not going to Colleen's birthday party. And I don't like Jeff, either, and I'm never going to do my homework, ever, and I'm going to fail all my tests.

CARLA: It wasn't me who magically changed your life. The magic is in you. You're not Cinderella and I'm not Prince Charming.
(*She touches his shoulder. He jerks away and she backs off.*)

BRADLEY: You're not allowed in here.

CARLA: I'd like to see you one more time before I go. Maybe we can make a party out of it.

BRADLEY: This is the boys' bathroom. You're going to get in trouble.

CARLA: Will you come and see me one more time? (*She exits.*)

BRADLEY: (*Quietly, after Carla's gone.*) I hate you.

END SCENE 8

Scene 9

    Bradley's bedroom. Bradley is sitting on the floor with a thermometer in his mouth. His parents enter. Mrs. Chalkers takes thermometer out of Bradley's mouth and reads it.

MRS. CHALKERS: Ninety-eight point six.

BRADLEY: I'm sick.

MRS. CHALKERS: You're not sick. You're normal.

BRADLEY: I'm not normal!

MR. CHALKERS: (*Trying to be funny.*) Well, I have to agree with Bradley there. He's not normal. (*Laughs at his own joke.*)

MRS. CHALKERS: (*Gives her husband a serious look.*) He's upset because of his counselor. (*To Bradley, warm but firm.*) You have to go to school. You've already missed one day.

BRADLEY: I hate school!

MRS. CHALKERS: I know how much you liked your counselor.

BRADLEY: I didn't like her. I hated her. I'm glad she's gone. She's so mean. All she does is talk, talk, talk. And she's got bad breath! It's because she eats dog food. (*Holds his nose.*) It stinks in her room.

MR. CHALKERS: Bradley, you can talk to us.

MRS. CHALKERS: I know it's not the same but anything you said to your counselor, you can say to your dad and me.

MR. CHALKERS: Where's that list of topics you made. We'll just start at the top and work our way right through it.

BRADLEY: Leave me alone! Just leave me alone.

(*His parents look at him, then exit. Bradley hugs Ronnie.*)

BRADLEY: Oh, Ronnie, what are we going to do?

END SCENE 9

Scene 10

The classroom. Mrs. Ebbel is at the front of the room everyone else is already in their seats when Bradley enters.

BRADLEY: (*Walking past Mrs. Ebbel.*) I was sick. Call my mother if you don't believe me.

(*Mrs. Ebbel glares at him, but doesn't say a word. Bradley takes his seat. He immediately starts to scribble on his desk with a pencil.*)

JEFF: Hi, Bradley. Where were you yesterday. Were you sick.

BRADLEY: Sick of you! (*Laughs at his own joke. He keeps scribbling.*)

MRS. EBBEL: This morning we will be having our math test. Now we've been studying the multiplication of fractions for –

(*Bradley gets up from his desk and goes to the pencil sharpener. He loudly sharpens his pencil.*)

MRS. EBBEL: You know, Bradley, yesterday we had a very quiet and productive day here. Probably the nicest day this class has had all year. I wonder why that was.

(*Bradley stares defiantly at her. He takes a half-step back toward his desk, then stops and sharpens his pencil again. He returns to his seat.*)

JEFF: I was thinking. How about we go to Colleen's birthday party together. I kind of feel funny going to a girl's house alone.

BRADLEY: (*Looking down at his desk as he scribbles on it.*) I'm not going to her stupid birthday party. I hate her!

JEFF: Oh.

MRS. EBBEL: Melinda, will you please pass out the math test. (*To the class.*) You have forty-five minutes.

(*She gives pile of tests to Melinda who proceeds to pass them out.*)

JEFF: (*While Melinda is still passing out the test.*) I saw Carla. I went to her office to say good-bye. She said she'd like to see you. She asked me to tell you that.

(*Bradley doesn't respond.*)

JEFF: Don't you even want to say good-bye to her? It's not her fault she was fired.

BRADLEY: (*Automatically.*) It was too! (*Then, after it registers.*) She was fired?

(*By now, he has his test, and starts scribbling across it as he speaks to himself.*) So? I still hate her. It wasn't my fault she was fired. I hate her. I hate her. I hate her.

(*He scribbles so hard he rips his test. The other kids in the class try to ignore him as they work on their tests, but keep glancing back at him. Bradley looks at the torn test, and reads the first question aloud, in a mocking voice.*)

BRADLEY: What is three-fourths of two-thirds? (*His eyes widen as he starts to get excited.*) What is three-fourths of two-thirds! (*He raises his hand, but doesn't wait to be called on before speaking.*) Mrs. Ebbel. Can I have a new test, please? Mine got torn.

(*Mrs. Ebbel hesitates, then gives him a new test. He is seen thinking, and carefully writing.*)

END SCENE 10

Scene 11

The counselor's office. There are boxes everywhere again. The only picture left on the wall is Bradley's monster. Carla is packing up. She looks at the picture on the wall, then starts to take it down, but doesn't finish. The picture hangs crooked, held up by only one tack in the corner. Bradley enters holding a wrapped present. Carla doesn't notice him.

BRADLEY: It's a pleasure to see you today.

CARLA: Bradley!

BRADLEY: Well I went to Colleen's birthday party. (*Sets present on table.*)

CARLA: How was it?

BRADLEY: The best one I ever been to.

(*They both laugh.*)

BRADLEY: Remember, you told me to give Colleen a gift from the heart. Well, you know what I gave her? A heart! A real heart. Well not a real one. It was a model of a heart. You can take it apart and put it back together and see what the insides look like. The way the blood goes.

CARLA: Sounds neat.

BRADLEY: It was my dad's idea. I didn't know what to get a girl. I told him what you said – a gift from the heart. You know what? He once gave my mom a model of a heart for Valentine's Day. That was before they married. I mean, I'm not going to marry Colleen or anything. I just thought it sounded like a neat gift.

CARLA: (*Gesturing toward the present.*) So, why –

BRADLEY: (*Quickly, with embarrassment.*) Oh, that's for you. Kind of a going away present.

CARLA: For me? Thank –

BRADLEY: Guess what?

CARLA: What?

BRADLEY: We had a math test. I got a hundred per cent. I'd show it to you, but I can't, know why?

CARLA: Why?

BRADLEY: Because it's hanging on the wall in Mrs. Ebbel's room.

(*Carla goes to Bradley as if to hug him, but he holds out his hand for her to shake. She gives him a firm handshake.*)

BRADLEY: Well. I have to go. (*Somewhat proudly.*) Mrs. Ebbel asked me to clean the erasers. (*He shrugs and awkwardly starts to leaves, then stops.*) Her name is Ronnie.

(*He exits. Carla stares out after him, then remembers the present. She slowly unwraps it, opens the box and pulls out Ronnie the Rabbit.*)

END OF PLAY

APPENDIX

OPTIONAL BIRTHDAY PARTY SCENE
May be inserted after Act Two, Scene 10.

>*No scenery is necessary. Colleen enters balancing an egg on a spoon. Melinda appears a moment later, also carrying a spoon with an egg. The girls, with Colleen in the lead, carefully walk from one end of the stage to the other, then back. It's a race. Other kids can be heard off stage rooting for Colleen or Melinda. Lori is rooting for Melinda. Jeff is rooting for Colleen, but other voices should be heard as well. Bradley's voice is not heard. The audience should be wondering if Bradley will be there or not. Lori and Jeff enter and wait off to the side.*

LORI: Faster Melinda. Don't let her beat you!

JEFF: That's the way, Colleen. Don't drop it.

>(*Colleen hands her spoon to Jeff. He gets about halfway across the stage when Melinda finishes her lap. However, she does not give her spoon to Lori. Bradley nervously enters wearing a party hat. He is the only one wearing a hat. Melinda gives him her egg and spoon. The spoon wobbles in his hand as he makes his away across stage weaving from side to side. Note: The egg can be attached to the spoon so it will not fall.*)

MELINDA: C'mon Bradley!

COLLEEN: Go Jeff!!

LORI: Faster Bradley. Don't drop it. Faster!

>(*The girls continue to shout, Bradley continues to wobble. Jeff makes it to the end of the stage, then turns and comes back. Bradley makes it to the end of the stage and turns to come back. Jeff is far in the lead when his egg falls off the spoon and splats on the floor of the stage. As Bradley continues, Melinda and Lori cheer for him, while Colleen is trying to distract him.*)

COLLEEN: Bradley, your shoe's untied!

LORI: Don't listen to her. C'mon Bradley!

>(*Bradley makes it all the way across. Lori and Melinda cheer.*)

LORI: (*Jumping up and down and clapping her hands.*) Yay!

MELINDA: Way to go Bradley!

COLLEEN: (*While Lori and Melinda are congratulating Bradley.*) Darn, we lost!
>(*To Jeff.*) Thanks to you.
>(*Jeff shrugs.*)

COLLEEN: Good job, Bradley.

JEFF: Nice, goin' Bradley.

BRADLEY: I thought I was going to drop it. I just don't know about birthday parties.

JEFF: You're doing fine.

BRADLEY: Really?

JEFF: Really.

BRADLEY: I've never carried an egg on a spoon before. Just on a fork. But not with the shell on!

LORI: We won! That's two points!

BRADLEY: Huh?

LORI: See, everybody on the winning team gets two points, and everybody on the losing team gets one point.

MELINDA: It would come out the same if they just gave one point to the winners and nothing to the losers, but this way the losers don't feel so bad.

BRADLEY: That's nice.

LORI: *I'm telling him!* After each race we trade teams, and then at the end of all the races, Colleen's mother counts up all the points and the girl with the most points gets first pick from the basket of prizes. Then the girl with the second most gets second pick.

MELINDA: And so on. Colleen's mother has a chart with everyone's name on it to keep track of the points.

LORI: I'm telling him! Colleen's mother has a chart.

COLLEEN: Okay. The next race will be a backwards race.

(*She and Jeff exit apparently to where the next race will be run.*)

BRADLEY: A backwards race! Are all birthday parties this much fun?

(*Lori and Melinda look oddly at each other, then at Bradley.*)

MELINDA: Haven't you ever been to a birthday party?

BRADLEY: No. Not for a long time, anyway. They kicked me out of the last one because I sat on the cake.

(*Lori cracks up.*)

BRADLEY: I saved the hat. (*Points to his hat.*)

(*The girls look at Bradley and laugh. They follow after Colleen and Jeff.*)

LORI: Well, if you have any questions just ask me.

MELINDA: Or me.

LORI: I've been to more birthday parties than Melinda.

MELINDA: You have not. (*To Bradley.*) She hasn't.

LORI: What about Holly's birthday party? You didn't go to that one.

(*Bradley exits.*)

MELINDA: That was because we were on vacation.

LORI: So, you still didn't go.

(*Lori and Melinda exit.*)

END OF OPTIONAL BIRTHDAY PARTY SCENE

Anne of Green Gables

by R. N. Sandberg

Adapted from L. M. Montgomery's Novel

ORIGINAL PRODUCTION

Anne of Green Gables was originally produced by Seattle Children's Theatre on February 22, 1991. It was directed by Rita Giomi with the following cast:

DIANA	Reiko Aylesworth
MRS. BARRY	Barbara Benedetti
ANNE SHIRLEY	Anne Christianson
STATIONMASTER, SCHOOLTEACHER, DOCTOR	Mark Drusch
GILBERT	Henry Lubatti, Jr.
MRS. LYNDE, MRS. BLEWETT	Cristine McMurdo-Wallis
MATTHEW CUTHBERT	Todd Jefferson Moore
MARILLA CUTHBERT	Jayne Taini

CHARACTERS

ANNE SHIRLEY, an orphan
MARILLA CUTHBERT, a spinster
MATTHEW CUTHBERT, her bachelor brother
DIANA BARRY, a young girl
GILBERT BLYTHE, a young boy
MRS. BARRY, Diana's mother
MRS. LYNDE/MRS. BLEWETT
STATIONMASTER/MR. PHILLIPS, the schoolteacher/doctor

SETTING

Primarily, Green Gables – a unit with dining room and Anne's room, all surrounded by trees and flowers.

Various other locations in Avonlea, a small town on Prince Edward Island, Canada, about 1900.

Anne of Green Gables

Act One

Scene 1

The dining room at Green Gables. Marilla is setting the table as Rachel Lynde bursts in.

RACHEL: Marilla, is Matthew ill? I saw him heading for town. He's not off to the doctor's is he?

MARILLA: He's gone to the train station, Rachel. We're getting a little boy from the orphan asylum in Nova Scotia.

RACHEL: You can't be in earnest.

MARILLA: Yes, of course I am. We've been thinkin about it for some time. You know how hard it is to get hired help.

RACHEL: Yes, but –

MARILLA: Mrs. Peter Blewett's bringing him on the 5:30 train. She was going to the orphanage to pick up a girl for her cousin, so we just told her to pick us up a boy.

RACHEL: Well, Marilla, I'll just tell you plain that I think you're doing a mighty foolish thing. You're bringing a strange child into your house and you don't know a single thing about him. Why, it was only last week I read in the paper how a man and his wife up west of the Island took a boy out of an orphan asylum and he set fire to the house – set it on purpose, Marilla – nearly burnt them to a crisp in their beds.

MARILLA: There's risks in pretty near everything a body does in this world.

RACHEL: But this.

MARILLA: Matthew was terrible set on it. You know he seldom sets his mind on anything, so when he does I always feel I ought to give in to it.

RACHEL: You and your brother don't know a thing about bringing up a child.

MARILLA: Neither do people who have their own when they start. Anyway, this boy's from Nova Scotia, right close to the Island. It isn't as if we're getting him from England or the States. He can't be much different from ourselves.

RACHEL: I heard of an orphan child over in New Brunswick who put strychnine in the well and the whole family died in fearful agonies. And in that instance it was a girl.

MARILLA: Well, we're not getting a girl. I wouldn't dream of taking a girl to bring up. We need someone to help work this farm.

RACHEL: Well, I hope it turns out all right. Only don't say I didn't warn you if Green Gables burns down or you both die of strychnine.

MARILLA: I appreciate your concern, Rachel.

(*The lights crossfade as the sound of a train whistle fades away in the distance.*)

Scene 2

Avonlea Station. A small figure, a child, sits on a battered suitcase. The child wears a too large overcoat and a cap covering its head. We can see only the child's back as the lights come up. The child wraps the coat more tightly around itself and turns towards us for the first time: she is a girl, a simple, tattered dress under her coat. The Stationmaster comes to pick up a mailbag and notices the girl.

STATIONMASTER: Now, look, my girl, we've got a Ladies Waiting Room, and that's where you ought to be. You've been out here long enough.

ANNE: I prefer to stay outside. There's more scope for imagination. (*Looking off.*) Like with that wild cherry tree. If no one comes for me, that's where I'll sleep tonight. All white with bloom in the moonshine. I'll imagine I'm dwelling in marble halls. (*Pointing off.*) Oh, look, look at it now – as the wind's blown it. What does it make you think of?

STATIONMASTER: A cherry tree blowing in the wind.

ANNE: My goodness, no!

STATIONMASTER: And all the fruit that'll fall off and be squashed. What a mess I'll have to clean up.

ANNE: It looks just like a bride! With a lovely misty veil. I've never seen one but I can imagine what she would look like. I don't ever expect to be a bride myself. I'm too homely. But I hope that someday I shall have a white dress. That is my highest ideal of earthly bliss.

(*An older man, very tentative and shy, enters. He stands diffidently off to the side looking around for something at first, then focuses in on Anne and hears her last few lines.*)

STATIONMASTER: (*Sees the man and goes to him.*) About time you got here, Matthew.

MATTHEW: Will the 5:30 train be long?

STATIONMASTER: Been in and gone half an hour. (*Indicating Anne.*) There she is. (*Confidently.*) She's a case. Got a tongue runs longer than a freight train to Ottawa.

MATTHEW: (*Puzzled.*) Is Mrs. Peter Blewett about?

STATIONMASTER: Couldn't wait. Had to get the other girl to her cousin's. Said you and your sister were adopting this one.

MATTHEW: (*More puzzled still.*) I was expecting a boy.

STATIONMASTER: Well, she's not a boy, Matthew, and I don't have any more orphans here.

ANNE: Excuse me, are you Mr. Matthew Cuthbert of Green Gables?

STATIONMASTER: (*To Anne.*) Looks like you won't be sleeping in the trees after all. (*To Matthew.*) Good luck, Matthew. (*Exits.*)

ANNE: I'm very glad to see you. I was beginning to be afraid you weren't coming for me and I was imagining all the things that might have happened to prevent you. It's so wonderful that I'm going to live with you. I've never belonged to anybody – not really. I feel pretty nearly perfectly happy. I can't feel exactly perfectly happy because – well, (*She sets down her bag and pulls off her hat.*) what color would you call this? (*She holds out one of her braids to him.*)

MATTHEW: It's red, ain't it?

ANNE: Yes, it's red. Now, you see why I can't be perfectly happy. I cannot imagine that red hair away. I do my best. I think to myself, "Now my hair is a glorious black, black as the raven's wing." But all the time, I know it's just plain red, and it breaks my heart. It will be my lifelong sorrow.

(*She picks up her bag. Matthew does not move.*)

ANNE: Shouldn't we be going?

MATTHEW: Well, now, you see, I'm confused about that.

ANNE: (*A moment of fear.*) Is it because I'm talking too much? People are always telling me I do. Would you rather I didn't talk? If you say so I'll stop. Could we go if I do? I can stop when I make up my mind to it, although it's difficult.

MATTHEW: Oh, I don't mind the talkin. You can talk as much as you like.

ANNE: Oh, I'm so glad. It's such a relief to talk when one wants and not be told that children should be seen and not heard. Shall we go?

(*Matthew doesn't answer. Her voice trembles.*)

ANNE: We are going to Green Gables, aren't we?

MATTHEW: Well, now, you see –

(*Anne clutches her bag. She is terrified.*)

MATTHEW: You're not like other girls, are you? Not like girls around here.

ANNE: I don't know. I guess I'm not. But I do have my good points. I'm sure you'll find them out once you get to know me.

MATTHEW: Well, now I expect that's so. All right. Come on.

ANNE: (*As they start to go.*) Have you ever imagined what it must feel like to be divinely beautiful?

MATTHEW: (*His voice trailing off in the distance.*) Well, now, no, I haven't.

(*The lights are cross fading back to the dining room.*)

Scene 3

 Green Gables. Marilla sits anxiously at the table. We hear Anne talking before she and Matthew enter.

ANNE: This Island is the bloomiest place! But those red roads are so funny. (*As they enter.*) What does make the roads so red?

MATTHEW: Well, now, I dunno.

ANNE: Well, that is one of the things to find out, sometime. Isn't it? (*Sees the house for the first time.*) Oh, I must be in a dream.

 (*Matthew goes into the dining room. Marilla looks at him and Anne. Anne takes off her cap.*)

ANNE: Hello.

MARILLA: (*To Matthew.*) Where's the boy?

MATTHEW: There wasn't any boy.

MARILLA: There must have been a boy. We sent word to bring a boy.

MATTHEW: There was only her.

MARILLA: Well, this is a pretty piece of business.

ANNE: You don't want me. You don't want me because I'm not a boy! I might have known it was all too beautiful to last. I might have known nobody really did want me. (*She bursts into tears.*)

MARILLA: Well, well, there's no need to cry about it.

ANNE: Yes, there is need. You would cry too, if you were an orphan and you came to a place you thought was going to be home and found that they didn't want you because you weren't a boy. Oh, this is the most tragical thing that ever happened to me.

MARILLA: (*An almost imperceptible smile tries to force itself onto her face.*) Well, don't cry anymore. We're not going to turn you out of doors tonight. We'll investigate this affair, tomorrow.

(*Anne's sniffles are subsiding.*)

MARILLA: What's your name?

(*Anne composes herself, becoming quite serious.*)

ANNE: Will you please call me Cordelia?

MARILLA: Is that your name?

ANNE: No-o-o, not exactly. But I would love to be called Cordelia. It's such an elegant name.

MARILLA: I don't know what on earth you mean. If Cordelia isn't your name, what is?

ANNE: Anne Shirley, but oh, please do call me Cordelia. It can't matter much to you what you call me if I'm only going to be here a little while, can it? And Anne is such an unromantic name.

MARILLA: Unromantic fiddlesticks! Ann is a good plain sensible name and that's what I'll call you.

ANNE: Well, then, could you please call me Anne spelled with an "e"?

MARILLA: What difference does it make how it's spelled?

ANNE: Oh, it makes such a difference. When you hear a name, can't you always see it in your mind? A-n-n looks dreadful, but A-n-n-e looks so much more distinguished. If you'll only call me Anne spelled with an "e," I shall try to reconcile myself to not being called Cordelia.

MARILLA: Very well, then, Anne with an "e," take off your coat and have some supper.

(*As Anne removes her coat and sets her bag aside, Marilla serves out the stew. Matthew hangs his coat up.*)

MATTHEW: Trip to the station's made me hungry.

(*Matthew and Marilla bow their heads for a moment in silent prayer. Anne doesn't quite know what to do. Matthew and Marilla begin to eat.*)

MARILLA: Did you ask Mrs. Peter Blewett why she'd brought a girl?

MATTHEW: Never saw her. She left (*He hesitates to get the pronunciation right.*) Anne with the stationmaster. He said she didn't bring no boys off the train. Didn't see how she could be left at the station, no matter what the mistake was.

MARILLA: Well, we'll straighten this out tomorrow. Mrs. Peter's going to the Barry's. I'll talk to her first thing. (*She looks at Anne who is sitting sadly at the table.*) You're not eating.

ANNE: I can't. I'm in the depths of despair. Can you eat when you're in the depths of despair?

MARILLA: I've never been in the depths of despair, so I can't say.

ANNE: Well, did you ever try to imagine you were in the depths of despair?

MARILLA: No, I didn't.

ANNE: Then I don't think you can understand what it's like. It's a very uncomfortable feeling. When you try to eat, a lump comes right up in your throat and you can't swallow anything, not even if it was a chocolate caramel. I had one chocolate caramel two years ago and it was simply delicious. I've often dreamed that I had a lot of chocolate caramels, but I always wake up just when I'm about to eat them. I hope you're not offended because I can't eat. Everything is extremely nice, but I can't.

(Marilla and Matthew look at each other.)

MATTHEW: I guess she's tired. Best put her to bed, Marilla.

MARILLA: I suppose. I made up the couch in the back room for the boy, but that won't do for her. *(As she lights a candle.)* We'll have to put you in the east gable, I guess. It's plain but it's clean. Bring your bag.

(Anne picks up her bag. Marilla starts out.)

MATTHEW: Anne.

(She turns back.)

MATTHEW: Sleep well.

ANNE: Thank you, Mr. Cuthbert.

(Anne and Marilla exit to Anne's room. It is very austere. Marilla holds a candle.)

MARILLA: I suppose you have a nightgown?

ANNE: Yes, the matron of the asylum made it for me. It's fearfully skimpy, but you can dream just as well in it as in a lovely trailing one with frills round the collar.

MARILLA: Well, undress as quick as you can and go to bed. I'll come back in a few minutes for the candle. I daren't trust you to put it out yourself. You'd likely set the place on fire. Good night. *(Turns to go.)*

ANNE: How can you call it a good night when you know it must be the very worst night I've ever had?

MARILLA: That's a good, old bed, nice and firm. And you've a room all to yourself. I expect this is a far better night than most you had back in that orphan asylum. Good night. *(She goes.)*

(Anne looks around the room. She shivers and tries to hold back her tears, but they burst forth as she throws herself on the bed. After a moment, she gathers

her strength and sits up with conviction. She blows the candle out and lies down.)

Scene 4

> *As the lights come up, a rooster crows. Bright sunlight. Anne dresses as Marilla puts breakfast on the table. Matthew enters from outside, dirty from having already begun work. He grabs a biscuit.*

MARILLA: Mrs. Peter Blewett'll be at the Barry's by nine. I'll talk to her direct, this time. The child'll have to be sent back.

MATTHEW: (*Reluctantly.*) Yes, I suppose so.

MARILLA: You *suppose* so! Don't you know it?

MATTHEW: Well, now, it's kind of a pity sending her back when she's so set on staying.

MARILLA: Matthew Cuthbert, you don't mean to say you think we ought to keep her?

MATTHEW: Well, now, no, I suppose not – not exactly. I suppose – we could hardly be expected to keep her.

MARILLA: I should say not. What good would she be to us?

MATTHEW: We might be some good to her.

MARILLA: I believe that child has bewitched you! It's plain as plain that you do want to keep her.

MATTHEW: Well, now, she's a real interesting little thing. You should have heard her talk coming from the station.

MARILLA: I don't want an orphan girl, and if I did, she isn't the style I'd pick. No, she's got to be sent back straight away.

ANNE: (*Bursts into the room.*) Good morning, Miss Cuthbert! Good morning, Mr. Cuthbert! Oh, isn't it wonderful? Don't you feel as if you loved the world on a morning like this? I'm not in the depths of despair, anymore. I've just been imagining that it was me you really wanted after all and that I was to stay here for ever and ever. It was a great comfort while it lasted.

MARILLA: Sit down and eat your breakfast.

> (*Matthew exits.*)

ANNE: I'm pretty hungry, this morning. The world doesn't seem such a howling wilderness as it did last night. I'm so glad it's sunshiny. But I like rainy mornings real well, too. All sorts of mornings are interesting, don't you think? But it's easier to be cheerful and bear up under affliction on a sunshiny day.

MARILLA: For pity sakes, hold your tongue! You talk entirely too much for a little girl.

(*Anne is stopped short. She begins to eat slowly in silence.*)

MARILLA: Can you wash dishes right?

ANNE: Pretty well. I'm better at looking after children. It's a pity you haven't any here for me to look after.

MARILLA: I don't want any more children than I've got at present. What's to be done with you I don't know. Matthew's a most ridiculous man.

ANNE: I think he's lovely. He's so very sympathetic. I felt he was a kindred spirit as soon as I ever saw him.

MARILLA: You're both strange enough if that's what you mean. When you wash the dishes, take plenty of hot water, and be sure you dry them well. After you finish the dishes, we'll go to the Barry's and settle what's to be done with you.

ANNE: (*Softly, to herself.*) I'm not going to think about going back. I'm going to enjoy my breakfast and these trees and – oh, look, there's one little early wild rose out! Isn't pink the most bewitching color in the entire world? I love it, but I can't wear it. Redheaded people can't wear pink, not even in imagination. Did you ever know of anybody whose hair was red when she was young, but got to be another color when she grew up?

MARILLA: No, I don't know as I ever did, and I shouldn't think it likely to happen in your case, either.

ANNE: Well, there's another hope gone. My life is a perfect graveyard of buried hopes. That's a sentence I read in a book once. I say it to comfort myself whenever I'm disappointed in anything. It's so nice and romantic, don't you think.

MARILLA: Since you're bent on talking, you might as well talk to some purpose. Tell me what you know about yourself. Where were you born and such?

ANNE: Bolingbroke, Nova Scotia. My father was Walter Shirley, and he was a teacher in the high school. My mother was Bertha Shirley. Aren't Walter and Bertha lovely names?

MARILLA: A person's name doesn't matter as long as she behaves herself.

ANNE: (*She talks matter of factly as she eats.*) My mother was a teacher, too, but Mrs. Thomas said they were a pair of babies and poor as church mice. They went to live in a teeny-weeny, little yellow house. I never really saw it, but I've imagined it thousands of times. Honeysuckle over the parlor window, lilacs in the –

MARILLA: I don't need your imaginings. Stick to the bald facts.

ANNE: Mrs. Thomas said I was the homeliest baby she ever saw, nothing but eyes. But my mother thought I was perfectly beautiful. I'm glad she was satisfied with me, because she didn't live long, you see. She died of fever when I was just three months old. My father died four days after. There was no family to take me in, and nobody wanted me. But finally, Mrs. Thomas took me, even though she had a drunken husband. I lived with them until I was eight. I helped look after their children – there were four of them younger than me. Then Mr. Thomas was killed falling under a train, and his mother offered to take Mrs. Thomas and the children but she didn't want me. Finally Mrs. Hammond took me since I was handy with children. She had two when I came, and afterwards twins three times in succession. When Mr. Hammond died, she broke up housekeeping, divided her children among her relatives and went to the States. I had to go to the asylum because nobody would take me. I was there four months. And then, Mrs. Blewett came. Those are the facts.

(*Silence for a moment.*)

MARILLA: (*With difficulty.*) Were those women good to you?

ANNE: O-o-oh, they meant to be – just as good and kind as possible. And when people mean to be good, you don't mind very much when they're not quite – always. They had a good deal to worry them, you know. It's very trying to have a drunken husband and to have twins three times in succession. But I feel sure they meant to be good to me.

(*Marilla looks away from Anne. Anne picks up her plate.*)

ANNE: I'll wash the dishes, now.

MARILLA: Why don't you go outside for a little, first. You can do the dishes after.

(*Anne looks at the door but doesn't go.*)

MARILLA: What's the matter?

ANNE: If I go out there – well – there's no use in my loving Green Gables if I can't stay. I'll do the dishes and we can go.

Scene 5

    The front porch of the Barry house. In a rocking chair sits an attractive young girl, Diana Barry, just Anne's age. She is rocking a baby wrapped in a blanket. Marilla and Anne with her bag enter. Neither are in good spirits.

DIANA: Why good morning, Miss Cuthbert? Won't you come on in? Mother's just taking some muffins out of the oven.

MARILLA: Thank you, Diana. Has Mrs. Peter Blewett come yet? Your mother said she'd be stopping by, this morning.

DIANA: Why yes. She's just arrived. Shall I get her for you?

MARILLA: Thank you. I'll go in.

(*Diana is looking at the downcast Anne.*)

MARILLA: This is Anne Shirley. This is Diana and her sister, Minnie May, Anne.

ANNE: (*Perking up.*) Diana. What a perfectly lovely name. Diana was a goddess, you know. I'm Anne with an "e" on the end. It's much more elegant.

MARILLA: Let's go in, Anne.

(*Mrs. Barry, followed by Mrs. Blewett comes out before they can.*)

MRS. BARRY: I thought I heard your voice, Marilla. How good of you to stop by.

MRS. BLEWETT: Well, I see you got the girl, all right. I couldn't waste time waiting for Matthew, last night.

MARILLA: The girl's why I've come, Mrs. Peter. You see there's been a mistake: we wanted a boy. We told your brother Robert to tell you we wanted a boy.

MRS. BLEWETT: You don't say. Well, Robert sent word by his daughter Nancy and she said you wanted a girl. She's a terrible, flighty thing, that Nancy. I can't count the times I've had to chastise her for heedlessness. It's not my fault, Miss Cuthbert.

MARILLA: We should have come to you ourselves on such an important matter, not trusted to a message. But anyhow, the mistake's been made and the only thing to do now is to set it right. Can we send the child back to the asylum? I suppose they'll take her, won't they?

MRS. BLEWETT: I suppose so – but you know, that may not be necessary. All the way back, yesterday, I was thinking, "now, why didn't I get one of those orphans to come work for me." You know how hard it is to keep good help. I swear the girls I hire don't know what it means to work. Think they've come to eat my food and let the children run wild.

MRS. BARRY: Your children have a lot of energy, Mrs. Peter.

MRS. BLEWETT: That's why I've got the serving girls there – to get that energy out of them!

MRS. BARRY: (*Rocking the baby.*) Ssshh.

MRS. BLEWETT: (*To Anne.*) Let me look at you, girl. What was your name again?

ANNE: Anne Shirley.

MRS. BLEWETT: That's right. There's not much to you without that coat wrapped around. (*To Marilla.*) They practically shoved her at me, said she'd be a good worker, though they seemed a little too eager to get rid of her to my mind. She is wiry, though. Wiry ones are the best.

ANNE: Do you have any twins, Mrs. Blewett?

MRS. BLEWETT: What business is that of yours? If I take you, you'll have to be a good girl – good and smart and respectful. I've four boys and a little girl and you'll earn your keep. There's no mistake about that. You've experience caring for children, haven't you?

ANNE: (*Softly.*) Yes.

MRS. BLEWETT: Well, then I suppose I might as well take her off your hands, Miss Cuthbert. That slaggard I have now is just about to run off. I saw it in her eyes, this morning. (*Referring to Anne.*) Having one like this'll save me the trouble of trying to find a new girl every month. If you like, I'll take her home, right now.

(*Marilla looks at Anne. Anne's eyes are downcast.*)

MRS. BARRY: (*To her baby.*) Sshh, Minnie May, it's all right. Sshhhh.

MARILLA: (*Slowly.*) Well, I don't know. I didn't say that Matthew and I had absolutely decided not to keep her. In fact, Matthew is disposed to have her stay. I oughtn't to decide without consulting him. If we decide not to keep her, we'll send her over to you, tomorrow night. Will that suit you, Mrs. Peter?

MRS. BLEWETT: I suppose it'll have to. (*She turns and abruptly goes back into the house.*)

MRS. BARRY: Come in and have some tea, Marilla. You, too, Anne – there's warm muffins.

MARILLA: Thank you, but I told Matthew I'd be home right away.

MRS. BARRY: (*With a laugh.*) I've rarely seen you so solicitous of Matthew, Marilla. Come on, Diana, we don't want to keep Mrs. Peter waiting. (*She exits.*)

DIANA: (*Staring at Anne.*) Well, perhaps, I'll see you again, sometime. (*Exits.*)

MARILLA: (*To Anne.*) Come on, now.

ANNE: Oh, Miss Cuthbert, would you really let me stay at Green Gables?

MARILLA: (*Crossly.*) It isn't decided yet. Perhaps we will conclude to let Mrs. Peter Blewett take you after all. She certainly needs you much more than I do.

ANNE: I'd rather go back to the asylum than live with her. She looks exactly like a – like a gimlet.

MARILLA: A little girl like you should be ashamed of talking so. You hold your tongue and behave as a good girl should.

ANNE: I'll try to do and be anything you want, if you'll only keep me.

MARILLA: You can practice keeping your thoughts to yourself, then, as we go back to Green Gables.

ANNE: (*As they exit.*) You shall see how strong I can be, Miss Cuthbert. I'll be the model of golden silence. I shall be as quiet as the leaves when the wind's stopped blowing after a storm.

(*They're gone but Anne's voice can still be heard.*)

ANNE: That's a lovely, cool quiet, isn't it? Even the insects seem to be waiting to make sure...

(*The lights have shifted.*)

Scene 6

Green Gables. The dining room. After dinner. Marilla, sewing, and Matthew, oiling his boots, sit at the table. Anne enters drying her hands with a towel.

ANNE: That's the last of the dishes, Miss Cuthbert, and I believe they are dried very well. It does make one feel satisfied to have completed a task down to every detail in just the way it was supposed to be done.

MARILLA: It's time for bed, now Anne.

ANNE: I'm still bursting with energy, Miss Cuthbert.

MARILLA: It's time for bed.

ANNE: Good night, Mr. Cuthbert.

MATTHEW: Good night, Anne.

ANNE: I look forward to seeing your smiling face in the morning. (*She exits.*)

MATTHEW: (*Stares at Marilla for a moment. She just keeps sewing.*) I wouldn't give a dog to that Blewett woman, let alone a child like that.

MARILLA: I don't fancy Mrs. Peter Blewett's style either, but it's that or keep the child ourselves. I know that's what you want, and I've been thinking over the idea. I dare say I'd make a terrible mess of bringing up a child, especially a girl.

MATTHEW: Well, now, I reckoned you'd come to see that we should keep her. She's such an interesting little thing.

MARILLA: I have not said we'll keep her and it would be more to the point to say she was a useful little thing.

MATTHEW: She's done fine by the dishes.

MARILLA: She'd have to be trained to everything. And there'd be no interfering from you. An old maid doesn't know much about bringing up a child, but I guess she knows more than an old bachelor.

MATTHEW: You can have your way, Marilla. Only be as good to her as you can without spoiling her. I kind of think she's the sort you can do anything with if you only get her to love you.

MARILLA: Who'd have ever thought you'd be talking like that. Little girls have been your mortal fear since you were five years old.

MATTHEW: Well, now, I don't know that it's since I was five. And this one's different.

MARILLA: We'll both be in for it if we do this.

MATTHEW: (*Smiling.*) We will.

MARILLA: I have not agreed to keep her.

MATTHEW: I know.

(*Marilla goes to Anne's room. Anne is in bed, imagining.*)

MARILLA: Have you said your prayers, Anne?

ANNE: I never say any prayers.

MARILLA: Don't you know it's terrible wicked not to say your prayers every night?

ANNE: Mrs. Thomas told me that God made my hair red on purpose and I haven't cared about Him since.

MARILLA: While you are under my roof, you must say your prayers.

ANNE: Why, of course, if you want me to. But you'll have to tell me what to say.

MARILLA: You must kneel down.

ANNE: Why must people kneel to pray? If I really wanted to pray, I'd go out into a great big field all alone and I'd look up into the sky – that lovely blue sky that looks as if there's no end to its blueness – and I'd just feel a prayer. Well, what am I to say?

MARILLA: Most children would start with, "Now I lay me down to sleep." (*She hesitates.*) But I think you're old enough to pray for yourself. Just thank God for your blessings and ask Him humbly for the things you want.

ANNE: I'll do my best. Gracious Heavenly Father, I thank thee for the trees with their lovely blossoms and the woods and the flowers and the Lake of the Shining Waters – that's what I've decided to call that beautiful pond by the Barry's. I'm extremely grateful for them. That's all the blessings I can think of just now. As for the things I want, they're so numerous that it would take a great deal of time to name them all, so I will only mention the two most important. Please let me stay at Green Gables; and please let me good looking when I grow up. I remain, yours respectfully, Anne Shirley. There, did I do all right? I could have made it much more flowery if I had a little more time to think it over. Oh, I should have said "Amen" instead of "Yours respectfully." Do you suppose it will make any difference?

MARILLA: I – I don't suppose it will. Go to sleep now like a good child. Good night. (*She starts to go.*)

ANNE: Miss Cuthbert? If you do allow me to stay, might I call you Aunt Marilla? I've never had an aunt or any relation and it would make me feel as if I really belonged to you.

MARILLA: I'm not your aunt.

ANNE: We could imagine you were.

MARILLA: When the Lord puts us in circumstances He doesn't mean for us to imagine them away.

ANNE: I don't know what I would have done all my life if I couldn't have imagined myself away from my circumstances.

MARILLA: (*Starting to go again.*) Go to sleep, now.

ANNE: Miss Cuthbert? Won't you please tell me if you are going to send me away or not?

MARILLA: If I tell you we're going to send you away you won't sleep for crying and being in the depths of despair. If I tell you we're going to keep you you won't sleep from excitement. A night of sleep's too important to be lost, especially for a child. I'll tell you in the morning.

ANNE: But, Miss Cuthbert, if you don't tell me, I shan't sleep one wink. I'll spend the entire night imagining the life that may lie before me. If I'm to be sent away, I'll sleep to gather strength to face Mrs. Blewett. If I'm to stay, I'll sleep to thank you for your generosity. So can't you please tell me?

MARILLA: Well – I suppose I might as well. You are next door to a perfect heathen, Anne. There are so many things you need to be taught. If you stayed, I should have my hands full. (*She pauses.*) I have had a pretty easy life of it so far, but I suppose we can't get through this world without our share of trouble. Matthew and I have decided to keep you. That is, if you will try to be a good girl.

(*Anne cannot respond.*)

MARILLA: Why, child, whatever is the matter?

ANNE: I'm crying. I can't think why. I'm glad as I can be. I'll try to be so good, Miss Cuthbert. I promise you. But it will be uphill work, I expect, for Mrs. Thomas told me I was desperately wicked.

MARILLA: You're not wicked, child. But I'm afraid you cry and laugh far too easily.

ANNE: I'll do my best, Miss Cuthbert. My very best.

MARILLA: And we will try to do right by you. Good night, now.

ANNE: Miss Cuthbert? Since I can't call you Aunt Marilla, what am I to call you?

MARILLA: You may call me just plain Marilla.

ANNE: Won't that sound awfully disrespectful?

MARILLA: If you're careful and speak respectfully it will sound just fine.

ANNE: Good night – Marilla.

MARILLA: Good night.

ANNE: Marilla. I can say good night tonight with a clear conscience.

MARILLA: (*Blows out the candle.*) Good night, Anne. (*Exits.*)

ANNE: (*With great joy.*) Good night.

Scene 7

The dining room. Rachel Lynde is sitting at the table. Marilla is pouring tea.

MRS. LYNDE: You've got your hands full, now. It's too bad there was such a mistake made. Couldn't you have sent her back?

MARILLA: I suppose we could, but we decided not to. Matthew took a fancy to her, and I must admit she's a real bright little thing.

MRS. LYNDE: It's a great responsibility you've taken on. There's no guessing how a child like that will turn out.

(*Anne comes running in from outside.*)

ANNE: (*Babbling rapidly even before she's through the door.*) Oh Marilla, Matthew! I've been invited to visit Diana Barry! Oh Marilla, Mrs. Barry said Diana wants me to come over on Saturday! Do you think I might wear your Amethyst brooch when I go, Marilla? I know it's precious but –

(*Anne stops short seeing Mrs. Lynde. Rachel is giving her the once over.*)

MARILLA: This is Mrs. Rachel Lynde, Anne.

MRS. LYNDE: Well, they didn't pick you for your looks, that's sure and certain. She's terrible skinny and homely, Marilla. Come here, child, and let me have a closer look at you.

(*Anne does not move.*)

MRS. LYNDE: Lawful heart, did anyone ever see such freckles? I said come here, child.

MARILLA: Anne?

MRS. LYNDE: And hair as red as carrots! What a sight! The children'll have a time taunting those looks, and I don't blame em. Red!

ANNE: I hate you! I hate you, I hate you, I hate you! How dare you call me skinny and ugly? How dare you say I'm freckled and red-headed? You're a rude, impolite, unfeeling woman!

MARILLA: Anne!

ANNE: (*To Rachel.*) How would you like to be told that you're bony and clumsy and haven't a spark of imagination?

MARILLA: Anne!

ANNE: I don't care if I hurt your feelings! And I'll never forgive you, never!

MARILLA: Anne! Go to your room, and stay there until I come up.

(*Anne exits.*)

MRS. LYNDE: Did anybody ever see such a temper! I don't envy your job bringing that up, Marilla.

MARILLA: You shouldn't have twitted her about her looks, Rachel.

MRS. LYNDE: Marilla Cuthbert, you don't mean to say you're upholding a display of temper like that?

MARILLA: No, I'm not trying to excuse her. But she's never been taught what's right. And you were hard on her.

MRS. LYNDE: Well, I see I'll have to be very careful what I say after this. Since the fine feelings of orphans, brought from goodness knows where, have to be considered before anything else.

MARILLA: Rachel –

(*Matthew looks in as Rachel gathers up her things to leave.*)

MRS. LYNDE: Oh, no, I'm not vexed – don't worry yourself. I'm too sorry for you to leave any anger in my mind. You'll have your own troubles with that child. But if you take my advice – and I've raised ten children and buried two – you'll use a fair sized birch switch on that one. Good morning, Marilla, Matthew. I hope you'll come down to see me often as usual, but don't expect me to visit here again in a hurry. (*She exits.*)

(*Matthew looks at Marilla as the lights cross fade to Anne's room. Anne is facedown on the bed. Marilla enters.*)

MARILLA: Anne. (*No response.*) Anne. Get off the bed with those boots, and listen to what I have to say.

(*Anne gets up.*)

MARILLA: Aren't you ashamed of yourself?

ANNE: She hadn't any right to call me ugly and redheaded.

MARILLA: You hadn't any right to fly into a fury and talk to her that way. I was ashamed of you, Anne. I wanted you to behave nicely and you disgraced me. I don't know why you should have lost your temper because she said you were redheaded and homely. You've said it often enough yourself.

ANNE: There's a difference between saying a thing yourself and hearing other people say it. You may think it's so but you hope other people think otherwise. Oh, Marilla, I couldn't help it. When she said those things, something just rose up inside and choked me. I had to fly out at her.

MARILLA: Well, you've made a fine exhibition of yourself. It's a dreadful thing to lose your temper like that.

ANNE: Just imagine how you would feel if somebody told you you were skinny and ugly.

MARILLA: I understand how you feel, Anne. I understand it very well. And I don't say that I think Mrs. Lynde was exactly right in saying what she did to you. But she was a stranger, your elder and a visitor – all reasons why you should have been respectful to her; and you were rude and saucy. You must go to her and tell her you are very sorry for your bad temper and ask her to forgive you.

ANNE: I can never do that. You can punish me in any way you like, Marilla. You can shut me up in a dark, damp dungeon inhabited by snakes and toads and feed me only on bread and water and I shall not complain. But I cannot ask Mrs. Lynde to forgive me.

MARILLA: We're not in the habit of shutting people up in dark, damp dungeons, especially as they're rather scarce in Avonlea. But apologize to Mrs. Lynde you must. You said you would try to be good if we kept you at Green Gables, but it certainly doesn't seem like it, now. (*She exits into the dining room.*)

(*Matthew who has been listening in the dining room is stifling a laugh. He puts on a serious face as Marilla goes by him and out of the room. He makes sure she's gone and then tentatively enters Anne's room.*)

MATTHEW: (*Whispering.*) Anne? How are you?

ANNE: All right.

MATTHEW: Well now, Anne, don't you think you'd better do it and have it over with? It'll have to be done sooner or later, you know, for Marilla's a dreadful, determined woman – dreadful, determined. Do it right off, I say, and have it over with.

ANNE: You mean apologize to Mrs. Lynde?

MATTHEW: Yes – apologize – that's the very word. Just smooth it over so to speak.

ANNE: I don't know how I can. It would be true enough to say I am sorry, because I am sorry, now and quite ashamed. But it would be so humiliating. I couldn't think of going to Mrs. Lynde unless – (*She hesitates.*)

MATTHEW: Yes?

ANNE: Well – if you really wanted me to – I suppose I could do it to oblige you. I'd do anything for you.

MATTHEW: Well, now, of course, I really want you to. Just go and smooth it over.

ANNE: Should I?

MATTHEW: Yes.

ANNE: Yes, all right.

MATTHEW: But don't tell Marilla I said anything. She might think I was putting my oar in and I promised not to.

ANNE: I understand. Wild horses won't drag the secret from me. (*She stops.*) How would wild horses drag a secret from a person, anyhow?

MATTHEW: Well, now, I dunno.

(*They share a laugh.*)

ANNE: Thank you, Matthew.

Scene 8

Outside Mrs. Lynde's house. Marilla and Anne enter. Marilla wears a black shawl and an amethyst brooch. Anne seems particularly cheerful, perhaps humming and skipping.

MARILLA: Well, here we are. (*She looks at Anne who is smiling broadly, lost in her thoughts.*) What are you thinking?

ANNE: I'm imagining out what I must say to Mrs. Lynde.

MARILLA: Well, I must say you look awfully happy about it.

ANNE: Marilla, your amethyst looks so beautiful in the sun. Might I wear it when I visit Diana?

MARILLA: No, Anne.

(*Mrs. Lynde enters carrying gardening items. Anne throws herself down on her knees before Mrs. Lynde, holding out her hands beseechingly.*)

ANNE: Oh, Mrs. Lynde, I am so extremely sorry. I could never express all my sorrow, no, not if I used up a whole dictionary. I behaved terribly to you – and I've disgraced my dear friends, Matthew and Marilla, who are letting me stay at Green Gables although I'm not a boy. I'm a dreadfully wicked and ungrateful girl, and I should not have flown into a temper because you told the truth about me. What I said about you was true, too, but I should not have said it. Oh, Mrs. Lynde, please, please, forgive me. If you refuse, it will be a lifelong sorrow for me. You wouldn't like to inflict a lifelong sorrow on a poor little orphan girl, would you, even if she had a dreadful temper? Oh, I am sure you wouldn't. Please, say you forgive me, Mrs. Lynde.

MRS. LYNDE: There, there, get up child. Of course, I forgive you. I guess I was a little too hard on you, but I'm an outspoken person. It can't be denied your hair is a terrible red, but I knew a girl once whose hair was every mite as red as yours when she was young, but when she grew up it darkened to a real handsome auburn. I wouldn't be surprised if yours did too.

ANNE: Oh, Mrs. Lynde! You have given me hope. I shall always feel that you are a benefactress. Oh, I could endure anything if I only thought my hair would be a handsome auburn when I grew up. Thank you, Mrs. Lynde. May I go into the garden while you and Marilla talk. There's much more scope for imagination there.

MRS. LYNDE: Laws, yes, child, and pick a bouquet of them white lilies if you like.

ANNE: Oh, I can weave them into a crown for Diana Barry. I'm going to visit her, you know. They'll look lovely in her hair. (*Anne exits.*)

MRS. LYNDE: She's a real odd little thing, Marilla. But there's something kind of taking about her. I'm not surprised you and Matthew decided to keep her.

MARILLA: (*Stares off after Anne.*) I hope we haven't made a mistake. I'm not sure the child is honest.

Scene 9

The dining room. Matthew is eating his lunch. Anne enters.

ANNE: I don't suppose you know much about hair, do you? About making it look like something other than a volcano erupting.

MATTHEW: Well, now, I've always liked the way your hair looks.

ANNE: You are the spirit of kindness, Matthew, but you have no understanding of the pain one experiences upon feeling the world's scorn for red hair.

(*Marilla enters. Anne does not see her.*)

ANNE: I am to venture out to meet the beautiful Diana Barry but how can I go with hair that looks like old, dried up red licorice.

MARILLA: You're just going for a visit, Anne. You needn't make such a fuss over it.

ANNE: She's *invited* me, Marilla. No one's ever invited me to their house before. Perhaps, she longs for a bosom friend like I do. I've imagined a friend who'd care for me more than anyone else in the world. And I always imagined she'd have black hair. Like Diana. That's why I'm so frightened to go looking like I do. She's probably invited me out of pity. Or to find out what an orphan's like.

MARILLA: Don't let your mind run away with you. (*Handing Anne a little bundle.*) Here's some shortbread for the two of you. You have a good time. Oh, before you leave, have you seen anything of my amethyst brooch? I thought I stuck it in my pincushion, yesterday, but I can't find it anywhere.

ANNE: I – I saw it this morning when I walked past your door. I even went in to look at it.

MARILLA: Did you touch it?

ANNE: Y-e-s. I pinned it on my breast just to see how it would look. To see if it would make me somehow more attractive. I was still hoping I might wear it, this afternoon.

MARILLA: You had no business to do anything of the sort. You shouldn't have gone into the room and you shouldn't have touched the brooch. Where did you put it?

ANNE: On the bureau. I hadn't it on a minute. Truly.

MARILLA: It isn't anywhere on the bureau.

ANNE: I'm perfectly certain I put it back. I just don't remember if I put it in the pincushion or on the china tray.

MARILLA: The brooch is gone, Anne. By your own admission, you were the last person to handle it. Now, what have you done with it? Tell me the truth.

ANNE: I never took it out of your room, Marilla, and that is the truth.

MARILLA: You are telling me a falsehood, Anne.

ANNE: I'm not.

MARILLA: You are. Just like that made up apology to Rachel Lynde. Saying whatever you think you need to say to get what you want. Don't you say anything more unless you are prepared to tell the whole truth.

ANNE: But I have told you the truth.

MARILLA: Go to your room and stay there until you are ready to confess.

ANNE: But what about Diana? I'll stay in my room as long as you like afterwards. But I must meet Diana.

MARILLA: You'll not go to the Barry's or anywhere else until you've confessed.

ANNE: But, Marilla!

MARILLA: Nowhere – I will not have a liar in my house!

(*Anne throws the shortbread on table and exits.*)

MATTHEW: You're sure it hasn't fallen down behind the bureau?

MARILLA: I've moved the bureau and taken out the drawers and looked in every crack and cranny.

MATTHEW: Well, I don't suppose she meant to steal it. Probably just to play with, to help along that imagination of hers. I suppose she's lost it and is afraid to own up for fear she'll be punished.

MARILLA: She's dishonest, Matthew. How can we trust her if she's dishonest? And if we can't trust her, how can we care for her? How can we...(*She tries to hold back her feelings.*) I've got to go to the Barry's and explain. Please get me my black shawl. It's in the trunk by my bureau.

(*Matthew exits. Marilla picks up the shortbread and tries to collect herself. Anne enters.*)

ANNE: I'm ready to confess, Marilla.

MARILLA: Well get on with it.

ANNE: I took the amethyst brooch, just as you said. I didn't mean to take it when I went in, but it looked so beautiful when I pinned it on that I was overcome by temptation. I imagined how perfectly thrilling it would be to play Lady Cordelia Fitzgerald with it on – walking through my enchanted forest. And I took it. I thought I could walk through the woods and put it back before you came home. When I was going over the bridge across the Lake of the Shining Waters, I took the brooch off to have another look at it.

(*Matthew re-enters with the shawl.*)

ANNE: And as I was leaning over the bridge, it just slipped through my fingers – and went down – down – down all purply-sparkling, and sank forever more beneath the Shining Waters.

MARILLA: This is terrible. Terrible. My mother gave me that brooch. You are the very wickedest girl I ever heard of.

ANNE: Yes, I suppose I am. And I know I'll have to be punished. Would you please get it over right off because I'd like to meet Diana with nothing on my mind.

MARILLA: Diana, indeed! There'll be no Diana, today, Anne Shirley. That shall be your punishment. And it isn't half severe enough!

ANNE: But you promised I could go, Marilla! I must go. I might never have a chance again.

MARILLA: You're not going anywhere, and that's final.

(*Anne goes off to the front yard, crying.*)

MARILLA: I'm afraid Rachel Lynde was right from the first. The child is utterly bad.

MATTHEW: Well, she's never had any bringing up.

MARILLA: She's getting it now. (*Marilla grabs the shawl from Matthew. As she does, something pricks her hand.*)

MARILLA: Ow! (*She removes a pin that is tangled in the shawl.*) Dear life and heart, here's the brooch safe and sound. Whatever did she mean by saying she lost it? Oh, I remember now. I laid this shawl on the bureau for a minute before I put it away. I suppose the brooch got caught in it somehow.

(*Matthew coughs. She looks at him. He is looking straight at her. They both look toward Anne. He hands Marilla the shortbread; she gives him the shawl. She goes to Anne.*)

MARILLA: Anne Shirley, I've just found my brooch hanging to my black shawl. Now I want to know what this rigamarole you told me meant.

ANNE: You said you'd keep me here. I confessed so I could visit Diana. I made it as interesting as I could but...

MARILLA: Anne, you do beat all! But I was wrong – I see that now. Of course, it wasn't right for you to confess to a thing you hadn't done, but I drove you to it. It's a hard thing to say one's sorry but if you'll forgive me, Anne, I'll forgive you and we'll start square again.

ANNE: Oh, Marilla! Five minutes ago I was so miserable I was wishing I'd never been born and now I wouldn't change places with an angel!

(*Anne rushes to embrace Marilla, but Marilla stops her by holding out the bundle of shortbread.*)

MARILLA: Don't forget this. It'll be a treat for the two of you.

ANNE: Thank you. (*A pause.*) Marilla, I wasn't lying when I apologized to Mrs. Lynde. It's just that I'm not a very impressive person. So if I want something to have sufficient impact, I have to make it as dramatic as I can.

MARILLA: Just say what you feel and the impact'll take care of itself.

ANNE: Is that what you do?

MARILLA: It's the way people should be.

(*Anne and Marilla look at each other. There's something they want to say.*)

MARILLA: Go on, now. Diana's waiting.

(*The lights start to fade. There's still something unresolved between them. Just before the blackout –*)

ANNE: (*Runs off.*) To the Lake of the Shining Waters.

END OF ACT ONE

ACT TWO
Scene 1

The woods.

ANNE: Oh, just smell the pine, here. Can't you imagine fairies dancing on the smell as if it were a magic carpet?

DIANA: Not really.

ANNE: I don't know how people live without flowers and trees. I expect people in desolate climates must be extremely depressed all the time. They've nothing lovely to look at or smell.

DIANA: Perhaps, they don't notice. They've never seen them, so they don't miss them.

ANNE: I've imagined all kinds of lovely places even though I've never seen them.

DIANA: Really? I never imagine anything. (*An awkward pause.*) I think we should be getting back.

ANNE: Would you like a shortbread?

DIANA: It's starting to get dark.

ANNE: Just one, then we'll go. They're very good. Marilla uses extra butter.

DIANA: All right.

ANNE: Marilla's an excellent cook. I even like her vegetables.

DIANA: These are delicious. Like something the Queen might eat. Can I have another?

ANNE: (*Handing her one.*) Do you really never imagine things?

DIANA: I haven't the knack for it.

ANNE: But you said these were the kind of thing the Queen might eat.

DIANA: That's not real imagining.

ANNE: You mean like fantastic wizards and terrible monsters?

DIANA: Yes.

ANNE: Don't you ever imagine that things are different in your life? Your mother, for instance?

DIANA: I suppose. But that really doesn't take much imagination.
(*They look at each other and laugh.*)

ANNE: It can be fun, sometimes, to imagine from real life. Like these woods. Imagine what happens here at the very dead of night.

DIANA: We should go before the light's completely gone.

ANNE: I expect it's pitch black, then. The kind of place that ghosts might choose for their revelry. The way those branches hang down. They seem to be moving even though there's not a breath of wind.

DIANA: Let's go, shall we?

ANNE: Don't you think a haunted wood is very romantic?

DIANA: This wood isn't haunted.

ANNE: You do believe in ghosts, don't you?

DIANA: Charlie Sloane says that his grandmother saw his grandfather driving home the cows one night after he'd been buried a year.

ANNE: So there could be ghosts here. Look at the way that tree's swaying. It's as if a lady's walking slowly along the bank, nodding her head, wringing her hands, uttering wailing cries. Listen. Do you hear it?

DIANA: Yes.

ANNE: Soft, wailing cries. There's a death in her family. A little murdered child.

DIANA: Oh!

ANNE: There's a light gleaming between the boughs! It's a skeleton.

DIANA: A headless horseman!

ANNE: Do you feel it?

DIANA: What?

ANNE: Something cold on your neck.

DIANA: Yes.

ANNE: Like icy fingers creeping slowly around, slowly around.

DIANA: They're going to squeeze!

(*They scream. They run off and collapse on the ground. They look at each other and burst out laughing together.*)

DIANA: That was wonderful.

ANNE: You can imagine, you see.

DIANA: I'm glad you've come to Green Gables.

ANNE: Do you think, Diana – do you think you can like me a little – enough, perhaps, to be my bosom friend?

DIANA: Why, I guess so. It will be jolly to have a friend. There isn't any other girl who lives very near, and my sister's such a little bitty thing.

ANNE: Will you swear to be my friend for ever and ever?

DIANA: I don't mind.

ANNE: We must join hands – so. I'll recite the oath first. I solemnly swear to be faithful to my bosom friend, Diana Barry, as long as the sun and the moon shall endure. Now you say it and put my name in.

DIANA: I solemnly swear to be faithful to my bosom friend, Anne (with an "e") Shirley, as long as the sun and the moon shall endure.

(*Anne turns away.*)

DIANA: Anne?

ANNE: (*Wiping away a tear.*) It's nothing.

DIANA: (*Hesitates, then.*) It's a raindrop.

ANNE: Yes. A salty raindrop.

DIANA: An ocean raindrop.

ANNE: A flood of them.

DIANA: An ocean of rain.

ANNE: A ferocious storm about to overwhelm us.

DIANA: We'd better run.

ANNE: Yes, run. Run for the palace.

DIANA: Run for home.

(*They run off, laughing.*)

Scene 2

The schoolyard. Mr. Phillips, the teacher, rings a hand school bell and looks at his watch. He is not in a good mood. Anne and Diana enter, chattering away.

DIANA: And the cutest by far of all the boys is Gilbert Blythe. He's always playing tricks and teasing the girls.

ANNE: I'm glad he won't be at school.

DIANA: Not til his uncle's better, anyway.

MR. PHILLIPS: (*Accusingly.*) Miss Barry.

(*Anne and Diana are stopped in their tracks.*)

DIANA: Oh, good morning, Mr. Phillips.

MR. PHILLIPS: It would be a much better morning if you had been punctual, Diana Barry. The first day of school is hardly a day for tardiness.

DIANA: I'm sorry, Mr. Phillips.

MR. PHILLIPS: You have been a model student, Diana. I assume this morning's behavior is attributable to (*He throws a quick glance towards Anne.*) circumstances beyond your control, and I shan't hold it against you. You will find a textbook on your desk and the assignment on the board. I suggest you begin working immediately.

DIANA: Yes, Mr. Phillips. Come on, Anne.

MR. PHILLIPS: I would like to speak to this young lady alone for a moment.

DIANA: This is Anne Shirley, Mr. Phillips. She's –

MR. PHILLIPS: I am well aware of who she is. You may go in, Diana.

DIANA: Yes, Mr. Phillips.

(*She and Anne exchange a look and Diana exits.*)

MR. PHILLIPS: I am an understanding and compassionate man, Miss Shirley. But the world is neither understanding nor compassionate. It asks only, can you do the job? This morning, you have failed to do it, my girl. Your lateness has started you off with a black mark. I want no repetition of this. Our scholars are not to be led into your errant ways.

ANNE: Diana and I came as fast as we could, Mr. Phillips. We were both just so –

MR. PHILLIPS: Excuses undo nothing. I understand you have been taught no discipline, that you have led a fragmented life and have not had to bind yourself to the grindstone.

ANNE: I know what it is to work hard, Mr. Phillips.

MR. PHILLIPS: You shall know what it is, my girl. And if you thrive on it, we shall get along famously. I do not expect you to be a scholar, Miss Shirley. All I expect of a girl of your background is that you behave well.

ANNE: But you see Mr. Phillips, that's just it. I'll read and write all you want but as for behavior, well, I'll try but –

MR. PHILLIPS: You shall do better than merely trying, Miss Shirley, or both of us shall wish for your return to that pathetic institution from whence you've come.

(*He points the way to school and they walk off to class.*)

Scene 3

Green Gables. Outside. Matthew has been waiting for Anne.

MATTHEW: Well, now.

ANNE: Hello, Matthew.

MATTHEW: Well, how was it?

ANNE: It started off quite badly.

MATTHEW: Yes, but how did it end up?

ANNE: Mr. Phillips, who imagines himself a kind of Roman Emperor of education, gave me these unbearably simple lessons to do all day long, as if I were a mere child. Finally I had to say to him, "Mr. Phillips, I really would prefer to be challenged." He didn't say anything, but after that he began giving me the same lessons as Diana.

MATTHEW: And on your first day, too.

ANNE: He wasn't impressed. All he said when I left was, "Make certain you're on time, tomorrow, Miss Shirley."

MATTHEW: But you'd done real well.

ANNE: Dazzlingly. Of course, it was only reading and history. We haven't gotten to mathematics, yet.

MATTHEW: You'll dazzle them in mathematics, too.

ANNE: Thank you, Matthew.

MATTHEW: The teacher already knows who you are.

ANNE: How could he miss me, being late and looking like I do.

MATTHEW: They never learned my name til almost the end of the term. Maybe that's why I stopped going.

ANNE: Well, nothing he does is going to make me stop going. I'll show him that I'm a match for any of his regular scholars. Diana, Charlie Sloane, or his oh so highly esteemed Gilbert Blythe. And when the end of the term concert comes, I shall be up on the podium reciting. That's what the top scholars get to do, to make a speech or recite a poem. I shall wear a flowing white gown, with blossoms in my hair and the light shining off my face. And no one, no one will think of me as…(*She stops.*)

MATTHEW: What, Anne?

ANNE: They'll be glad I'm here.

Scene 4

The schoolyard. There is laughter and commotion, offstage (in the classroom). A boy, Gilbert Blythe, leaps over the wall of the schoolyard, and holds in his laughter until he is clear of being heard, then it bursts forth from him. Diana comes after him. She is laughing, too.

DIANA: Gilbert, what did you do to Ruby?

GIL: (*Holding up a large pin.*) Pinned her hair around the back of her chair.

DIANA: You didn't?

GIL: Did you hear her scream? I'll bet she thought her hair was being yanked out by the roots.

DIANA: You shouldn't do such things, Gilbert Blythe.

GIL: I wouldn't to someone like you, Diana.

DIANA: Oh, yes.

GIL: But to a prissy thing like Ruby Gillis? Her hair's as yellow as straw. She reminds me of a scarecrow – except she cries all the time.
(*Mr. Phillips enters.*)

MR. PHILLIPS: (*Sternly.*) Mr. Blythe.
(*Gil and Diana are startled.*)

MR. PHILLIPS: I would like to speak with you if you please.

GIL: Yes, sir. (*He starts to go back in.*)

MR. PHILLIPS: No, not in there. Let the silly creatures vent their immature energy.

(*Diana moves off a bit as Mr. Phillips leads Gilbert away.*)

MR. PHILLIPS: It's very good to have you back, my boy. As I expected, missing the first month of school hasn't hurt you one bit. Is your uncle in New Brunswick all right, now?

GIL: Yes sir, thank you.

MR. PHILLIPS: It's really as if you haven't been gone. You'll move right to the head of the class.

GIL: I've still plenty of work to do, Mr. Phillips. The new girl seems quite intelligent.

MR. PHILLIPS: Yes, you're finally going to have a run for the top scholar prize.

GIL: I welcome the competition, sir.

(*Mr. Phillips and Gil move off as Anne comes on. She carries her slate and is writing furiously on it.*)

DIANA: Oh Anne! I thought I was going to burst. Did you see the look on Ruby's face when she screamed? Gil Blythe's the only one who could think up something like that and get away with it. Mr. Phillips had no idea.

(*Anne nods her head and keeps on writing.*)

DIANA: Anne!

ANNE: Just a minute.

DIANA: He's aw'fly handsome, isn't he?

ANNE: Who?

DIANA: Gilbert Blythe, of course.

ANNE: Yes, he's handsome, but he's far too bold. It isn't good manners to wink at a strange girl.

DIANA: He winked at you?

ANNE: Just after he'd pulled the pin out of Ruby's hair. He knew I saw him and he was showing off. But I just turned away.

DIANA: That must have been a shock for him, a girl turning away.

ANNE: It's his name, that's written up on the porch wall with Julia Bell's, isn't it?

DIANA: (*Playfully.*) With the big "Take notice" heart over it.

(*She and Anne giggle as Gilbert returns.*)

GIL: Who's your new friend, Diana.

DIANA: This is Anne Shirley, Gil. Anne spelled the elegant way – with an "e."

GIL: Well, how do you do, Miss Elegant Anne Shirley.

(*She ignores him.*)

GIL: Why she's taking no notice of me!

DIANA: (*Giggling.*) She "took notice" of the writing on the porch.

(*Anne shoots Diana a look but focuses right back on her slate.*)

GIL: Ah, the lovely Julia Bell. Yes, she and I are inextricably bound together. I learned my multiplication tables by counting the freckles on her face.

ANNE: That's very cruel. And so was what you did to Ruby Gillis.

GIL: Yes, I can see why you wouldn't appreciate jokes about hair and freckle.

(*Anne throws herself back into her work, totally ignoring him.*)

DIANA: Charlie Sloane is dead gone on Anne, you know.

ANNE: I hate Charlie Sloane.

DIANA: Jane Andrews told me that Minnie McPherson told her that she heard Charlie telling Ruby Gillis that Anne had a very pretty nose.

GIL: Charlie Sloane is one of the least perceptive people in Avonlea, but in this case I must say I agree. She does have a lovely nose.

(*Anne does not respond.*)

GIL: If it weren't so stuck up in the air.

(*She continues focusing on her slate.*)

GIL: Watch out you don't bruise that lovely nose from pressing it too hard to the grindstone. Though I suppose grinding your nose into that slate is your only choice if you're going to try to match me. Particularly with hair like this. (*He holds onto one of her braids.*) Carrots is what I call it.

DIANA: Gil!

GIL: (*Calling offstage.*) Look everybody, carrots! carrots! carrots!

ANNE: You mean, hateful boy! (*She cracks Gilbert over the head with her slate.*)

DIANA: Anne!

(*Mr. Phillips enters.*)

MR. PHILLIPS: Anne Shirley, what is the meaning of this?

(*Anne, who is still shaking, does not respond.*)

MR. PHILLIPS: Answer me.

DIANA: It wasn't her fault, Mr. Phillips.

MR. PHILLIPS: Whose fault was it?

GIL: It was mine, sir. I teased her.

MR. PHILLIPS: Teasing does not warrant violence. I'm appalled to see a student of mine displaying such a vindictive spirit. You shall write a hundred times, "Anne Shirley has a very bad temper. Anne Shirley must learn to control her temper." You'll learn this is not the way Avonlea children behave, Anne Shirley. Now, come in and begin immediately. (*He exits.*)

GIL: We'd better go before he gets madder.

(*Anne refuses to acknowledge him.*)

DIANA: Go on, Gil.

GIL: (*To Anne – he can barely get it out.*) I'm awful sorry, Anne. Honest I am. (*She does not respond. He exits.*)

ANNE: I shall never forgive Gilbert Blythe. The iron has entered into my soul.

DIANA: He makes fun of all the girls, Anne; and I've never heard him apologize for anything before. He laughs at my hair because it's so black. He's called me crow a dozen times.

ANNE: There's a great deal of difference between being called crow and being called carrots. He's hurt my feelings excruciatingly. (*Mr. Phillips returns.*)

MR. PHILLIPS: I instructed you to begin immediately, Anne Shirley. You're not in an institution where you can do as you please any longer.

ANNE: I was a model pupil at the orphanage, Mr. Phillips, but then there were no children there as rude as Gilbert Blythe.

MR. PHILLIPS: You could learn a great deal from Gilbert Blythe – and in fact, you shall. From now on, you shall sit next to Gilbert. Perhaps that will teach you to moderate your temper and your pride. (*He exits.*) (*Anne and Diana are in shock.*)

Scene 5

> *Green Gables. Marilla is sweeping. Rachel Lynde enters in a flurry.*

MARILLA: Why, hello, Rachel.

RACHEL: Has Anne come home, yet?

MARILLA: No, not yet.

RACHEL: Well, Ruby Gillis happened to stop by on her way home from school, and she said…

MARILLA: Yes?

RACHEL: Perhaps, you should wait until Anne comes.

MARILLA: Nothing's happened to her, has it?

RACHEL: No, not exactly.

> (*Anne enters. She carries her school satchel. She notes that Mrs. Lynde is there and goes straight to Marilla.*)

ANNE: Marilla, I will tell you this right out. Today, a very rude boy called me an unmentionable name and I hit him over the head with a slate. Mr. Phillips gave me an assignment as punishment, which I accepted. But then to further humiliate me, he forced me to sit next to the boy and declared that I must sit there until I had undergone a change of personality. I won't suffer such humiliation, Marilla. I have vowed to Diana and I am informing you: I will never return to that school. Never.

MARILLA: Nonsense.

ANNE: It isn't nonsense at all. Don't you understand, Marilla? I've been insulted.

MARILLA: Insulted, fiddlesticks! You'll go to school tomorrow as usual.

ANNE: Oh, no. I'm not going back, Marilla. I'll learn my lessons at home and I'll be as good as I can be and hold my tongue all the time if it's possible at all. But I will not go back to school I assure you.

(*Anne stares up unflinchingly at Marilla. Marilla ponders for a moment.*)

MARILLA: You'd best get busy with your chores.

(*Anne drops her satchel on the table and exits by Matthew who is coming in from the field.*)

MATTHEW: Hello, Anne. How was school, today?

ANNE: Intolerable. (*She exits.*)

MATTHEW: (*Coming to Marilla.*) What's happened?

MARILLA: She's had a run-in at school. She claims she's not going back.

MATTHEW: What are we going to do?

MARILLA: There's no use trying to reason with her. She's too worked up.

MATTHEW: But what are we going to do?

MARILLA: I don't know. When I looked in her face, well, I don't think I've ever seen a person that determined. She may be a child but there's an awful stubbornness in her.

RACHEL: (*Looking straight at Marilla.*) Like another little girl we all knew many years ago.

(*Marilla and Rachel stare at each other for a moment.*)

MARILLA: What did you do with her when she was like this?

RACHEL: Don't you remember?

MARILLA: Left me alone. Completely alone.

RACHEL: It always seemed to work.

MATTHEW: Not always.

RACHEL: Well, in this case, that's what I'd do. There are times when you can drum sense into a child's head and there are times when they've got to learn it themselves. Just humor her a little.

Scene 6

Anne alone in her room. She holds a lap desk and is doing her homework. Marilla enters.

MARILLA: Supper's ready.

ANNE: All right.

MARILLA: (*She sees Anne's been crying.*) How did you make out with your work, today?

ANNE: Fine.

MARILLA: Nothing you need to ask Mr. Phillips?

ANNE: No, I'm progressing quite well.

MARILLA: What's the matter, Anne? Do you miss school? Do you want to go back?

ANNE: No, Marilla. It's just – When I lived with Mrs. Thomas, there was a bookcase with glass doors. One of the doors was broken. Mr. Thomas smashed it one night when he was slightly intoxicated. But the other was whole and I used to pretend that my reflection was a little girl who lived in the bookcase. She was my comfort and consolation. But when I look in the mirror here – I keep thinking of Diana. Once you've had a real friend, you can't pretend anymore.

MARILLA: I might as well tell you this, now. On Saturday, when Mrs. Barry and I go to market, we've arranged for Diana to come over to tea. If you're willing to have her.

ANNE: Oh, Marilla, thank you. Thank you. You don't know how you've relieved my soul. I've been languishing and now I shall have a joyous occasion to sustain me through the rest of the week.

MARILLA: And perhaps, next week, you'll feel sufficiently relieved to go back to school.

Scene 7

The dining room. Anne and Diana, who is quite dressed up, enter. They are playing at Ladies Having Tea.

ANNE: Won't you please come in.

DIANA: Why thank you.

ANNE: Won't you please sit down.

DIANA: Why thank you.

ANNE: I greatly enjoyed our stroll round your lovely Lake of the Shining Waters, this afternoon.

DIANA: Why thank you. I know I shall enjoy your hospitality greatly.

ANNE: Why thank *you!* Oh, this is such fun, isn't it, Diana? Do you know what Marilla said we could have for tea? Fruitcake, cherry preserves and – raspberry cordial!

DIANA: I love raspberry cordial!

ANNE: Well, then, my dear, may I serve you a glass?

DIANA: I'd be ever so grateful.

ANNE: I shall bring it directly. (*Anne goes to the cabinet.*) Marilla said it was right here.

DIANA: It's been so awful without you at school, Anne. You've missed ever so much. Ruby Gillis charmed her warts away with a magic pebble that she got from old Mary Jo.

ANNE: Here it is, I believe. (*She gets the bottle from the hutch and brings it to the table.*)

DIANA: Charlie Sloane's name was written with Em White's on the porch wall; she was real mad about it. And Gilbert Blythe did the most awful thing to Tillie Boulter...

ANNE: (*Interrupts her.*) Please, Diana.

DIANA: You're really being silly, Anne.

ANNE: I shall never forgive Gilbert Blythe.

DIANA: He's truly sorry.

ANNE: Let's not spoil our one afternoon, together. (*She hands Diana a glass of cordial.*)

DIANA: All right.

ANNE: I'll get the tea. (*She starts off.*)

DIANA: (*Sipping daintily.*) This is awfully nice raspberry cordial, Anne.

ANNE: (*Off.*) I'm real glad you like it. Take as much as you want.

DIANA: (*Takes a very large drink.*) Mmm, the nicest I ever drank. (*She drains the glass, and pours herself another.*) This raspberry cordial is ever so much nicer than Mrs. Lynde's although she brags of hers so much. (*She drinks most of the glass down.*) It doesn't taste a bit like Mrs. Lynde's. (*Drinks.*)

ANNE: (*Re-entering.*) I should think Marilla's would prob'ly be much nicer than Mrs. Lynde's. Marilla is a famous cook. Will you have some more?

DIANA: Thank you.

(*As Anne talks, she pours Diana's drink, then proceeds to make and pour the tea, and cut and serve the cake and preserves. While Anne talks and does all this, the "cordial" has begun to effect Diana: she gradually becomes quite woozy and ill. Anne who is involved with her story and tasks does not really notice Diana's illness.*)

ANNE: Marilla's trying to teach me to cook, but it's uphill work. There's so little scope for imagination in cookery. You have to go by rules. The last time I made a cake I forgot to put the flour in. I was imagining a lovely story about you and me. You had smallpox and I was nursing you back to health. The cake was a dismal failure. Flour is so essential to cakes, you know. Marilla was very cross, and I don't blame her. I'm a trial to her. Last week, Marilla made a pudding sauce to serve to Mr. and Mrs. Chester Ross. She told me to put it on the shelf and cover it, but when I was carrying it I was imagining I was a nun taking the veil to bury a broken heart and I forgot about covering the sauce. When I finally remembered to cover it, I found a mouse drowned in it. I took the mouse out, of course, but Marilla was milking at the time and I forgot to tell her until I saw her carrying the sauce to the table. I screamed, "Marilla, you mustn't use that pudding sauce. There was a mouse drowned in it, and I forgot to tell you." Marilla and Matthew and Mr. and Mrs. Ross all just stared at me.

DIANA: I – I – don't feel so well. I – need to go home.

ANNE: You mustn't dream of going home. You haven't had your tea.

DIANA: I've got to go home.

ANNE: What about your cake and preserves?

(*Diana groans.*)

ANNE: Lie down for a little and you'll feel better. Where do you feel bad?

DIANA: I'm – I'm awful sick.

ANNE: Oh, Diana, do you suppose you really are taking the smallpox? If you are, I'll never forsake you. But I do wish you'd stay till after tea.

DIANA: (*Getting up.*) I'm dizzy. (*She falls.*)

ANNE: Diana!

(*Diana holds her stomach and groans. Marilla and Mrs. Barry enter.*)

MRS. BARRY: Diana!

MARILLA: What is going on, Anne?

ANNE: Diana's sick, Marilla. We were having a lovely tea when suddenly she became terribly ill.

MRS. BARRY: She's not ill. She's drunk!

ANNE: Drunk?

MRS. BARRY: How did this happen Diana?

ANNE: All she'd had is that raspberry cordial Mrs. Barry. Diana thought it was lovely. Better than Mrs. Lynde's. She had two glasses.

DIANA: Three.

MARILLA: This isn't raspberry cordial, Anne.

ANNE: I got it from the cabinet, just like you said. It was the only bottle there.

MRS. BARRY: (*Who has gone to the table to examine the bottle.*) This is currant wine! (*To Anne.*) You awful girl, you've given my Diana wine!

ANNE: But I didn't mean to. I thought it was raspberry cordial. Oh, Diana, I'm so sorry.

MRS. BARRY: You stay away from her. You've done enough damage.

MARILLA: It's not her fault. I told her the bottle was in the cabinet when I'd forgotten that I'd moved it down to the cellar.

MRS. BARRY: A proper household wouldn't have wine around in the first place.

MARILLA: And a proper child wouldn't drink three tumblerfuls at a time of anything.

MRS. BARRY: You're not coming back to this house, Diana.

ANNE: Don't say that, Mrs. Barry.

MRS. BARRY: You're a thoroughly wicked little girl and Diana shall never play with you again.

ANNE: Oh, please, forgive me, Mrs. Barry. I didn't mean to intoxicate Diana. I would never do that.

MRS. BARRY: I won't have your orphan ways ruining my child.

(*Mrs. Barry drags Diana out. Anne cries.*)

MARILLA: There, there, child, don't cry. You weren't to blame.

ANNE: I am to blame. I'm always causing trouble, and I shall never see Diana again.

MARILLA: Don't be foolish. Mrs. Barry's just upset. She'll think better of it tomorrow.

ANNE: She won't. Diana is the only person in the world who might ever have possibly liked me and now she's gone. My whole life's ruined. I'm ugly and stupid and an orphan and nothing will ever be right. I should just run away so I'm all alone like I deserve.

MARILLA: (*Sternly.*) You're not ugly and you're not stupid. But if when things go wrong, you cry or get angry or go off into your imagination because you're afraid you really don't deserve anything good – then nothing good will happen to you. And you will end up alone. (*Marilla turns and goes as the lights shift.*)

Scene 8

The schoolyard. Early morning. Mr. Phillips sitting on the bench, reading a book. He shivers a bit and pulls his coat tighter about himself. Anne enters. She carries her books and supplies.

ANNE: Good morning, Mr. Phillips.

MR. PHILLIPS: You never arrived this early when you were a student in this school, Anne Shirley.

ANNE: I thought I might need extra time for a discussion, this morning. To gain your permission to return to class. I also tend to walk faster when the sun starts breaking over the horizon. I find it exhilarating.

MR. PHILLIPS: Yes, I often sit here rather than inside with the hope the rays will fill me with inspiration. Our mutual appreciation for the sun, however, doesn't seem sufficient reason to allow you to return to school. After two weeks, I'm afraid you're just too far behind.

ANNE: Gilbert Blythe was gone a month, and he had no trouble catching up. Besides, I don't believe I am behind. (*She begins handing him papers.*) Here are my spelling and vocabulary assignments, the mathematics problems and three book reports. I've also written a collection of poems and two stories, as well as an essay on the place of Prince Edward Island in Canadian History.

MR. PHILLIPS: (*Looking through the papers.*) You've gone ten pages ahead in mathematics and three full lessons in spelling.

ANNE: The vocabulary I believe is done for the full term.

MR. PHILLIPS: Well, given what you've accomplished, I see no need for you to return to school. You should just continue working at home.

ANNE: I want to return, Mr. Phillips. I want to be with the other students.

MR. PHILLIPS: No one to crack over the head at home, is that it?

ANNE: I vow to you that I shall be a model student if you allow me to return.

MR. PHILLIPS: I don't think you're capable of being a model student, Anne. Your mind's too active. Sometimes for the good, other times well…If you could learn to discipline your mind instead of letting it take you off in some far-flung direction, I suspect you could become quite an exciting scholar. A top scholar, even. With a chance to recite at the end of term concert. If you could tolerate standing on the stage next to Gilbert Blythe.

ANNE: I wouldn't mind who I was next to if I could recite.

(*Diana enters.*)

MR. PHILLIPS: You're quite determined, aren't you.

ANNE: I want to learn, Mr. Phillips.

MR. PHILLIPS: You've surprised me at every turn, Anne Shirley. I might as well discover the full extent of your surprises. (*He exits.*)

ANNE: Diana!

DIANA: My mother has said I'm not to talk with you, Anne. She says you're not fit company and I'm not to associate with you.

ANNE: Oh, Diana.

DIANA: I know. It's awful.

ANNE: Won't she relent?

DIANA: I've cried and cried and told her it wasn't your fault, but she won't be swayed. I'm never to play with you again. But Anne, she can't stop us from thinking of one another. We shall still be near each other in the classroom and whenever we want we can look at each other with a special look and imagine ourselves off in the woods on a great adventure.

ANNE: You really do care for me.

DIANA: I'm your bosom friend.

ANNE: Oh Diana, I didn't think anybody could care for me. Nobody ever has since I can remember.

DIANA: I'm devoted to you Anne.

(*They embrace. They separate.*)

ANNE: Fare thee well, my bosom friend. Henceforth we must be as strangers living side by side. But my heart will ever be faithful to thee.

(*Diana runs off before she cries. Anne goes to pick up her school satchel when Gilbert enters.*)

GIL: Hello, Anne.

(*She looks up at him, then looks away.*)

GIL: I'm glad you're back. I've wanted to tell you how sorry I was about what happened. I tried to apologize, that day, but I know you were too upset to hear me.

(*She stays turned away.*)

GIL: You're not still mad, are you?

ANNE: I'd appreciate it if you'd leave me alone, Gilbert.

GIL: Are you going to be mad at me for keeps? I promise I won't ever tease you about your hair again. I swear it.

ANNE: I'd just like to be alone for a little.

GIL: It must be hard coming back – after stayin away like you did. You're real stubborn, aren't you. (*He laughs.*) Look, if you're worried about the work you missed, I'd be glad to help you out with it. It's quite a bit – some of it real tricky – but I bet I can get you through it.

ANNE: I don't need your help, thank you.

GIL: You really are something, aren't you? A fella tries to be nice to you, and you just cut him right off.

ANNE: I'm just not concerned about what you have to say right now.

GIL: That's real friendly.

ANNE: Well, we're not friends as far as I can tell.

GIL: Whoever said we were. Just cause I offered to help you out. You think you're so much better than everybody else, lord knows why. Well go ahead – do it all yourself. You can fail for all I care, Anne Shirley.

ANNE: For your information, Gilbert Blythe, I'm ahead in most of my lessons and finished the vocabulary for the term. And Mr. Phillips was so pleased with my work that he said he was hoping to see me reciting at the end of term concert.

GIL: He did not.

ANNE: He as much as said he expected me to win the top scholar prize if I set my mind to it.

GIL: Well, we'll just see about that.

ANNE: Yes, we will, won't we?

Scene 9

The dining room. Anne is sitting at the table, working at her studies. Matthew sits off to the side, looking at a catalogue. Marilla is putting on a coat, bundling herself up.

MARILLA: (*To Matthew.*) I hope to be home by nine, as usual, but this may not be a usual meeting. We're going to be discussing the Blewett children, though I don't know there's anything the Church Aid Society can really do.

MATTHEW: Replace the mother.

MARILLA: (*Gives him a look then turns to Anne.*) What are you working so hard on?

ANNE: Geometry. I've got to improve.

MARILLA: I don't see how you can do better than you've been doing.

ANNE: I have to if I'm going to recite at the end of term concert.

MARILLA: Fiddlesticks. Your learning is your reward. You don't need to be showing off in public.

ANNE: But I have hope of making it my most glorious revenge.

MARILLA: Revenge isn't a fit thing for a little girl to be speaking of. Not fit for a grown person, either. I don't think there'll be any concerts, this year.

ANNE: Marilla!

MARILLA: Make sure you put out your candle, tonight. I may be home late and I don't want it burning down. (*She exits.*)
(*Anne is crushed.*)

MATTHEW: Well, now. That concert is almost a month away, isn't it? And who knows what can happen in a month's time.

ANNE: Thank you, Matthew, but it's probably better that I not get my heart set on it. I'd look ridiculous standing before an audience reciting. I hardly have the appearance of a dignified public figure. I probably won't be selected in any case with all this geometry. Did you ever study geometry when you went to school?

MATTHEW: Well, now, no I didn't.

ANNE: I wish you had because then you'd be able to sympathize with me. It's casting a cloud over my whole life.
(*Abruptly, Diana Barry bursts into the room. She is clutching Minnie May, wrapped in a blanket. A hoarse child's coughing comes from the blanket.*)

DIANA: Oh, Anne, Minnie May is awful sick – she's got the croup – and father and mother went to Church Aid and there's nobody to go to the doctor and I don't know what to do I'm so scared.
(*Matthew gets up, puts on his coat and leaves.*)

ANNE: Don't worry Diana.

DIANA: She's so bad Anne. It's like she can't breathe. It came on her all of a sudden.

ANNE: Matthew's going for the doctor, Diana.
(*The coughing grows worse.*)

ANNE: I know exactly what to do for croup. (*She exits to the kitchen for the ipecac.*) When you look after three sets of twins, you get lots of experience. Bringing a child out in the air would be awful for pneumonia but it sometimes helps croup. You've had her out in the air and Minnie May's still coughing. She's got a bad case. But we'll just get this ipecac down her.

DIANA: She's going to die!

ANNE: Hush, Diana!

DIANA: I know she is!

ANNE: Get that cloth and wipe her forehead.

DIANA: I can't!

ANNE: Diana.

DIANA: I can't!

ANNE: Diana! Get the cloth. Now, come wipe her forehead. You see, you're helping her.

(*More coughing.*)

ANNE: You've got to take this, Minnie May. It's a magic elixir. It comes from the fairies. They make it from the most beautiful flowers in the world. And they only let children drink it when they really really need it.

(*Anne and Diana slowly put their heads on each other's shoulders as lights fade. When they come back up, Anne and Diana are asleep in the chairs. The baby is still in Anne's arms. Matthew followed by the Doctor, enters.*)

MATTHEW: There she is.

(*The Doctor takes the baby from Anne's arms and begins examining her. Anne followed by Diana wakes up.*)

MATTHEW: (*To Anne.*) Sorry it took so long. Had to go all the way to Spencervale.

ANNE: (*As the Doctor continues the examination.*) I was awfully near giving up in despair, Doctor. She got worse and worse, sicker than ever the Hammond twins did. I gave her every drop of ipecac in that bottle and when the last drop went down, I said to myself – I didn't want to worry you, Diana, but I had to relieve my feelings – "This is the last lingering hope and I fear tis a vain one." But in about three minutes, she coughed up the phlegm and then she fell asleep.

(*Marilla has entered into the front yard during Anne's speech. She has stayed outside looking at the stars. Now, Mrs. Barry enters, running by Marilla and rushing into the dining room.*)

MRS. BARRY: My baby, my baby! (*She rushes to the baby. The Doctor hands the baby to her.*) My Minnie May. Is she going to be all right, doctor? Is she going to be all right?

DOCTOR: I expect she is.

MRS. BARRY: Oh, thank you, thank you.

DOCTOR: Don't thank me. Thank that little red-headed girl. She's the one saved your baby's life. Never seen such skill and presence of mind in a child that age. (*Sitting at the table.*) I'll write you a prescription for some syrup. (*As he writes.*)

ANNE: (*Yawns.*) Oh, I don't know how I'm going to keep my eyes open at school, tomorrow.

MARILLA: Don't you worry about school. You just sleep in.

ANNE: I can't. I'll fall behind.

MATTHEW: You go to bed and have a good sleep. I'll do your chores, tomorrow.

ANNE: Good night.

MRS. BARRY: Anne. Thank you. And I hope you'll forgive me for misjudging you.

ANNE: I have no hard feelings, Mrs. Barry. I assure you I didn't mean to intoxicate Diana and henceforth I shall cover the past with a mantle of oblivion.

MRS. BARRY: Yes, well…when you're rested, I'd like you to come over and play with Diana.

ANNE: (*Loudly, waking up Minnie May.*) Oh Mrs. Barry!

(*Matthew and Marilla smile at Anne as she and Diana hug.*)

Scene 10

> *Bright sunlight. Outside Rachel Lynde's house. Matthew is pacing. Mrs. Lynde enters.*

MRS. LYNDE: Why, Matthew Cuthbert, what in the world are you doing here?

MATTHEW: Well, now, that's a good question.

MRS. LYNDE: Has Marilla sent you, Matthew?

MATTHEW: Well, now, actually, I don't believe she has. You see, you know how Anne saved Little Minnie May? Well, I was thinking she deserved something for that. You know like a reward. And, well, I've been watching Anne, you see. (*He stops.*)

MRS. LYNDE: Yes?

MATTHEW: Well, she don't quite look like the other girls. Not because of how she looks, I mean, herself – but because of what she wears.

MRS. LYNDE: Those awful dresses Marilla makes for her. They're positively ridiculous and I've longed to tell Marilla so, but I've held my tongue because I can see she doesn't want advice.

MATTHEW: Well, now, I was thinking that it's only a few weeks to the end of the term and there'll be that concert and all and Anne might just be asked to recite and if she was gonna be up there in front of all those people – well she ought to look like a dignified public figure.

MRS. LYNDE: You want me to make her a new dress.

MATTHEW: Well, now, I'll pay you for it. Pay you whatever you think's fair.

MRS. LYNDE: It's fine you've come, Matthew. I'd be glad to make the dress. If Marilla made it – well, Anne would probably get wind of it and your surprise'd be spoiled.

MATTHEW: Well, now, I'm much obliged. Much obliged.

MRS. LYNDE: I'll take care of everything. She'll have it for the concert.

MATTHEW: Uh-huh.

MRS. LYNDE: Don't you worry.

MATTHEW: No, I won't.

MRS. LYNDE: Good. I'll bring it to you without Anne or Marilla knowing a thing. You can be sure.

MATTHEW: Well, now, that's just fine. (*He's hesitating.*)

MRS. LYNDE: Is there something else, Matthew?

MATTHEW: Well, now, I dunno – but, uh, don't they make them sleeves different nowadays from what they used to?

MRS. LYNDE: How do you mean, different?

MATTHEW: Oh, I dunno. Sorta like all like uh, you know (*He indicates with his hands.*)

MRS. LYNDE: I'm not sure I do.

MATTHEW: (*Pulls a scrap of paper from his pocket.*) Well, like this.

MRS. LYNDE: Where did you find this?

MATTHEW: Magazine.

MRS. LYNDE: Why, Matthew Cuthbert, thinking about dresses and looking through ladies magazines! My word! Anne's dress will have puffed sleeves so big, Marilla will be stunned into silence. And it'll be our little secret. (*Matthew beams.*)

Scene 11

On the bank of the river. Anne and Diana are in a small boat in the water. Diana is happily rowing. Anne is slightly nervous. They wear heavy coats.

DIANA: This is ever so much fun, isn't it Anne?

ANNE: Yes. But I do wish I knew how to swim.

DIANA: This tub may be old as the dawn but I don't think it's in danger of sinking, just yet.

ANNE: There's an awful lot of water seeping in. Oh, it's cold.

DIANA: Yes, a body wouldn't last five minutes in the water. Not quite the ideal for a picnic. But end of term deserves some kind of celebration.
(*Diana pops out of the boat and pulls it on the bank. Anne, who climbs out quickly, holds a picnic basket.*)

ANNE: One more week.

DIANA: Yes, you'll know on Friday whether you've beaten Gilbert or not.

ANNE: What's important is we're together again.

DIANA: If you win top scholar will you forgive him?

ANNE: I don't want to discuss it.

DIANA: Think how you felt when my mother wouldn't forgive you.

ANNE: I don't care how he feels.

DIANA: You expect everyone to care about how you feel.

ANNE: Oh we're in luck. Hot cocoa and Marilla's special muffins.

DIANA: He's apologized. He's never teased you again. In fact, he's been overly nice to you. What does he have to do, Anne?

ANNE: He's just so arrogant.

DIANA: He's sure of himself, that's all. No reason he shouldn't be. He's always been top.

ANNE: Well, he won't be this year. I've mastered geometry and all that's left is the recitation. I'm going to make sure mine is so powerful that no one will have any doubt who is the winner. I'm going to recite "The Lady of Shallot."

DIANA: Oh, that's so romantic! Floating down the river to Camelot, drawn by Lancelot from her seclusion to her death. You'll be wonderful, Anne.

ANNE: I shall be more than wonderful. I shall become the Lady of Shallot. When I finish, everyone will have seen that awful combination of death and beauty reflected right on my face.

DIANA: Oh, that's ghastly! How will you do it?

ANNE: (*Pauses, then looks towards the boat.*) I shall experience her pain, first-hand. Come on. (*She goes to the boat.*)

DIANA: What are you going to do?

ANNE: (*Taking off her coat.*) Down she came and found a boat.

DIANA: Anne!

(*Anne takes the paddle out of the boat.*)

ANNE: Beneath a willow left afloat,

And round about the prow she wrote (*Looks at Diana.*)

DIANA: The Lady of Shallot.

ANNE: (*From in the boat.*) Well, push me off.

DIANA: Into the river?

ANNE: Yes.

DIANA: No!

ANNE: Diana, I've got to float down the river, singing my mournful, holy song.

DIANA: And dying!

ANNE: (*Getting up.*) All right, I'll push myself off. I thought as my bosom friend you'd want to be part of this. This is entering the world of Camelot, of Lancelot, of –

DIANA: The Lady of Shallot

ANNE: Yes.

DIANA: All right. Lie back down.

(*Anne does. She walks slowly toward the boat, starts to undo the rope from shore.*)

DIANA: Lying robed in snowy white,

That loosely flew to left and right –

(*Rachel Lynde enters. She carries a large bundle.*)

DIANA: The leaves upon her falling light –

Thro' the noises of the night –

MRS. LYNDE: What are you doing, Diana?

(*Diana, startled, screams. Anne, startled by Diana's scream, pops up in the boat and screams. Mrs. Lynde, startled by Anne's appearance, screams. They all stare at each other, breathing hard.*)

MRS. LYNDE: Oh my heart. My heart. (*She catches her breath.*) I should have known this was some trick of yours, Anne Shirley. I came the back way purposefully not to meet you, and of course here you are.

ANNE: I'm sorry, Mrs. Lynde. We weren't trying to scare you.

DIANA: You scared us just as much as we did you.

MRS. LYNDE: I suppose I did. Well, my feet are on the ground, anyway, not under it, so I suppose there's no damage done, thank goodness.

ANNE: Why didn't you want to meet me, Mrs. Lynde?

MRS. LYNDE: (*Pulling the bundle closer to her.*) Never you mind. Go on back to your silly game. But mind you don't scare anyone else. (*She exits.*)

ANNE: She didn't want me to see what she had in that bundle. It's connected with the concert, I can feel it. It's an omen, Diana.

DIANA: A bad omen. You shouldn't go out in the boat, Anne. The river's so deep here, and the currents –

ANNE: (*Lying down.*) Come on, push me off.

DIANA: Anne, I really think –

ANNE: And as the boat-head wound along

The willowly hills and fields among,

They heard her singing her last song –

Diana!

DIANA: All right. (*Pushing the boat off.*) The Lady of Shallot.

(*As Anne recites, the boat floats away – upstage. Diana anxiously watches.*)

ANNE: Heard a carol, mournful, holy,

Changed loudly, chanted lowly,

Till her blood was frozen slowly,

And her eyes were darkened wholly,

Diana!

DIANA: What?!

ANNE: (*Stands in the boat, soaking wet.*) It's leaking! The water's flooding in!

DIANA: Row to shore, Anne! Quick, row!

ANNE: The paddle's there.

DIANA: Oh no!

ANNE: I'm sinking. Run for help, Diana, run!

DIANA: (*As she runs.*) Don't get in the water! You'll freeze.

(*Anne stands shivering in the boat, cold and fear both taking their toll. She begins to recite to give herself courage.*)

ANNE: For ere she reached upon the tide

The first house by the waterside

Singing in her song she cried –

The Lady of Shallot.

(*She leaps from the boat to the piling in the river.*)

ANNE: Under tower and balcony,

By garden-wall and gallery,

A gleaming shape she floated by,

Dead-pale between the houses high,

Silent into Camelot.

(*She is hanging on for dear life. Gilbert comes on, poling in his boat. Anne's back is to him as he poles towards her.*)

ANNE: Out upon the wharfs they came.

Knight and burgher, lord and dame,

And round the prow they read her name,

The Lady of Shallot.

ANNE AND GIL: Who is that? and what is here?

GIL: And in the lighted palace near

Died the sound of royal cheer;

And they crossed themselves for fear,

All the knights at Camelot.

(*He has poled to Anne. As he reaches up and helps her down from the piling.*)

GIL: But Lancelot mused a little space;

He said, "She has a lovely face;

God in his mercy lend her grace,

The Lady of Shallot."

(*She drops down into the boat exhausted.*)

GIL: What were you doing?

ANNE: I was in the Barry's boat and it sprang a leak. Diana went for help. Could you take me to shore?

(*He poles to shore. They are both silent. As they reach the shore, he offers to help her out, but she climbs out on her own. She quickly puts on her coat.*)

ANNE: I'm very much obliged to you.

GIL: Anne, look here. It's been such a long time. It was only a silly stupid joke I made. And besides, I think your hair's awfully pretty, now. Awfully pretty. (*He reaches up and almost touches it.*) Honest I do.

(*She hesitates, looking into Gil's eager face, wanting to get herself to agree, not quite knowing how. She looks away to get up the courage. Gil, put off a little, smiles and tries to joke.*)

GIL: I swear I won't call you "carrots" ever again. And I'll come save you whenever you need. (*With a grand gesture.*) I'll be your Lancelot, my romantic "Lady of Shallot." (*He laughs.*)

ANNE: I shall never be friends with you, Gilbert Blythe.

GIL: All right then! (*He climbs back in his boat.*) And I'll never ask you again, Anne Shirley. (*Poling off.*) And I don't care either! You're the one who should have been apologizing to me!

(*He's gone. Anne wraps her coat around herself and sits dejectedly. Diana comes running on in a frenzy.*)

DIANA: Oh, Anne, Anne! I thought you were drowned. I felt like a murderer, because I pushed you off. I was in hysterics!

(*Matthew runs on, out of breath.*)

MATTHEW: You're all right?

ANNE: Yes, Matthew. I'm sorry I frightened you.

(*Matthew drops to the ground to catch his breath.*)

DIANA: How did you escape?

ANNE: Gilbert Blythe came along in a dory and brought me to land.

DIANA: Oh, Anne, how splendid of him! How romantic!

ANNE: It was not romantic. I do not ever want to hear the word romantic again.

DIANA: Well, at least, you'll be speaking to him, now.

ANNE: I won't. Not ever.

(*Matthew and Diana are both looking at her.*)

DIANA: He saved your life, Anne.

ANNE: He only wanted to mock me.

DIANA: You're impossible. When you've done something wrong, everyone's expected to say it's all right. But when someone's done something to you, there's no way to make up for it. How can anyone be friends with you?

(*Diana exits. Matthew is looking hard at Anne.*)

ANNE: Diana?! Well it's too bad for her if she doesn't want to be my friend. I don't need her anyway.

MATTHEW: I guess you don't need anybody.

(*Anne is struck to the core. She stares at him.*)

MATTHEW: I guess maybe you just need to be all on your own. (*He exits.*)

(*Anne sadly picks up the picnic as the set shifts back to Green Gables. When it's in place, she sets the blanket on the dining room table and goes to her room.*)

Scene 12

  Lights up on Anne's room. Anne comes slowly in. She reaches under her bed and pulls out her old, battered suitcase and opens it. She begins packing her things.

ANNE: They're right. Everyone'd be happier if I'd never come.

(*Lights up on the dining room. Matthew and Marilla enter. Matthew carries the bundle from Mrs. Lynde.*)

MARILLA: Are you all right?

MATTHEW: I suppose.

MARILLA: You're not mad at her for almost drowning, are you?

MATTHEW: No.

MARILLA: What's wrong, Matthew?

MATTHEW: You've spent the last forty years mindin your own business, Marilla. I don't think you need to change, now.

(*Marilla exits to Anne's room.*)

MARILLA: You'd best get out of those wet things. (*Marilla helps Anne change as she talks.*) Matthew said the Blythe boy saved you. He's a nice looking fellow. Reminds me of his father. We used to be real good friends, his father and I. People even called him my beau.

(*Anne looks at her for the first time.*)

MARILLA: But we had a quarrel and I wouldn't forgive him when he asked. I meant to after awhile, but I was sulky and angry and I wanted to punish him. He never came back – and I always felt rather sorry. Wished I'd forgiven him when I had the chance.

(*Anne looks away.*)

MARILLA: I'll make some tea to warm you up. (*She exits to the dining room.*)

(*Diana followed by Gilbert enters the front yard and comes to the dining room.*)

MATTHEW: Why, hello, Diana.

DIANA: Hello Mr. Cuthbert, Miss Cuthbert. This is Gilbert Blythe.

MARILLA: How do you do.

(*Gil nods.*)

(*Anne enters from bedroom.*)

DIANA: Anne! I won't let your stubbornness ruin our friendship, and the friendship you should have with Gil.

ANNE: I can't always do what everyone else does, Diana. I'm not like you and Gil. I say and think wild, embarrassing things. I have fits of temper. I'm incorrigible.

GIL: You're not so different from us, Anne. A lot of people would say I'm just as incorrigible as you. (*With a sly grin.*) I think it's a compliment to both of us. We always make things exciting. I'm looking forward to standing beside you at the concert, no matter who wins.

ANNE: Thank you, Gil.

GIL: Are we going to be friends, now?

ANNE: You've always treated me like a friend; I've just been too foolish to realize it.

DIANA: I'm so glad we've come. (*She hugs Anne.*)

ANNE: (*Holding on tightly.*) I shall never forget you, Diana. Never. (*She releases Diana and exits to bedroom.*)

DIANA: Anne!

MARILLA: I think we're all a bit frayed from the excitement. Thank you for coming over.

DIANA: Good night. (*Shouts to bedroom.*) See you tomorrow, Anne.

GIL: Good night.

MARILLA: Good night.

(*They leave. Anne enters the dining room with her suitcase.*)

ANNE: I was going to leave a letter for you, but that wouldn't be fair. I've got to face up to it. You've done everything you could for me but I've been nothing but a burden to you. I can't go on living here, any more. I've got to leave.

MATTHEW: No, Anne.

ANNE: You're the gentlest soul alive, Matthew. I don't want to bring you any more pain. I couldn't bear to see you look like you did, this afternoon, and I know I would. I know I would hurt you again. It's better if I go.

MATTHEW: No.

ANNE: I don't belong here.

MARILLA: Why?

ANNE: Because I don't.

MARILLA: Because you're ugly and have red hair? Because the devil's in you? Because you're an orphan?

ANNE: Yes.

MARILLA: When I was young, I was always being teased about my looks. I didn't like myself much, was sure I was ugly. So I tried to imagine that ugliness away. I didn't do it like you, all romance and fantasy and show. I turned to work. Tried to put people out of my life. Until you came. You're part of this family, Anne.

ANNE: I don't deserve this.

MATTHEW: You do. You deserve everything. You're smart and pretty and loving, too, which is better than all the rest. You've been a blessing to us, and there never was a luckier mistake than what Mrs. Blewett made.

ANNE: If I'd been the boy you sent for, I could have helped you so much more.

MATTHEW: I'd rather have you than a dozen boys. You mind that, Anne – rather than a dozen boys. You're my girl.

MARILLA: And mine. It's never been easy for me to say things out of my heart, but I love you as dear as if you were my own flesh and blood. I need you here, Anne.

(*Marilla opens her arms for Anne. Anne runs to her.*)

MATTHEW: (*As he pulls the dress from the bundle and holds it up.*) And everyone's gonna know how good you are. (*Seeing the dress.*) Oh!

ANNE: (*Screaming as she runs to Matthew and grabs the dress.*) Look at those sleeves! Look at those sleeves! (*She holds the dress up to herself, then turns to them. Very simply.*) I am gonna make you so proud. So very proud.

(*They hug her.*)

(*Curtain*)

END OF PLAY

ALTERNATIVE DOUBLING

The pages that follow allow Mrs. Blewett to be doubled with Mrs. Barry rather than Mrs. Lynde. The Scene 5 that follows replaces the original Scene 5 and the new Scene 6A is inserted after the original Scene 6.

The advantages of this doubling are that the actress playing Mrs. Barry has a much more satisfying acting task in the show and that Anne's internal struggle and her attempt to leave Green Gables at the end of Act II have a clearer set-up.

However, since this change requires adding a brief additional scene and since the play is already quite long for many youth theaters, I have chosen to provide this as an alternative rather than the standard version of the script.

Scene 5

The front porch of the Barry house. In a rocking chair sits an attractive young girl, Diana Barry, just Anne's age. She is rocking a baby wrapped in a blanket. Marilla and Anne with her bag enter. Neither are in good spirits.

DIANA: Why good morning, Miss Cuthbert? Won't you come on in? Mother's just taking some muffins out of the oven.

MARILLA: Thank you, Diana. Has Mrs. Peter Blewett come yet? Your mother said she'd be stopping by, this morning.

DIANA: Why yes. She's just arrived. Shall I get her for you?

MARILLA: Thank you. I'll go in.

(Diana is looking at the downcast Anne.)

MARILLA: This is Anne Shirley. This is Diana and her sister, Minnie May, Anne.

ANNE: *(Perking up.)* Diana. What a perfectly lovely name. Diana was a goddess, you know. I'm Anne with an "e" on the end. It's much more elegant.

MARILLA: Let's go in, Anne.

(Mrs. Blewett comes out before they can.)

MRS. BLEWETT: I thought I heard your voice, Miss Cuthbert. I see you got the girl, all right. I couldn't waste time waiting for Matthew, last night.

MARILLA: The girl's why I've come, Mrs. Peter. You see there's been a mistake: we wanted a boy. We told your brother Robert to tell you we wanted a boy.

MRS. BLEWETT: You don't say. Well, Robert sent word by his daughter Nancy and she said you wanted a girl. She's a terrible, flighty thing, that Nancy. I can't count the times I've had to chastise her for heedlessness. I thought I was bringing you what you wanted. It's not my fault, Miss Cuthbert.

MARILLA: We should have come to you ourselves on such an important matter, not trusted to a message. But anyhow, the mistake's been made and the only thing to do now is to set it right. Can we send the child back to the asylum? I suppose they'll take her, won't they?

MRS. BLEWETT: I suppose so – but you know, that may not be necessary. All the way back, yesterday, I was thinking, "now, why didn't I get one of those orphans to come work for me." You know how hard it is to keep good help. I swear the girls I hire don't know what it means to work. Think they've come to eat my food and let the children run wild.

MARILLA: Your children have a lot of energy, Mrs. Peter.

MRS. BLEWETT: That's why I've got the serving girls there – to get that energy out of them!

DIANA: (Rocking the baby.) Ssshh.

MRS. BLEWETT: (To Anne.) Let me look at you, girl. What was your name again?

ANNE: Anne Shirley.

MRS. BLEWETT: That's right. There's not much to you without that coat wrapped around you. (To Marilla.) They practically shoved her at me, said she'd be a good worker, though they seemed a little too eager to get rid of her to my mind. She is wiry, though. Wiry ones are the best after all.

ANNE: Do you have any twins, Mrs. Blewett?

MRS. BLEWETT: What business is that of yours? If I take you, you'll have to be a good girl – good and smart and respectful. I've four boys and a little girl and you'll earn your keep. There's no mistake about that. You've experience caring for children, haven't you?

ANNE: (Softly.) Yes.

MRS. BLEWETT: Well, then I suppose I might as well take her off your hands, Miss Cuthbert. That slaggard I have now is just about to run off. I saw it in her eyes, this morning. And after less than a week. (Referring to Anne.) Having one like this'll save me the trouble of trying to find a new girl every month. If you like, I'll take her home, right now.

(Marilla looks at Anne. Anne's eyes are downcast.)

DIANA: (To her baby.) Sshh, Minnie May, it's all right. Sshhhh.

MARILLA: (Slowly.) Well, I don't know. I didn't say that Matthew and I had absolutely decided not to keep her. In fact, Matthew is disposed to have her stay. I just came over to find out how the mistake had occurred. I think I'd better take her home again and talk it over with Matthew. I oughtn't to decide without consulting him. If we decide not to keep her, we'll send her over to you, tomorrow night. Will that suit you, Mrs. Peter.

MRS. BLEWETT: I suppose it'll have to.

(*She turns and abruptly goes back into the house. An awkward moment then Marilla starts to go.*)

MARILLA: Come on, Anne.

DIANA: Aren't you going to come in, Miss Cuthbert?

MARILLA: No, thank you. I told Matthew I'd be home right away.

DIANA: (*Staring at Anne.*) Well, perhaps, I'll see you again, sometime.

MRS. BARRY: (*Off.*) Diana? You and Minnie May come on in.

DIANA: (*To Marilla.*) I'll give mother your regards. (*To Anne.*) Goodbye. (*She exits.*)

MARILLA: (*To Anne.*) Come on, now.

ANNE: Oh, Miss Cuthbert, did you really say that perhaps you would let me stay at Green Gables?

MARILLA: (*Crossly.*) Yes, you did hear me say just that and no more. It isn't decided yet. Perhaps we will conclude to let Mrs. Peter Blewett take you after all. She certainly needs you much more than I do.

ANNE: I'd rather go back to the asylum than live with her. She looks exactly like a – like a gimlet.

MARILLA: A little girl like you should be ashamed of talking so about a lady and a stranger. You hold your tongue and behave as a good girl should.

ANNE: I'll try to do and be anything you want, if you'll only keep me.

MARILLA: You can practice keeping your thoughts to yourself, then, as we go back to Green Gables.

ANNE: (*As they exit.*) You shall see how strong I can be, Miss Cuthbert. I'll be the model of golden silence. I shall be as quiet as the leaves when the wind's stopped blowing after a storm.

(*They're gone but Anne's voice can still be heard.*)

ANNE: That's a lovely, cool quiet, isn't it? Even the insects seem to be waiting to make sure...

(*The lights have shifted.*)

Scene 6a

Anne is happily staring into the pond.

ANNE: My dear Princess of the Shining Waters, I know you're smiling at me from the depths of your watery home because you believe I'm going to stay forever and ever. But you musn't get your heart set on my always being here. Some day, I may have to leave. I may go on adventures. I may seek out a devoted prince. I may just tire of – this lovely home. So let's not dwell on our future. Let's just try to enjoy whatever time we have together.

(Mrs. Barry has entered, staring at Anne.)

MRS. BARRY: Are you Anne?

(Anne, startled, can only nod.)

MRS. BARRY: I didn't expect to find you here.

ANNE: I'm sorry. I wasn't doing anything. I was just enjoying the lake.

MRS. BARRY: Is that what you were doing.

ANNE: I'll go.

MRS. BARRY: Wait a moment. I was just on my way to Green Gables to find you.

ANNE: To find me?

MRS. BARRY: Yes. Diana would like you to come over Saturday to play.

ANNE: Diana.

MRS. BARRY: Yes. I'm Diana's mother. You will come, won't you?

ANNE: Oh, yes. Yes. Yes! *(Running off.)* Marilla! Marilla!

Afternoon of the Elves

by Y York

for Marin Elf

Afternoon of the Elves by Y York. ©1993 by Y York PAu 1-922-830. Adapted from the novel *Afternoon of the Elves* by Janet Taylor Lisle. ©1989 by Janet Taylor Lisle. Reprinted by permission of the Publisher, Orchard Books, New York. All inquiries should be addressed to Kathy Alm, Seattle Children's Theatre, PO Box 9640, Seattle, WA 98109-0640 or Joyce Ketay Agency, 1501 Broadway, Suite 1910, New York, NY 10036.

ORIGINAL PRODUCTION

Afternoon of the Elves was originally produced by Seattle Children's Theatre on September 23, 1993. It was directed by Linda Hartzell with the following cast:

ALISON/MRS. CONNOLLY..Whitney Lee
JANE ....Felicia Loud
MR. LENOX...Todd Jefferson Moore
MRS. LENOX...Peggy Poage
SARA KATE CONNOLLY...................................Rebecca Ann Rothstein
HILLARY LENOX...Annette Toutonghi

CHARACTERS

Jane and Alison are stars of the fourth grade; they have recently allowed Hillary to join their ranks. Sara Kate is an upperclassman who has been held back for a second try in the fifth grade. Mr. and Mrs. Lenox are Hillary's parents. Mrs. Connolly is Sara Kate's mother; she is a person unable to cope.

SETTING

The main settings are the amazingly well manicured Lenox backyard that abuts the atrocious Connolly backyard that is filled with old appliances, car motors, tires, general junk, and brambles; in the midst of the mess is the elf village. Another important setting is inside the deteriorated Connolly house. Secondary settings are outside of the school and on the town, both of which can be implied with sound and lights. A simple design that allows each setting to use the whole stage is recommended.

AFTERNOON OF THE ELVES

ACT ONE
Scene 1

> *Outside of school, Friday afternoon. A bright fall day. Jane Webster and Alison Mancini, dressed alike with matching hairdos, leaving school with books, giggling, etc.*

HILLARY: (*Off.*) Wait up!

ALISON: (*Playing.*) Do you hear something, Jane?

JANE: (*Ibid.*) Not a thing, Alison.

HILLARY: (*Off.*) It's me, Hillary, wait!

ALISON: Oh, it's *Hillary*, Jane. Do you think we should wait for *Hillary*?

JANE: Hillary-who-didn't-do-her-hair?

HILLARY: (*Off.*) I didn't have time!

ALISON: *We* had time.

JANE: We *made* time.

> (*Hillary enters. She is dressed as they, but with different hair. She carries a book bag.*)

HILLARY: (*Out of breath, defensive.*) My mother didn't have time.

JANE: You let your mother do your hair?

ALISON: I don't let my mother *touch* my hair. She *pulls* it, then when I scream and run she says, "Alison Mancini, get in this chair or I'm going to call your *father* at the *office*." I tremble, Mother, I just tremble. I do my own hair.

JANE: I do, too.

ALISON: (*To Jane.*) You *have* to do your own hair.

JANE: (*Defensive.*) So what?

ALISON: So nothing.

HILLARY: How do you do it by yourself?

ALISON: With two mirrors and a chair.

JANE: (*To Alison.*) And a hairbrush.

HILLARY: I don't think I can do it.

ALISON: Well you have to learn so we can be the Mighty Three.

HILLARY: Guess what? I heard Mr. Decker call us the Three Musketeers; I heard him say so to Mrs. Gray this morning. "Well, I see you've got the Three Musketeers in your class," he said.

JANE: Too-too good.

ALISON: Write it down, Hillary.

HILLARY: I already did (*Hugs book bag.*).

ALISON: We're getting famous. That's what happens when there's three of you; people start to notice you; you get famous.

JANE: And three's the right number.

ALISON: Yes, if you're four, people think you're a gang.

JANE: (*Rhyme, rap.*) The number four is very poor!

ALISON: Oh, stop it, already. We all know you can rhyme.

JANE: I have to keep in practice.

HILLARY: Practice for what?

ALISON: Jane's father only lets her watch TV if she rhymes.

HILLARY: Wow, that's crummy.

JANE: It won't last; his new girlfriend is a poet. (*Rhyming.*) The number two is one too few.

ALISON: Yeah. Two is no good. If there's only two, it's the same as one; nobody notices.

HILLARY: We, the Mighty Three.

JANE: (*Singing.*) Alison, Hillary and Me. Hey! Maybe we should be a band. We already match.

ALISON: You (*Jane.*) could write the songs. Let's start right away, this afternoon.

JANE: I need to think up a song first.

ALISON: Tomorrow then. We'll meet at…(*Hillary.*) your house.

HILLARY: I can't sing.

JANE: That doesn't matter.

ALISON: (*At the same time.*) That doesn't matter.

JANE: Pididdle!

ALISON: (*At the same time.*) Pididdle!

JANE: I said it first.

ALISON: (*At the same time.*) I said it first.

JANE: Who said it first, Hillary?

HILLARY: Um. Alison.

ALISON: I win. Okay, okay. Name ten…stars.

(*Jane names ten current rock, movie, and TV stars, while Alison punches her in the arm.*)

ALISON: Ten! I'm exhausted. (*From punching.*)

JANE: Let's go get something to eat.

ALISON: All you do is eat.

JANE: Do not. I couldn't finish my lunch. Sara Kate Connolly sat down next to me – made me lose my whole appetite. She is gross.

ALISON: She is *mental.* That's why she got held back. She's supposed to be *two* years ahead.

HILLARY: She lives behind my house.

JANE: Yuk.

ALISON: Her mother drank pesticide before she was born.

JANE: Have you seen what she eats? Mush in a thermos. Yuk.

HILLARY: If her mother drank pesticide she'd be dead.

ALISON: Maybe she *is* dead. Nobody's ever seen her.

HILLARY: *I've* seen her.

ALISON: Maybe that's just a ghost; the ghost of Sara Kate's mother, oooo.

JANE: Sara Kate Connolly is a magician.

ALISON: She is not.

JANE: It's true; whenever Sara Kate Connolly is around, people's things *disappear.*

(*Alison and Jane giggle.*)

JANE: She stole a *bike* and used it to deliver newspapers. She delivered a paper to a policeman's house.

(*Sara Kate enters.*)

ALISON: Oh, no. It's *her*, it's Sara Kate.

JANE: Don't say her name!

ALISON: If we ignore it, maybe it will go away.

JANE: Oh, no, she's coming, she's coming.

(*Sara Kate joins them. She is dressed in ill-fitting trousers, shirt, down vest, work boots.*)

ALISON: Look, Jane, look, Hillary, look who has come over to talk to us. Sara Kate Connolly. What a nice surprise.

JANE: Sara Kate Connolly. Why, I haven't seen you since –

SARA KATE: Since school let out, five minutes ago.

ALISON: Can you tell me exactly where you got those amazing boots? I'm dying to get some exactly like them for a trip to the Arctic Circle.

JANE: And I need a pair for my trip to the Peruvian desert.

ALISON: But what do you need them for, here, in America, Sara Kate
Connolly?

JANE: For a job in a gas station?

ALISON: Are you going to get a job in a gas station now that you don't have a
bicycle to ride on a paper route anymore? Huh?

SARA KATE: I need to talk to you.

ALISON: You need to talk to who?

SARA KATE: Not you. (*Hillary.*) You.

HILLARY: Why do you need to talk to me?

SARA KATE: I need to talk to you *alone*.

JANE: Oh, brother.

ALISON: Well you can't.

SARA KATE: It's actually very important. And private.

JANE: She'll tell us later.

SARA KATE: Maybe. Maybe not.

HILLARY: I don't have anything to say to you.

SARA KATE: Of course you don't have anything to say to me. I have something
to say to you. But you will have to tear yourself away from these two
chaperons.

HILLARY: (*Mad.*) They're not chaperons! (*Beat.*) What are chaperons?

SARA KATE: Body. Guards. For the young and frightened.

HILLARY: I'm not frightened.

SARA KATE: Then let's talk. You. And me. Over there.

HILLARY: (*To Jane and Alison, whisper.*) I better talk to her or she'll never go
away.

ALISON: Are you sure?

HILLARY: Yeah, it's okay. I'll see you tomorrow.

ALISON: Okay. Bye. Bye, Sara Kate Connolly, see you at the gas station.

(*Alison and Jane exit. Pause.*)

SARA KATE: Why were they saying all those famous names and hitting each
other?

HILLARY: What names? Oh! It was a pididdle.

SARA KATE: A *what?*

HILLARY: A pididdle. They said the same thing at the same time. Then Alison
said pididdle so Jane had to name ten stars while Alison punched her
until she got done.

SARA KATE: That doesn't even make sense!

HILLARY: It's just a game.

SARA KATE: It's a stupid one!

HILLARY: (*Pause.*) What do you *want*?

SARA KATE: (*Formally.*) Are you Hillary Lenox?

HILLARY: You know who I am. Our backyards touch.

SARA KATE: I can't be sure who you are, you're dressed exactly like Alison Mancini and Jane Webster. Girls of a predatory and evil nature. You should hope they never commit a crime; you might get blamed.

HILLARY: Why?

SARA KATE: You dress like them; the witness might identify *you* by mistake.

HILLARY: Well, it's me, Hillary.

SARA KATE: If *you're* Hillary Lenox, I need to talk to you about a matter concerning our touching backyards. (*Pause.*) Have you peeked through the vegetation into my backyard lately?

HILLARY: (*Annoyed.*) I *never* have peeked into your backyard, through the *vegetation or* the bushes.

SARA KATE: Then, it's as I thought. (*Beat.*) I am the only one who knows.

HILLARY: (*Annoyed.*) What? The only one who knows what?

SARA KATE: About the elves.

HILLARY: What are you talking about?

SARA KATE: In my backyard that touches your backyard, even as we speak, there is a village of tiny houses built for and by elves.

HILLARY: That's crazy.

SARA KATE: You haven't *seen* it.

HILLARY: Is this some kind of trick?

SARA KATE: No, it's not a trick. I don't blame you for not believing; I wouldn't believe either if I hadn't seen with my own eyes. Right in the yard, tiny little houses that nobody but a tiny elf could live in.

HILLARY: Well, let's go take a look.

SARA KATE: Not yet. Come after four.

HILLARY: I want to go now.

SARA KATE: Well you don't get what you want. Come to my house after four.

HILLARY: Maybe I will; maybe I won't.

SARA KATE: (*Beat.*) You will. Don't come to the front. Come to the backyard. After four.

• • •

Scene 2

> *Friday afternoon. The lights reveal the Lenox backyard, a stoop and a back door to the house, a shed, tools and catalogs on stage. This yard is manicured and sculpted. A new birdbath. Mr. and Mrs. L and then Hillary.*

MR. L: (*About birdbath.*) Do you think it's alright here?

MRS. L: Frank, it's fine, it's great. It's been great every place we've put it in the last hour. Let's leave it there.

MR. L: (*Looks at a catalog.*) It looks bigger in the picture.

MRS. L: There's nothing around it to compare it to in the picture.

MR. L: I should have ordered the biggest one.

MRS. L: This one is fine.

MR. L: Do you really think it looks okay?

MRS. L: Yes, it looks okay!

MR. L: *Just* okay?

MRS. L: It looks…fabulous. Authentic.

MR. L: Yeah, I guess I think it does, too.

MRS. L: Can we address the mess behind the garage now?

MR. L: Now, Honey, I'm going to get to that, I told you I would. All things in good time.

> (*He leaves the catalog on the stoop with the others. Hillary enters with book bag, sees birdbath, begins skipping.*)

HILLARY: Wow, that is too-too good.

MR. L: Hillary, honey, don't skip on the grass, skip on the cement. You're tearing up the lawn.

HILLARY: Sorry, Dad. Looks good, really nice. A lot nicer than the picture.

MR. L: Thanks, honey. Do you think it looks good here?

HILLARY: Well…

MRS. L: Yes, you do, you do.

HILLARY: Yeah, looks good, Dad.

MRS. L: (*About book bag.*) Did they give you homework over the weekend?

HILLARY: No. It's just my diary inside. (*Beat.*) Can Alison and Jane come over tomorrow?

MRS. L: Sure. You can play in the yard.

MR. L: – I gotta move it.

MRS. L: No!

MR. L: No, I gotta. I can't have little girls poking it and knocking it.

HILLARY: We don't do that.

MRS. L: Never mind, Honey. Your Dad has temporarily lost his reason. (*Beat.*) Were the girls mad we didn't do your hair?

HILLARY: …It was okay.

MRS. L: I'll do it tomorrow.

HILLARY: I can do it myself.

MRS. L: Was it fun to dress alike?

HILLARY: Too-too fun, Mom. Everybody noticed.

MR. L: And that's good?

HILLARY: Dad! Of course it's good. It's too-too good. Jane and Alison know all about it. They've been doing it for a long time, and everybody in school knows who they are.

MR. L: And that's too-too good?

HILLARY: *Yeah*, it's too-too good.

MRS. L: (*Beat.*) Are they nice to you, honey?

HILLARY: They let me *dress* like them!

MRS. L: They've been friends for a long time. You're kind of the outsider.

HILLARY: Mom, they're *nice* to me, it's *fine*.

MRS. L: Okay. Do you want a snack?

HILLARY: No. I'm going to visit Sara Kate.

MRS. L: (*Surprised.*) Sara Kate? Sara Kate Connolly?

MR. L: I thought you were friends with Alison and Jane.

HILLARY: I'm not *friends* with Sara Kate; I'm only *visiting* her.

MRS. L: Why don't you invite her over here instead?

HILLARY: Because she doesn't go places.

MRS. L: That house looks like it's going to fall down.

HILLARY: I'm not going in the *house*; we're going to play in her *yard*.

MR. L: (*Sarcastic.*) The yard, great. You'll probably come home with some disease.

HILLARY: There's no disease over there.

MR. L: Or lice. Or poison ivy. We should call the Health Department.

HILLARY: Dad, you can't call the Health Department! You can't!

MR. L: Don't raise your voice to me, young lady.

HILLARY: Oh, I tremble, I just tremble!

MRS. L: Hillary!

HILLARY: Whaaat?!

MRS. L: …We're not going to call the Health Department. Your Dad is just having an opinion. (*Beat.*) How come Sara Kate invited you? What's the occasion?

HILLARY: No occasion. She invited me and I want to go. (*Beat.*) You're always saying how we should be nice to the less fortunate.

MRS. L: (*Beat.*) Alright. But go get a snack. I think you're having low-blood sugar. Eat some protein.

HILLARY: Yes, ma'am.

(*Hillary exits.*)

MR. L: "I tremble. I just tremble"?

MRS. L: I don't know where she comes up with these things.

MR. L: Where do you come up with low-blood sugar?

MRS. L: I don't know. (*Beat.*) Do you think we should have had more kids?

MR. L: Ask me on a different day.

MRS. L: Not for *us*; for her.

MR. L: She's fine, honey, she's just fine. (*Beat.*) Except we'll probably have to de-louse her when she gets home from Sara Kate's.

MRS. L: Don't I recall some stories about *you* and head lice?

MR. L: (*Defensively.*) We all had 'em.

MRS. L: And we all survived. She'll be okay.

MR. L: (*Beat.*) What about that bike business?

MRS. L: Honey, we don't even know if that story was true; let's give Sara Kate the benefit of the doubt.

• • •

Scene 3

Sara Kate's backyard. This yard is the antithesis of the Lenox yard. There are old appliances, car engines, tires, brambles. There, in the midst of the mess, is an orderly elf village. Little houses built with sticks, string, rocks, and leaves; separated by rows of rocks into an elf development. A well in the center of "town." Sara Kate is working on the elf village. Hillary enters with her book bag through the hedge; without looking at Hillary, Sara Kate speaks.

SARA KATE: I first saw it a couple of days ago, it just sort of appeared. They must work all though the night, but it isn't done. You can see where a couple of houses aren't finished, and there's places made ready for houses with no houses on them yet.

HILLARY: How did you know I was here?

SARA KATE: Do you want to see the village or not?

HILLARY: Okay. (*Impressed.*) Wow. Too-too good. Look, they used sticks and leaves for roofs. And rocks to separate the little houses. It's a little neighborhood.

SARA KATE: Yeah, they took rocks from our driveway.

HILLARY: They stole them?

SARA KATE: Yeah, there's rocks gone from our driveway.

HILLARY: Should we put them back?

SARA KATE: No, the elves *need* them, and we don't even *have* a car anymore.

HILLARY: You don't have a *car?*

SARA KATE: No. So what?

HILLARY: Nothing. (*Beat.*) Well, they shouldn't steal. Even rocks.

SARA KATE: The elves don't think so.

HILLARY: (*Shocked.*) They don't think it's wrong to steal?

SARA KATE: Elves have different rules.

HILLARY: They *steal?!*

SARA KATE: Just stuff nobody is using. Or stuff from mean rich people.

HILLARY: How do they know who's mean?

SARA KATE: They just know.

HILLARY: Look, a well, a tiny little well. Let's haul up some water.

SARA KATE: Leave it alone. It's very fragile.

HILLARY: It *all* looks real fragile. What happens when it rains?

SARA KATE: They rebuild and repair. Elves are at the complete mercy of earth forces.

HILLARY: (*Pause.*) How do you know so much?

SARA KATE: ...I think the elves sneak stuff into my brain.

HILLARY: What do you mean?

SARA KATE: I tried to haul up some water and all of a sudden I was thinking "the elves won't like this."

HILLARY: (*Beat.*) Sara Kate, are you sure elves built this? Maybe this was built by mice. Mice could live in these houses quite nicely.

SARA KATE: Mice! That is really – that is just – that is so *stupid!* When did you ever hear of mice building houses?!

HILLARY: Or even a person could have built these houses.

SARA KATE: Look, I didn't have to invite you here today, and I didn't have to show you this. I thought you might like to see an elf village for a change. If you don't believe elves built this, that's your problem. I *know* they did.

HILLARY: I never saw elves in *my* backyard.

SARA KATE: Well, of course not.

HILLARY: What do you mean?

SARA KATE: (*Sincere, kind.*) Elves would never go in your backyard, no offense,

Hillary, but your backyard would not offer any protection. See, elves need to hide, they hate it when people see them. In the olden days, it didn't matter so much, but now, there's too many people, and too many bad ones; elves can't risk being seen by a bad person.

HILLARY: (*Worried.*) Why? What would happen?

SARA KATE: There's no telling, but it would be very terrible. They know they're safe here, there's a million places to hide in this yard.

HILLARY: (*Looks around, impressed.*) Yeah. I see what you mean.

(*Hillary sneaks up on things and peeks behind them, looking for elves, as she begins to believe Sara Kate's elf information.*)

SARA KATE: Where, for example, would they find stones in your yard to make these little private lots?

HILLARY: (*Realization.*) Right. Our driveway is all paved with cement. There's no rocks anywhere in our yard. And Dad rakes the leaves the second they fall; so there's nothing to make a roof out of! (*She begins to skip.*) Wow. Your yard is perfect for elves! Look at all the junk to hide in, and strings and wire to make the houses, and rocks, and leaves for roofs. (*She stops skipping abruptly.*) Oh, is it alright to skip?

SARA KATE: What are you talking about? (*Sara Kate skips and jumps and prances about.*) Of course it's alright to skip. It makes the elves really happy.

HILLARY: It does? (*She skips.*)

SARA KATE: Yes! And if you make them happy enough, they trust you and let you peek at them. (*Stops suddenly.*) Listen! I hear them laughing now.

(*Hillary stops skipping. They listen.*)

SARA KATE: Their language is like earth sounds. But if you listen real careful, you can hear that it's really elves.

(*Both girls are affected by a felt presence. Hillary is amazed.*)

HILLARY: (*Whispers.*) Sara Kate? I think they're here.

SARA KATE: Yes, I feel it too. Don't talk about them or they'll go away. Act natural.

(*Hillary tries to act natural. She hums and opens her book bag.*)

SARA KATE: (*Disdain.*) Are you doing *homework?!*

HILLARY: (*Whispers.*) I was going to write something down. In my diary.

SARA KATE: Don't whisper, whispering isn't natural. What are you going to write?

HILLARY: About the elves. I keep a record, a written record of everything. I document my life.

SARA KATE: Why do you want to do that?

HILLARY: In case we get famous – me and Alison and Jane. I have all our documentation in my diary.

SARA KATE: I don't want to be famous. (*Beat.*) I'm going to straighten the rocks.

HILLARY: I can do that, too.

SARA KATE: I don't want to interrupt your documenting.

HILLARY: It's no interruption.

(*Hillary puts diary in book bag. The girls start to straighten rocks at one of the "lots."*)

HILLARY: Oh, look.

SARA KATE: Little steps.

HILLARY: (*At the same time.*) Little steps!

SARA KATE: Oh! Orion's belt, the Big Dipper, the Little Dipper, the Pleiades, Virgo, Gemini, Aquarius, Libra, Pisces, Capricorn. Ten! (*Beat.*) How come you didn't punch me?

HILLARY: What are you talking about?!

SARA KATE: Ten stars. We said the same thing at the same time. You're supposed to punch me while I say ten stars.

HILLARY: (*Realizing.*) Sara Kate, you're supposed to say "pididdle," and then make *me* say ten of something, and punch *me*. You don't have it right at all.

SARA KATE: (*Flares up.*) Who cares?! It's *your* stupid game. I just did it because I thought *you* liked it, *I* don't like it, it's a stupid game. Who cares?!

HILLARY: (*Trying to end the argument.*) I'm sorry. I didn't mean – you're right! It *is* a stupid game, you're right. Who cares?

SARA KATE: Yeah, who cares.

(*Pause. Hillary walks near the elf houses.*)

HILLARY: (*An idea.*) The elves must think we're giants!

SARA KATE: (*Impressed.*) What?!

HILLARY: Yes! They think we are kindly human giants! (*Stands on something to look around.*) Kindly giant sisters who watch over elves.

SARA KATE: (*Pretending to keep watch, a giant voice.*) The kindly giant sisters scan the horizon for signs of danger! All clear on the western bank!

HILLARY: (*Playing along.*) All clear on the eastern bank.

(*Hillary walks in a large fashion. A lumbering, giant walk. Sara Kate does too.*)

HILLARY: The kindly giant sisters walk the land, keeping watch.

SARA KATE: The ground quakes with their steps.

HILLARY: But the elves have no fear.

(A figure appears in a window. It is a thin woman wearing a nightgown; she is clearly very ill, with wild hair.)

SARA KATE: No dangerous humans in sight.

HILLARY: Only the kindly *giant sisters*.

SARA KATE: *(At the same time.)* – *Giant sisters.* All elves may proceed to their homes.

(Hillary sees the figure in the window. She is frozen in fear.)

SARA KATE: Elves may continue construction on the village. The kindly giant sisters will lift and carry objects of great size –

(Sara Kate notices Hillary and looks to the house where she sees the figure.)

SARA KATE: You have to go.

HILLARY: What is – who is –

SARA KATE: Just go. You have to go.

HILLARY: But I –

SARA KATE: No buts. Get going.

HILLARY: But you shouldn't –

SARA KATE: Here! Here's your bag. Just take it and go. Go home Hillary.

(Hillary leaves through the hedge. Sara Kate sighs and turns toward the house, where the figure has disappeared.)

• • •

Scene 4

Immediately following. The Lenox backyard. Hillary enters her backyard again, out of breath and confused. She is glad to see all the familiar, friendly, neat garden. She sits under the back stoop light, removes diary from her book bag and records her confused, scattered thoughts.

HILLARY: There's a ghost in Sara Kate Connolly's yard. We were playing with the elves, I mean their village. I didn't think it would be real. Why would elves build in Sara Kate's yard? She is a human mess. She's bony and dirty and dresses bad. There's nothing magical about her. Elves should live in a yard of someone...beautiful or...soft. I don't know why they chose Sara Kate's brain to leave messages in or Sara Kate's yard to live in. Unless they like haunted houses. Jane said Mrs Connolly is dead and maybe she is because I just saw a ghost in the window – It looked more like a ghost than a person. A skinny, creepy, sickly –

MR. L: *(At the door.)* Hillary?

HILLARY: Oh!!

(*Hillary gasps and jumps away in fright, dropping her diary to the ground. Mr. Lenox enters.*)

MR. L: Boo.

HILLARY: (*Relieved.*) I thought you were a ghost.

MR. L: Not yet. You better get on in, honey; *somebody* hasn't set the table yet!

HILLARY: Oh, man, the table!

(*Hillary takes her book bag but leaves the diary where it fell. Mr. Lenox picks up his catalogs, absently snatches the diary, puts everything in a small shed that is attached to the side of the house. He enters the house. Lights fade. A person carrying a candle is seen in the Connolly window.*)

• • •

Scene 5

Saturday morning, the next day. The Lenox backyard. Mr. and Mrs. Lenox are working in the yard. They are happy.

MR. L: I should have been a gardener.

MRS. L: You are a gardener.

MR. L: I mean a for-real gardener. On somebody's gigantic estate. The gardener, taking care of the big boss's flowers and shrubs.

MRS. L: And what would I be doing?

MR. L: You'd be a corporate lawyer. How else could I afford to be somebody's gardener?

MRS. L: Oh, great, you get to garden and I have to slave in some corporate office. This isn't sounding fair.

MR. L: Yeah, but now we both slave in offices, and nobody's having any fun.

MRS. L: This is fun.

MR. L: This…is making me *hungry*. Where's our kid?

MRS. L: Out like a light.

MR. L: I wish I could sleep like that.

MRS. L: You have to be a kid to sleep like that.

MR. L: Let's make pancakes; that'll get her up.

(*Hillary runs into the garden in her nightgown. Mr. L grabs her.*)

MR. L: Whoa.

HILLARY: Mom, Dad, I was having the best dream, it was the best dream, all about elves. It was so real. There was an elf Mayor, and elf villagers, and an elf ballerina. I want to go see.

MR. L: Honey, it was a dream.

HILLARY: Yeah, but there are elves. Over there. (*Points.*)

MRS. L: Maybe, you should get dressed first.

HILLARY: (*Looking at her nightgown, surprised.*) Oh, man. I was going next door in my nightgown. I need to get dressed. I need to wake up.

MRS. L: What time are Alison and Jane coming?

HILLARY: Alison and Jane are coming! I forgot. I completely forgot. I got to do my hair.

(*Hillary runs toward the house.*)

MRS. L: Don't forget to get dressed.

HILLARY: Oh, Mother!

(*Hillary exits.*)

MRS. L: I recognize that tone of voice. I think I used it on *my* mother.

MR. L: (*Joking.*) Was your mother as unreasonable as you?

MRS. L: Probably.

MR. L: (*Beat.*) I don't remember elves in my youth.

MRS. L: Your youth is too far away to remember.

MR. L: I wish they'd play in our backyard. Where it's neat, and clean and safe.

MRS. L: Neat and clean and safe is no fun.

(*Alison and Jane come into the yard; they are wearing matching jackets. Alison carries a department store bag. The girls are overtly polite to parents; the parents are tolerant, but not fooled.*)

JANE: Good morning, Mrs. Lenox; good morning Mr. Lenox.

ALISON: We hope we're not disturbing you.

JANE: Hillary invited us.

MRS. L: We know. We're getting the yard ready.

JANE: Oh, we don't need anything special.

MR. L: It isn't for you, it's for the yard.

MRS. L: Frank. Nice jackets.

ALISON: Oh, Mrs. Lenox, I'm so glad you like them. We just got them, just now, this morning.

JANE: My Dad dropped me off early at Alison's.

ALISON: Too early to come here. So Mom took us to Mildred's.

JANE: These were on sale.

ALISON: Really inexpensive.

JANE: Mrs. Mancini paid for them. She said they were on her because they were so cheap. We got one for Hillary.

ALISON: I hope it's okay.

MR. L: How do you know she'll like it?

ALISON: She'll like it; *we* like it.

(*The parents exchange a look.*)

MRS. L: It's okay, but next time, ask in advance.

ALISON: Oh, we will. This was an emergency.

MR. L: Now girls, this is new sod. No running and jumping and carrying-on that's going to rip it up. And be careful of the birdbath, it isn't cemented in yet. And watch where you walk, there's new ground cover planted.

MRS. L: (*High irony.*) Yes, girls, Mr. Lenox is working hard on the yard so Hillary has a nice place to *play*.

MR. L: (*To Mrs.*) Now, Honey, it isn't ready for play yet, when it's ready for play, then they can play as hard as they want. In the meantime, they have to be careful. Now, here, right here, you can play, do whatever you want, right here.

JANE: Where, Mr. Lenox?

MR. L: Right here, between here and here.

(*The girls walk to the safe patch. It's very small.*)

ALISON: Here?

MR. L: Yeah.

MRS. L: We were on our way to some pancakes. Have you girls eaten?

JANE: Yes.

ALISON: Uh huh.

MRS. L: Okay.

MR. L: Have fun.

ALISON: Thank you.

(*Alison and Jane smile until the Lenoxes go inside, then they start jumping on the safe patch.*)

JANE: You can play right here.

ALISON: Play where it's safe!

JANE: Don't knock over the birdbath!

ALISON: Don't tear up the sod!

JANE: Don't rip up the ground cover.

ALISON: What *is* ground cover?

JANE: What's *ground cover?* What's *sod?*

(*They are laughing when Hillary comes out. Her hair matches theirs. She has her book bag.*)

HILLARY: Hi.

JANE: We got you a jacket.

(*Alison gives her the box. Hillary opens it and puts on jacket.*)

HILLARY: Wow.

ALISON: Just like ours. Your mother says it's okay.

HILLARY: Too-too good.

ALISON: Your hair looks good.

HILLARY: I did it myself.

JANE: See.

HILLARY: Two mirrors, like you said. Look, it fits. (*Beat.*) What do you want to do?

JANE: I want to knock over the birdbath.

> (*Jane and Alison laugh.*)

HILLARY: Dad worries a lot about the garden.

JANE: He said we could stand right here, between here and here. Come here, let's see if we even all fit.

> (*They try.*)

JANE: Closer, closer!

ALISON: Inhale and we'll all fit.

> (*They don't fit, they giggle.*)

ALISON: Your father is mental, Hillary.

JANE: Not mental, demented.

HILLARY: All fathers are demented.

ALISON: My father's never *been* in our yard. The only yard he goes on is the golf course. He goes every weekend.

JANE: My father hires somebody.

HILLARY: Dad's pretty fussy.

JANE: Demented. Hey! I forgot. What happened with Sara Kate yesterday?

ALISON: Oh, yeah. What was her big secret?

HILLARY: Something she wanted me to see in her yard is all.

ALISON: What?

HILLARY: It's this little town. She says elves built it.

ALISON: Elves?! Is she nuts or what?

JANE: There's no such thing as elves.

ALISON: Did you go over there? (*Hillary nods.*) By yourself?

HILLARY: Just for a minute.

ALISON: Yuk.

JANE: Next time, wait for us. (*Rhymes.*) The Migh-tee Three visit Sara Kate Con-no-ly. Hey! Does anybody want to hear my song?

ALISON: Oh! Its too-too good, Hillary.

HILLARY: Sing it.

> (*Jane sings, Alison sings along for some.*)
> We are the Mighty Three,
> Alison, Hillary and Me.
> We dress alike and we never fight,

Don't listen to you cause we know we're right.

We are three friends for sure.

And we don't want any more.

We are the Mighty Three,

Alison, Hillary and Me.

HILLARY: That is too-too good.

ALISON: We can sing it at the next assembly.

HILLARY: Then we'll really be famous.Did you write down the words?

JANE: No, they're in my head.

ALISON: You should document them, Hillary.

HILLARY: Yeah. (*She looks in her book bag.*) My diary's gone.

ALISON: Oh, brother.

HILLARY: Maybe it's in my room.

JANE: Forget it; you can write the words later.

HILLARY: (*Worried.*) I wonder what I did with it.

ALISON: Oh, it doesn't matter.

HILLARY: Yes, it does. I had it yesterday. I wrote what Mr. Decker said about us. I always put it in here.

ALISON: Did you take it next door?

HILLARY: I take it everywhere.

ALISON: Well, that's where your diary went, Hillary.

JANE: Oh, yeah. Sara Kate Connolly made it disappear.

HILLARY: No she didn't.

ALISON: Sure she did. You're going to have to buy a new diary, Hillary. That's all there is to it.

(*Sara Kate enters from the shrubbery.*)

ALISON: Don't look now, Hillary, but your new best friend has arrived.

HILLARY: What do you want?

JANE: Were you listening behind the bushes?

SARA KATE: I need to talk to Hillary.

JANE: (*Snide.*) Did you bring her diary?

SARA KATE: What?

HILLARY: Where's my diary?

(*Pause. Sara Kate enters the yard. She looks around the yard, amazed by what is to her great opulence.*)

SARA KATE: I need to talk to Hillary.

HILLARY: What? What do you want?

ALISON: We don't have any secrets. Talk.

HILLARY: It's true, we don't have secrets; talk, or get out.

SARA KATE: There's been a surprising development in the elf village.

HILLARY: (*Excited, in spite of herself.*) What is it? Did you see elves?

JANE: Or the Easter Bunny?

ALISON: Or Santa?

SARA KATE: I didn't see them, but they've been there.

HILLARY: (*Torn.*) Well, how do you know?

ALISON: Oh, brother.

SARA KATE: They've *been* there! They built something. Something…impressive.

JANE: Let's go see.

SARA KATE: No. Only Hillary is invited.

ALISON: Well, Hillary won't go.

JANE: Not unless you invite us, too.

SARA KATE: Hillary? Do you want to come see what the elves built?

HILLARY: Yes…but only if Alison and Jane can come, too.

SARA KATE: Suit yourself. (*Walks in front of each, counting and pointing.*) One, one, one.

(*Sara Kate exits through the hedge. The girls are momentarily stunned. Pause, then.*)

JANE: Weird, she's *weird*. One, one, one, what? Is that as high as she can count?

ALISON: She's mental. She's too-too mental for me.

JANE: You don't believe in elves, Hillary.

HILLARY: (*Hesitating.*) No. But there is something in Sara Kate's yard. A little town. Somebody had to build it.

JANE: Yeah, somebody. Somebody Sara Kate Connolly.

ALISON: We have a song to practice, Hillary. We don't have any time for elves. Okay?

HILLARY: Yeah. I know.

(*Jane and Alison begin the song. Hillary hesitates, then joins in.*)

• • •

Scene 6

The Connolly backyard. Sara Kate. An elf-sized ferris wheel made from bicycle tire rims, quite amazing. There are other changes as well. Hillary, carrying her old jacket and book bag, comes quietly through the hedge, Sara Kate couldn't possibly hear.

SARA KATE: Isn't it beautiful?

HILLARY: I didn't make a sound; how did you know I was here?

SARA KATE: I don't *know*; I just…know. (*About the wheel.*) What do you think?

HILLARY: (*She drops her jacket and book bag and walks around and admires it.*) It's really something. Tiny little seats.

SARA KATE: Elf size.

HILLARY: How did they carry the tires?

SARA KATE: Many many of them working together.

HILLARY: How do you know?

SARA KATE: Information gets into my brain.

HILLARY: Is it a voice gets in your brain?

SARA KATE: Yes.

HILLARY: What's it sound like?

SARA KATE: It sounds…like me. (*Beat.*) The tires are from that old bike. See? The bike tires are gone. These are those tires.

HILLARY: How are you going to ride it?

SARA KATE: It's an old piece of junk; nobody could ride it. See this?

(*Something that might be a tiny swimming pool.*)

HILLARY: A swimming pool. Oh my goodness! They made a little swimming pool.

SARA KATE: Or something.

HILLARY: You know what? I bet they're going to make a whole amusement park. Right in your backyard. Merry-go-round, roller coaster. It's perfect. The elves will ride the rides until they get hot, and then they'll go for a swim.

SARA KATE: (*Unconvinced.*) Maybe.

HILLARY: What do you mean "maybe?"

SARA KATE: Elves are not tiny human beings. They're elves, completely different from humans. It's possible to jump to wrong conclusions.

(*Hillary considers the pool.*)

HILLARY: (*An idea.*) It's a power source.

SARA KATE: (*Impressed.*) Aaaaah, yesssss; combination hydro and photovoltaics.

HILLARY: Yeah, a power source.

SARA KATE: (*Playing.*) The power streams down from the sun –

HILLARY: (*Playing.*) And the stars, too. It never stops coming down, a never ending source of power –

SARA KATE: If you're feeling a little energy drain, stop at the power pool –

HILLARY: For a fill up. (*Sticks her finger in the pool; she expands.*) I'm filling up with energy. Pow, pow.

SARA KATE: Don't explode!

HILLARY: Now I'm full of energy. Energy to heat the houses.

SARA KATE: Except elves don't get cold.

HILLARY: No way!

SARA KATE: Well, they dooooo, but not until it's freezing. When they finally get so cold they can't stand it, they move into empty human houses. (*Neatens the village.*) Come on; the kindly giant sisters must help the elves again.

HILLARY: The Hillary giant lines up the scattered stones around the elf houses.

SARA KATE: The Sara Kate giant gathers berries for the elves' dinner.

HILLARY: And the Hillary giant helps her.

(*Sara Kate eats berries. Hillary sees and tries some; they're terrible.*)

HILLARY: Yuk. These are terrible, yuk. Poison I bet.

SARA KATE: (*Playing.*) Not to an elf. (*Pops a berry in her mouth.*)

HILLARY: (*Serious.*) Don't eat that, Sara Kate. (*Beat.*) Are you hungry?

SARA KATE: (*Serious.*) I'm not hungry.

HILLARY: You can eat at my house.

SARA KATE: (*Subdued.*) No. I eat with my mom. (*The game again.*) Here. Put leaves and little sticks in this box, Hillary giant.

(*Sara Kate suddenly turns, as if to see something. Hillary looks, too, but the elves are gone.*)

SARA KATE: Gone.

HILLARY: I wish I could see an elf.

SARA KATE: You have to sort of see them out of the corner of your eye.

(*Hillary looks forward, trying to see sideways.*)

SARA KATE: Don't worry if you don't see one right away. It might take them a long time to trust us. Move your bag.

(*Hillary picks up her book bag, remembers her diary. Starts looking around.*)

HILLARY: If the elves took the tires and all, but they need them to cool off and stuff, I think that's alright.

SARA KATE: (*Not really paying attention, walking in the giant way.*) Of course, it's alright.

HILLARY: But it would probably be wrong if they took somebody's personal stuff.

SARA KATE: Human rules don't work for elves. What are you doing way over there?

HILLARY: If there was something that a human being *owned* and *needed* and *loved*, and an elf didn't need it or love it or anything. It would be wrong for that elf to take it.

SARA KATE: What are you *doing?* There's no building materials over there.

HILLARY: I'm looking for something.

SARA KATE: What?

HILLARY: My diary. I'm looking for my diary.

SARA KATE: Your diary isn't over there.

HILLARY: (*Hopeful.*) Where is it?

SARA KATE: How should I know? Is that what this is about? Your diary? (*Beat.*) You *do* think I stole your diary.

HILLARY: (*Too fast.*) No. No. I...I lost it. I can't find it. And I had it here yesterday, so I thought, maybe..

SARA KATE: What?! You thought, what?!

HILLARY: I thought...maybe...I *left* it here. By mistake.

SARA KATE: You think I sneaked into your stupid book bag and stole your stupid diary. Boy, you *are* the same as Jane and Alison. Every time something happens, you blame it on me. You are sickening.

HILLARY: (*Getting mad.*) What am I supposed to think? The last time I ever saw it I was here –

SARA KATE: (*Shouting.*) Who cares what you think? You're a stupid little girl with stupid little friends.

HILLARY: (*Shouting.*) I am not stupid and my friends are not stupid. We have a song –

SARA KATE: A stupid song to show how stupid your brains are –

HILLARY: Don't you call us stupid. You got held back. You're the only one's stupid around here.

SARA KATE: Get out. Get out of my yard.

HILLARY: I was going to give you my jacket. I brought my jacket all the way over here to give it to you.

SARA KATE: Who wants your stupid jacket?! Get out.

(*The ferris wheel spins by itself, whirs, dazzles. The girls are silent, amazed. Hillary stops it.*)

SARA KATE: (*Gently.*) Why did you stop it?

HILLARY: It scared me.

SARA KATE: (*Sympathizing.*) Oh, don't be scared of elves. Elves can't hurt people. People can hurt elves is all.

(*The window shade on the house is pulled to one side.*)

HILLARY: Do you want my jacket? My mother said I could give it to you. I got this new one.

SARA KATE: So you could match your good friends.

HILLARY:...You never wear a coat.

SARA KATE: I don't...get cold.

HILLARY: Like an elf.

(*Sara Kate notices the window shade.*)

SARA KATE: Oh, man. I gotta go before the bank closes. Do you want to go shop with me?

HILLARY: Do you go to the corner, to Mr. Neal's?

SARA KATE: No. I go to the supermarket. Things are cheaper, and it's…just better to go to the big stores.

HILLARY: My mother would kill me if I went all the way to the supermarket.

SARA KATE: So don't go, no skin off my nose.

HILLARY: No, okay, I'll go. I'll go with you.

• • •

Scene 7

> *Immediately following. The girls walk into the big city. There is a bigness all around them, a large city with its accompanying city/store sounds. Tall buildings, traffic. A bigness in which a little girl can move anonymously. Hillary stands back and watches and listens amazed at Sara Kate. Sara Kate talks to unseen functionaries.*
>
> *At the bank. Sara Kate downstage, front; Hillary watches slightly upstage.*

SARA KATE: (*Ultra sweet.*) Hello, I need to cash my mother's check, ma'am. See? she signed it right on the back. Her signature is on file here and you can look it up. *I* cash the checks because she works and can't come here, and it's real convenient for me to do it because the bank is right near our house. (*Worried.*) I *always* do it, ask anybody….(*Relieved.*) twenties will be fine.

(*Sara Kate and Hillary walk. Street sounds. Then they enter the pharmacy. Hillary watches as Sara Kate talks.*)

SARA KATE: (*Worried.*) I *know* the prescription has run out, but the person who was here yesterday *promised* to call the doctor to OK the refill. This is very terrible. You see, my mother needs her medicine and she's already gone a whole day without it, because that *other* man, he said he'd call the doctor. Could you just give me one refill for one month's supply?… Great, great.

(*At the grocery store. Walking with Hillary.*)

SARA KATE: (*To Hillary.*) In the grocery store, you only buy *plain* boxes of stuff, no brands because they cost more money. If you buy the stuff in the plain boxes it costs a lot less. Cream of Wheat in the plain box lasts a long time and it really fills you up when you're hungry. That way you have enough to send some money to the electric company and the phone bill; you don't want them turned off because to get them turned back on you gotta give them *more* money, for a *deposit.*

HILLARY: What's a deposit?

SARA KATE: It's a whole bunch of money that you don't get anything *for*. Only poor people have to pay one.

HILLARY:…That doesn't make sense.

SARA KATE: You're tellin' me.

(*Hillary is amazed.*)

• • •

Scene 8

Lenox yard. Saturday dusk. Mrs. Lenox is puttering. Hillary enters from the hedge. Hillary is nervous because she knows her mother would be furious if she knew she'd been shopping with Sara Kate.

MRS. L: It's about time you were home.

HILLARY: Why?

MRS. L: It's getting dark is why. It's time you were home.

HILLARY: Well, I *am* home.

MRS. L: And you should be.

HILLARY: Well I *am*.

MRS. L: Hillary!

HILLARY: Whaaat?

MRS. L: (*Beat.*) I think being with Sara Kate is making you cross.

HILLARY: (*Cross.*) I'm not cross.

MRS. L: If Sara Kate is going to put you in a bad mood, we're not going to let you go over there.

HILLARY: Mom, you have to let me.

MRS. L: No, we don't have to.

(*Mr. L enters from house. He carries an envelope.*)

MR. L: (*To Mrs. L.*) Honey, did you pay the phone bill last month?

MRS. L: Sure I did.

MR. L: This says second notice.

MRS. L: (*Testy.*) I guess I forgot, I don't know.

MR. L: Okay, I just don't want, you know, the old credit rating to slip.

MRS. L: (*Testy.*) I'm sorry.

HILLARY: Don't worry. They don't turn off the phone unless you skip *two* months.

MR. L: I didn't know that.

HILLARY: Yeah, and if they *do* cut it off, there's a kind of phone service you can get for free.

MR. L: What kind is that?

HILLARY: It's a kind of phone service that you can only call *out* on.

MR. L: Why would I want that?

HILLARY: It's for emergencies; Sara Kate says the phone company *has* to let you have one. It's so you can call for help at 911. But nobody can call you.

MR. L: What else does Sara Kate say?

HILLARY: She says you can get water from the hydrant for free.

MR. L: Oh?

HILLARY: Yeah, and the electric bill, if you just pay a little bit, they won't turn it off, they're not allowed to if you're trying to pay.

MR. L: Oh, boy.

(*Parents exchange a look.*)

HILLARY: What?

MR. L: Hillary, what happens if everybody does that?

HILLARY: I don't know!

MR. L: Somebody has to pay for that electricity. The way it gets paid is everybody else's rates go up.

HILLARY: Poor people have to pay a deposit!

MR. L: (*Pause, gently.*) Hillary, I think you shouldn't play with Sara Kate anymore.

HILLARY: But, Dad –

MR. L: No, I think it would be better if you don't see her anymore.

HILLARY: But you don't even know her.

MR. L: Honey, life is hard enough if people play by the rules; it's impossible if they don't.

HILLARY: But Dad –

MR. L: Hillary. No. Everybody has to do their part. It's like a *relay* race – if somebody on the team doesn't run their part, the whole team loses.

HILLARY: We don't even have races like that at my school.

(*Brief pause.*)

MRS. L: Hillary, honey, go wash up for dinner.

(*Hillary sighs, goes inside.*)

MR. L: Don't say it.

MRS. L: She's a little kid.

MR. L: She's not too little to learn.

• • •

Scene 9

Alison enters, mad, sits in a huff. Jane enters, then Hillary, who is walking like a giant.

ALISON: How *could* you, how *could* you, after we practiced all *week*? We practiced *all week*.

HILLARY: I looked into the audience and all of a sudden I couldn't remember the words or anything.

JANE: What are you *doing*?

HILLARY: (*Caught.*) Oh! I was walking like a giant.

ALISON: Walking?! Pay attention, Hillary. We worked so hard on the song to make it right. And it was stupid. What's the point of practicing if we're stupid?

JANE: What were you thinking about, Hillary?

HILLARY: I was wondering what to do when the toilet gets stopped up.

ALISON: The toilet! You are mental; you're mental!

JANE: You call your father, that's what you do.

ALISON: Kids don't have to fix toilets, Hillary.

HILLARY: Some kids do I bet.

ALISON: Well *we* don't.

HILLARY: We're pretty lucky. We're lucky.

ALISON: We're *not* lucky.

HILLARY: We are. Our parents can buy us stuff, and we have outfits. Everybody doesn't have outfits. Or dinners.

ALISON: Oh boy, wrap it up and send it to the starving children around the world, Hillary.

HILLARY: I'm just saying.

ALISON: Are we supposed to stand around and feel bad because we're not starving?

HILLARY: I don't know.

ALISON: Well I know. And it's stupid to feel bad because somebody else is starving.

HILLARY: Sara Kate doesn't have it so good.

ALISON: Is that what this is about? Sara Kate!?

(*Jane holds a pencil to her nose and prances around.*)

JANE: Hey, hey! Who am I? Who *am* I?

HILLARY: What are you doing?

JANE: I was being Sara Kate Connolly.

ALISON: (*To Hillary.*) Sara Kate took a math test with her pencil taped to her nose.

HILLARY: No!

ALISON: For sure. Right before she *disappeared!*

HILLARY: Maybe she had a...fit or something. Maybe that's why she hasn't been in school.

JANE: I never heard of a fit where you tape pencils to your nose.

HILLARY: There's all *kinds* of fits! Maybe she's really sick.

ALISON: She *is* really sick, Hillary. That's what we've been telling you.

JANE: She's mentally sick.

HILLARY: Sometimes I think *you're* mentally sick.

JANE: *What* did you say?

HILLARY: I was *joking.*

ALISON: Ha Ha.

HILLARY: I mean if somebody is really sick then somebody should visit her.

JANE: You better not.

HILLARY: I mean who's taking care of the elf village?

ALISON: Oh, brother.

JANE: Your parents will get really mad if you go over there.

ALISON: Let's go to Jane's and practice.

HILLARY: I can't. I have to go straight home. (*Beat.*) I said I would.

JANE: (*To Alison, exiting.*) Come on, Alison, you and me can go practice.

ALISON: (*Exiting.*) We don't need to practice; *we* didn't forget the words.

HILLARY: Bye.

(*Hillary watches until the girls are out of sight, then runs off.*)

• • •

Scene 10

Inside the Connolly house. It is very run down. A knock at the door.

HILLARY: (*Off.*) Hello? Is anybody home? Sara Kate?
(*Hillary pushes open the door and sticks her head in.*)

HILLARY: Hello, your door is open. (*Enters and gasps.*) Wow, they're gone. They're all moved away!
(*She enters, finds it a scary, uncomfortable place, starts to exit, hears something (the sound of a rocking chair on wood.).*)

HILLARY: Sara Kate?
(*The sound continues. She looks toward the sound.*)

HILLARY: Elves! It's the elves.
(*Hillary crosses the stage in the semi-darkness, following the sound, which grows louder. Pushes open "a door," where in full window light she sees Sara Kate in rocking chair with her mother. Mrs. Connolly is a thin, sick, frightened creature. Mrs. Connolly and Sara Kate look toward Hillary. Hillary gasps. She is confused. She starts to babble.*)

HILLARY: I thought no one was here. I thought the sound was elves. What's wrong with your mother?
(*Sara Kate carefully gets up so as not to startle her mother, as Hillary continues to babble.*)

HILLARY: You weren't in school, I thought you were sick; I thought the elves needed help. The ferris wheel is knocked over. I saw it in the yard. I'm not allowed to come here anymore. What's wrong with your mother?!

SARA KATE: (*Whispers, practically hissing.*) Get out. Get out of my house. Don't ever come back. And don't you tell anybody. Don't you dare tell anybody.

HILLARY: Sara Kate, it's me, Hillary.

SARA KATE: You get out and don't you come back. You forget you ever were in this house. You forget it, erase it from your mind, it didn't happen.
(*Hillary runs out. Sara Kate and Mrs. Connolly, alone. Mrs. Connolly covers her face with her hands; Sara Kate comforts her. Blackout.*)

END OF ACT ONE

ACT TWO
Scene 1

A week later, the Lenox yard. Home from school, Hillary reads the diary entry she just wrote.

HILLARY: Dear Diary. (*Beat.*) Dear Diary *Substitute*, Or Journal, or whatever you are. I'm not mad at Sara Kate anymore about my real diary she stole, even though I know I ought to be. I can't be mad at her anymore. Once I almost told Alison and Jane what I saw, but I promised not to. Even if I did tell about it, I don't know what I would say; sometimes I think maybe it wasn't real. Maybe it was another elf dream. A bad one this time.

(Mr. Lenox enters from the gate with a gigantic trellis.)

MR. L: Hey, there's my girl.

HILLARY: Dad! What are you doing home?

MR. L: I took the afternoon off. Look what I got. I'm going to plant a trumpet vine next spring. Now it will have something to grow on.

HILLARY: Next spring is a long way away, Dad.

MR. L: Nah, it's right around the corner. Trumpet flowers are gorgeous.

HILLARY: I don't think I know what they look like.

MR. L: Gorgeous. Last night I dreamt I *was* one. What do you think of that?

HILLARY: That's pretty weird. Did you come home early just to work in the garden, Dad?

MR. L: Just! Just to work in the garden?! Yeah, I did.

HILLARY: Wow. Too-too good.

MR. L: I'll say, too-too good. Plants don't talk back.

HILLARY: Plants don't talk at all.

MR. L: Even better. Where should we put the trellis?

HILLARY: I don't know.

MR. L: How about by the hedge?

HILLARY: Okay.

(They put the trellis in front of the hedge. Hillary stands back to look.)

HILLARY: (*Sad.*) Oh. Oh, Dad, can we put it somewhere else?

MR. L: What's wrong with here?

HILLARY: I just – I don't – It's like we're putting up bars between us and Sara Kate.

(Hillary turns abruptly, gasps slightly.)

MR. L: What?

HILLARY: Did you see something over there?

MR. L: No.

HILLARY: I thought I saw something. Right there.

MR. L: It was probably a bird.

HILLARY: Maybe.

(*Hillary is silent. Mr. L moves the trellis away from the hedge.*)

MR. L: We'll put the trellis somewhere else.

HILLARY: Okay.

MR. L: I didn't know you were still thinking about Sara Kate.

HILLARY: Dad. I *want* to forget about her; I want to forget all about her, but she's always in my brain. I think I see her out of the corner of my eye, but then I turn to look, and she's not there.

MR. L: You weren't friends very long.

HILLARY: Dad. Dad. I know, I *know*. And sometimes it wasn't even very fun to be friends with her. But it was special. She's special.

MR. L: (*Beat.*) I guess I didn't realize. (*Beat.*) Hey, let's plant some bulbs. It'll clear our brains.

HILLARY: Now? In the cold?

MR. L: Yeah, plant them in the fall for flowers in the spring.

HILLARY: Okay.

MR. L: Get the bulb thing out of the shed.

(*Hillary looks in the shed.*)

MR. L: There's a lot of gardening to be done in winter. Planting bulbs, pruning trees.

HILLARY: (*At shed.*) I don't see the bulb thing.

MR. L: Look on the shelf. It's much less traumatic to the tree if its branches are cut in winter when the sap is slow.

(*Hillary crosses back to Mr. Lenox with her diary.*)

MR. L: Whatcha got there? That's not a bulb thing.

HILLARY: Dad, this is my diary. What's my diary doing in the shed?

MR. L: *That's* your diary? Oh. Oops. I put it there; I put it in the shed. I didn't think.

HILLARY: Oh, man, oh, no, oh, Dad. Oh, Dad. Sara Kate thinks I think she stole my diary.

MR. L: Why does she think that?

HILLARY: Because I *did* think it. Oh, man.

MR. L: Sorry, Honey, really.

HILLARY: I'm an idiot.

MR. L: (*Beat.*) Well, maybe you better get over there and apologize.

HILLARY: Really?

MR. L: Yeah, okay, go on.

• • •

Scene 2

The Connolly backyard, near dusk. Hillary comes through the hedge connecting the two yards. The elf village is in disarray; the ferris wheel is on its side. She walks around for a moment, Sara Kate enters, she wears no coat in spite of the cold.

SARA KATE: Hello.

HILLARY: (*Startled.*) Oh. Oh. Sara Kate, it's you. I didn't hear you. You're here!

SARA KATE: Of course I'm here.

HILLARY: I thought – I don't know, I haven't seen you. (*Beat.*) How's your mother?

SARA KATE: She's fine. How should she be?

HILLARY: Sometimes she's sick.

SARA KATE: Sometimes everybody is sick.

HILLARY: When she gets sick, you take care of her.

SARA KATE: So what? When I get sick, she takes care of me.

HILLARY: But that's different –

SARA KATE: No. It's the same.

HILLARY:…How are the elves?

SARA KATE: They're okay.

(They are quiet, not knowing what to say. Sara Kate rights the ferris wheel.)

HILLARY: Is it broken?

SARA KATE: No, it's fine.

HILLARY: What a mess.

SARA KATE: Yeah, I've been real busy. I'm trying to clean up.

HILLARY: Can I help?

SARA KATE: Here. (*Hands her a box.*) Pick up the junk.

HILLARY: Okay. Your yard looks sooooo good.

SARA KATE: You just said it's a mess.

HILLARY: No, it's a great mess. An elf mess. There's nothing like this anywhere else.

SARA KATE: That's why the elves come.

HILLARY: I know. Some things only make sense here.

SARA KATE: Yes.

HILLARY: (*Beat.*) Sara Kate? Did you tape a pencil to your nose?

SARA KATE: Yes. So what?

HILLARY: What for?

SARA KATE: So it wouldn't *fall off* when I took the *math test*.

HILLARY: Yeah, but, *why* did you *take* a math test with a pencil taped to your nose?

SARA KATE: I was practicing. You can do anything if you practice. You can learn anything. They read us that story about Pierre the Package. You know that story?

HILLARY: No, they didn't read us that story.

SARA KATE: Yeah, it's for older kids. Pierre doesn't have any arms or legs. Nothing. He's just a head and a body. So when he needs to write, somebody tapes a pencil to his nose so he can type.

HILLARY: Why don't they just type the letter for him?

SARA KATE: A million reasons why! Maybe it's a love letter; or maybe he wants to write it himself. If he wants to do it himself, he should be allowed.

HILLARY: It must be very hard.

SARA KATE: Lots of things are hard. You have to learn how to do them is all.

HILLARY: Like taking care of a house. (*Beat.*) I found my diary.

SARA KATE: (*Sarcastic.*) Congratulations.

HILLARY: Remember? I thought I left it here.

SARA KATE: You thought I stole it.

HILLARY: Yeah. I'm sorry.

SARA KATE: Who wants to read about the Mighty Three?

HILLARY: I don't write about that anymore.

SARA KATE: I don't see what's so great about being the same as them.
(*Mrs. Connolly appears in the window. Sara Kate sees her.*)

HILLARY: I'm not the same as them. They're not even the same as each other.
(*Mrs. Connolly disappears.*)

SARA KATE: (*Sighs.*) I have to go in.

HILLARY: Is it your mother?

SARA KATE: Yes. She wants me to come in.

HILLARY: Do you want me to go home?
(*Sara Kate looks closely at Hillary.*)

SARA KATE: Listen –

HILLARY: Yes.

SARA KATE: Can you keep a secret?

HILLARY: I can. I can keep one forever.

SARA KATE: Okay. My mother has been worse lately and she likes to have me stay near. Do you have any money?

HILLARY: A little.

SARA KATE: We're out of stuff. Food. My mother likes coffee and milk. And sugar. We need bread and fruit. She likes fruit. And aspirin.

HILLARY: What else?

SARA KATE: Whatever you can get.

· · ·

Scene 3

> *Hillary crosses the partially darkened stage, is daunted by the enormity of the task, jams her hands in her pockets, takes a big breath, and begins to walk into the sounds of the city.*

· · ·

Scene 4

> *Later that day, inside the Connolly house. It is cold and barren. A knock. Sara Kate runs to the door, peeks out, and opens it for Hillary, who enters completely out of breath carrying two large shopping bags.*

SARA KATE: Look at all this stuff.

HILLARY: (*Out of breath.*) Yeah, I got a real lot.

SARA KATE: I thought you said you only had a little money.

HILLARY: I broke up my bank. Forty bucks. I had to stop and rest a lot of times.

SARA KATE: You should have swiped a cart.

HILLARY: Oh. I didn't know.

SARA KATE: (*Pause.*) You didn't tell, did you?

HILLARY: No, I didn't tell!

SARA KATE: (*Emptying a bag.*) You got everything! Milk and cereal. You got the kind with raisins!

HILLARY: Yeah. Sorry. I couldn't find the plain white boxes, the cheap ones you said are better.

SARA KATE: Oh, no, don't apologize, this is fine, really great! Bread and bologna! You got bologna!

HILLARY: Yeah. Boy, stuff costs a lot.

SARA KATE: I know. (*Beat.*) I got to take some stuff to my mother.

HILLARY: Okay.

> (*Sara Kate puts some stuff in the empty grocery bag and exits. Hillary takes the rest of the groceries out. She opens the refrigerator, finds the light doesn't go on and that it is not working.*)

HILLARY: Oh, man. Gross. This is gross.

(Shuts refrigerator, sees a bug, jumps. Stands on a chair. Sara Kate returns.

SARA KATE: What are you standing there for?

HILLARY: I'm cold.

SARA KATE: Yeah, it gets cold. The furnace broke.

HILLARY: What do you do when the furnace breaks?

SARA KATE: First you call the oil company. Then they send a guy who says how much it costs. Then you tell them never mind because it's so much.

HILLARY: How do you keep warm?

SARA KATE: The stove. Upstairs I got three electric heaters and electric blankets.

HILLARY: Electric blankets give you cancer!

SARA KATE: Yeah, but if you don't keep warm you freeze to death.

HILLARY: How's your mother?

SARA KATE: She's okay. Let's have sandwiches, bologna sandwiches.

HILLARY: *(Looks toward roaches.)* I'm not hungry.

SARA KATE: Suit yourself. I love white bread. *(Finds mayonnaise.)* And mayonnaise! You need mayonnaise on bologna sandwiches.

HILLARY: Yeah, you do. I think I changed my mind.

SARA KATE: Two bologna sandwiches coming up!

HILLARY: I thought all you ate was berries off trees.

SARA KATE: Why eat berries off trees when you have bologneeee!?

HILLARY: *(Happy.)* I don't know. I saw roaches.

SARA KATE: They don't hurt anybody. Roaches are misunderstood.

HILLARY: *(Laughs.)* Somebody sprays our house.

SARA KATE: We used to get that. Now we try to get along with them.

HILLARY: Yuk.

SARA KATE: Roaches are very clean. I saw it on TV. Before they took the TV back. Here's a sandwich. Yippee, bologneee.

HILLARY: Who took the TV back?

SARA KATE: That's what happens when you don't have any money; people come and take your stuff away.

HILLARY: That's crummy.

SARA KATE: Yes, it's very terrible. I try to keep things paid. But sometimes, the money's just *gone*.

HILLARY: Man.

SARA KATE: But it helps when I send the bill people letters. I write and say I'll send them money next month.

HILLARY: *(Slowly.)* You. You do everything.

SARA KATE: No. I mean. I *help*...sometimes. I *help*.

HILLARY: No. You do everything. You pretend that your mother tells you what to do, like everybody else's mother. But that's not right. She doesn't tell you anything. She's too sick. You're the one taking care of her.

SARA KATE: So what! (*Pause.*) I learned how; I can do it.

HILLARY: Don't be mad. I was just trying to imagine it. What happens with the big stuff – I mean, the big stuff?

SARA KATE: I do it...I do the big stuff, whatever happens, I do it. I sign it; I write it; I talk on the phone. I tell people what to do, and if they don't do it, I find some other way. My mother gets so upset when we run out of money.

HILLARY: Don't *you* get upset?!

SARA KATE: Sometimes my father can send money and sometimes he can't. When he can't we just have to manage.

HILLARY: But how?

SARA KATE: People leave stuff. There was a whole cart full of food in the supermarket parking lot one time. At school there's lost and found.

HILLARY: They give you lost and found?

SARA KATE: Sure, I say it's mine, and they give it to me.

HILLARY: You should tell. If people knew you were taking care of your mother by yourself, they'd do something about it.

SARA KATE: No! They'd take my mother away.

HILLARY: You can't take care of her forever.

SARA KATE: I've been doing it for a year, and nobody even knows.

HILLARY: (*Quietly.*) A year.

SARA KATE: People are stupid. They don't have a clue to what's going on right in their own backyards.

HILLARY: (*To herself.*) I know.

SARA KATE: People don't like anybody who is sick. They put us where they can't see us.

HILLARY: Like the starving people around the world.

SARA KATE: Yeah, so if you're thinking of getting help for us, forget it.

HILLARY: My parents aren't like other people; we could ask my –

SARA KATE: No. No, Hillary. Somebody like you can ask for help; somebody like me has to steal it.

HILLARY: (*Beat.*) Sara Kate? Are you an elf?

(*A loud knock at the door.*)

SARA KATE: Oh, no.

MRS. L: (*Off.*) Hillary? Sara Kate? It's Mrs. Lenox. Mrs. Connolly, are you there?

SARA KATE: Get rid of her.

(*Hillary peeks through the door.*)

HILLARY: Hi, Mom, I'm coming. Bye, bye, Sara Kate.

(*Hillary tries to exit.*)

MRS. L: Just a minute, Hillary.

HILLARY: Let's go, Mom.

MRS. L: Where is Sara Kate?

HILLARY: Come on, Mom.

MRS. L: Hillary! Just a minute.

(*Mrs. Lenox sees into the room.*)

MRS. L: What is…? Sara Kate? What have you girls done to this room?

HILLARY: It's nothing; it's just Sara Kate.

MRS. L: What have you been doing? Where is your mother?

(*Sara Kate performs with practiced courtesy.*)

SARA KATE: Hello, Mrs. Lenox. I'm so glad to be seeing you again. It's been a long time, hasn't it. My mother is fine, but she's upstairs having a nap, now. I know this room looks terrible. We're having it fixed. That's why everything is moved. I'm sorry you had to come looking for Hillary.

MRS. L: (*Confused.*) I tried to call…

SARA KATE: Yes, the phone's been turned off since this morning, which you probably found out. There must be a line down somewhere. There's a man coming to fix it.

MRS. L: Is the heat off, too?

SARA KATE: Yes. They had to turn off the heat. Just for an hour or so. They're working on pipes.

MRS. L: Pipes?

SARA KATE: Yes. So they had to turn off the heat. They always do that.

MRS. L: Who?

SARA KATE: Workmen. The workmen who fix pipes.

MRS. L: (*Pause.*) I would like to see your mother.

SARA KATE: She can't be bothered. She'll call you when the phone is fixed.

MRS. L: Is she upstairs?

SARA KATE: Of course. She's taking a nap.

MRS. L: I'm going to go up.

SARA KATE: No! No. You can't go up.

MRS. L: Sara Kate, I need to speak with your mother.

SARA KATE: Would you please go away?! Just go away!

MRS. L: No, I'm not going to go away. I'm going to go talk to your mother.

(*Mrs. Lenox exits.*)

HILLARY: Do something. Can't you do something? She'll find out. She'll see your mother. Fix it.

SARA KATE: I don't know how to fix this. I should never – never –

HILLARY: Never what? Should never what?

SARA KATE: I should never have invited you.

HILLARY: To see the elves?

SARA KATE: People ruin everything.

HILLARY: I didn't. I didn't mean to.

SARA KATE: What you meant doesn't matter. It's all ruined.

(*Sara Kate puts her face in her hands.*)

HILLARY: It'll be okay. Mom's not like that. You'll see. Don't cry.

SARA KATE: (*Crying.*) I...I'm so tired.

(*Mrs. Lenox reenters greatly subdued.*)

HILLARY: Mom. What are you going to do?

MRS. L: Sara Kate. Sara Kate, stay with your mother. I'll be right back, do you understand? I'm going to take Hillary home, and then I'll be right back. Don't worry, Sara Kate. We're going to take care of your mother. Come on, Hillary.

(*Mrs. Lenox leads Hillary to the door. Hillary turns back.*)

HILLARY: I'm sorry. I'm sorry, Sara Kate.

(*Sara Kate does not acknowledge Hillary, but looks out blankly.*)

• • •

Scene 5

A week later, the Lenox garden. The bright sunny daylight contrasts strongly with the cold evening light of the previous scene. It's the comfort of daylight after a bad dream. Hillary, with a pencil taped to her nose, writes the last word, then reads diary entry.

HILLARY: Dear Diary. I stayed home again today. Mom and Dad act like I'm sick. If I don't eat enough dinner they bring something special to my room, like soup with meatballs and crackers. Mom even made pie. But I hardly ate any. I guess I have to go back to school soon, but I don't want to. I don't want to see anybody. Nobody understands. They all have stuff and food and all.

(*Alison and Jane arrive at the gate. They are dressed alike. Hillary puts down diary, and begins to rake leaves.*)

ALISON: (*Pause.*) Hi.

JANE: Can we come in?

HILLARY: It's a backyard, anybody can come in.

JANE: We brought your homework.

HILLARY: (*Sarcastic.*) Great.

JANE: It's really hard. It's math and it's new.

ALISON: You should get your father to put in a swing set back here.

HILLARY: He says I'll outgrow it and then we'll still have the cement pilings.

ALISON: Your father is mental.

JANE: Too-too mental.

HILLARY: He likes his yard is all.

JANE: When you coming back to school? We miss you.

ALISON: We thought you were sick.

HILLARY: You knew I wasn't sick.

JANE: But you haven't been at school. Not since they found out Sara Kate kept her mother a prisoner.

HILLARY: She did not keep her mother a prisoner.

ALISON: That's what it said in the *paper*. It said she kept her mother from getting medical attention.

HILLARY: Sure, medical attention in some asylum.

ALISON: What's the matter with you, Hillary?

JANE: Alison, be quiet. Want some help, Hillary?

HILLARY: I don't care.

JANE: (*Gets rake from shed.*) Hey! My Dad's getting married, and guess what?

HILLARY: (*Not interested.*) What?

JANE: I get to be in the wedding ceremony and you and Alison get to go as my guests.

ALISON: What should we wear, Hillary?

HILLARY: I don't know.

ALISON: Maybe we should dress like Jane in her flower-girl dress.

HILLARY: I don't know if I can go.

JANE: No, you can't dress like me; people won't know who is me. I have to be separate.

HILLARY: I might be sick that day.

JANE: Hillary, don't worry if you still feel a little bad about Sara Kate. She was even worse than we thought. And you're tied up in knots about it.

ALISON: You shouldn't feel stupid because you fell for all her lies, even though me and Jane never did.

JANE: Sara Kate was very terrible; she made up the whole thing about elves and how they live and what they eat and stuff.

ALISON: Don't worry. We don't blame you at all. It wasn't fair to pick on someone so much younger. We blame Sara Kate.

HILLARY: I don't blame Sara Kate. I blame you. You don't know anything about it; you don't know anything about elves.

JANE: If elves are so great, why did Sara Kate leave the village behind?

HILLARY: (*Making it up.*) She left it for me. She knows I'll take care of it.

ALISON: She didn't leave it for you; she didn't have time to take it with her when she ran away, is all.

HILLARY: (*Pause.*) She ran away?

ALISON: She didn't want to go to a foster home. (*Beat.*) It says so in the *paper*.

HILLARY: Do you believe everything it says in the stupid newspaper?!

ALISON: Newspapers never lie.

HILLARY: They do; all the time.

ALISON: Don't be stupid, Hillary. You're being an idiot over nothing.

HILLARY: Sara Kate is not nothing.

(*Mrs. L. appears at the back door.*)

MRS. L: Hey! What's all this yelling?

ALISON: We didn't do anything; it's Hillary.

JANE: We didn't start it.

MRS. L: Start what? Jane put down that rake.

JANE: I didn't do anything.

MRS. L: I think you girls better go home.

JANE: When is Hillary coming back to school?

MRS. L: Soon. She'll be back soon.

(*The girls exiting.*)

JANE: Bye, Hillary. Sorry.

ALISON: We don't have to apologize; we didn't do anything.

(*Mrs. L and Hillary are quiet for a moment.*)

MRS. L: What was that all about?

HILLARY: They said Sara Kate ran away. Because she didn't want to go to a foster home. She doesn't have to go to a foster home, does she?

MRS. L: Hillary, Sara Kate is on her way to Kansas. To her father.

HILLARY: Because if she didn't have any place to stay, well, she could stay with us.

MRS. L: Sara Kate is a very troubled little girl.

HILLARY: She's very smart. She took care of her whole house.

MRS. L: I know, Hillary. But what she did, the letters, the lying –

HILLARY: She was afraid, Mom. And she was right.

MRS. L: Hillary…Mrs. Connolly needs to be in a hospital.

HILLARY: Everything she was afraid would happen happened.

MRS. L: Her mother wasn't getting better; she was getting worse.

HILLARY: They took her mother, Mom. Just like Sara Kate said. Her mother.

MRS. L: Hillary, she was too little to take care of her mother herself. She was too little to take care of herself, herself. Now they both have a chance to get better.

HILLARY: Could I write to her?

MRS. L: We'll wait and see if she writes to you.

HILLARY: She'll probably ask about the elf village.

MRS. L: She probably will. Why don't you bring it over here? So you can keep an eye on it for her.

HILLARY: What? Are you nuts?

MRS. L: Hillary!

HILLARY: I'm sorry I'm sorry. I didn't mean – Mom. Mom. Dad would, Dad would, he'd –

MRS. L: It's Dad's idea.

HILLARY: Dad's?

(*Mr. L at the door.*)

MR. L: Yeah, your *Dad's*.

HILLARY: Dad!

MR. L: People are coming to haul the junk out of the yard, thank goodness.

MRS. L: Then they're going to start showing it to people. To buy.

MR. L: I don't think anybody's going to want to have an elf village in his backyard.

HILLARY: (*Looks around; it's not possible.*) Oh, man. Thanks, thanks really. But I don't think it'll work out. Our yard's too neat. The elves won't come here.

MRS. L: How about behind the garage? It's a mess back there.

HILLARY: Yeah. (*Beat.*) Yeah! It's a disaster back there. It's perfect.

MR. L: I knew I had some reason for not cleaning it up.

HILLARY: That's great. That's great. Thanks, thanks a lot.

• • •

Scene 6

Immediately following, the Connolly yard. The village is in disarray. Hillary starts to pack up the village.

HILLARY: (*Whispering.*) You elves are very untidy. Oh! Don't whisper.

Whispering is unnatural. (*Beat.*) Maybe you aren't untidy, maybe it's earth forces messing up your village each time.

(*Hillary gasps and turns to see an elf, but it's gone.*)

HILLARY: Someday you'll let me see you. I won't have to work at it at all; one day I'll see an elf. (*Beat.*) How'd I know that? (*Realizes.*) The elves are sneaking information into my brain! Hey, elves! Sneak information into Sara Kate's brain – a message from me.

(*Hillary remembers playing with Sara Kate. She speaks to her as if she were really there.*)

HILLARY: Sara Kate? The elves are going to live in the mess behind my garage. There's plenty of places for them to hide back there. I'll take extra rocks to separate their little lots. They're starting to trust me a little. I almost saw one.

(*As lights fade and music cue sounds, Sara Kate appears on stage. Hillary is not at all surprised to see her.*)

HILLARY: You don't have to worry at all; I remember everything you said. I will be one kindly giant sister, making sure no evil forces harm the elves or their village. I will climb the tallest hill and scan the horizon, waiting for your return.

(*The ferris wheel turns. The girls walk in the giant way, as lights fade.*)

END OF PLAY

the Portrait the Wind
the Chair
by Y York

for r
sweet and low

the Portrait the Wind the Chair by Y York. ©1994. PAu 1-937-459.
Reprinted by permission of Dramatic Publishing. All inquiries
should be addressed to Dramatic Publishing, 311 Washington Street,
Woodstock, IL 60098, or Joyce Ketay Agency, 1501 Broadway,
Suite 1910, New York, NY 10036.

ORIGINAL PRODUCTION

the Portrait the Wind the Chair was originally produced by Seattle Children's Theatre on March 3, 1995. It was directed by Mark Lutwak with the following cast:

CHAIRMAN..Eric Ray Anderson
TERROBA/MINNIE..Olga Sanchez
LUCY ....Annette Toutonghi

CHARACTERS

Played by 3 actors.

TERROBA, Female, 14, stuffy, nervous. Also plays MINNIE in the dream,
    fearless, fun, a tomboy.

LUCY, Female, 10, worried, impertinent.

CHAIRMAN, Male, ageless. A chair.

PLACE

A combination living room/dining room in an old house. This room is slightly transformed to become a little island in the middle of a creek.

TIME

The present.

THE PORTRAIT THE WIND THE CHAIR

ACT ONE

The living room/dining room of a house, a little rundown, simply furnished and with a lot of house plants. There is a life-size portrait of a teenage girl with short, curled hair, white socks, saddle oxfords, flare skirt, sweater, and pearls (circa 1950). It is a comfortable room. The sound of a ferocious wind storm. Winter.

Lucy, carrying her book bag and the mail, opens the door, sticks in her head, shouts.

LUCY: Terroba! *(Pause.)* Hey! *(Pause.)*
    (Lucy comes in cautiously, carefully locks the doors behind her. She stands there a moment, not knowing what to do. Then she uses her coat as a barrier between herself and the portrait, as she goes to the kitchen.)

LUCY: Don't look at me like that. I don't even see you up there. And your stupid chair isn't going to get me either. *(She punches the chair.)* So there!
    (Exits to kitchen.)
    (Terroba, 14, enters, she looks exactly like the girl in the portrait. She is angry with herself.)

TERROBA: Stupid, stupid, stupid. *(She hangs up her coat, then self mocking.)* "Hey Emily, wanna come over and do homework like the old days." Stupid, stupid, stupid.
    (Unseen, Lucy stands in the kitchen doorway, still with letters, book bag, and also a broom.)

LUCY: Who you talking to?

TERROBA: *(Screams.)*

LUCY: *(Screams.)* Don't scare me! Don't scare me!

TERROBA: Scare *you*?! *(Beat.)* What are you doing here?! You have tutoring!

LUCY: No tutoring. Because of the storm.
    (Terroba starts upstairs.)

TERROBA: *(With finality.)* I've got homework.

> *(Lucy remains where she is with coat on, throws newspaper and mail on the floor. Terroba stops.)*

TERROBA: What? What now?

LUCY: You know what.

TERROBA: *(Sighs.)* You have to get over this.

LUCY: Well, I'm not over it *yet.* Okay?!

> *(Terroba opens closet.)*

TERROBA: *(Over loud for Lucy's benefit.)* What have we here? Coats coats and more coats. And overshoes, and boots. And coat hangers. All monsters have taken up residence elsewhere.

> *(Terroba starts to close closet.)*

LUCY: Not so fast.

> *(Lucy pokes in closet with broom. She jumps back frightened.)*

LUCY: Oh!

TERROBA: What?

LUCY: *(Realizing.)* Oh, it's just a jacket. Okay.

TERROBA: Give me your coat.

> *(Terroba tries to take Lucy's coat.)*

LUCY: Don't touch me.

TERROBA: I was just going to hang it up.

LUCY: Here.

> *(Lucy tosses the coat on floor. Terroba hangs it up.)*

TERROBA: You are so messy. Put that stuff *(Letters.)* on the table.

LUCY: I don't know why I have to bring in the letters every day.

TERROBA: Because it's your job.

LUCY: I'm not allowed to read them, why should I have to bring them in?

TERROBA: *(For the 10th time.)* You bring them in so the house looks occupied. If you leave letters in the box, we're sitting ducks.

LUCY: We're sitting ducks just from letters?

TERROBA: Letters in the box make you a target.

LUCY: Then the mailman shouldn't leave them!

TERROBA: It's his job to leave them. It's your job to bring them in so the house looks occupied. I'm going upstairs.

LUCY: *(Worried.)* No. Poke under the chair first.

> *(Lucy holds out the broom. Terroba takes it and pokes under the chair.)*

TERROBA: Poke, poke, poke. Okay?

LUCY: You'll thank me when there's something under there some day.

TERROBA: There's nothing under anything, Lucy. Should I poke under the sofa?

LUCY: Why?

TERROBA: In case there's something under it!

LUCY: Don't be ridiculous. Nothing's under the *sofa*.

   (Lucy kicks the chair.)

TERROBA: Lucy!

LUCY: Who cares! It's a crummy old chair. Send it to the dump.

TERROBA: Gramma liked it.

   (Terroba sits and sinks down into the chair.)

LUCY: *(To chair.)* Oh no. Let her go! You let her go!

TERROBA: What?!

LUCY: Give me your hand! I'll pull you out!

TERROBA: I can get out. Lucy, calm down.

LUCY: Oh. I thought it was pulling you down.

TERROBA: No. It's not pulling; it's fine. *(Bounces.)* A little lumpy maybe, but fine.

LUCY: It's *a lot* lumpy. How could Gramma even stand to sit in it?

TERROBA: Maybe the lumps fit her behind.

LUCY: Well they don't fit mine.

TERROBA: *(To chair.)* You sure are a lumpy chair.

LUCY: *(Mad.)* Oh great, now *you're* talkin' to the chair! Are you gonna turn loopy like Gramma before she died? "Looks like it's just you and me; these grandchildren are just too busy for us. Don't mind me, Lucy, me and my old chair are having a little chat."

TERROBA: Probably because *you* wouldn't talk to her.

LUCY: Stop blaming me!

TERROBA: Nobody's *blaming* anybody. *(Beat, examining chair.)* This chair is a wreck. Maybe we could get it reupholstered or something.

LUCY: I hate it.

TERROBA: We'll add it to the list of stuff you hate around here. *(As she starts upstairs.)* Don't make a mess. Mom's gotta talk to the chairman today.

LUCY: She's gonna be in a bad mood.

TERROBA: That's why don't make a mess.

LUCY: *(To keep Terroba in the room.)* Yeah, she hates the chairman.

TERROBA: *(Returning.)* She doesn't *hate* him. Where do you come up with these things?

LUCY: She does. Because of the suit thing – the suit thing.

TERROBA: What – ? ...Suit affliction?

LUCY: Yeah; he's got *suit affliction*. A fatal case.

TERROBA: Lucy – Suit affliction is a *joke* – when nobody respects you, you put on a suit to get some respect.

LUCY: I don't hear a joke in that.

TERROBA: You're too little.

LUCY: You hate the chairman, too. He makes you so nervous you can't study.

TERROBA: I don't hate him; he doesn't *have* to give money for getting A's.

LUCY: Would he give me a hundred dollars for college if I get an A?

TERROBA: *(Exasperated.)* Its a program. Any kid gets an A, gets a hundred dollars. But the way you study, his hundred dollars is pretty safe. *(Heading upstairs.)* No mess, Lucy, no kidding.

LUCY: Let me come be in your room.

TERROBA: No.

LUCY: I'll be silent. Not a word. Zip.

TERROBA: That's what you said last time.

(Terroba exits upstairs, leaving the broom behind. Lucy gets an idea. She takes the broom for protection, makes threatening gestures to the chair and portrait as she goes. Lucy drags dining room chairs away from the table, takes an afghan from the back of the sofa, tosses it on the chairs to make a cave. Goes to the closet with her broom, gingerly opens it, pokes inside, takes out Mom's suit jacket and ties up the chair with it. All of her unspoken activities are punctuated by her own soundtrack [humming].)

LUCY: *(To chair, while tying it up.)* You won't stay in our house if I have anything to say about it. You'll go right in the soonest garbage truck. There! That should hold you forever.

(She pulls an old suitcase from the closet, opens it, takes a half slip from inside and puts it on her head, wearing the slip like it's hair; takes out alligator shoes, growls, places them strategically. Walks in a queenly fashion.)

LUCY: The Queen of the Amazon proclaims tomorrow a no-school day for all public school children in America.

(Terroba enters with her book.)

TERROBA: Do you want something to eat – what's on the chair?

LUCY: That is not a chair; that is a prisoner of war. Caught trying to assassinate her highness.

(Terroba unties the chair and hangs up the jacket.)

TERROBA: You're gonna ruin Mom's good jacket.

LUCY: She never wears it.

TERROBA: You're still not allowed to play with it.

LUCY: The Queen of the Amazon may play with anything she likes.

TERROBA: The Queen of the Amazon wears a slip on her head?

LUCY: This is my long flowing hair. *(Big voice.)* You must obey my every commandment.

TERROBA: Like: thou shalt not slay thy bossy little sister?

LUCY: *(Big voice.)* Don't enrage the Queen, or you wilt be sorry.

TERROBA: Is this the mess I told you not to make? *(Suspicious.)* Where did you get Gramma's alligator shoes?

LUCY: Not shoes. Dangerous man-eating reptiles along the river bank.

TERROBA: Is that Gramma Minnie's slip?

LUCY: Hair!

TERROBA: Is it Gramma's?

LUCY: It was in her suitcase.

TERROBA: You're not supposed to be in Gramma's stuff.

LUCY: Why? She doesn't need it.

TERROBA: Chill, Lucy. Just chill.

LUCY: I can play with it if I want.

TERROBA: Mom won't like it.

LUCY: Well, who's going to tell her, snitch face?

> *(Terroba crosses and looks in suitcase as Lucy gets large books from the book case which she spreads along the floor in a long path. She steps from book to book. They talk over the action.)*

LUCY: *(Lying.)* Besides, Gramma said I could have anything I want. Anything in her suitcase. She said so.

TERROBA: *(Suspicious.)* When did you two have this conversation?

LUCY: *Before she died.* When do you think? Yesterday?

TERROBA: You never even went in her room. The whole time she was sick.

LUCY: I'm little; I don't have to talk to sick people.

TERROBA: It was fun to talk to her.

LUCY: It wasn't fun. It was scary.

TERROBA: You weren't too scared when she took you to the lake. You weren't too scared when she took you to the movies.

LUCY: I was too scared. The whole time.

TERROBA: You weren't. Not 'til she got sick. As soon as Gramma couldn't take you places – Zip! – you don't go in her room. I don't know why she wanted you to have anything.

LUCY: She didn't give me anything.

TERROBA: She gave you this house.

LUCY: Mom still has to pay the mortgage, and besides she didn't give it to *me;* she hated me.

TERROBA: If she hated you then why did she want you to have the ring with the beautiful blue stone?

LUCY: Because the ring with the beautiful blue stone doesn't exist, that's why. It's easy to give somebody something that doesn't exist.

TERROBA: *(To herself.)* She gave me the tiny little diamond.

LUCY: There's no tiny little diamond, either. It was fever dreams.

TERROBA: I know! *(Beat.)* She was pretty sick there at the end.

LUCY: Sick and mean.

TERROBA: What did Gramma ever do to you.

LUCY: She *died*, she died to me.

TERROBA: She couldn't help it. You are a crumb.

LUCY: I'm not – listen, if she wanted me to have a ring with a beautiful blue stone, she for sure wanted me to have her *slip*.

TERROBA: You better not hurt Mom's law books.

LUCY: I must step carefully from rock to rock so I don't get eaten. *(Referring to shoes.)* The River Amazon is full of alligators.

TERROBA: Not really. It's too full of pollution now.

LUCY: Well, *my* River Amazon is full of alligators!

TERROBA: *(Thoughtful, at suitcase.)* Maybe Gramma always wanted a tiny little diamond, or something. Hey! Maybe there's a secret hidden compartment. For rings.

(Lucy goes to the suitcase. They poke around; find pearls, scarves.)

LUCY: It's just an old cardboard suitcase. There's no secret compartment.

TERROBA: She let me wear these pearls once.

LUCY: Big deal.

TERROBA: *(At portrait.)* No, they're very old. She's got them on in her picture. That's how old.

LUCY: How come you got to wear them?

TERROBA: It was for the Halloween I was an oyster.

LUCY: Oh, yeah, *weird!*

TERROBA: No, it was very clever. It was Gramma's idea.

LUCY: *(Mad.)* Yeah, she's the one talked me into being a mushroom.

(Lucy takes a cushion from the sofa and puts it on her head. It makes her look remarkably like a toadstool.)

TERROBA: I thought that was your own stupid idea.

LUCY: Nope. *(Points to portrait.)* Hers. She guaranteed nobody else would be one. *(Sarcastic.)* She was right!

TERROBA: Let's put this stuff away. You've turned the living room into a dump.

LUCY: No I haven't; dumps are outside. Let's play with it before we put it away.

TERROBA: The house has to be nice for when Mom gets home.

LUCY: Come on, just for a little while. Then I'll help you straighten up. Come on.

(Lucy tempts Terroba with a second slip.)

TERROBA: *(Checks clock.)* Oh, alright, but just for a little while.

(Terroba puts slip on head. Lucy is excited that she's tricked Terroba into playing.)

LUCY: I'll be in my queen cave. You must come and pay my homage.

TERROBA: Pay your homage?

LUCY: Yeah, come to my cave and pay it. You can pay it with your fabulous silken scarves.

TERROBA: That's not what pay homage means.

LUCY: Who cares?

TERROBA: Well, not you, if your vocabulary score is evidence.

LUCY: Be careful of the alligators. Step only on the rocks.

TERROBA: I, Terroba, Queen of the lesser Amazon, come to the cave of Lucy –

(Lucy threatens Terroba with the alligator shoes; she growls.)

TERROBA: Are you a Queen or alligators?

LUCY: *(Growls.)*

TERROBA: Alligators are silent, Lucy.

LUCY: Don't call me Lucy. Lucy is too stupid for a queen.

TERROBA: Not as stupid as Terroba. I told Mom and Dad to call you Lucy or don't bring you home from the hospital.

LUCY: It's stupid.

TERROBA: It was the best I could do on short notice. Mom and Dad were going to call you End-all-war.

LUCY: Call me something better.

TERROBA: I, Terroba, Queen of the lesser Amazon, come to the cave of *Lucinderoba,* *(Lucy squeals with delight and runs to cave.)* Queen of the Major Amazon, to pay homage and give her my fabulous silken scarves.

LUCY: Hum something.

(Terroba hums as Lucy marches along the rocks in a grand fashion.)   •

LUCY: I, Lucinderoba, Queen of the Amazon, do take your fabulous homage.

(There is a terrible crash. The girls scream and grab each other.)

LUCY: *(Gaining control of herself.)* Let me go.

TERROBA: You hugged me first.

(Terroba crosses to the door.)

LUCY: *(Worried.)* Where are you *going*?

TERROBA: I want to see what that was.

(They cross to the front door. Open it. It's monstrous windy, loud. They see that a tree has fallen. They are impressed and scared. Close door.)

LUCY: Man! That was *close*!

TERROBA: *(To cover fear.)* It's not so close.

LUCY: It almost fell on the house!

TERROBA: It wouldn't have fallen on the house even if it fell the other way.

LUCY: Right into the living room!

(Lucy runs toward the upstairs steps.)

TERROBA: Don't go up there.

LUCY: I want to take a picture of the tree.

TERROBA: You don't need a picture; you can *see* it.

LUCY: No, so we can show everybody at school.

TERROBA: *(With authority.)* No. I'm in charge. Remember?! Me! Come down here, now.

LUCY: *(Surprised.)* Okay, you're *in charge*, big deal.

TERROBA: You can't go outside and take a picture. Trees are falling down. Do you have homework?

LUCY: Of course.

TERROBA: Get it. We'll do homework.

LUCY: Together?! You and me? In the same room?

TERROBA: Yes.

(Lucy gets book bag.)

LUCY: Yay! I get to go to your room.

TERROBA: No. We'll do homework right here.

LUCY: That's no fun.

TERROBA: But that's what we're gonna do.

LUCY: *(A pout.)* I thought I could go in your room.

TERROBA: Well you were wrong.

(Terroba sits on the sofa. Lucy takes her work to the cave.)

LUCY: *(Pause.)* Do you hate homework? *(No reaction.)* I hate homework. *(No reaction.)* All the really really *cool* kids hate homework. *(No reaction.)* What *is* your homework?

TERROBA: It's *reading*, which I can't do while you're *talking*.

LUCY: What's it about?

TERROBA: It's about inventors who had things named for them. Zeppelins, named for Count von Zeppelin. Sandwich, named after the Earl of Sandwich.

LUCY: Earl of Sandwich?! Was his first name Baloney?

(Terroba ignores her. After a pause, Lucy stands.)

LUCY: I gotta have my colored pencils.

TERROBA: Lucy, sit down.

LUCY: No, I have to do this in colors; He *said*. I need to go get my pencils.

(Lucy starts for the stairs.)

TERROBA: Do something else.

LUCY: You're the one says I have to do homework, and this homework has to be done in colors.

TERROBA: You're not going upstairs and that's final.

(Lucy makes an exasperated sigh, returns to the cave, then suddenly:)

LUCY: You're afraid a tree is going to fall on the house!

TERROBA: *(Too fast.)* No I'm not.

LUCY: Yes! That's why I can't go upstairs. That's why I get to do my homework together. I have to get out of here.

(Lucy heads to the door. Terroba grabs hold of Lucy – by a belt or something. Lucy struggles to go forward. Terroba drags her back to the living room.)

LUCY: Let me go, let me go!

TERROBA: Calm down, Lucy, calm down! You're safer in here than you are out there.

LUCY: Not if a tree falls on us.

TERROBA: Listen, this is a solid old house that trees never fall on. You can't go outside or upstairs and that's that. Now. I'm gonna let you go, but you have to stay put, okay? *(No reaction.)* Okay?!

(Lucy nods. Terroba returns to the sofa. Lucy gets her homework from the cave and sits close to Terroba for security.)

LUCY: I want a tree to fall on the house when we're *not* here.

TERROBA: Where would we live? In some crummy apartment like before?

LUCY: I like an apartment.

TERROBA: *Sharing* a room? No thanks.

LUCY: I like sharing a room.

TERROBA: Four flights of steps?

LUCY: No, not that.

TERROBA: Cigarette smoke coming in from Laurie's?

LUCY: That was gross.

TERROBA: Well, what exactly is it that you *like* so much about an apartment?

LUCY: I like it all little.

TERROBA: I love it here. Plenty of room.

LUCY: Plenty of big spooky dead person room.

TERROBA: If you want a smaller room, you can have mine as soon as I move into Gramma's.

LUCY: Mom's never gonna let you.

(Lucy walks over to Gramma's room, it's on the same floor, and looks toward it.)
Because Gramma's room is not empty. Gramma's still in it.

TERROBA: She is not.

LUCY: Dad's in it, too. All the dead people we know are in it.

TERROBA: Dad never even lived here. There's no such thing as ghosts, Lucy. No such thing.

LUCY: Then how come when I come downstairs for a drink of water that picture never takes her eyes off me?

TERROBA: Get your water from the bathroom if you don't like Gramma's picture.

LUCY: I like refrigerator water. With the fresh-made ice cubes.

TERROBA: Then don't complain.

LUCY: We should get rid of it. Get some nice fun picture. Like the one of Great Aunt Hattie when *she* was a little girl.

TERROBA: *(Sarcastic.)* Sure, if it looks like you, it's *nice*, if it looks like me, it's *scary*.

LUCY: This picture is scary no matter who it looks like. Scary and mean.

TERROBA: The only mean thing in this house is you.

LUCY: No such thing.

TERROBA: I can't even remember the last time you said or did anything nice.

LUCY: I'm funny!

TERROBA: Then how come I'm not laughing?

LUCY: Because you don't get jokes. Just like her! *(Beat.)* Let's put it in the basement.

TERROBA: We're not going to put it in the basement. Maybe Mom'll let me put it in my room.

LUCY: Upstairs?! No way! Then upstairs will be just as scary as downstairs. *(Beat.)* Hey!

(Lucy takes the table cloth from the table.)

LUCY: Help me cover it up.

TERROBA: Why can't it wait?

LUCY: Because it's a good idea. I should have thought it up before.

(Lucy stands on a chair, trying to cover the painting with the tablecloth. Terroba helps Lucy cover up the picture.)

TERROBA: Alright, alright. You make me insane. "Help me, help me. I'm too little. Do it, do it."

(They cover the picture.)

TERROBA: Okay? Is everything okay now? Nothing under chairs? Nobody looking out of paintings?

(Terroba exits to kitchen.)

LUCY: Where are you going?

TERROBA: To get something to eat. Go upstairs and you're murdered.

(Terroba goes to kitchen. Lucy gets an idea. She sneaks a look at Terroba's book.)

LUCY: Boring, boring; stupid and boring.

(She kicks the chair, which catches her.)

LUCY: *(Scream.)* No, no! Let me go! You let me go! Hey, help me!

(Terroba rushes in from the kitchen.)

TERROBA: What?!

LUCY: The chair, the chair!

TERROBA: Lucy –

LUCY: Look, look.

(Terroba looks under the chair.)

TERROBA: There's nothing –

LUCY: It grabbed me, it grabbed me. Don't tell me it didn't grab me.

TERROBA: What grabbed you?

LUCY: Right there, the chair.

(Terroba examines it. Finds a burr.)

TERROBA: It's a burr. It's a sticky burr. Probably from your pants.

LUCY: Do they have burrs in winter?

(Terroba attempts to make a joke)

TERROBA: Sure; Burr, Burr.

(Lucy thinks it is not a joke worth acknowledgment.)

LUCY: Let's call Mom. See if she can come home early.

TERROBA: We're not going to bother Mom at work.

LUCY: No we can because the weather's so bad. Nobody will mind. *(Whine.)* Please.

TERROBA: Oh, alright.

(Terroba dials phone.)

TERROBA: *(Surprised.)* It's the voice mail.

LUCY: Why!?

TERROBA: *(Listening.)* Hush. *(Listening.)* Everybody went home at 1:30 because of the storm.

LUCY: Yay! Yay! Mom's coming, Mom's coming.

TERROBA: *(Relieved.)* Let's do dinner as a surprise.

LUCY: Peanut butter waffles.

TERROBA: *(Sarcastic.)* Oh, yeah, Mom's favorite.

LUCY: She likes them.

TERROBA: *(Disappointed, realizing.)* She won't get to talk to the chairman.

LUCY: Why is she talking to him, anyway?

TERROBA: No reason.

LUCY: *(Jealous.)* Some other big chance for college money?

TERROBA: It isn't about *me*.

LUCY: Is it about me?! What is it?!

TERROBA: Mom doesn't want you to get your hopes up.

LUCY: Well they're up; it's too late.

TERROBA: You don't even know what to hope for.

LUCY: *(Loud.) Tell meeeeeee!*

TERROBA: About changing her schedule. To work at home some days.

LUCY: Oh yes! Let her work at home. I'll be so good, so quiet. Zip.

TERROBA: Now see? Your hopes are all up. I wasn't supposed to tell you.

LUCY: Just like a mouse.

TERROBA: It isn't because you're noisy Mom has to go to the office.

> *(The cuckoo clock sounds four o'clock.)*

TERROBA: *(Brief pause.)* I wonder where she is.

LUCY: *(Holding her ears.)* Don't make me worry.

TERROBA: The traffic's probably bad.

> *(They've done this before. Terroba tries to reassure Lucy.)*

LUCY: But she *didn't* have an accident.

TERROBA: No, she didn't have an accident. It's just bad traffic.

LUCY: Like during rush hour.

TERROBA: Just like rush hour. Plus people always drive slower in a bad storm.

LUCY: And this one is very bad. Bad enough to knock over an old old tree, so the cars are just creeping along.

TERROBA: *(Realizes.)* Lucy! *(Crosses to the window down front.)* This could be the wind storm of the century. Like Gramma Minnie said about Hurricane Donna, from when she and Great Aunt Hattie were kids.

> *(Lucy kicks off her shoes and climbs onto the table, as if getting out of the way of rising water.)*

LUCY: Big Hurricane Donna flooding the creek by Gramma and Great Aunt Hattie's house.

TERROBA: Get off the table.

LUCY: I took off my shoes.

TERROBA: You have no respect for our furniture.

LUCY: I must climb into my trusty canoe so that I'm not swept away by the hurricane water.

TERROBA: It was a *raft*, and the storm was *over* when Gramma went down the creek.

LUCY: *Great Aunt Hattie* went down the creek.

TERROBA: Great Aunt Hattie didn't even want to go.

LUCY: *Did!*

TERROBA: She didn't. Gramma made her.

LUCY: *(Riding the table, acting this.)* I, Great Aunt Hattie, ride in this canoe during a mighty Hurricane because I *want* to.

TERROBA: Great Aunt Hattie never wanted to go anywhere because she was too scared.

LUCY: *(High drama.)* I float away from my bossy older sister, Gramma Minnie. Get away, Minnie, who needs you?

(The wind rattles the house.)

TERROBA: *(Re wind noise.)* Gramma said the hurricane wind felt like a big monster shaking the house.

LUCY: *(Scared, climbing off the table.)* It's a good thing we don't get hurricanes.

(Lucy is clearly worried.)

TERROBA: Hey! We're okay; we're fine. *(Trying to distract Lucy.)* Let's do something else; let's play something else.

(Terroba goes to a shelf where there are games.)

LUCY: I don't want to play anything.

TERROBA: How about your spell game?

(Terroba picks up the spell game.)

LUCY: That's not a game. It's a trick to make me learn my vocabulary list.

(Lucy walks on her "rocks.")

TERROBA: It is too a game. Me and Mom played it.

LUCY: Loud, so you would trick me!

TERROBA: No. It's cute; little tiny letters; they're cute.

LUCY: Yuk. *(Beat.)* Remember when we walked on the rocks at the zoo?

TERROBA: Yeah. Do you want to play walking-on-the-rocks-at-the- zoo?

LUCY: No, I want to *go* to the rocks at the zoo. You and me and Emily. Taking a bus. By ourselves. On a Saturday. Three good friends walking the river walk in the Amazon River Basin habitat. We had a really, really good time.

TERROBA: *(Sullen.)* I don't remember a good time.

LUCY: Yeah. Really good. We should all go some place again.

TERROBA: Fat chance.

LUCY: No, it would be really easy.

TERROBA: It's not gonna happen.

LUCY: No, you should let me go with you.

(Terroba is silent.)

LUCY: I'd be really good. Zip. Speak only when spoken to. Not wander off. Not cry. Not stick my hand in the cage. Not drip my ice cream cone.

TERROBA: Lucy, stop it.

LUCY: Please let me Please let me Please let me Please let me, please say you'll let me, please –

TERROBA: Emily doesn't want to go some place with me anymore.

LUCY: Yes, she loves to.

TERROBA: She has a new best friend.

LUCY: When did that happen?

TERROBA: Who knows who cares.

LUCY: *(Accusingly.)* What did you do?

TERROBA: I didn't do anything. I still like *her*.

LUCY: People only like you if you don't care if they like you.

TERROBA: That is not true.

LUCY: Truuuuue.

TERROBA: How do you know?

LUCY: Everybody knows that. It's better not to like people so much. You're probably really nice to her, hug her and stuff.

TERROBA: I don't.

LUCY: Doooo! Nobody can stand that. Show me what you do.

TERROBA: There's nothing to show.

LUCY: I know what you do. *(Acting.)* "Hi, Emily, boy I really miss being friends with you, I really still love you a wholllle lot."

TERROBA: *(Shocked because Lucy's right.)* I never did that.

LUCY: Sure you did. You're nice to everybody in America except *me*, and *I'm* the only one who wants to be around you. You should let me show you how to be with your friends.

TERROBA: You don't know how I should be.

LUCY: Sure I do. I pay attention and figure it out. You should say this. *(Starts to act something.)* "Boy, Emily, isn't it a drag – "

TERROBA: Stop it. I don't take advice from you.

LUCY: No, you should. Everybody likes *me* because *I don't care* if they like me.

TERROBA: You're deranged if you think everybody likes you. Your teacher told Mom you're completely asocial.

LUCY: A social what?

TERROBA: Asocial. It means no friends.

LUCY: My teacher didn't say that. He just didn't.

TERROBA: He said you're a pain.

LUCY: I'm funny!

TERROBA: You're the only person who thinks you're funny.

LUCY: Then how come everybody's always laughing?

TERROBA: Where are they? Where are all these people who are always laughing? Because they're never *here*.

LUCY: *(Lying.)* At school.

TERROBA: If you had any friends, you wouldn't always want to follow me and Emily.

LUCY: You're just mad because everybody likes me and nobody likes you. I have huge numbers of friends.

TERROBA: You have *zero* friends. None. You have to be *queen*, you have to be *boss*, you have to be *first*. You're a cranky little bossy selfish person and you never ever talked to Gramma after she got sick!

LUCY: I had homework!

TERROBA: You're not even sorry.

LUCY: I didn't do anything.

TERROBA: It's a good thing you're not sorry, because she can't accept your apology.

LUCY: I'll write her a letter!

TERROBA: And send it where?!

LUCY: *(Sincerely.)* To the dead letter office.

TERROBA: *(Brief pause, she can't believe Lucy said that.)* Go upstairs, *go* outside, maybe a tree will fall on you or the wind will blow you to Utah. Don't talk to me; I'm not going to talk to you anymore, I'm not going to be your only friend.

LUCY: I don't need friends. What's so great about friends? What did you and Emily ever do that was so great? Talk on the telephone? Sit around at her house and watch TV?

TERROBA: *(Defensive.)* We didn't just watch TV. We ordered out pizza.

LUCY: *(Impressed.)* You ordered out pizza?

TERROBA: Sure, why not?

LUCY: And they bring it?

TERROBA: Sure. We have to pay for it, but they bring it.

LUCY: Would they bring it to me?

TERROBA: You could try it. Unless you're too scared.

LUCY: I'm not scared. I'm gonna get pizza.

 (Lucy goes to phone.)

LUCY: What's the number?

TERROBA: *(Triumphant.)* You have to look it up.

LUCY: I'm gonna ask information.

 (Lucy picks up phone.)

LUCY: There's no sound. *(Worried.)* There's just nothing.

(Terroba crosses to phone.)

TERROBA: It's dead.

LUCY: Phones don't *die.*

TERROBA: Well, this one did.

LUCY: *(Grabbing phone.)* Hello??? Hello. Dead.

(They are silent. The big sounds of the wind.)

TERROBA: Maybe we should go across the street.

LUCY: Yuk!

TERROBA: We'll knock on their door and ask if we can stay until Mom gets home. We'll take our books; that'll impress them.

LUCY: They've never even talked to us.

TERROBA: Mr. Jones said hi once. Let's go.

(While they put on their coats, gather their homework. Cross to the door.)

LUCY: How will Mom know?

TERROBA: We'll leave her a note. Don't be nasty, and remember your manners. If they give us dinner, chew with your mouth closed. And when you get squishy vegetables, don't spit them out!

(When they open the door, the force from the wind blows the door open, knocks them back, traps Lucy behind door, knocks things down; it takes all their effort to close it again.

TERROBA: Close it! Close it!

(Nobody is going anywhere. Lucy looks out the window, down front.)

LUCY: Man. Just look at it. Man.

TERROBA: *(Looking too.)* Is that our trash can?

LUCY: I think so. Should we go get it?

TERROBA: No way.

(Terroba crosses back to closet. Hangs up coat.)

TERROBA: We're gonna have to stay put, Lucy. Don't worry; it's okay. We're fine.

LUCY: Then how come you wanted to go across the street?

TERROBA: *(Making it up.)* So I wouldn't have to cook. Give me your coat.

(Lucy gives Terroba her coat; sits on sofa, very still.)

TERROBA: *(A serious tone, kindly.)* Listen, Lucy.

LUCY: *(Covering her ears.)* Don't scare me; don't scare me! You're going to say something bad.

TERROBA: *(Still kind.)* In Hurricane Donna –

LUCY: *(Desperate.)* This *isn't* a hurricane!

TERROBA: Okay. This isn't a hurricane. But when you have a really big wind, it can knock down some trees; like the one outside.

(Lucy is very still.)

TERROBA: Sometimes they can fall on the roads, so the cars can't get by. Then the drivers have to wait until somebody moves the trees.

(A brief pause. Then Lucy jumps up and starts pacing back and forth quickly across the living room.)

LUCY: Mom is coming home! She *is*. She is coming home.

TERROBA: *(Forced calm.)* But it might take longer.

LUCY: *(Tears.)* No. Oh, please no, please no.

TERROBA: It's okay, Lucy, it's really okay.

LUCY: A tree did not fall on her car!

TERROBA: No, it didn't, only in the road in front, maybe.

LUCY: Mommeeeee.

(Terroba holds Lucy.)

LUCY: Let me go, let me go. Don't touch me.

TERROBA: I was just trying –

(Lucy runs to the bad chair and starts to hit it from her anger and her fear.)

LUCY: You you you you you you you you –

TERROBA: *(Over.)* Lucy, Lucy, Lucy. It's okay, it's the *same*, it's the same as a minute ago.

(Lucy stops hitting the chair.)

TERROBA: *(Continued.)* Hey, we'll *play*; we'll play queen of the Amazon, come on, we'll wear slips on our heads. We'll play with all Gramma's stuff.

LUCY: *(Very subdued.)* It *isn't* the same. The phone died.

TERROBA: Wanna play? Wanna be queen in the cave? Wanna wear a slip on our heads?

LUCY: No. It's a stupid game. I hate it.

TERROBA: *(Idea.)* Show me how to be.

LUCY: What are you talking about?

TERROBA: You said you could. You said you could show me how to be. Go ahead. I'll be…

LUCY: *(Instantly into it.)* You be Emily! And I'll be you. This is how you're *supposed* to act, not the dumb way you act.

TERROBA: What should I do?

LUCY: Okay. I'm you. You be Emily walking by. Go on.

TERROBA: Hi, Terroba.

LUCY: No! She's not *talking* to you, remember?! Be Emily being mean. Chew gum, she chews gum.

TERROBA: We don't have gum.

(Lucy quickly reaches in her pocket for gum, then thinks better of it because gum's not allowed.)

LUCY: *Pretend*, this is pretend. Walk right past me. I'm you. Go on.

(*Lucy jumps on sofa being Terroba. Terroba walks past as Emily, haughty.*)

LUCY: *(As Terroba.)* Isn't it a drag, Emily?

TERROBA: *(As Emily, mean.)* Isn't *what* a drag, Terroba?

LUCY: *(As Terroba.)* I can't stand that our parents have to sign our homework.

TERROBA: *(As Emily, still mean, suspicious.)* Who cares?

LUCY: *(As Terroba.)* Now I have to hear about it twice! Once when my Mom reads it and once when the teacher reads it.

TERROBA: *(As Emily, acting a little distant.)* I don't know which time is worse.

LUCY: *(As Terroba.)* Mom won't even let me go outside until she's seen the homework, and by then, it's too dark to go out and play.

TERROBA: *(As Emily.)* Yeah, my mother already said I can't go out until she signs my homework.

LUCY: *(As Terroba.)* That's whacked. This is what I think we ought to do, Emily. Tell our parents they changed the rule back, and nobody has to sign anymore. Then we can play outside until it's dark, come in and do the homework, and sign our parents' name the next day when we get to school.

TERROBA: *(Interrupts, as herself.)* Lucy –

LUCY: Call me Terroba.

TERROBA: Lucy, I'm not going to tell Emily to lie to her parents.

LUCY: No, you should. *You* don't have to lie; just *say* it, it's cool; she'll think you're cool. Doooo it.

TERROBA: What's supposed to happen if I do it?

LUCY: People will *like* you. Emily will *like* you. You're always so prissy.

TERROBA: What?!

LUCY: So proper. You do what you're told. You're good all the time.

TERROBA: I'm not good all the time.

LUCY: Yes, you're too good, *and* you're too serious – all the time. You should talk about fun stuff so they'll like you.

TERROBA: *(Mad.)* What do you know about it?

LUCY: I *listen*. Nobody cares about *pollution*, Terroba. You should talk about *fun* stuff, then after kids are your friends, you can *sneak in* boring stuff in little little bits.

(*The lights flicker, then go out; it is still day, so the room is filled with gray light. Lucy falls to the ground where she stands.*)

LUCY: Oh no, oh no, oh no…

TERROBA: Okay, it's okay…it's just a…a power outage – (She gets out matches, lights a candle, tries to be positive.) It happens a lot in storms — the electricity goes out and then it goes back on; it always goes back on.

LUCY: *(Miserable, hiding her face.)* Nooooo.

TERROBA: Well. This is...cozy. I'll get snacks. We can eat in the living room. By candle light. Won't that be fun?

LUCY: I don't want food.

TERROBA: What do you want?

LUCY: I want lights. I want TV.

TERROBA: You know what Mom says about TV.

LUCY: *(Takes candle.)* If we had TV we could watch it by candle light.

TERROBA: *(Decides not to correct her; beat.)* I got an idea. Let's go to sleep. If we go to sleep, we won't notice that the lights are out.

LUCY: We can't even go upstairs!

TERROBA: We'll go in Gramma's room.

LUCY: Never!

TERROBA: Okay, okay. We'll stay out here. I'll get covers, and we'll stay right here.

LUCY: Don't leave me!

TERROBA: Come stand here. You can watch me. We'll talk the whole time.

(Lucy watches as Terroba exits to get bedding.)

TERROBA: *(Off.)* Do you want a nightgown?

LUCY: Not from a creepy dead person.

TERROBA: *(Off.)* I got the fluffy cover.

LUCY: I don't care.

(Terroba reenters with bedding.)

TERROBA: Come on. You can sleep on the sofa.

(Lucy takes a blanket to her cave.)

LUCY: No. It's *supposed* to be dark in here. So I won't notice more.

TERROBA: Do you want me to be in there with you?

LUCY: No, there's no room for you; there's just room enough for me. *(Goes into cave.)*

TERROBA: *(Disappointed.)* Okay. I'm right here. I'll be right here.

(Terroba wraps herself in covers, lays down, is clearly very frightened. Blows out candle, just as the storm is hitting a noise peak, the sound of a tree cracking. Blackout.)

END OF ACT ONE

ACT TWO

Light as if it were dawn, the room is not fully lit. The chair is gone, and the actor playing the ChairMan sits in a chair frame and wears a chair-upholstered costume. The cuckoo goes off announcing 12 o'clock. The cuckoo is not the friendly sound we heard at four, but is the caw of a crow. Other than the caws, it is silent – no wind. After a few caws from the cuckoo, Lucy pokes her head out of her cave, comes out stretching, looking around.

LUCY: Twelve o'clock. Is it noon or is it midnight? Terroba? Man, it's freezing. Turn up the heat.

(Lucy notices the silence.)

LUCY: Hey. It's over. The storm's over.

(She crosses to the door, opens it. A huge treetop slowly pushes through the door, trapping Lucy against the wall. Only her arm is visible. She shouts for help.)

LUCY: Help! Terroba, help me. Wake up, already!

(Minnie [Gramma Minnie as the young girl in the portrait] comes out of the tablecloth-covered painting, stretches, like she's been in one position for a long time. Minnie looks just like Terroba except for her hair and her clothes. For Minnie, it is 1950, and Lucy is her little sister Hattie.)

MINNIE: I am sooooo stiff.

(She does a little twirl, a dance. Looks around.)

LUCY: Help meeeee!

MINNIE: *(Looking at tree.)* This is tree mendous!

LUCY: Hey! Hey, help. I'm smashed against the wall.

MINNIE: Oh boy, Hattie, what have you got yourself into this time?

LUCY: Let me out of here; come on.

MINNIE: Here I come, girl.

LUCY: Move this stupid tree.

MINNIE: This is a major problem. A job for lumberjacks. *Log*arithms, maybe.

LUCY: Stop teasing.

MINNIE: Maybe what is required is another big wind.

(Minnie blows at the tree.)

MINNIE: Well, that didn't work.

LUCY: Will you quit fooling around?

MINNIE: Okay, already.

(Minnie squeezes between the door and the tree.)

MINNIE: Okay, push your way out.

(Lucy squeezes out. Lucy thinks Minnie is Terroba.)

LUCY: It took you long enough.

MINNIE: You're lucky you're free at all. I should leave you stuck so you don't try to follow me.

LUCY: Why are you dressed like that?

MINNIE: For my *portrait!* Isn't this the worst? You're gonna have to wear all this junk now. It's your turn! Ha ha ha ha haaaaa.

(Minnie puts the pearls on Lucy and "adjusts her" for the portrait.)

MINNIE: And you're gonna have to stand *still*, and hold your hands like this – don't scratch your nose! Now smile; keep smiling. Smile for an hour in a row. Smile forever, smile until your cheeks crack. Put these on.

(Minnie gives Lucy the rings she is wearing.)

MINNIE: Don't lose them, or Mom'll frost ya.

(Minnie takes off her dress to reveal her dungarees. Lucy puts on the rings and has a realization.

MINNIE: Look! I had on my dungarees the whole time.

LUCY: The beautiful blue stone and the tiny little diamond! What – ?! You – ? Gramma Minnie! Get back in there!

(Lucy points to painting.)

MINNIE: No can do, kiddo; I barely sneaked out of the house as it is. Mom's scared a tree is gonna fall on us. How'd you get out?

LUCY: Go back!

MINNIE: I say no can do; not me, not in that house, not today. Listen, Hattie, I'm taking the raft down the creek; it's movin' like a river. Don't fink on me or you're toast, okay?

LUCY: *(Shouting.)* Terroba! I want Terroba!

MINNIE: Hey, girl, quiet down. Since I rescued you, the least you can do is not snitch.

LUCY: Snitch what?

MINNIE: About me going to the creek.

LUCY: There's no creek.

MINNIE: Since when, ding bat?

LUCY: There is no creek. There was a creek by your house in Washington DC. There's no creek here. I am not your little sister. You are my Gramma and I want you to go back into your painting.

MINNIE: *(Beat.)* Hattie, have you been sneaking off and watching somebody's television set? It'll burn you up. Mom says so.

LUCY: My Mom hates television, too.

MINNIE: You'll catch radioactivity.

LUCY: *Nooooo.* Your brain rots and you turn into a yes man.

MINNIE: What's a yes man?

LUCY: That's what my Mom says.

MINNIE: *Your* Mom? Hattie? We got the *same Mom.*

LUCY: No! My Mom is your daughter and you're dead.

MINNIE: I'm sure gonna miss you when they put you in the insane asylum.
    (Minnie puts a slip on her head.)

LUCY: I invented that, Gramma.

MINNIE: Stop it, Hattie, now just stop it! You're giving me the willies.

LUCY: What am I *supposed* to call you?

MINNIE: Call me Minnie or I'll frost ya. Gramma sounds ridiculous. *(She picks up the broom.)*

LUCY: *(Ducks.)* Don't hit me.

MINNIE: Hit you? Why? *(Beat, suspicious.)* Hattie! What did you do?

LUCY: *(Guilty.)* Nothing.
    (Minnie grabs the broom and heads toward the table.)

MINNIE: You're just lucky I'm in a hurry, girl. Bye bye, Loony Tunes.

LUCY: *(Scared.)* Where are you going?

MINNIE: To the creek. Tell on me and you're toast.

LUCY: You can't leave me all alone.

MINNIE: Just watch me.
    (Minnie heads for the raft [table].)

LUCY: Nooooo. Wait. *(Idea.)* I'll *tell.* I'll *tell* somebody. I'll tell *everybody.*

MINNIE: Oh, brother. Okay. Grab some headgear, girl, and let's go.
    (Lucy gets the other slip.)

MINNIE: We gotta beat it before they come lookin' for us.
    (Lucy climbs onto the table and Minnie helps. Lucy starts to sit in front.)

MINNIE: Hey, hey, get behind, pipsqueak.

LUCY: How come I have to be behind?

MINNIE: Because I'm the queen.

LUCY: You? Who am I?

MINNIE: Queen worshiper.

LUCY: Don't want to be.

MINNIE: Lady-in-waiting.

LUCY: No.

MINNIE: Navigator. Here; navigate or man overboard!

LUCY: I won't go overboard.

MINNIE: You will if you get *pushed.*

LUCY: *(She paddles once, then.)* Is this a raft or a canoe?

MINNIE: Canoe?! Girl, you have lost your mind.

LUCY: I guess I got the story wrong.

MINNIE: Be quiet and navigate.

LUCY: I'm too little to navigate.

MINNIE: Just hold the paddle like a rudder. *(Beat, amazed.)* Boy, I never saw the water so high.

(Lucy sees creek for the first time.)

LUCY: Yikes!

MINNIE: What?

LUCY: A creek, a creek!

MINNIE: Yeah so?

LUCY: No, a *real* creek. Where are we going?!

MINNIE: *(Sarcastic.)* I'm dropping you at St. Elizabeth's Mental Institution. Then I'm going to the little island in the middle.

LUCY: How will we get back?

MINNIE: We'll worry about that later, Hattie.

LUCY: Don't call me Hattie!

MINNIE: What do you want me to call you *today*.

LUCY: Call me Lucy. No! Call me…Lucinderoba.

MINNIE: *(Impressed.)* Sure; that's a great name. Lucinderoba. I'll call you that; just stop calling me Gramma. Give me the paddle.

(Minnie takes the broom. Paddles.)

MINNIE: Hang on, girl. I've wanted to get to this island for a long time. It's *uninhabited.*

LUCY: Does that mean no people?

MINNIE: Exactly.

LUCY: *(Stands.)* I don't want to go where there's no people. I want to go back.

MINNIE: We can't paddle up stream; just relax.

LUCY: Take me back.

(Lucy "rocks the boat.")

LUCY: I want to go back.

MINNIE: Hattie! Watch it!

(The raft "tilts," and Lucy slides off.)

LUCY: *(Sliding off.)* Oh, no.

MINNIE: Hang on! Oh, brother! Where did she go?! *(Shouting.)* I'm a hundred percent murdered if you're drowned. Where are you?

LUCY: Over here. *(On a book.)* I'm on a rock.

MINNIE: Okay, keep talking.

LUCY: Hey, I'm okay. I'm okay; I'm walking.

MINNIE: In the water?

(Lucy is wearing shoes in the shape of alligators.)

MINNIE: Wow, what are those?

LUCY: Alligator shoes! They go right on top.

(Minnie extends broom to Lucy.)

MINNIE: Pull us to the island.

LUCY: Me?!

MINNIE: You can do it, girl. Pull, Hattie!

LUCY: Not Hattie!

MINNIE: Pull, Lucinderoba, great strong brave girl.

(Lucy makes effort-filled sounds as she pulls them ashore.)

LUCY: *(Annoyed.)* First I have to paddle and now I have to pull?!

MINNIE: Pull, pull, pull, Lucinderoba.

(They get to the "island." Minnie jumps to "shore." The girls look around. At that point, the sun comes out from behind the clouds, the walls of the house become transparent, revealing foliage of which the house plants become a part, and the face of the ChairMan.)

MINNIE: Good going, girl. Come on. Jump outta them shoes.

(Lucy takes off the shoes.)

MINNIE: Let's find a safe place to put these.

LUCY: I'll do it! They're mine.

MINNIE: Okay, but keep them safe, we'll need them to go back.

(Lucy crawls around briefly looking for a safe place to put the shoes while Minnie looks around. Lucy shoves the shoes under the ChairMan's upholstery. She doesn't notice him; he watches with interest.)

MINNIE: Listen.

(A pause.)

LUCY: What?

MINNIE: No cars, no buses, no people. Just us.

LUCY: Creepy.

(Minnie does a little twirl of excitement. Runs up the hill (steps) to get a better view.)

MINNIE: As far as the eye can see, not another living soul.

CHAIRMAN: What am I? Dead wood?

MINNIE: *(To Lucy.)* Not another living soul, except *us*.

CHAIRMAN: By *us*, do you mean *me*, too?

MINNIE: *(To Lucy.)* Of course I mean you, too. That's what *us* is, you, too. If it was not *you too*, I'd say "not another living soul, just me."

LUCY: What are you talking about?

MINNIE: What am *I* talking about? What are *you* talking about? *(Mimics ChairMan's voice.)* "Does *us* mean *me, too?*"

LUCY: *(Worried.)* I didn't say that.

MINNIE: You did; I heard you.

CHAIRMAN: *I* said it.

MINNIE: I know you said it.

LUCY: *(Worried.)* I didn't say that either.

MINNIE: Enough already! Let's go investigate.

LUCY: I won't investigate!

    (Lucy sits down on the ChairMan.)

CHAIRMAN: I know you.

LUCY: I didn't say that.

MINNIE: Didn't say what?

LUCY: I didn't say "I know you."

MINNIE: I *heard* you say I know you.

CHAIRMAN: No. *I* said "I know you." She said, "I didn't say that."

    (Lucy slowly turns and sees the ChairMan's face. She tries to flee, but he grabs her by the clothing,. just like the burr in Act One.)

LUCY: It's the Chairman! *(Realization.)* The Chair-MAN! Eeeeeeeee. Let me go; let me go, let go of me. *(Continue throughout as necessary.)*

MINNIE: Let her go; hey you, ChairMan, let her go, or I'll fix your wagon.

CHAIRMAN: I don't think so.

MINNIE: I'll whack you one.

CHAIRMAN: Whack me all you will; I know torture; I've lived with children.

MINNIE: *(Sneaks behind chair.)* I'm warning you, ChairMan, you're looking for trouble if you don't release my sister. You may know torture, but do you know this?!

    (Minnie tickles chair.)

CHAIRMAN: Oh, no, not that, hee hee, ho ho, hee hee, ho ho. That is too cruel. Hee hee, ho ho.

    (ChairMan lets go, and Lucy escapes. Minnie takes her hand, and they flee.)

CHAIRMAN: Oh, no, don't go. I was only playing. I never get to go. Stuck in the same place year in and year out. How would you like it?!

    (Hidden, Lucy and Minnie watch and listen to the ChairMan's lament.)

CHAIRMAN: Little kids kicking and sticking and wiping, dripping and leaking on you. Chair abuse is rampant in the land. And is there a lobby, a coalition, a reform movement? Is chair relief the order of the day? Not on your life. I have to hear about reupholstering! Tear off my covers! Stretch new fabric! Stick me with pins! Sew on a new skin! Toss away my tired but trusty old cushion and implant a firm new foam appliance. Just so human behinds can be happy! Or, worse, redecorate entirely and just toss the old chair out. Boy, the stories I could tell about people if I could only talk. *(Pause.)* Wait a minute. I can talk. I am talking. I just have to…move. I have to walk. I *will* walk. Let me just – *(Pulls self free.)* I can walk. I can talk. Where is that little chair kicker? I'm going to have a discussion with her about the rights of chairs. And what's this?

(ChairMan picks up alligator shoes.)

CHAIRMAN: Ah, their transport; they can't escape me now.

(ChairMan exits with shoes. As girls walk on from the other direction. Minnie thinks it was fun. She begins to investigate the island: testing before she steps on sofa [bog] chairs [rocks] books [river rocks]. Lucy follows.)

LUCY: That was really close!

MINNIE: That was really a hoot.

LUCY: He coulda got me. Thanks, Gramma.

MINNIE: Don't start with that Gramma business!

LUCY: And I never did anything nice for you at all.

MINNIE: Oh, come off it; it's not that big a deal.

LUCY: *(Desperate.)* I'm sorry.

MINNIE: Sorry for what?

LUCY: I'm sorry…for something in the future.

MINNIE: *(Very suspicious, turns to her.)* Girl. What are you planning?

LUCY: It isn't a plan; it just happens. Can you forgive me in advance?

MINNIE: *(Continues investigating.)* No can do. Not 'til I know what it is.

LUCY: You won't believe me.

MINNIE: If this is more of that Gramma stuff, Hattie –

LUCY: Can't you just forgive me?

MINNIE: I say no can do.

LUCY: But what if, what if I do something bad – or mean, like not go in your room and talk to you for a long time – and then I never see you again. Just for instance.

MINNIE: You're giving me the willies, girl.

LUCY: Come on!

MINNIE: Forget it, Hattie. Now, what did you do to that ChairMan?

LUCY: *(Lying.)* I never saw him before in my life.

MINNIE: Then how come he said "I know you."

LUCY: I didn't do anything! He grabbed *me.*

MINNIE: Maybe it wasn't a grab; maybe it was a greeting. Think about it, sitting in one spot all day long. Somebody finally sits down, you want to give them a little hug.

LUCY: I don't. I don't want to give anybody a little hug.

MINNIE: Since when?

LUCY: No, you shouldn't hug. You shouldn't like people too much. Then you feel too bad when they die.

MINNIE: Hattie – You can't be an insane girl you just can't. You have no idea how hard it will be on me if they have to put you in St. Elizabeth's.

LUCY: Hard on *you*?!

MINNIE: Yes, hard on me. It's tough being the oldest. Every time I turn around, some parent says "where's your little sister? Watch out for your little sister."

LUCY: Well excuse me for living!

MINNIE: Oh, come off it, girl. Let's find that ChairMan so you can apologize to *him*.

LUCY: Find the ChairMan?! *(Scared.)* No way.

MINNIE: No, it's fun to talk to a chair.

LUCY: I'm not moving from here.

MINNIE: *(Sarcasm.)* Great. This will be real fun.

LUCY: There's no fun. The fun doesn't start until I'm grown.

MINNIE: *(Sarcasm.)* Oh, sure. Grow up, have kids, cook, clean. That's real fun.

LUCY: No. Be big, be brave. Go to college.

MINNIE: Now I know you've lost your whole mind.

LUCY: I'm going to college.

MINNIE: No, Hattie, you're not. Not a chance. Don't you listen to the parents talk nights? "Thank goodness the girls don't have to go to college." There's no Big chance for us.

LUCY: Well, that's not fair.

MINNIE: I'll say. If I ever have a daughter I'll make her go to college, be a doctor.

LUCY: No, you let her be a lawyer. I guarantee it.

MINNIE: *(Nodding.)* Lawyer's okay. Something hard with a lot of school. So she can make some dough.

LUCY: No dough.

MINNIE: Sure; lawyers make dough.

LUCY: Not *your* one. She's a lawyer for poor people.

MINNIE: I say stop giving me the willies.

LUCY: It's true.

MINNIE: *(Beat.)* Okay, big shot. How come you know so much all of a sudden?

LUCY: …Because of my game. My game I made up.

MINNIE: *(A challenge.)* How's it go?

(Lucy adjust her slip, acts this.)

LUCY: I am Lucinderoba – from the land of tomorrow.

MINNIE: You *have* been watching television.

LUCY: Yes! Yes! A fun TV game.

MINNIE: What's TV?

LUCY: *(Beat, big voice.)* TV is what us people from the future call television.

MINNIE: *(Impressed.)* Hey! You've got this all worked out; neat, Hattie. Let's hear it.

(They use big voices and act their parts, variously.)

LUCY: I, Lucinderoba, from the future world of humans, bring knowledge of the future to…Minnie –

MINNIE: Minnieroba.

LUCY: Yeah! Minnieroba! From the world of the *paaast*.

MINNIE: Tell me some things about the future, oh Lucinderoba.

LUCY: It is one true future fact that you get into very big trouble for taking the raft to the little island in the middle.

MINNIE: That's one safe bet.

LUCY: But you will survive it because your parents are so happy when you get found.

MINNIE: Tell me more, oh future girl.

LUCY: In future world, most kids watch TV many hours, except for your granddaughters, Lucy and Terroba, who don't get to watch at all.

MINNIE: My granddaughters?! You thought up granddaughters for me! You sure been busy, Hattie, I mean – Lucinderoba. What else do "my granddaughters" do besides watch "TV?"

LUCY: They order out pizza.

MINNIE: What's pizza?

LUCY: Pizza is future food. A favorite of kids.

MINNIE: What's order out?

LUCY: That's when they bring it to your house in a big truck.

MINNIE: Do future kids go on raft adventures and get to wear their dungarees when they play outside?

LUCY: Future kids get to wear dungarees all the time. To school, even. They call them jeans, though.

MINNIE: Girls too?!

LUCY: Girls do everything the same as boys in future world. In future world, girls go to college.

MINNIE: *(Normal voice.)* This is some future you've dreamed up, Hattie.

LUCY: Lucinderoba!

MINNIE: No, I'm really impressed.

LUCY: Now, I must ask you questions, oh young-human-girl-from-the-past. Who is in your house when you return from school every day?

MINNIE: *(Bowing.)* Various people, Future Girl, usually Mom and Hattie – my deranged younger sister.

LUCY: What do you do when you get home from school?

MINNIE: First the boring stuff of homework and chores, then I am free to play outside until dark.

LUCY: Who do you play with, Past Girl?

MINNIE: Sometimes I must play with the idiot sister, but usually I am free to play with my many friends.

LUCY: How many friends are there?

MINNIE: Many many.

LUCY: What is their number?

MINNIE: *(Normal voice.)* You want me to count them?

LUCY: Count them!

MINNIE: *(On her fingers.)* Well, there's Rudy, Julia, Randall, Holly, Marsue, Jonathan, Willie –

LUCY: Stop it! Are you making this up?

MINNIE: You know I'm not. There's: Sylvia, Noel, Morris –

LUCY: *(Real voice.)* Why do they all like you?

MINNIE: *(Pause, notices Lucy isn't playing.)* I don't know. I never thought about it.

LUCY: What *do* you think about?

MINNIE: I think – I like them, so I play with them.

LUCY: What if they don't like you?

MINNIE: If they don't like me, then they don't have to play with me, but I can't think about that – thinking about what somebody else might be thinking about makes me dizzy – quick, ask me something else!

LUCY: *(Big voice.)* One more future question. Humans in future world are very scared. What advice can you give future humans, Minnieroba?

MINNIE: *(Big voice.)* They should cut it out.

LUCY: They don't know how.

MINNIE: Well, Lucinderoba, can you tell me what everybody's so scared about?

LUCY: Robberies and guns and people dying and nobody's there when you get home from school, and the chair pounces.

(Minnie gives a big sigh. Walks up and down, as she tries to figure out how to help.)

LUCY: I, for example, am very scared in my future life.

MINNIE: *(Serious.)* Hattie –

LUCY: Don't call me –

MINNIE: Okay, okay. *(Beat.)* What's the worst thing that could happen, oh Future Person, Lucinderoba?

LUCY: *(Quietly.)* I could die.

MINNIE: Okay, you're dead. Now what?

LUCY: Well, that's really scary.

MINNIE: No. Everybody's really *sad*, particularly *me* because Mom and Dad are never gonna let me go anywhere, if *you* die. But it's not scary.

LUCY: Mom could die.

MINNIE: That's sad, too. But not scary. Don't be scared in advance, Hattie. Don't waste your time on stuff that might not even happen.

LUCY: You could die.

MINNIE: Oh, girl. Not for years. And I sure don't want to waste any time thinking about it.

LUCY: And you didn't tell the ChairMan to get me?

MINNIE: I don't even know this ChairMan.

LUCY: *(Pause, then big voice again.)* I have a commandment for you, oh, Young Girl InThe Past. You must obey.

MINNIE: Yes, oh Future Girl. Your wish is my commandment.

LUCY: You must forgive Lucinderoba for her future mistake. You must do it now!

MINNIE: No can do, Future Girl, uh uh.

LUCY: *(Pleads.)* Come onnnn.

MINNIE: No no no no no, uh uh.

(It starts to rain little letters on them. Lucy catches some in her hand.

MINNIE: Uh oh, rain. I hope the hurricane isn't coming back.

LUCY: This rain isn't wet.

MINNIE: *(Checks.)* Dry rain, whaddayaknow?

LUCY: This *isn't rain*. It's letters! Oh no, letters, it's little letters. Quick, hide them, hide them.

MINNIE: Why?

LUCY: Letters make us a target.

MINNIE: They're great! They're trying to spell something; right in my hand.

LUCY: He'll find us, the ChairMan; he'll see us. We gotta hide.

MINNIE: You should find out what this ChairMan's problem is.

LUCY: No!

MINNIE: Uh oh. There he is, he's coming.

(Lucy looks around, desperate.)

LUCY: We gotta, we gotta! Hey!

(*Lucy pulls the slip off her head and pulls it on up to her armpits.*)

LUCY: Quick! Do this, like meeee! Mushroom!

MINNIE: I beg your pardon?

LUCY: Mushrooms! Mushrooms, ninny!

MINNIE: (*Playing.*) What's mushrooms ninny?

LUCY: Pretend you're a toadstool. Disguise yourself. Quick!

(*Minnie puts on slip, too; not scared. The girls put cushions on their heads.*)

MINNIE: Okay, I don't think it's gonna help, though.

(*They wear their mushroom cushions. ChairMan enters.*)

CHAIRMAN: The letters are falling right here. What do they say? (*Reads.*) "Sitting ducks." But I don't see sitting ducks or sitting anything else. Except these toadstools. I don't remember toadstools. I think I'll have a little rest; chairs never get to sit on stools, except in the odd tumbling routine. I'll lean on one of these.

(*Chair leans on Lucy, she pushes back, there is a bit of back and forth.*)

CHAIRMAN: I never knew sitting could be so much fun! No wonder people are always sitting.

LUCY: You're too heavy!

CHAIRMAN: I'm sorry. (*Stands.*) I know exactly what you mean. Even the littlest person is eventually too heavy. Maybe I, too, should try a vocal complaint. "You're too heavy. Stand up. You're breaking my spine! Off, off, at once!" (*Surprised.*) That felt so good. I will; I'll talk back to them. (*To stools.*) Thank you. Which one of you spoke? (*Pause.*) Something odd about these stools. Well, I'm looking for two little sisters. One littler than the next. Have you seen them?

(*Girls shake their heads no.*)

CHAIRMAN: No? If they should return, give a shout, will you?

(*ChairMan starts to exit.*)

MINNIE: What do you want them for?

LUCY: Don't talk to him!

CHAIRMAN: I want to teach them a lesson.

LUCY: See!

MINNIE: What kind of lesson?

CHAIRMAN: History! That littler one has no respect for furniture history.

MINNIE: What did she do?

LUCY: Don't listen to him.

CHAIRMAN: Punching and kicking and tying up.

MINNIE: You *should* teach her a lesson or two.

CHAIRMAN: Just one.

>*(Lucy tries to exit.)*

CHAIRMAN: Where are you off to?

MINNIE: Nowhere. She's staying right there. Why don't you tell us the lesson? For practice.

CHAIRMAN: How kind of you. No one ever listens to me. *(Clears throat in preparation.)* Have you heard of Sir Lap, the Earl of Chair?

LUCY: The Earl of Chair?

CHAIRMAN: Yes, the inventor of chairs. The good Earl saved the human world from a day spent in toil. Before chairs, it was vertical all day long until nightfall when humans fell into exhausted horizontal sleep. They couldn't even go to a movie, before my Earl got involved. After the chair, he discovered human laps. The chair, the lap, the buffet dinner tray – all because of the Earl.

MINNIE: Is this the lesson you want to teach her? The littler little girl?

CHAIRMAN: In its entirety.

MINNIE: Would you excuse us for a moment?

CHAIRMAN: Certainly.

>*(The two mushrooms cross away from the ChairMan.)*

MINNIE: I say talk to him.

LUCY: What if he leans on me again?

MINNIE: So what?

LUCY: He's one heavy dude.

MINNIE: No, I say work this out. Go talk to him.

LUCY: What are you going to do?

MINNIE: I'll watch. I'll be right over here. Go on.

>*(Minnie exits. Lucy, from a safe distance, takes off her disguise.)*

LUCY: Hi, Chair.

CHAIRMAN: Lowboy, actually. *(Beat.)* I think I know you.

LUCY: I know you, too.

CHAIRMAN: Yes, turn around, would you? *(Lucy does.)* Oh, yes! Lucy. You're Lucy.

LUCY: You know me from behind?

CHAIRMAN: Everyone always turns their back on a chair.

LUCY: Well, of course.

CHAIRMAN: It doesn't do much for the old ego.

LUCY: No?

CHAIRMAN: No! They walk right up, turn around and sit on me.

LUCY: I'm sorry.

CHAIRMAN: Sorry to which part?

LUCY: All of it; the turning around, the sitting, the kicking, the tying up, the gum stuck underneath.

CHAIRMAN: Was the gum you?!

LUCY: Yeah, Mom was coming and I'm not allowed.

CHAIRMAN: Thank you, it was my favorite flavor.

LUCY: (Surprised.) Oh! You're welcome. I got other flavors, too, but I only stick it on you when I'm about to get caught.

CHAIRMAN: Glad to be of help. (Approaches her.) But in return, do you think, it would be nice, so very nice, I don't think it would be so much trouble –

LUCY: Stop right there, Chair.

CHAIRMAN: What?! What did I do? Was I big? Was I scary? I feel so misunderstood.

LUCY: Yeah, you're big. Yeah, you're scary. Nobody knows what's underneath.

CHAIRMAN: What should I do?

LUCY: Shorten your skirt.

CHAIRMAN: (Makes a deal.) If I shorten my skirt, will things improve for me?

LUCY: No more punching, hitting, kicking, or tying.

CHAIRMAN: Dare I ask for some affection? A little pat, instead of a swift kick.

LUCY: (Tentative, pats chair.) There, there.

CHAIRMAN: And something nice to wear.

LUCY: You mean like new upholstery?

CHAIRMAN: No! No more pins.

LUCY: Oh. (Idea.) Oh! How about a slip cover? There.

(Lucy puts slip on the chair.)

CHAIRMAN: Very nice.

LUCY: And you can wear these.

(She puts pearls on the chair.)

CHAIRMAN: (Touched.) Oh my, oh my. How do they look on me?

LUCY: Pretty great. I'll place them so they won't poke you when people sit.

CHAIRMAN: I feel my confidence growing.

LUCY: Here, take these rings, too.

(Lucy takes off the rings.)

CHAIRMAN: (Awed.) Do I dare hope to have those?

LUCY: Sure, I'll put them on one of your pre-existing safety pins. I'll be very careful not to re-stick you.

CHAIRMAN: I'd hate for you to get into trouble; are you sure it's alright?

LUCY: What's the use of having stuff if you can't give it away?

CHAIRMAN: Let me give you these in return.

(ChairMan gives her the alligator shoes.)

LUCY: Thanks. You're gorgeous, chair.

(Lucy gives the chair a hug.)

CHAIRMAN: And one last thing.

LUCY: What's that?

CHAIRMAN: Respect.

LUCY: *(Sad.)* I have no respect for furniture.

CHAIRMAN: Why not?

LUCY: I don't know.

CHAIRMAN: Is it something I did?

LUCY: No.

CHAIRMAN: Didn't do?

LUCY: No.

CHAIRMAN: Said?

LUCY: No.

CHAIRMAN: Didn't say?

LUCY: No.

CHAIRMAN: *I* know. Wait right here. I'll be right back.

(ChairMan exits through closet.)

LUCY: *(Shouts.)* Maybe Gramma knows how to respect furniture. Ask Gramma. *(Beat.)* Where is Gramma? *(Lucy looks for Minnie.)* Gramma? I mean, Minnie? Where are you? Hey, come back. Minnie! You can't investigate without me, you can't! Come back here.

(Minnie enters.)

MINNIE: Hey, girl! Just wait until you see the other side of the island. What's all the shouting?

LUCY: Big news. Big. I talked to the ChairMan. It's all settled. An arrangement. It's got affection, and consideration, and slip covers. Lot's of changes.

MINNIE: I say good going, girl.

(The ChairMan re-enters wearing Mom's suit jacket, which has split down the sides.)

CHAIRMAN: Hello there, hello young ladies.

(Minnie drags Lucy to one side to whisper.)

MINNIE: Whoa! What's with the suit jacket?

LUCY: I don't know.

MINNIE: That's what you said last time; turned out you *did* know.

CHAIRMAN: I have something to say to you.

LUCY: To me?

CHAIRMAN: No, not you. *(Points to Minnie.)* You.

MINNIE: Not me.

LUCY: Hah! Now he wants you. Now *you're* scared.

MINNIE: Who me? *(Scared.)* Scared of a suit? Don't be ridiculous. Go find out what's what. I'll wait…right here.

(Lucy crosses to the ChairMan.)

LUCY: Hey you, ChairMan! Why are you wearing that suit jacket?

CHAIRMAN: Isn't it obvious?

LUCY: Not to me.

CHAIRMAN: Well it will be. Just you listen to me talk with this suit jacket on. Watch. See if you don't respect me. I'm going to talk to Terroba.

LUCY: That's not Terroba. Terroba is – Terroba is far away.

CHAIRMAN: Now, now, don't play games. Watch me give her the big chance. Her one big chance. From me, the ChairMan.

LUCY: Oh, man. This is Terroba's one big chance?

CHAIRMAN: It is, it is.

LUCY: Wait a second.

(Lucy crosses to Minnie.)

LUCY: *(To Minnie.)* This is the big chance.

MINNIE: To do what?

CHAIRMAN: To get a suit. Go to Utah. Law school. College.

MINNIE: I get to go to college?

CHAIRMAN: You do. Maybe.

MINNIE: Oh wow. I don't know.

LUCY: No, go ahead, take it, take your big chance.

MINNIE: I'm not ready. I don't know what to say.

CHAIRMAN: Time's a wasting.

MINNIE: *(Upset.)* No can do. Not ready. Not prepared. Uh uh.

LUCY: Listen, *girl*, I say yes, can do. If this ChairMan in a suit jacket is not impressed with you, he isn't worth a hoot, and I,…your little sister, declare it.

MINNIE: I don't have what it takes to impress a suit.

LUCY: *(Idea.)* Hey! Wait, wait right here. Keep him here. Keep him talking.

(Lucy crosses to little letters and gathers the A's. Minnie crosses to ChairMan.)

MINNIE: Say, ChairMan, what's a ChairMan in a suit jacket do?

CHAIRMAN: Gets to sit on the board.

MINNIE: We don't have a board here. Wanna sit on our raft?

CHAIRMAN: Why, thank you.

(ChairMan climbs on the table.)

MINNIE: Doesn't look like such a tough job to me.

CHAIRMAN: That's because you're not wearing a suit jacket. Many things come clear when you slip your arms into a suit jacket. You get a greater clarity of vision. I highly recommend it.

LUCY: *(To Minnie.)* Pssst. Hey, come here.

MINNIE: *(To Lucy.)* I don't think he's impressed with me at all.

LUCY: No, he's just got suit affliction. Show him these.

MINNIE: Look at all these A's!

LUCY: Yeah, that'll impress him for sure. Keep some with you at all times. Then you'll always be ready for your big chance.

MINNIE: I'll keep some in my pocket. *(Beat, to ChairMan.)* Hey, Mr. ChairMan, what's all that about a chance?

CHAIRMAN: A *big* chance. Do you want it?

MINNIE: Probably a few A's would help.

CHAIRMAN: Well, of course. Everyone is impressed with A's.

MINNIE: Well, I got a few.

(She tosses them like rice at a wedding.)

CHAIRMAN: Whoa! You have A's to spare. A's galore. More A's than I can even count. I'm impressed! *(They shake hands; then to Lucy.)* There! Can you respect me now?

LUCY: I can. I *do*. Very impressive.

(The storm begins again.)

MINNIE: Whadda you know? I got my chance.

LUCY: I want to investigate the other side of the island.

CHAIRMAN: *(To Lucy.)* What impressed you the most?

LUCY: So many things. I can't even choose.

CHAIRMAN: *(Really happy.)* Oh. Oh.

MINNIE: Come on you two. *(Getting raft.)* Lets investigate.

CHAIRMAN: How about when I said, "clarity of vision"?

LUCY: That was a good one.

(Big wind. The letters blow.)

MINNIE: Uh oh. I don't think anybody's going anywhere for a while. Come on, come in here.

LUCY: *(Protests.)* We have to save the little letters.

MINNIE: Come on, girl, no time. Let's go in this cave.

LUCY: There's no room. It's too little.

MINNIE: Plenty of room. Come on. *(Minnie goes in cave.)*

CHAIRMAN: I'll gather up the letters.

LUCY: Wouldn't you rather come into the cave?

CHAIRMAN: Certainly not. We ChairMen can sit out, or out sit, any storm.

LUCY: Okay. Here I come. Here I come.

(*Lucy goes into the cave. The storm sounds escalate. The stage darkens, the room becomes a real room again. The room is a mess. The chair now wears pearls, slip, torn suit jacket, and unseen to us, rings; the alligator shoes are replaced with Gramma's alligator shoes. Morning light comes from the downstage window. The normal cuckoo sounds for eight o'clock. After a moment Lucy climbs out of the cave. She is confused, touches chair, walks around, sees the items from the dream: cave, letters, slips. Runs to front door; carefully peeks out, fearing the tree, then opens it all the way to look outside. The storm is over. Terroba comes out of the cave.*)*

LUCY: Here I come. Here I come.

TERROBA: (*Confused.*) What? Do you want to come back in here?

LUCY: Gramma?

TERROBA: (*Pause.*) Noooo.

LUCY: I want to investigate the other side of the island.

TERROBA: (*Surprised.*) The *island!?*

LUCY: (*Fiercely.*) Call me Lucy. I'm *Lucy.*

TERROBA: I know you're Lucy.

LUCY: (*Runs to the chair.*) I respect you, I respect you, now.

TERROBA: What island are you talking about?

LUCY: (*Beat, realizes.*) Terroba?

TERROBA: That's me.

LUCY: (*Amazed.*) I had a big dream.

TERROBA: I did, too.

LUCY: *You* had a dream?

TERROBA: Yep. Must have been all the wind.

LUCY: What did you dream?

TERROBA: There was…A storm. And a raft. And something about a Chance.

LUCY: What?!

TERROBA: Yeah. And there was an *island.* What did you dream?

LUCY: It was…wow, it's all slipping away.

TERROBA: Yeah, I hardly remember mine, either.

LUCY: My dream is fading all away.

TERROBA: Well, it must have been something. You made a big mess.

LUCY: I did?

TERROBA: Yeah; Gramma's stuff is all over the place. And you dumped your spell game.

LUCY: All my little letters.

(*Lucy picks up Mom's torn jacket from the chair.*)

TERROBA: We'll find them; don't worry. What happened to Mom's jacket?

LUCY: I don't know.

TERROBA: Good thing Mom doesn't wear it.

LUCY: Let's put more pretty things on the chair.

(Lucy looks around for something else to put on the chair instead of slips, see the covered painting.)

LUCY: Gramma! Gramma! She escaped from her painting; we got to get her back.

(Lucy runs to the portrait and takes the table cloth off of it. It is unchanged.)

LUCY: *(Surprised.)* Oh.

TERROBA: She's still in her painting, Lucy.

LUCY: *(Looks closely at painting.)* What's she wearing under her dress?

TERROBA: I never noticed. What is it?

LUCY: Looks like blue jeans.

TERROBA: I don't know if they had them back then.

LUCY: Hi, Gramma.

TERROBA: She can't hear you, Lucy.

LUCY: *(Beat.)* Did Gramma ever go to college?

TERROBA: Yeah. She got a scholarship.

LUCY: *(Beat.)* Let's put the tablecloth on the chair.

TERROBA: Okay.

(They put table cloth on chair, Lucy finds the rings.)

LUCY: Look!

TERROBA: Oh, Man. Wow. The tiny little diamond and the beautiful blue stone. It's a good thing we didn't throw this chair away.

LUCY: We're not ever gonna throw this chair away. *(Handing Terroba the little diamond.)* Thanks 'Roba.

TERROBA: Why?

LUCY: *(Beat.)* I gotta thank somebody.

TERROBA: *(Pause.)* You're welcome. And thank *you*. *(For the tiny little diamond.)*

LUCY: You're welcome. Let's fix the chair.

(Lucy takes the pearls from the chair and they drape the tablecloth, put the pearls back on the chair. The telephone rings.)

BOTH: Mom!

(They run for the phone. Terroba gets it.)

TERROBA: Mom?! Hi, Mom; we're fine. No, we were never scared.

LUCY: Let me talk.

TERROBA: We went to sleep so we wouldn't notice so much. *(Listen.)* You did? *(To Lucy.)* She slept at a school. *(Listen, to Lucy.)* There were fifty other stranded people and neighbors brought over blankets and pillows and dinners. *(Listen.)*

Oh, Mom, you didn't have to worry about us. We were never scared. Goodbyeiloveyou. Here.

(Hands phone to Lucy.)

TERROBA: Hurry up, so she can come home.

LUCY: Mom! I was never scared, well, maybe once, when the tree fell down. And when the phone died. And when the lights went out. But I'm not scared now. *(Listen.)* The big tree in the yard. *(Looks around room.)* Listen Mom, don't hurry home, drive *carefully*, we're not scared, really not. Goodbyeiloveyou.

(The sunlight comes through the window downstage. Lucy walks downstage to look out the window. Terroba does, too. The girls look out. The light hits the portrait behind them. Lucy puts her arm around Terroba. Terroba is really surprised, but doesn't say anything. After a second, she puts her arm around Lucy. They are happy.)

TERROBA: *(Happy.)* What a mess. We're going to have to pick up the yard and the alley.

LUCY: Find the trash can.

TERROBA: There's probably a lot of trees down.

LUCY: Yeah. *(Beat.)* Let's go out.

TERROBA: Yeah! Oh; maybe we should wait.

(Lucy runs to the closet and goes inside it.)

LUCY: No, let's go out. Let's go…*investigate* our street. Where's your coat?

TERROBA: The closet. Don't you want me to get it?

LUCY: No, I got it; here. *(The girls suit up.)* Now, be careful out there. Keep your eyes peeled for loose branches and stay close. Then we'll come back and clean up; we'll make it beautiful. I'll help.

TERROBA: Great.

LUCY: We'll cook breakfast. We'll call up Emily. Tell her to come over for breakfast.

TERROBA: She won't come.

LUCY: She will if it's peanut butter waffles. Nobody can resist peanut butter waffles.

TERROBA: We can try.

LUCY: Sure. We can do anything.

(They exit through the front door. The lights fade except on the portrait and the chair where they linger for a moment, and blackout.)

END OF PLAY

Mother Hicks
by Suzan L. Zeder

Mother Hicks is dedicated to Mary Ellen Bridges,
whom I never met, but feel as though I know.

AUTHOR'S NOTE

This play came from somewhere and passed through me on its way to somewhere else. The idea first presented itself after I read a collection of oral lore from the W.P.A. Federal Writer's Project, written during the Depression. I was struck by the number of witch tales which provided supernatural explanations for natural disasters, and by the need of communities to create witches as scapegoats in troubled times and landscapes.

The writing of this play has been a joyous voyage of discovery for me. The witch stories, locations, and details of place and period are real and historically accurate. The characters and storyline are original and have shaped themselves through me. This play has always moved with its own power. It has told me where it needed to go next, and whenever I came to my desk there were characters waiting to talk to me.

I have one deep and serious production concern with this play. I strongly urge potential producers and directors to cast a deaf or hearing impaired actor in the role of Tuc. Although it may take a little extra time and effort to find and work with this actor, the benefits are overwhelming. It is the difference between someone copying choreographed movements and someone dancing in the language of their soul. The use of sign in this play is a language as precise as any of the words spoken aloud. If sign language is to have dramatic impact it must have meaning; it must be real and specific if it is to have emotional eloquence and physical poetry.

I have had a special relationship with this play. I wish you the same. May it help you "see the sharp sting of honey and taste the sunrise."

Suzan L. Zeder
Dallas, Texas
1986

ORIGINAL PRODUCTION

Mother Hicks was originally produced by Seattle Children's Theatre May 6, 1983. It was directed by Rita Giomi with the following cast:

GIRL	Emily Jenkins
TUC	Keith Dahlgren
MOTHER HICKS	Toni Cross
BOYD BOLLINGS, JAKE HAMMON	Kevin Cavanah
HOSIAH WARD, RICKY RICKS	Brian Faker
IZZY SNIPES	Cecilie D. Keenan
RINDY SUE RICKS, LIBRARIAN	Sheri Lee Miller
ALMA WARD	Carmen Roman
WILSON WALKER, HOWIE HAMMON	Christopher Tolfree

CHARACTERS

TUC, a deaf man, in his 20's
GIRL, a foundling, 13 years old
MOTHER HICKS, an ageless woman in her 40's
CHORUS (who translate for Tuc and play the following roles)
RICKY RICKS, 12 years old
IZZY SUE RICKS, his mother
JAKE HAMMON, farmer
HOWIE HAMMON, his son, 11 years old
CLOVIS P. EUDY, shopkeeper
WILSON WALKER, writer for the WPA
HOSIAH WARD, mortician
ALMA WARD, his wife

SETTING

The town of Ware, in southern Illinois:
Act One: Various locations in and around town
Act Two: Dug Hill, the store, a street, Cairo, the graveyard

TIME

Late Spring, 1935

MOTHER HICKS

ACT ONE

The set consists of a large open area on a gently raked stage. Downstage there are two tall telephone poles with terminals and cables. The wires stretch diagonally upstage and connect with another smaller pole. There is a feeling of uncluttered vastness reaching toward a disappearing horizon.

Opening music is a folk song of the Depression: an upbeat kind of song: not too city, not too country; that reflects the tension and trouble of the time. House lights fade with the music and a tinkling bell is heard in the silence of the darkness. A rosey hued cyclorama floods the stage.

A figure is seen silhouetted against the cyclorama. Tuc pulls a large wagon, ringing the bell as he crosses downstage. As lights come up we see that the wagon is loaded with odd pieces of furniture, hung with miscellaneous costume pieces, and rigged with a variety of props. From this wagon will come many of the costume and prop pieces used by the Chorus as they take their various roles and move the action from scene to scene. Tuc pulls the wagon to a spot center-stage, and steps into a bright pool of light. The Chorus enters behind him.

Tuc signs in silence for a beat or two, then the Chorus speaks his words.

CHORUS: Mother Hicks is a witch, people say.
    And she lives all alone at the top of Dug Hill
    And she works her magic on the town below.
    When cracks is seen in the dry creek bed
    When the corn burns up
    When a calf's born dead
    Mother Hicks is a witch, people say.
    When a child falls sick
    And there ain't no cause
    And there ain't no cure
    Then everybody knows that it's witched for sure.
    Mother Hicks is a witch…people say.
    (*During the following, Chorus members come forward, speak a few lines, take an article of clothing from the wagon, and exit. Tuc continues signing.*)

CHORUS: This time is Spring in 1935

A year of fear in the Great Depression.

This place is Ware. W.A.R.E.

The Mississippi River's over there.

This is southern Illinois,

But we call it Egypt.

(*A single Chorus member remains; comes forward and shares the edge of the spotlight with Tuc. All subsequent translations of sign language will be handled this way: the interpreter shares the light, but gives focus to the sign.*)

CHORUS: My name is Tuc.

I cannot speak. I cannot hear.

I use my hands and the words appear.

I hang these words in the air for you

To tell a story that I know is true;

'Cause I heard every word with my eyes.

It is deep in the early,

Just before dawn.

(*Lights fade to blackout, a low throbbing electrical hum pulsates in the darkness. The sound is pierced by the shrill sound of a whistle. Lights come up on Girl at the top of the telephone pole.*)

GIRL: A dare is a dare and done. Dare and double dare, to sneak over the fence at the power station and fetch the quarter that Ricky threw there. Up and over the fence and then drop down into the cool wet grass. (*She drops down a rung.*)

Then I heard it, that stinging, singing sound; racing through them wires, and round them coils and cables; like the electricity wanted to be out like lightning bolts. It's true fact, that I do dares of mortal danger. Things that no one else in town would dare to do, or dare to tell they'd done 'em.

A dare is a dare and done!

(*From out of the darkness, a voice is heard off-stage. It is Ricky Ricks, a boy about Girl's age.*)

RICKY: Girl! Hey...You here, Girl?

(*Girl ducks behind the pole and hoots like an owl. Ricky enters.*)

RICKY: Dang it, Girl come out! If my Ma finds out I'm not in bed...

(*Girl jumps out of the tree and startles him.*)

RICKY: You just made me jump to Jesus!

GIRL: You should have guessed, Ricky, them hoot owls live in trees.

RICKY: It's five o'clock in the morning, and I don't exactly feel like guessing!

(*Girl flips a quarter in the air and catches it.*)

GIRL: A dare is a dare and done!

RICKY: My quarter.

GIRL: Nope, my quarter.

RICKY: I was sure you'd get electrocuted doing that dare.

GIRL: A dare ain't a dare unless there's danger. You got the money?

RICKY: I don't know why we had to do this so early. Why couldn't we wait 'till...

GIRL: Cause I need the money now!

RICKY: Then hand 'em over.

GIRL: (*Evasive.*) Uhhh Ricky, you know how you always wanted a pet, but your Mama wouldn't let you have a dog cause it'd slobber up the house?

RICKY: Yeah.

GIRL: Well, I decided to sell you my frogs.

RICKY: Your frogs?

GIRL: I raised them since they was squiggles, they're good hoppers, and they all got names.

RICKY: Names?

GIRL: I figure frogs with names is worth more than regular.

RICKY: A deal's a deal! You promised to sell me your Tom Mix Wrangler Badge, the Buck Rogers pocket watch, and the Orphan Annie Secret Society code book.

GIRL: I did a million dares to get all that stuff.

RICKY: ...*And* all the seals you collected from the Ovaltine jars.

GIRL: I had to go through all the garbage in the whole city dump to get those...

RICKY: Deal's a deal! I also want the Jack Armstrong Whistle Ring!

GIRL: But Jake gave me that whistle, he sent for it with Wheaties box tops.

RICKY: No whistle, no deal.

GIRL: But it's the only thing that ever came through the mail just for me.

RICKY: (*Turning to leave.*) Guess you don't want my money.

GIRL: I need that money, Ricky, I need it bad.

RICKY: Not bad enough.

GIRL: You can have the whistle! Hell-fire! You can have anything you want except my quilt piece. (*Girl takes off her whistle-ring and gives it to him. She unfolds her quilt piece which contains her treasures in a small bundle.*)

RICKY: Who'd want that dirty old thing?

GIRL: That shows how much you know! This here's fine embroidery on these here initials: I.S.H. fine embroidery, by someone's own hand!

RICKY: Let's go see those frogs, maybe I'll buy 'em for a penny a piece. (*Ricky starts out.*)

(*Girl follows.*)

GIRL: Penny? They's worth a least a nickel!

RICKY: I kin catch 'em myself.

GIRL: With names? Kin you catch them with names...and trained?

(*Girl and Ricky exit. Lights pick up Tuc and a Chorus member. Tuc signs.*)

CHORUS: A baby girl was found in town,

About thirteen years ago.

People took her in and raised her

Here, and there, and all around.

And so, she goes...

In and out of people's houses,

Like so many times before.

She rests a while inside a family,

Until they can't keep her anymore.

And then...she goes again.

(*There is the sound of distant thunder. From off-stage Jake is heard.*)

JAKE: Girl! You come here, Girl! (*He enters carrying a duffle.*) I want to get off before the storm!

(*Girl enters at a run, she is clutching an old sock.*)

GIRL: I got it. Jake! I got it!

JAKE: (*Not listening to her.*) Now, I told you, I need to be in Cairo by this afternoon and I can't go until I see you safely to the Wards.

GIRL: Sit down, Jake.

JAKE: Ellen and Becca packed up all your things, all they could find.

GIRL: Sit down.

JAKE: No, Girl. This one time you're not going to get me buffaloed I've got to get going.

GIRL: No, you don't!

JAKE: Girl, I told you.

GIRL: I got it for you. I got the money.

JAKE: What?

GIRL: I been collecting bottles at a penny a piece; I run groceries for Mr. Eudy, pulled weeds for Miz. Snipes, and sold some stuff. I got six dollars and forty-three cents.

(*Girls hands him the sock proudly. Jake sits on a stump.*)

JAKE: Girl, that's real fine; and Ella and me, we're grateful, but I need a bit more for the mortgage.

GIRL: How much?

JAKE: Two hundred and fifty six dollars.

GIRL: (*Simply.*) That's a lot of frogs.

JAKE: Huh?

GIRL: I kin earn it. I kin get me a real job...

JAKE: It's over. They took the farm and they'll sell it for back payments. I can't stay where I can't work.

GIRL: Bob Ricks digs ditches on the county road, Ricky told me.

JAKE: That's a WPA job. WPA stands for "we piddle around!" I wouldn't take a handout from those crooks in Washington if my life depended on it. There are jobs in Cairo, real jobs.

GIRL: (*Pleading.*) Take me with you.

JAKE: I can't.

GIRL: I could get a job in Cairo. I could give you and Ella all the money.

JAKE: I wish we could take you. Hell, I like you better'n some of my own kids. But you're not kin and I can't take responsibility for another living soul right now.

GIRL: I won't take up much room and I won't eat hardly nothing.

JAKE: Girl, neither God nor nature ever sent me anything before that I couldn't handle. Last year, when the flood came, I built a wall with sandbags. When we had that tornado, I knew how to get everyone in the shelter and wait it out. Even a war's got enemies with bullets; but there's something happening in this country now, like a terrible silent storm. I can't see it, or hear it, and I don't know how to fight it, and it scares me. (*There is a pause. Girl knows she can't change his mind. He hands her back her money.*)

GIRL: (*Very vulnerable.*) I got used to your family, Jake.

JAKE: Hush, now.

GIRL: I never got used to anything before. (*Jake pulls out a plug of Red Man chewing tobacco, Girl holds out her hand for some too.*)

JAKE: Chewing tobacco is one bad habit you'll have to break. Alma Ward will probably have a heart attack first time you spit.

GIRL: (*Suddenly angry.*) I ain't going to live with no grave digger.

JAKE: Mortician.

GIRL: He digs graves, don't he?

JAKE: At least, Hosiah Ward will never be out of work.

GIRL: I won't go to the Wards. He smells like chemicals and she's got a face like somebody's foot.

JAKE: Alma Ward is a nice woman and they can afford to give you a good home.

GIRL: I won't go!

JAKE: They're the only one's in town who'll take you. You just about used up everybody else.

GIRL: I'll run away. I'll hitch me a ride to Cairo and I'll find my people.

JAKE: I told you, Girl, we can't...

GIRL: I mean my *real* people!

JAKE: (*He has heard this before.*) Oh, Girl...You better roll up that tired old dream and put it away. Your people are long gone, or never were.

GIRL: (*Very upset.*) That's all you know! Maybe they're rich, Jake! Maybe they got a truck bigger'n yours; maybe they got a family, better'n yours! Maybe they got jobs and lots of money!

JAKE: If they're so rich, how come they never found you?

GIRL: 'Cause I'm hard to find!

(*She throws the money at him and runs off. He picks it up and takes off after her.*)

JAKE: Dang it, Girl! You come back...

(*Lights return to Tuc and Chorus member. Tuc signs.*)

CHORUS: There's a certain kind of spell

In the air, everywhere.

You can tell, very well, that it's fear.

Things begin to disappear.

Gone is the money in the bank.

Gone are the jobs.

Gone are the homes, and the families and their plans.

But they seemed so safe!

But they seemed so sure!

All of a sudden, everybody's poor.

Where did it go?

Who took it all away?

Mother Hicks is a witch, people say.

(*Ricky Ricks enters at a run from the opposite side and nearly collides with Tuc. Ricky backs off, frightened, and ducks behind a tree stump. From offstage his Mother, Izzy, calls.*)

IZZY: Ricky Ricks, you get back here and eat your oatmeal! You'll get it for supper, see if you don't! (*She enters, sees Tuc, shouts and waves to him.*) Tuc! Oh, Tuc, I've got something for you! Now you wait right there. (*To herself.*) I don't know why I do that. I know perfectly well that boy is deaf as a fire plug, but I always call out to him!

(Izzy exits back into her house as Howie enters looking for Girl. Ricky pulls Howie down behind the stump hiding from Tuc, who busies himself with his cart.)

HOWIE: Ricky! You just about yanked my arm off.

RICKY: Sorry.

HOWIE: You seen the Girl, my Pa's lookin' everywhere for her.

RICKY: I thought you were leaving today.

HOWIE: That's why I'm lookin'. She's got the keys to his truck. I gotta go.

(He starts off and Ricky yanks him back.)

HOWIE: Ricky!

RICKY: You got time for one last dare.

HOWIE: Ricky!

RICKY: Dare and double dare, I did the last one!

HOWIE: You did?

RICKY: You dared me to piss on the electric fan while it was running.

HOWIE: You were so stupid you did it.

RICKY: Well, now, you gotta sneak up behind Tuc and touch him without him seein' you.

HOWIE: That ain't nothin'.

RICKY: But you got to use your whole hand and not just one finger.

HOWIE: *(Not so sure.)* You do it.

RICKY: It's your dare.

HOWIE: I ain't got time, and my Pa's really mad, and...

(Howie starts to rise and Ricky yanks him back again.)

RICKY: Dare and double dare.

HOWIE: Okay! Okay! *(Howie starts moving toward him and hesitates.)*

RICKY: What's the matter?

HOWIE: I'm going...I'm going...

(Howie inches toward Tuc, Ricky pulls back his sling shot and takes aim at Tuc, Howie looks back and sees what he's up to.)

HOWIE: Ricky Ricks, you dumb ass, if you hit him he'll probably kill you.

RICKY: I'm just giving you some cover.

HOWIE: Yeah, sure.

RICKY: Go on.

(Slowly, Howie inches toward Tuc and just as he gets there, almost touching him, Ricky lets the stone fly, which hits Tuc who whirls around. Tuc makes a face at Howie who screams and races back to the stump. Ricky doubles up with laughter. Girl springs from nowhere and lands on Ricky, beating him up.)

GIRL: That dare was to touch him, not to hurt him.

HOWIE: Girl!

(*Tuc starts toward them as Jake enters at a run and pulls them apart.*)

JAKE: It's Okay, Tuc. I got 'em.

(*Tuc nods, gestures and crosses back to his wagon but continues to watch.*)

JAKE: (*To Girl.*) Wouldn't you know I'd find you fighting.

HOWIE: I found her for you, Pa! I found her!

GIRL: No you didn't.

HOWIE: Yes, I did.

GIRL: Shut up, Howie. (*To Jake.*) They was throwin' rocks, trying to hit…

RICKY AND HOWIE: No, I wasn't.

HOWIE: It was Ricky, he's the one with the…

RICKY: Shut up, Howie…

JAKE: Now, Girl…

(*Ricky picks up the car keys which have fallen in the scuffle. Howie snatches them away.*)

HOWIE: I found 'em for you Pa, I found the keys!

RICKY: No, you didn't.

HOWIE: Yes, I did.

JAKE: Shut up, Howie. Now, Girl, you are coming with me to the Wards, and you are coming, now.

HOWIE: (*Taunting.*) We're going to Cairo, and you can't go! We're going to Cairo, and you can't go! We're going to…

JAKE, RICKY, AND GIRL: Shut up Howie!

HOWIE: Yes, sir!

JAKE: You get on home and tell your Mother I'll be right there.

HOWIE: Yes, sir.

JAKE: And round up all the other kids, I'm not waiting on *anyone,* understand me?

HOWIE: Yes sir!

(*Howie exits and Izzy enters with an arm load of old clothes.*)

IZZY: Well, Jake Hammon, I thought you and all those kids were long gone to Cairo.

JAKE: We're trying, Izzy, We're trying!

IZZY: Well, good luck to you.

JAKE: I figure I'm due a little good luck.

IZZY: I expect you are.

(*Jake nods and exits with Girl, practically dragging her off.*)

GIRL: Hellfire, Jake, it weren't my fault…It weren't my…

(*Izzy crosses to Tuc with the clothes.*)

IZZY: (*Shouting.*) This here's clothes…*Old clothes.* (*She pulls out a pair of overalls and shouts even louder.*) I swear you can see daylight through the knees of these overalls, but I expect you'll find some use for them. (*She takes Ricky by the hand.*) They say he reads lips, but I ain't so sure.

(*Tuc smiles, indicates his thanks. Izzy exits. Tuc comes forward and signs. A Chorus member speaks for him.*)

TUC: Handed-down people and
Handed-down clothes
Passed from one to another
When the wear starts to show.
They give to feel good,
And then go on their way.
They don't know how it feels
To be given away.

(*Chorus sets up Clovis P. Eudy's General Mercantile: a counter with a cash register and candy jars, a few barrels, etc. Clovis enters with a crate. Whenever he talks to Tuc, Clovis uses a loud exaggerated tone. Tuc reads his lips.*)

CLOVIS: And these crates here, move them over there. Here to there. Understand? Comprendez? Got it?

(*Tuc nods. Wilson Walker enters, just as horn is heard off-stage.*)

WILSON: (*To Clovis.*) Excuse me, could you tell me if this place is called Ware?

CLOVIS: This place is called Clovis P. Eudy's General Mercantile; the town's Ware…

(*Horn honks again.*)

CLOVIS: …and that's the mail truck.

(*Clovis exits, Wilson crosses to Tuc who is moving crates.*)

WILSON: I beg your pardon; my name is Wilson Walker and I'm from the University at Carbondale. I'm doing some research on folklore.

(*Tuc continues to work, unaware that Wilson is talking to him.*)

WILSON: I'm collecting tales and legends and stories and sayings, that kind of thing, for a book about this region.

(*Tuc notices him and hands him a card which Wilson reads.*)

WILSON: "My name is Tuc. I am deaf and mute." (*Embarrassed, shouts at Tuc.*) Oh, My God, I'm sorry!

(*Tuc turns the card over and hands it back to him. Wilson reads.*)

WILSON: "Please do not shout. If you speak slowly I can read your lips."

(*Clovis enters.*)

CLOVIS: Leave him alone, he's working.

WILSON: I'm sorry, I didn't realize.

CLOVIS: What do you want?

WILSON: Information.

CLOVIS: Figures; information's free.

WILSON: My name is Wilson Walker and I'm from the Federal Writer's Project.

CLOVIS: From the government?

WILSON: Sort of.

CLOVIS: I've got nothing to say.

(*Clovis turns away. Before Wilson can respond, Girl bursts into the store.*)

GIRL: Mr. Eudy, Mr. Eudy, afternoon mail here yet?

CLOVIS: Still in the bag.

GIRL: Anything for me?

CLOVIS: You think I got X-ray eyes?

GIRL: I'm expecting a very important letter from Jake Hammon; see he promised to send for me, just as soon as he got to Cairo…

CLOVIS: Girl, you seen the last of that dirt farmer and his family. Now, the Wards is nice people and you've got a good home…

GIRL: It ain't my home!

CLOVIS: Well, you go along there anyway.

GIRL: I can't!

CLOVIS: Why not!

GIRL: They sent me for groceries! Here's the list from the stiff house!

CLOVIS: Girl…

GIRL: And one more thing that should be on this list, a plug of Red Man.

CLOVIS: Girl. I can't sell you chewing tobacco. I'll check the mail.

(*Clovis touches Tuc and hands him the list. They exit. Girl scopes out Wilson.*)

GIRL: Hi.

WILSON: Hi.

GIRL: You're new around here.

WILSON: Just passing through.

GIRL: You chew?

WILSON: Huh?

GIRL: (*Meaning tobacco.*) I don't suppose you chew, do you?

WILSON: Oh yeah, sure…Have a stick of Wriggley's.

(*Wilson hands her a stick of gum, she takes it but is obviously disappointed.*)

GIRL: Thanks. What's your name?

WILSON: Wilson Walker.

GIRL: Two last names? That's dumb.

WILSON: (*Amused by her.*) Oh, yeah? What's yours?

GIRL: Girl.

WILSON: I can see that, what's your name?

GIRL: (*Touching her quilt piece.*) Iswa Shunta Ho.

WILSON: Huh?

GIRL: It's a Cherokee name, you know, like these initials here on this Cherokee Indian blanket. I'm practically three quarters Cherokee.

WILSON: So how'd you get over here to Illinois, Cherokee?

GIRL: In a trunk.

WILSON: A trunk?

GIRL: My people was Vaudeville and they was always having babies in trunks and...

WILSON: I thought you said they were Cherokee Indian.

GIRL: They was Cherokee vaudeville.

WILSON: Oh!...so, where is everybody today, or is the town usually this dead?

GIRL: They're all at the funeral. Zollie Phelps got himself witched.

WILSON: Witched?

GIRL: That's what everybody says.

WILSON: Looks like I came to the right place.

GIRL: Oh, yeah.

WILSON: Well today, I'm hunting witches.

GIRL: Oh, yeah?

WILSON: Yep, I figure I've hunted down fifteen, maybe twenty witches between Carthage and Karnack.

GIRL: What do you use to hunt them with? Cross, silver bullet, holy water, Bible?

WILSON: I trap 'em here in this notebook and hold 'em tight in these pages, so people can read about 'em forever.

GIRL: You talk like a loon.

WILSON: I'm with the WPA...

GIRL: WPA? I wouldn't take a handout from those crooks in Washington if my life depended on it!

WILSON: Handout? This is a job!

(*Wilson sits as Clovis enters with a letter and a package.*)

CLOVIS: Hey Girl.

GIRL: He wrote! I knew he would!

CLOVIS: This letter's for Hosiah and the package from Chicago's for Alma. You might as well take it home with you.

GIRL: I told you it ain't my home.

(*Ricky Ricks enters.*)

RICKY: Afternoon, Mr. Eudy, is my Ma here yet? I'm supposed to meet her here after the funeral.

CLOVIS: She'll be along. I expect they're just getting to the Amens and Hallelujahs.

(*Clovis turns his back to Ricky who steals a licorice whip, Clovis turns just in time to see him.*)

CLOVIS: Did you get any hail over to your place?

RICKY: Yes, sir. Hail stones big as knucklebones.

CLOVIS: Queer time of year for hail.

RICKY: 'Hail in June is a Devil's moon,' that's what my Ma says.

CLOVIS: I'll check on your order, Girl.

(*Clovis exits. Ricky swipes another piece of licorice. He sees Girl and brandishes his Jack Armstrong whistle-ring with a flourish and blows it.*)

RICKY: Hey, Girl, want to see a neat ring I got here?

GIRL: Not especially.

(*Ricky blows it again just to tease her.*)

GIRL: Hey, Ricky, how about if I come to live at your house for a while?

RICKY: You give me back my quarter?

GIRL: Yeah…

(*Girl tosses him the quarter, Ricky takes it.*)

RICKY: You kin sleep with the baby. She don't do nothing but cry and make bad smells.

GIRL: I don't mind.

(*Ricky sniffs in her direction.*)

GIRL: You got a cold, boy?

RICKY: I just wondered if you smelled like the dead yet.

GIRL: Get out of here.

RICKY: Well, you've been staying over to the grave-diggers.

GIRL: Ricky, I'm going to bust you one if you don't…(*Girl stops and sniffs herself.*) Do I?

RICKY: (*Seriously.*) Not so I can tell, of course I never smelled the dead.

GIRL: Neither have I!

RICKY: (*Teasing.*) They make you sleep in a coffin?

GIRL: Shut up, Ricky.

RICKY: You ever see any…bodies?

GIRL: I'm warning you.

RICKY: Alright!

(*Ricky turns away to steal a licorice whip just as Izzy enters.*)

IZZY: Ricky, stop stealing those licorice whips, you know I always wind up paying for them later.

RICKY: I like snitching them better!

IZZY: Ricky!

GIRL: Miz Ricks, I'm going to come and live with you for a while. Ricky said it was okay.

IZZY: But you're staying over with Alma and Hosiah Ward.

GIRL: You don't want me, huh?

IZZY: (*Simply.*) We can't afford you, not now. I'm sorry.
(*Girl turns away. Clovis enters.*)

CLOVIS: Morning, Izzy. You feeling any better today?

IZZY: Oh, not hardly. I feel like I'm something sent for that couldn't come. If I didn't know better I'd swear I'd been hexed.

CLOVIS: How was the funeral?

IZZY: Poor old Zollie, he sure did look...oh, I don't know...dead. It was witch-work, Clovis, witch-work.

CLOVIS: You think?

IZZY: I know! Last time she came to town, Zollie cursed her for making his cows go dry. From that day on, he was a dead man.

GIRL: Zollie Phelps was a drunk.

IZZY: You watch your mouth, Girl. He was my cousin.

GIRL: Jake Hammon always said, witches was bunk.

IZZY: Well, Hammon didn't know everything, young lady. There's not a sane person in this town would make light of witches, not in witch weather.

GIRL: Witch weather?

IZZY: When its cold like this, long past time for summer; when the thunder clouds roll in and the hail comes like frozen pieces of lightning, then it's Mother Hicks, up to her old tricks.
(*Wilson crosses down to them.*)

WILSON: Excuse me, did you say Mother Hicks?

IZZY: What if I did?

WILSON: My name is Wilson Walker, I'm with the Federal Writer's Project.

IZZY: Federal Writer's Project. I've heard of that! I heard Mrs. Roosevelt talking about it on the radio!

WILSON: Yes Mam, I'm with the Folklore Division: my subject is witchcraft.

CLOVIS: Witchcraft, you say.

WILSON: I was on my way to Jonesboro but I decided to stop and see if I could find out about this Mother Hicks.

IZZY: Well, you better look up on Dug Hill. You won't find her down here in town.

WILSON: People say this Mother Hicks is a witch.

IZZY: Mother Hicks is a witch alright, and she lives all alone at the top of Dug

Hill. And most every night at midnight she comes to the graveyard and casts spells with devil dolls and tiny little clothes and tiny little shoes.

WILSON: People say she used to be a midwife.

IZZY: Until she stopped birthing babies and started witching them.

CLOVIS: Babies got sick.

IZZY: Babies died!

CLOVIS: People say she used to have a child herself once.

IZZY: A little girl, but she gave that child to the Devil.

GIRL: Gaw!

(*Ricky and Girl listen, mouths agape.*)

IZZY: (*Tweeking Ricky's ear.*) Now, don't these little pitchers have the biggest ears?

RICKY: Cut it out, Ma.

GIRL: What about you, Two Names. Do you believe in witches?

WILSON: I've collected five notebooks full of stories.

GIRL: Stories or lies?

WILSON: The people who told them, told them as true. I believe every voice in these notebooks.

(*Girl takes a notebook from Wilson and glances through it. Tuc enters with a box. He works as they talk about him.*)

CLOVIS: You see that poor unfortunate man?

WILSON: Yes.

CLOVIS: Mother Hicks witched him, when she came to nurse him through the fever.

(*A hooded figure with a walking stick slowly approaches the store. The others, wrapped up in Izzy's story, do not notice.*)

IZZY: When he cried that fever cry, she touched his throat and caught that cry; then she looked at him with the evil eye and sucked up his sounds into silence. The last sound that boy ever heard was Mother Hicks singing to him. Mother Hicks is a witch alright.

GIRL: Mother Hicks *is* a witch!

WILSON: People say…

(*The figure raps sharply on the counter with the walking stick. All look up, startled. The figure walks directly to Clovis and hands him an empty box of shotgun shells. Izzy and Ricky turn away as she passes. Girl is frightened but curious. Wilson is confused at first, then fascinated.*)

WILSON: What's going on?

IZZY: Shut up, you damn fool.

WILSON: That's *her*, isn't it?

(*Wilson starts to speak to Mother Hicks, but she turns toward him and his mouth is dry as ash. She turns back to Clovis who hands her a full box of shells. She pays him and exits swiftly.*)

WILSON: (*Staring after her.*) I want to talk to her.

(*Izzy grabs his arm.*)

IZZY: Then you go up Dug Hill, all by yourself. Don't you see, she's down here because of the funeral. She must have smelled it all the way up witch mountain.

(*When Tuc finishes he touches Girl who is startled and screams.*)

GIRL: Ahhh!

(*They all jump.*)

GIRL: You just made me jump to Jesus!

CLOVIS: Your order's ready, Girl. You take the sack and I'll send Tuc along later with the heavy things. Now go straight home! (*Clovis exits.*)

WILSON: How do I get to Dug Hill?

IZZY: Just up the Jonesboro road.

WILSON: Good, that's the way I'm headed.

IZZY: But you won't find her, unless she wants to be found. Come on, Ricky. Good-bye, Mr. Wilson.

WILSON: (*Correcting.*) Walker.

IZZY: (*Flustered.*) Walker...Wilson...whatever! Good-bye. (*Izzy exits.*)

WILSON: Thank you, you've been most helpful.

(*Wilson starts out. Girl still has one of his notebooks.*)

GIRL: Wait!

WILSON: What?

(*Girl makes a decision to keep the book and hides it.*)

GIRL: Uhhhh, good luck, Two Names.

WILSON: So long Cherokee!

(*Wilson exits. Girl starts out.*)

RICKY: Hey, Girl, I know the dare of dares, the dare of dares!

GIRL: What?

RICKY: Go to the graveyard late tonight and touch Mother Hicks if she comes.

GIRL: Shut up, Ricky!

RICKY: Dare and double dare? (*He spits on his hand. Pause.*)

GIRL: Dare and double dare!

(*She spits on her hand and they shake. They exit.*)

(*Tuc comes forward and signs. Chorus member interprets.*)

CHORUS: That Girl never does what she is told
Instead she does a dare or two.

Like going down to the railroad track
When the Rock Island Rocket rips through,
Or going down to the quarry pool
Diving deep into cold black wells.
And nobody tries to stop her
Because there's nobody there
To tell her to be careful.
(*During this speech the Chorus has set up the Ward's dining room. Alma puts the finishing touches on the dinner table. Hosiah ties his tie, very precisely, looking in the mirror. He checks his watch.*)

HOSIAH: That's it, Alma. We start without her.

ALMA: Just five more minutes, Hosiah. I'm sure she'll be along.

HOSIAH: I've got to be there for the memorial service by 6:55.

ALMA: I'm sure she'll be…
(*Girl enters clutching the bag and the package.*)

ALMA: Finally, Girl! I was getting worried.

GIRL: (*Heading straight for the table.*) Oh, good! Supper's ready! I'm starved!
(*Alma takes the packages from her.*) Sorry about the package, it got a little ripped up on the barbity wire over to the quarry.
(*Alma exits into the kitchen with the groceries, she leaves the package on stage.*)

HOSIAH: Do you have any idea what time it is?

GIRL: (*She doesn't.*) Uh uh.

HOSIAH: It's 6:08.

GIRL: So?

HOSIAH: In this house dinner is served exactly at 5:30.

GIRL: Why?

HOSIAH: Because that's dinner time.

GIRL: At Jake's, dinner was whenever you got to the grub.
(*Alma enters with a plate of food.*)

ALMA: Do you want to change for supper?

GIRL: Change what?

ALMA: (*A bit amused.*) Never mind. You can wash up in the kitchen.

GIRL: Don't need to. I been swimming over to the quarry.

ALMA: (*On her way back to the kitchen.*) But the quarry's closed.

HOSIAH: And there's a big sign saying "No Trespassing."

GIRL: I wasn't trespassing. I was swimming.

HOSIAH: (*Calling out to Alma.*) Remember that memorial service, Alma. They can't get started without the ashes.

GIRL: That's disgusting.

HOSIAH: It's a business.

GIRL: That's disgusting.

HOSIAH: What are we supposed to do, let people decompose wherever they drop dead?

(*Alma enters with biscuits and hears this.*)

ALMA: That's disgusting.

(*Hosiah starts to dish up food with a serving fork.*)

GIRL: I don't see how you can do that.

HOSIAH: Do what?

GIRL: Touch food with hands that have touched the dead.

HOSIAH: I use a fork.

ALMA: (*Heading off an argument.*) Shall we say blessing?

(*All take hands, except Girl who reaches over Hosiah's hand to his wrist. They bow heads.*)

HOSIAH: Bless us, Oh Lord…

(*Girl isn't used to grace and starts for her food. Alma catches her eye.*)

HOSIAH: …For these thy gifts…

(*Girl starts for food again.*)

HOSIAH: Which we are about to receive through Thy mercy.

GIRL: Now?

ALMA: Now.

(*Girl digs in and begins to wolf down her food.*)

ALMA: I heard a queer thing from Izzy today. Folks are having trouble with their milking. Cows have gone dry morning and evening.

GIRL: (*Talking with her mouth full.*) I heard how a…

HOSIAH: *Don't talk with your mouth full.*

(*In all innocence, Girl spits her food into her hand and finishes her sentence.*)

GIRL: I heard once how a witch can milk a cow a mile away by wringing milk out of a clean white dish rag.

(*She pops the food back into her mouth, and wipes her hand on her knee. It does not go unnoticed by Hosiah. Alma just shakes her head.*)

ALMA: There is entirely too much witch talk in this town.

GIRL: Did you ever see Mother Hicks? People say she comes to the graveyard at midnight and does spells with…

ALMA: I don't want you going into the graveyard, Girl, not at night.

HOSIAH: Not at any time. You kids are always knocking over the gravestones and tearing up the plots. If I catch you in that graveyard, you're going to wish I hadn't.

(*Girl pushes away from the table and pouts.*)

ALMA: Can I give you another biscuit, Girl?

GIRL: No.

HOSIAH: (*Prompting.*) No what?

GIRL: No biscuit. I'm not hungry.

(*To break the tension Alma hands Girl the package.*)

ALMA: I was going to wait until after supper, but you might as well have this now.

GIRL: That package was for me?

ALMA: Since you've been so careless with this, I've half a mind not to give it to you.

(*Girl tears into the package and pulls out a new dress. She buries her face in it and smells.*)

GIRL: This is new ain't it?

ALMA: Yes.

GIRL: I kin tell because it don't smell like somebody else yet. I never had a new one, not one of my own.

ALMA: You need a new dress before you start at the big school next fall.

GIRL: I got no use for school. I'm going to Cairo to sell costume jewelry at Woolworths.

HOSIAH: Oh?

ALMA: You'll do no such thing; and speaking of school, we'll have to do something about your name.

GIRL: What about my name?

ALMA: If you're going to the big school you'll have to have a proper name.

GIRL: Why are you always trying to change me?

ALMA: I'm not trying to change you.

(*Girl tosses aside the dress.*)

GIRL: I like my old things better.

HOSIAH: (*To Girl.*) Pick it up.

ALMA: (*Picking up the dress herself.*) I just want you to be comfortable here.

GIRL: How can I be comfortable with you pickin' and peckin' at me all the time. I feel like a bird feeder.

HOSIAH: Young Lady, that is enough!

ALMA: It's alright, Hosiah…

HOSIAH: It is not alright. She comes into our house like a tornado and acts like a hooligan when you are just trying to give her something.

GIRL: I don't want anything! I don't want anything from *you.*

HOSIAH: Go to your room.

GIRL: It ain't *my* room. I'm going out. There's something I've got to do.

HOSIAH: The only thing you're going to do is to get to your room, before I let a spanking teach you some manners! Do you understand?

(*There is a moment of stand-off before Girl storms off.*)

HOSIAH: (*After a beat.*) I told you this wouldn't work, Alma.

ALMA: It might if you weren't so hard on her.

HOSIAH: Hard on her?

ALMA: It will work, we just have to be patient.

HOSIAH: We are just too old to be starting again with children.

(*Alma turns away, stung by his remark.*)

HOSIAH: And that one will tear you up! Alma, that kid was born bad and there's nothing you can do to break her of it.

(*Girl returns, sneaking out, but she hears the following.*)

ALMA: I can try.

HOSIAH: I give it another week, but then she goes.

ALMA: There's no where else for her to go.

HOSIAH: There's the State Home.

(*Girl hears this, and exits.*)

ALMA: Not while I have breath.

HOSIAH: The State Home is where that child belongs.

ALMA: Not while I have breath.

(*Lights change and Tuc steps into a spot. Chorus member speaks.*)

CHORUS: So I go and follow her.
> I have followed her before,
> As she runs down darkening streets,
> Until she can't run anymore;
> Or climbs a huge pecan tree
> To try to touch a star.
> I am there below in shadow
> Never seen, but never far,
> Should she fall
> Or suddenly be frightened.
> Out late, deep into night
> She goes to the graveyard
> In the pale moonlight.

(*During the last speech the stage has been cleared of everything but the telephone poles. This scene begins in deep shadow. In the distance there is the hooting of an owl and the cry of a loon. Crickets can be heard, softly at first, providing an understated tension. The lighting is eerie in the graveyard.*)

(*Girl enters, slowly, frightened. She moves through the graveyard with the utmost care. She stops for a moment and realizes that she is standing on a grave.*)

GIRL: Oh, my Lord! I'm standing on one…sorry! (*She steps aside gingerly.*) There's no such thing as spooks! There's no such thing as spooks!

(*Far downstage, to one side, Girl sits. She hums softly to herself. Tuc enters and watches the following at a distance, from the shadows.*)

(*For a few beats there is only the sound of crickets. Far upstage left the shrouded, hooded, figure of a woman enters and crosses downstage. She walks neither quickly nor slowly through the graveyard to a specific spot. She carries a basket. Under her breath she is muttering; only the rhythm and an occasional sibilant sound can be heard. The chirping of the crickets grows louder.*)

(*The woman kneels and carefully clears the ground in front of her, meticulously smoothing the earth. She removes a tiny baby dress from the basket, shakes it out, and places it on the ground. She removes a sweater from the basket, shakes it out and places it on top of the dress. A knitted cap, and two tiny soft moccasins are placed precisely in a human form. Suddenly, the woman stretches out her arms, catches her breath and slowly lowers herself onto the ground over the clothes. The cricket sound grows.*)

(*Girl rises slowly and moves toward the woman with an outstretched hand. The woman starts to rise, is aware of the presence and stops. Girl draws back into the shadow, but she drops her quilt piece. The woman kneels, Girl makes two feeble attempts to reach the piece and pulls back.*)

(*The woman gathers up the clothes quickly and turns toward the Girl's hiding place. She crosses slowly to the quilt piece, stops and picks it up. Girl is frozen with fear. The woman steps toward Girl and holds the cloth out to her. The crickets are deafening.*)

(*Girl reaches for the cloth and there is a split second when they both hold it. Girl looks up and they make eye contact. The woman drops the cloth, turns and exits back where she came from. Gradually the cricket sounds lessen, Girl steps out of the shadow, looks at the quilt piece and speaks.*)

GIRL: My heart is pounding. Louder than thunder, louder than Jesus. I close my eyes and see her eyes, shooting sparks. A witch can kill with a look. But then I see it, like a match, flare up inside her eyes, like she recognized me, like she knew me forever. And then her eyes go deep as wells and fill up with a kind of sadness.

She recognized me and I recognized her, too. She looked at me and knew me all my life. (*She looks at the quilt piece.*) I.S.H.…H, for Hicks?

(*A loon cries in the distance. Hosiah and the other Chorus members appear in the shadows.*)

HOSIAH: I thought I'd find you here. I told you to stay out of the graveyard!

GIRL: I go where I please.

HOSIAH: Girl, I warned you. (*Hosiah turns her over his knee. He spanks her in a stylized manner. He mimes three or four blows; his hand stops short of hitting her as the others clap providing the sound of blows.*)

(*Lights dim, all but a spot on Girl.*)

(*Girl rises slowly and looks toward the spot where Hosiah stands in shadow. She pulls out Wilson's notebook.*)

GIRL: Witches are never lonely or afraid because they got the power.

(*Lights dim. In the dark there is the sound of running water. Lights rise on Tuc and a Chorus member.*)

CHORUS: Early one morning, just before dawn,

I hitch up my cart and come down the long road.

Down to the town, from the hill where I stay.

I don't usually see much, but on this one day

I come to a clearing, near a stream and a tree,

And I saw the strangest thing I ever did see.

(*The water sound is louder as Girl comes down-stage with a sack. She carefully kneels and mimes the edge of the stream. She tests the cold water with her finger tips and shudders. She takes a white pan and a rusty knife out of the sack. She opens Wilson's notebook.*)

GIRL: (*She opens the notebook and reads.*) "This how you get to be a witch…Every morning just before dawn from Sabbath to Sabbath, go to a clear cold stream where the water runs east. Take a new white porcelain pan and an old knife gone red with rust. Wash that knife in water and pour a full pan of cold, clear water over your head and give your body to the Devil, saying…" (*Girl goes through the ritual as she speaks.*)

I swear that I do give

Everything betwixt me two hands

To the ways of witchcraft.

And I swear to do anything

The witch power asks of me.

(*Girl remains in her position and continues to mime the ritual as the scenes of her 'witching' are played around her. It should be clear that she is responsible for the various tricks and pranks, but she need not go through the actual business. Tuc signs. Chorus members speak.*)

CHORUS: That very next day.

I followed the Girl as she wandered around.

Strange things started happening

All over town.

Day One, Monday.

(*Girl reads from the notebook.*)

GIRL: "To make a witchball, gather up some cow hair, licked with cow spit. Mix with salt and tallow. Get some ashes from a burned down church, gather moss from a tombstone, and roll it all, in a ball, around a little piece of razor."

(*Upstage Izzy enters with a picnic basket. She looks in the basket and screams. Alma enters quickly.*)

IZZY: Oh, my Gawd! Oh, my Gawd!

ALMA: What in the world's the matter?

IZZY: Look there, what do you see?

ALMA: Why, Izzy, it looks like your supper for the church social.

IZZY: No, there, on top of the pecan pie! Look on top of the pie!

ALMA: Euuuuuuwwwww, it looks like a bug, a big, hairy, bug.

IZZY: It's a ball, it's a witchball!

(*Girl laughs. She remains in her position and repeats the ritual as the scenes of her witching are played behind her. Tuc signs each day as it passes.*)

CHORUS: (*For Tuc.*) Day Two, Tuesday.

GIRL: (*Reading from the notebook.*) "A spell is done by placing a witch wreath inside the hat of the person fer hex. The spell will grow around the person's head and he is sure to go mad."

(*Lights up on Hosiah and Clovis.*)

HOSIAH: It's a what?

CLOVIS: A witch wreath, made with feathers from a black hen.

HOSIAH: And you pulled that thing out of my hat?

CLOVIS: I think those headaches will stop now, Hosiah.

HOSIAH: You mean to tell me that bunch of feathers did a spell that caused my headaches?

CLOVIS: Nope, made your hat fit too tight.

CHORUS: (*For Tuc.*) Day Three, Wednesday.

GIRL: (*Reading.*) "A witch can turn herself into a black panther cat and prowl around unnoticed. If that cat steals something from someone, the witch will have power over them for sure."

(*Girl looks devilish and meows. Izzy crosses to Clovis.*)

IZZY: I tell you it was a cat, a big black panther cat, an unnaturally large panther cat and I heard it prowling around my washline and it stole a pair of my...personals.

CLOVIS: Now, let me get this straight. A cat stole your drawers and ever since, your vision's blurred, there's a ringing in your ears, you've got the chills, the shakes, the faints, and gas?

IZZY: That's right, Clovis.

CLOVIS: But Doc Gunner says there's not a thing wrong with you.

IZZY: That's how I know I'm doomed. When the Doctor can't find a thing wrong it's a sign that a person is witched. She's up to her old tricks.

CLOVIS: Mother Hicks?

IZZY: Mother Hicks!

(From here to the end of the scene, a low muttering of 'Mother Hicks' begins to build.)

CHORUS: *(For Tuc.)* Day Four, Thursday.

GIRL: *(Girl pours the water over her head again in the ritual. She is ill and shows it.)* I swear that I do give
Everything betwixt my two hands
To the ways of witchcraft...
(Alma crosses to Clovis.)

ALMA: When I woke the Girl this morning, she was burning up with fever, her hair was all wet and she was cold and clammy.

CLOVIS: What does Doc Gunner say?

ALMA: He's afraid it's pneumonia.

CLOVIS: Put a silver bullet in a bag and tie it around her neck.

ALMA: Whatever for?

CLOVIS: To protect her from witches.

ALMA: Doc Gunner says it's pneumonia.

(Muttering increases.)

CHORUS: *(For Tuc.)* Day Five, Friday.

IZZY: First it's dry enough to fry spit, then it floods the deluge.

CLOVIS: Radio says there's a tornado on the ground over in Jonesboro.

IZZY: The days of destruction are on us. Clovis, we've all been hexed by Mother Hicks.

(Izzy crosses to Clovis, Alma turns away.)

CLOVIS: It's just like it was in 1925.

IZZY: But in 1925 children died!

(Muttering increases, Alma, very upset, crosses to Hosiah.)

CHORUS: *(For Tuc.)* Day Six, Saturday!

ALMA: The Girl is going to the hospital, and she is going today!

HOSIAH: But Doc Gunner say's she's better off here at home.

ALMA: She's delirious! This morning she woke up screaming something about witchcraft!

(*Muttering increases to a chant: "Mother Hicks...Mother Hicks."*)

CHORUS: (*For Tuc.*) Day Seven, the second Sabbath!

(*Girl is extremely ill as she kneels by the stream and forces herself through the ritual. Throughout the next few lines, Tuc signs the numbers 1–7, one after another, as the scene builds in intensity.*)

GIRL: I swear that I do give

Everything...

IZZY: It's a witchball!

GIRL: Everything...

HOSIAH: I got these headaches!

GIRL: Everything...

ALMA: It's pneumonia!

GIRL: Everything!

CLOVIS: Children died!

GIRL: Everything betwixt my two hands

To the ways of witchcraft

(*Chanting builds to a crescendo.*)

And I swear to do anything

The witch power asks of me!

ALMA: (*Voice rising above the others.*) *This has got to stop!*

(*Silence. Girl picks up the notebook and reads, she is almost too ill to see the words.*)

GIRL: "Take a rust red knife

And cut the head off a living thing

Where the blood falls

The Devil will appear

And welcome you as a witch."

(*She is exhausted. She wraps her arms around her legs and holds herself together.*) But I don't want to be that kind of witch, the kind of witch that kills things. (*She spies a flower growing nearby.*) A flower is a living thing! (*She plucks the flower and holds it in front of her as she brandishes the knife above her head.*)

I swear that I do give

Everything betwixt my two hands

To the ways of witchcraft.

And I swear to do anything...

(*She brings the knife slashing down, misses the flower, but cuts a deep gash into her own leg. It is a serious wound and blood flows down her leg. She grabs at her leg in shock.*)

I cut myself...bad! I cut myself...BAD!

(*Tuc rushes from the shadows where he has been watching her. She sees him and screams. She faints, he catches her and lifts her up in his arms. Just as he turns upstage, a spot comes up on the shrouded figure from the graveyard. Mother Hicks holds her arms out as Tuc turns toward her. Blackout.*)

END OF ACT ONE

ACT TWO

Mother Hicks's cabin on Dug Hill.

With the addition of poles and canvas panels, Tuc's wagon is transformed into the cabin. All around are ceramic pots, baskets, jugs and small cages. Atop one of the poles is a wren roost. The area is lit by firelight from a large permanent campfire and several kerosene lamps around and about. A large smoking cauldron hangs above the campfire. Near the cauldron is a rocking chair.

Stage left is a makeshift pallet. Girl is asleep, wrapped tightly in blankets. She wears an old flannel shirt and sleeps fitfully. Near the pallet, Tuc squats on his heels and watches Girl. He has been there some time, keeping a silent vigil.

Girl stirs and moans and begins to cough deeply. Tuc rises and fetches Mother Hicks from the cabin. She crosses to the streaming cauldron and stirs a smoking cupful of the brew into a bowl. She crosses to Girl and hands the bowl to Tuc who puts it to Girl's lips.

MOTHER HICKS: Drink this.

GIRL: Don't hurt me.

MOTHER HICKS: Hesh.

GIRL: Where am I?

MOTHER HICKS: Dug Hill.

GIRL: I know who you are! You're...

MOTHER HICKS: (*Cutting her off.*) Drink!

GIRL: No!

MOTHER HICKS: Drink it or you'll strangle on your own phlegm.

(*Mother Hicks makes a sharp sign to Tuc; together they make Girl drink the brew. Mother Hicks strokes Girl's throat the way she might help an injured animal to swallow.*)

GIRL: What is it?

MOTHER HICKS: Brew of scaley bark, pokeweed, and rattlesnake yarb.

GIRL: Tastes terrible.

MOTHER HICKS: Better'n dying. (*Mother Hicks bends over her and loosens the blankets.*)

GIRL: This ain't my shirt. It smells foul.

MOTHER HICKS: Greased it good with hog fat and nutmeg.

GIRL: Why?

MOTHER HICKS: Reasons.

(*Mother Hicks draws back the cover and reveals the leg wound covered with a thick yellow mud. Mother Hicks draws a large hunting knife and passes the blade through the fire. Girl sees this and struggles.*)

MOTHER HICKS: Hold her. (*Mother Hicks signs as she speaks to Tuc. She repeats both the sign and the words with urgency.*) HOLD HER!

(*Mother Hicks approaches with the knife. Girl struggles as Tuc holds her down.*)

GIRL: Don't touch me! Don't hurt…

MOTHER HICKS: Hold Still! (*In one swift motion, Mother Hicks flips the mudpack off revealing a long healing scar. She crosses to the fire and reaches into a small bowl.*)

GIRL: What's that?

MOTHER HICKS: Hot yellow mud and vinegar, to draw the poison.

(*Mother Hicks slaps the poultice on Girl's leg. Girl cries out.*)

GIRL: Owwwwww!

MOTHER HICKS: Hesh up, you're not hurt. You're not hurt are you?

(*For the first time Girl realizes that she isn't.*)

GIRL: Some.

MOTHER HICKS: If I can't stop the festering, I'll have to cut it off.

GIRL: The mud?

MOTHER HICKS: The leg.

GIRL: No!

(*Girl struggles again. Mother Hicks signs to Tuc to hold her.*)

MOTHER HICKS: Now settle down and let that poultice dry. I'll have to tie you down if you don't.

(*Girl stops struggling and Tuc and Mother Hicks wrap her up in the blankets. Mother Hicks rises and checks the sky. As she speaks to Tuc, she signs.*)

MOTHER HICKS: We'll leave her out here while the weather holds; inside smells like skunk.

GIRL: What are you going to do with me?

MOTHER HICKS: (*With a crooked grin.*) Girl, I am doing with you now.

(*Mother Hicks exits into the cabin. Girl sinks back down as Tuc resumes his watch. Lights dim.*)

(*Pause.*)

(*In the darkness a shrieking sound is heard. It is just dawn, the sky is a bluish-red. Mother Hicks is kneeling over a large box. Tuc sits in the chair holding a lantern over her work. The shrieking sound comes from the box as does a thumping sound of struggle.*)

MOTHER HICKS: Hesh, Sister Kicker, hesh. 1, 2, 3, 4, 5 alive and come this dead one, stuck. There ain't no help for it, Sister Kicker, there ain't no help.

(*Girl wakes and sits up. Mother Hicks pulls the lantern toward her and lifts the chimney, she passes the blade through the flame.*)

GIRL: What are you doing?

MOTHER HICKS: Stay away!

GIRL: What's happening?

MOTHER HICKS: I said, stay...

(*Tuc is distracted and pulls the light away. Mother Hicks jerks his arm back.*)

MOTHER HICKS: Light, I need light!

GIRL: Stop it, please, whatever you're doing, stop it!

MOTHER HICKS: I can't.

(*At Tuc's encouragement, Girl inches toward them, horrified but fascinated at what is happening inside the box. Mother Hicks returns to the task at hand.*)

MOTHER HICKS: There, got it! Now, let 'em come. Snip, snip, snip and clip 'em off. Clip 'em clean!

(*After a beat, the sound subsides, Mother Hicks wipes her hands and knife on a rag; they are covered with blood.*)

GIRL: There's blood.

MOTHER HICKS: There always blood at a birthing.

(*Girl peers into the box.*)

GIRL: A rabbit?

MOTHER HICKS: Rabbits.

GIRL: I never heard a rabbit make such a sound before.

MOTHER HICKS: They only do when they're mortal scared or hurt.

GIRL: How many babies?

MOTHER HICKS: Five alive, three dead. (*Mother Hicks tosses three tiny objects into a pail.*)

GIRL: (*Pulling at the box.*) Can I see?

MOTHER HICKS: (*Protectively.*) If she gets riled, she'll eat 'em.

GIRL: Eat her own babies?

MOTHER HICKS: (*Peering into the box.*) Now, look at that, she's pushing them away, won't let them even get close to her.

GIRL: Why won't she nurse them?

MOTHER HICKS: Who knows why some critters don't take to their young? No reason, they just don't.

GIRL: Will she ever?

MOTHER HICKS: Likely not. (*Mother Hicks stands and stretches.*) Looks like the sky is getting ready to make itself a dawn. Come here!

(*Mother Hicks checks the fever. Girl pulls away.*)

MOTHER HICKS: I said, come here! The fever's broke…Good. But get back to bed before it's light.

(*Tuc carries her to the pallet.*)

GIRL: Can I name the rabbits?

MOTHER HICKS: No, but you can help.

(*Tuc sets her gently down and hands her the quilt piece tucked under her pillow. She is very pleased to see it.*)

GIRL: My quilt piece!

MOTHER HICKS: Go to sleep!

(*Girl goes back to sleep, lights dim.*)

(*Pause.*)

(*After a beat there is the sound of chirping birds. Lights rise on a morning scene. Mother Hicks kneels with several basins and baskets near her. She lifts an article of clothing out of a basin and wrings white liquid out of it. She shakes it out and we see it is a baby dress.*)

MOTHER HICKS: (*To the dress.*) So, there you are, all fresh and clean; all fresh and clean to go visiting. Tonight we'll go, just like I promised. Tonight we'll go.

(*Accidentally she squirts some water on herself. Girl wakes and listens.*)

MOTHER HICKS: None of that splashing, you hear? (*She splashes more water and laughs.*) And no spitting either!

(*Girl sits up.*)

MOTHER HICKS: Now, stop, I say, stop! If you can't keep from dousing your own…(*She is suddenly aware of Girl.*) What are you peeping at?

GIRL: Nothing.

MOTHER HICKS: You call me nothing?

GIRL: I didn't see nothing.

MOTHER HICKS: And if lies was food, there'd be no hunger in the world! (*Mother Hicks lifts out another article and wrings soapy water out of it.*)

GIRL: I know what you're doing!

MOTHER HICKS: What?

GIRL: You're milking a cow by magic! (*Mother Hicks pours a basin of soapy water into a bucket.*)

MOTHER HICKS: (*Gruff.*) Fever must be back if you can't tell milking from laundry.

GIRL: Laundry.

MOTHER HICKS: I save the soapy water for my yarbs.

GIRL: Oh…If it's laundry I can help. (*Girl limps over to Mother Hicks and tentatively takes an article and wraps it in a flannel cloth.*) I can take these flannel pieces and use 'em to wring the water out…These is baby clothes!

MOTHER HICKS: They is.

GIRL: There was all kinds of babies over at Jakes. Jakes is where I used to stay, and I used to love to play with 'em. They was all soft and white and plumped up, like dough before it's baked; soft little bread babies. (*She works as she speaks.*) This sure is fine linen, I can see right through it.

MOTHER HICKS: You be careful, mind?

GIRL: I mind.

MOTHER HICKS: Once there was a girl who wore that dress, and she had hair colored hair. You know how some folks go on about children and say they got hair blond as gold, or eyes blue as sky? Well, this little girl had hair colored hair, and eye colored eyes and she were beautiful.

GIRL: (*The question is important to her.*) What happened to that girl?

MOTHER HICKS: (*Bitter.*) Gone, taken with the rest.

GIRL: Gone where?

MOTHER HICKS: Just gone!

GIRL: Taken by who? Where was she taken?

MOTHER HICKS: (*Snaps at her.*) Watch how you touch that piece, you're strangling the life out of it.

GIRL: But I want to know!

MOTHER HICKS: Well, wantin' ain't gettin'! (*Tuc enters at a run, laughing and gesturing to Mother Hicks.*)

MOTHER HICKS: What in the…

(*Tuc signs something to her.*)

MOTHER HICKS: I don't know.

(*Tuc signs something else and they both laugh.*)

GIRL: (*Mystified.*) What are you laughing at?

MOTHER HICKS: This here fool.

GIRL: Jake always told me it weren't nice to laugh at him just because he's afflicted.

MOTHER HICKS: He told me a riddle.

GIRL: What?

MOTHER HICKS: He just make it up.

(*Tuc signs as Mother Hicks speaks.*)

MOTHER HICKS: What looks just like half a chicken?

GIRL: What?

MOTHER HICKS: (*As Tuc signs.*) The other half.

(*They both laugh, Girl is mystified.*)

GIRL: He told you that?

MOTHER HICKS: He did.

GIRL: How?

MOTHER HICKS: With them air pictures.

GIRL: You mean, all that fingering around means things?

MOTHER HICKS: (*Signs as she speaks.*) They teached him that over to the State School where he learned to lip talk. After he left the school and his people died, he came around and just stayed. He teached me some he learned at School, and I teached him some I made up, and we just built ourselves a talking way.

(*Tuc signs to her in a very animated manner. Girl is a bit taken aback.*)

GIRL: What's he doing now?

MOTHER HICKS: He's talking to you.

GIRL: To me?

MOTHER HICKS: He's trying to tell you something, but you're too ignorant to understand.

GIRL: I am not ignorant!

MOTHER HICKS: In his talk you are. He said…

(*Tuc signs and Mother Hicks translates.*)

MOTHER HICKS: You are my friend.

GIRL: Oh.

(*Tuc continues signing.*)

GIRL: What's he saying now?

(*Tuc signs the following speech as Mother Hicks translates. She places emphasis on what is being said rather than a word by word translation of the signs.*)

MOTHER HICKS: You look at me and only see things I cannot do, things I cannot be; but I can taste the cool spring water and know what month it is, I can smell the difference between the smoke of hickory and apple wood. I can see the sharp sting of honey, and I can taste the sunrise.

GIRL: Don't he mean he can taste the honey and see the sunrise?

MOTHER HICKS: He means what he says, that's the trouble with you town folks; you see and you hear, but you don't know nothing!

GIRL: Down in town, nobody knows he stays up here.

MOTHER HICKS: (*Suddenly bitter.*) I don't much care what they know in town.
(*Tuc signs something.*)

GIRL: What did he say?

MOTHER HICKS: He asked if we could put your old shirt on. You smell like a buzzard egg gone bad.

GIRL: (*Sniffing herself.*) I do!

MOTHER HICKS: Fever's broke, so I guess it will be alright. Go in, it's in the cabin.
(*Girl starts limping to cabin.*)

MOTHER HICKS: And watch how you walk on that leg!
(*Girl hops, on her good leg, into the cabin. There is the sound of geese and other animals. Tuc signs, "Girl stay here," to Mother Hicks.*)

MOTHER HICKS: No Tuc, as soon as she's well, she'll leave.
(*He signs it again.*)

MOTHER HICKS: She's just here for a spell.
(*He signs, "I want her to stay."*)

MOTHER HICKS: All critters come for the healing and then they go.
(*He signs, "I stayed," and Mother Hicks pats his cheek.*)

MOTHER HICKS: I know, Tuc, *you* stayed.
(*Girl comes out from the cabin wearing her own shirt. She also holds a large piece of quilted cloth which matches her quilt piece.*)

GIRL: There's a whole zoo in there!

MOTHER HICKS: Just the geese, a squirrel or two, and a family of skunks.

GIRL: Look what else I found. Do you know what this is?

MOTHER HICKS: Looks like you pulled down one of my curtains. What did you go and do that for?

GIRL: What does this look like?

MOTHER HICKS: It used to look like my curtains before you started tearing up my house – looks like it could use a wash.

GIRL: I'll do it.

MOTHER HICKS: Watch how you handle that piece, it's probably as old as you are.

GIRL: I know.

(*Tuc signs, "You are my friend," to Girl.*)

GIRL: Is he talking to me?

MOTHER HICKS: It appears that way.

GIRL: What's he saying?

MOTHER HICKS: I already told you once! You got the memory of a piss ant.

GIRL: (*Understands.*) Oh! (*She signs along with him.*) You are my friend.

(*Tuc signs "yes."*)

MOTHER HICKS: Look, I can't sit around here jaw jacking with you two. I got work to do.

GIRL: (*Curiosity peaked.*) Are you going to do…secret things?

MOTHER HICKS: (*Mysteriously.*) I am going to hang up this here laundry… (*Sharply.*)…if that is any of your business!

GIRL: I just wondered…

MOTHER HICKS: If you want to make yourself some use you can feed the rabbits and see if you can find their names.

GIRL: But I want to name them myself.

MOTHER HICKS: Every critter's got its own name inside 'em; you can't just make it up, but if you watch 'em close enough sometimes you can find it.

GIRL: I don't understand.

MOTHER HICKS: Don't matter, the rabbits do.

(*Mother Hicks exits with laundry. Girl and Tuc cross down to the rabbit box. Girl tenderly takes a tiny rabbit from the box and she and Tuc feed it with an eye dropper and a bowl of warm milk.*)

GIRL: (*To Tuc, pointing to the bunny.*) Sure is ugly, ain't it? Looks like a rat! (*Tuc teaches her the sign for 'rat.' With Tuc's help she feeds the bunny with an eye dropper.*)

GIRL: Wouldn't it be something if you could remember that far back, when you was as young as they is? If you could remember lying there and all of a sudden you see this big old milk nipple coming towards you and *Wham*…supper! (*She squirts the rest of the milk into her own mouth.*) Sometimes I can remember back that far, I really can. (*She puts the bunny back in the box.*) I can just barely see hair colored hair and eye colored eyes…(*Girl turns directly to Tuc.*) You remember your people, Tuc? Your Paw and your Momma?

(*Tuc signs "yes."*)

GIRL: They're dead ain't they?

(*Tuc signs "yes."*)

GIRL: You're lucky…Not on account of them being dead, that part's sad, but lucky you know where they are. You can close your eyes and see 'em live inside your mind. When you don't know about 'em...when you don't know, there's always something inside you that's hungry. (*Girl notices Tuc staring at her.*) When I see you staring at me, your eyes so big and round, I think I could fall right inside both your eyes and never be seen again. (*Tuc looks puzzled.*)

GIRL: Oh, don't mind me, I'm just talking loon talk. Loon talk, that's me!
(*Girl makes a circle near her ear and crosses her eyes, Tuc copies her gesture rolls over and laughs. Mother Hicks enters and spreads out the flannels, pours the soapy water into a bucket and generally busies herself. Girl crosses to her.*)

GIRL: Will you teach me things?
(*Mother Hicks does not respond.*)

GIRL: Teach me secret things?

MOTHER HICKS: Don't know any secret things.

GIRL: Some people call this place witch mountain.

MOTHER HICKS: Some people are stupid.

GIRL: I want to show you something, something special.
(*Girl fetches her quilt piece and holds it out to her. Mother Hicks focuses on her tasks.*)

GIRL: Have you ever seen this piece before?

MOTHER HICKS: Yep.

GIRL: You have?

MOTHER HICKS: When you first came, I practically had to pry it out of your hand.

GIRL: I mean before that, have you ever seen this before that?

MOTHER HICKS: (*Uncomfortable.*) I don't know, maybe, maybe not.

GIRL: I had this with me ever since I was born and see these initials here, these are sewn on with someone's own hand, and they stand for my name, see here I.S.H....what do you think the H could stand for?
(*Mother Hicks crosses to the rabbit box, Girl follows her.*)

MOTHER HICKS: (*Annoyed.*) I told you, I don't know. Now, cut out the jaw jacking and feed these babies, all this jabbering's gettin' them rabbits riled.
(*Mother Hicks places the eye dropper in Girl's hand and tries to get her to concentrate on the rabbits. Girl still wants answers.*)

GIRL: You *could* teach me things.

MOTHER HICKS: (*Exasperated.*) I wish someone had taught you how to feed a rabbit, you're squirting it up its nose! I swear of all the critters I got here you make the most noise and the least sense! (*Mother Hicks stands and crosses to the bucket.*) Now, I am going to water my yarbs and I want you to stay put! (*She signs to Tuc gruffly.*) Watch her!
(*Mother Hicks exits, Girl pouts and sits in the rocking chair.*)

GIRL: Is she always so mean?

(*Tuc turns her face to look at his.*)

GIRL: Is she always so mean?

(*Tuc shakes his head 'no,' and signs something much more elaborate.*)

GIRL: I don't understand.

(*Tuc signs "Mother Hicks," but Girl does not understand until he mimes her movements and Girl figures it out.*)

GIRL: Mother Hicks!

(*Tuc teaches Girl the sign for "Mother Hicks."*)

GIRL: Mother Hicks.

(*Tuc does the sign for "earth" Girl does not understand, so he gives her hints with gestures.*)

GIRL: Dirt.

(*He continues with different hints until Girl guesses correctly.*)

GIRL: Dirt, ground, world, earth!

(*Tuc repeats "Mother Hicks" and "earth."*)

GIRL: Mother Hicks...earth!

(*Tuc nods and signs "and."*)

GIRL: And.

(*Tuc nods and sign "air."*)

GIRL: Wind, blow, all over, AIR!

(*Tuc nods and repeats all three signs.*)

GIRL: Mother Hicks...earth and air!

(*Tuc nods and signs "and."*)

GIRL: And...

(*Tuc signs "fire" and points to campfire.*)

GIRL: Fire!

(*Tuc signs "and."*)

GIRL: And

(*Tuc signs "water" and gestures.*)

GIRL: Water!

(*Tuc nods and repeats all the signs. Girl tries to copy but tries to go too fast. Tuc laughs and slows her down. Tuc signs "and."*)

GIRL: And

(*Tuc signs "blood." Girl finally guesses it.*)

GIRL: Cut, hurt...blood!

(*Tuc signs "and."*)

GIRL: And.

(*Tuc signs "tears," tracing a tear down his cheek and then down Girl's cheek.*)

GIRL: Tears.

(*Tuc and Girl repeat the whole sequence, as they do, the words and signs take on meaning and deep significance for her.*)

GIRL: Mother Hicks *is* earth, and air, and fire, and water, and blood, and tears. Mother Hicks is…

(*Tuc signs "everything." Girl does not understand until he makes a more sweeping gesture.*)

GIRL: Everything!

(*Tuc signs "yes" as the lights dim. Pause. A spot comes up on Tuc as he moves into it and signs. A Chorus member enters and speaks.*)

CHORUS: But soon there came the morning when

It was time for me to go to town again.

I didn't want to go.

I was afraid somehow they'd know

That Girl was here with us, and then

They'd make me bring her back again.

(*Tuc moves a bit nearer to her and watches her sleep.*)

That morning, before I left,

I stood and watched her sleep.

I pressed my thoughts and feelings deep

Inside my memory.

(*Lights dim on Girl. Lights quickly come up on another area of the stage which indicates Clovis' store. The following scenes are played in fragmentary rapid succession similar to the witching scene at the end of Act I. Tuc moves through the groups of townspeople catching fragments of their conversations.*)

CLOVIS: (*To Tuc.*) And where in the blazes have you been? Take a little vacation did you? This whole town's been going to Hell and my stock boy decides to take himself a vacation?

(*Alma joins them.*)

ALMA: Morning, Clovis, any news?

CLOVIS: I went to the highway patrol station on my way in this morning. They haven't seen her, but they suggested you call the State Home, they keep runaways there sometimes. I'll call if you like.

ALMA: Thank you, Clovis, I'm grateful for your help.

CLOVIS: (*To Tuc.*) I got a week's worth of stock piled up, get with it, Boy!

(*Lights up on Izzy and Alma.*)

IZZY: So, where did Hosiah off to in such a hurry?

ALMA: He's gone to Cairo, he figures that's where Girl went looking for the Hammons.

IZZY: The whole time she was with them, they just let her run wild, let all those kids run wild, just wild things! Now, I'm sure that's where she went!

ALMA: She had pneumonia, she wouldn't have made it as far as the county line!

(*Hosiah enters, Alma rushes to him.*)

ALMA: Did you find her?

HOSIAH: Fool's errand! I've been to the Cairo employment office, the welfare department, and I called every Hammon in the whole city and not one has ever heard of Jake or the Girl.

(*She turns away.*)

HOSIAH: Alma, we've tried to find her.

ALMA: Not hard enough!

HOSIAH: There's nothing more we can do.

ALMA: When our boy was born dead, there was nothing we could do. When the scarlet fever took Sarah, there was nothing we could, but this time, Hosiah, this time there *is* something we can do. We can keep looking!

(*Tuc starts to exit and Clovis crosses to him and stops him.*)

CLOVIS: Hey, hey, hey! Where do you think you're going?

(*Tuc tries to sign something.*)

CLOVIS: Don't you go waggling your fingers at me. (*Clovis finds a plug of Red Man chewing tobacco in Tuc's top pocket of his overalls.*) Got yourself a new habit, Boy?

(*Tuc shakes his head.*)

CLOVIS: Help yourself, did you?

(*Tuc indicates he paid for it.*)

CLOVIS: What's the matter with you, boy. What's the matter with you anyway?

(*Lights dim to a spot. Tuc signs, Chorus member speaks.*)

CHORUS: Home late, long into the night,
Winding up the trail in the pale moonlight
With a feeling deep inside
Makes me want to run and hide.
So, I turn…nothing.
And I turn…no one.
Then I turn and I see
There ain't no one there but me,
But I run away.

(*Lights come up on the cabin. Mother Hicks sits near the fire, brushing Girl's hair. We hear the sound of tree toads. Tuc enters at a run and grabs Girl's blanket and runs into the cabin with it.*)

MOTHER HICKS: Hey!

GIRL: What's going on?

MOTHER HICKS: I don't know, but I aim to find out!

(*Tuc runs out of the cabin.*)

MOTHER HICKS: Whoa! Care to tell me what you're doing?

(*Tuc signs, "Girl sleep in cabin."*)

MOTHER HICKS: She can't sleep in there 'cause I got a whole family of skunks that won't take too kindly to being disturbed just because you got the willies!

GIRL: What's the matter?

MOTHER HICKS: He's just got the jumps. (*To Tuc.*) Now come and eat, you got black beans…burnt black beans. Now, sit and eat before you start making me feel goosey.

(*Tuc takes his bowl of beans but keeps a watchful eye all around. Mother Hicks sits in her chair and weaves a basket. Tuc tosses Girl the plug of Red Man.*)

GIRL: Hey, thanks! You was over in town today?

(*Tuc signs, "yes."*)

GIRL: Anything going on? Anyone say anything, you know, about me?

(*Tuc pauses and signs "no."*)

GIRL: Nobody?

(*Tuc repeats the "no."*)

GIRL: My whole life, I lived in that town and now, they don't even notice once I'm gone.

MOTHER HICKS: Down in town is a might measly place.

GIRL: But it's different here.

MOTHER HICKS: Here, my walls is made of tar paper, so creatures can come and go. There ain't no keepin' out and there ain't no holdin' in.

GIRL: (*Starting to take a plug of tobacco.*) Why do the animals come here?

MOTHER HICKS: They come for the healing, when there's a fester to lance, or something broken to be bound up or cut away. They come when they can't do for themselves.

(*Mother Hicks crosses to Girl and holds out her hand for the tobacco. Girl gives it to her.*)

GIRL: And after? What happens after they's well?

MOTHER HICKS: Tuc and me, we watch 'em close and find their names, then they can go and we'll always know 'em again. (*To Tuc.*) Now you bring back that bedding, so this little chicken can roost!

(*Tuc exits into the house.*)

GIRL: What if an…animal doesn't want to go?

MOTHER HICKS: Sooner or later they do, they all do.

(*Tuc enters with blankets and crosses back into the cabin.*)

GIRL: Will you wrap me up tight in them blankets, like when I first came here?

MOTHER HICKS: Why?

GIRL: I kinda feel like I'm a little tiny worm, all wrapped up in a cocoon.

MOTHER HICKS: Well, I ain't going to be expecting no butterflies at breakfast.

(*Tuc enters with a shot gun.*)

MOTHER HICKS: And what do you think you're doing with that?

(*Tuc signs "guarding."*)

MOTHER HICKS: Guarding? Against what?

GIRL: Something's wrong isn't it?

MOTHER HICKS: Sleep tight, little Rabbit, and don't worry about nothing, lessen it's Daniel Boone over there shooting his own foot off.

(*There is a rustling sound.*)

GIRL: I heard something.

MOTHER HICKS: What?

GIRL: I thought I heard something over there.

(*Clovis steps out of shadow.*)

MOTHER HICKS: Who's there? I said, who's there?

CLOVIS: So it is you, and you've got…

(*Tuc sees Clovis and shoots the shotgun in the air. Clovis turns and runs.*)

MOTHER HICKS: Tuc, you damned fool!

(*Tuc starts to run after him and she snatches the gun away. Tuc follows Clovis.*)

MOTHER HICKS: Tuc, it ain't no use!

(*Lights dim and come up immediately on the town. In the darkness we hear the party line ring of a telephone. Spot comes up on Clovis holding a phone receiver. Lights come up on Alma and Hosiah.*)

CLOVIS: Alma. It's Clovis.

ALMA: Clovis, that's the emergency ring on the party line.

CLOVIS: This is an emergency. I found her. I found the Girl.

ALMA: Where?

CLOVIS: Up on Dug Hill.

ALMA: Was she all right?

CLOVIS: I didn't get a good look.

ALMA: I am calling the State Police. State troopers don't take too kindly to witch stories or to trespassing!

CLOVIS: Trespassing? We are talking about kidnapping.

(Lights up on Izzy, she is holding a telephone receiver.)

IZZY: We are talking about witchcraft, Clovis.

ALMA: Izzy are you on here too?

IZZY: Well of course. A body's got a right to know what is going on. So, she's up on Witch Mountain you say?

CLOVIS: Looked like she was tied up or something.

ALMA: You can sit around here jaw jacking, but I'm going up that hill.

HOSIAH: You'll do no such thing.

IZZY: Tonight? Going up there tonight?

ALMA: Don't you dare try to stop me, Hosiah Ward!

HOSIAH: How do we know she was taken up there? How do we know she didn't just go.

ALMA: We won't unless we go up that hill. *(Back into the phone.)* Will you show me, Clovis, will you lead me back up that hill?

CLOVIS: Well...Alma...I...

ALMA: Clovis, I do believe you're scared.

IZZY: It just makes sense to be scared when you're dealing with a witch.

CLOVIS: *(Into the phone.)* Dealing with a shot gun!

IZZY: She shot you with a shot gun.

clovis: Well, somebody did.

ALMA: If you won't come with me, I swear I'll go alone.

CLOVIS: Alright, Alma, I'll be right over.

IZZY: Clovis P. Eudy! If you think I'm going to go traipsing up witch mountain in my condition...

CLOVIS: Then stay behind.

IZZY: And miss everything?

(Lights out on Clovis and Izzy. There is tension between Alma and Hosiah.)

ALMA: You don't want her to come back, do you?

HOSIAH: Oh, Alma.

ALMA: Do you?

HOSIAH: Not if she's just going to leave again. I don't want her to hurt you that way.

ALMA: I'll be alright and I have to know that she's alright.

(She touches his cheek. He nods.)

HOSIAH: I'll need my climbing boots.

ALMA: Better bring mine too...And Hosiah, you better bring your gun.

(He nods and exits as lights change back to the cabin.)

(Girl is asleep on her pallet. Mother Hicks paces. Tuc enters, out of breath and signing wildly.)

MOTHER HICKS: Slow down, I can't follow you…slow down.

(*Tuc takes a breath and signs, "Many people come. Very angry."*)

MOTHER HICKS: When?

(*Tuc signs, "Now."*)

MOTHER HICKS: But why?

(*Tuc signs, "Find Girl. Have Guns."*)

MOTHER HICKS: But they ain't got no cause, they ain't got no right.

(*Girl wakes and sits up.*)

GIRL: (*Alarmed.*) What's going on?

MOTHER HICKS: (*To Tuc.*) And they've got guns? Damned fools!

GIRL: What is it? What's happened?

(*Tuc runs into the cabin.*)

MOTHER HICKS: Tuc says some folks from town are on their way up here, he says they're riled and they got guns.

GIRL: But why?

MOTHER HICKS: Something to do with you.

GIRL: Let's witch 'em. All of 'em. Let's you and I witch 'em all.

MOTHER HICKS: What did you say?

GIRL: Let's throw them a spell to turn the road to slime and let 'em slide all the way back down to Main Street.

MOTHER HICKS: Hesh up, you fool.

GIRL: You can do it, and I can help. I know who I am.

MOTHER HICKS: You don't know anything!

GIRL: Yes I do! (*Mimes the witch ritual.*)

I swear that I do give

Everything betwixt my two hands

To the ways of witchcraft.

MOTHER HICKS: (*Angry.*) Stop that jabbering!

GIRL: I want to be a witch, like you!

MOTHER HICKS: I'll tell you witches, I'll tell you witchcraft! When the fever comes and makes the babies scream and burn up in their beds and die, that can't be scarlet fever, it's a hex. When a child's born all crippled up, or blind, or deaf, it can't be because its mother took no notice of the measles, it's a spell! When the hand of God strikes a good man down, or takes away his job, it must be someone's fault, it must be witchcraft!

GIRL: But, Mother Hicks…

MOTHER HICKS: (*Turns on her.*) Don't you *ever* call me that!

GIRL: Why not?

MOTHER HICKS: When they call me that in town, they don't mean mother.

GIRL: But I do.

MOTHER HICKS: Don't you ever say that to me again. (*She turns away from Girl.*)

GIRL: (*Simply.*) But I do. I know that I am your child.

MOTHER HICKS: My child was taken.

GIRL: They say you gave her to the Devil, but I…

MOTHER HICKS: (*Deeply grieved.*) I never gave her up! I held her when she screamed. I held her all the time she cried. I held her until she died of fever!

GIRL: She died?

MOTHER HICKS: And after, I held her in my own two arms, and then I laid her in the ground all by myself.

GIRL: (*Showing her the quilt piece.*) But look at this, you know you've seen this before, it's my name here and the H…the H it stands for Hicks!

(*Girl shoves the piece into her hands. Mother Hicks looks at her squarely.*)

MOTHER HICKS: It stands for Home.

GIRL: What?

MOTHER HICKS: Illinois State Home. (*There is a pause.*) I seen this piece before. I wrapped you in it just after you was born. Your Mother came here from the State Home, scared and all alone, hardly more than a child herself. I helped her with the birthing…

GIRL: (*In disbelief.*) No.

MOTHER HICKS: She stayed a spell, but then one day she ran and took you with her. She must have left you in the town on her way to somewhere else.

GIRL: And so I am…

MOTHER HICKS: The orphan child of an orphan child.

GIRL: That's not true!

MOTHER HICKS: Yes it is, Little Rabbit.

GIRL: Witches is powerful, witches can make things happen, witches is never lonely or afraid, because they've got the power. I am your child and you are a witch!

MOTHER HICKS: I am not a witch!

GIRL: Then what are you?

MOTHER HICKS: I'm just a left over person, just like you!

(*Tuc enters with an empty box of shotgun shells.*)

GIRL: That's not true!

MOTHER HICKS: (*To Tuc.*) I threw away the shells, I was afraid someone would get hurt! (*To Girl.*) Now, they are coming for you, and you'll go back to town with them, because that's where you belong!

GIRL: *No!*

(*Girl runs into the darkness. Tuc starts after her, Mother Hicks grabs the gun from him.*)

MOTHER HICKS: Let her go, Tuc! (*Mother Hicks paces for a minute, crosses to the rocker and sits with the gun in her lap.*) Let her go.

(*Voices of the townspeople are heard coming up the Hill.*)

RICKY: (*Offstage.*) Look there, just ahead! There's a fire!

(*Clovis, Alma, Hosiah, Izzy and Ricky enter clutching flashlights.*)

ALMA: Oh my God, Hosiah, there it is!

(*Mother Hicks stands at her doorway holding the shot gun in her arms.*)

MOTHER HICKS: Stop right there. One more step and you're on private property.

CLOVIS: (*Seeing the gun.*) Uhhhhhh, beg your pardon, Miz Hicks.

MOTHER HICKS: You got exactly three seconds to get your backsides down this hill.

ALMA: We understand that you're holding a child here against her will.

MOTHER HICKS: There ain't no one here.

ALMA: The Girl's been missing over a week and…

MOTHER HICKS: That's no concern of mine.

CLOVIS: We just want to look around.

MOTHER HICKS: You got a warrant?

ALMA: (*Advancing on her.*) Please I need to see for myself…

IZZY: Don't look at her, Alma! She'll witch you!

MOTHER HICKS: (*To Izzy.*) You never change, do you? What did I ever do to you, except give you a place to put your hate?

IZZY: (*Praying as a protection.*) You know what you did. In the name of the Father, and the Son…

MOTHER HICKS: (*Shouting.*) Be quiet!

CLOVIS: Can't stand to hear the word of God?

MOTHER HICKS: Prayers used that way is blasphemy!

IZZY: You cry blasphemy after witching our children?

MOTHER HICKS: I never hurt a child!

CLOVIS: But they died, you sang to those babies and they died.

MOTHER HICKS: It was the fever!

HOSIAH: (*Gun at the ready.*) Stand aside or use that gun, but we are coming in.

MOTHER HICKS: (*Raising the gun slightly.*) What gives you the right? What gives any of you the right, to talk, and talk, and talk, and call me a witch?

ALMA: We just want the Girl!

MOTHER HICKS: (*Putting her gun down.*) What's the use? You'll take whatever you want. You'll come in here with guns and call *me* criminal!

ALMA: We just want the Girl.

MOTHER HICKS: She's not here!

ALMA: Let me look. Please, I care for her.

MOTHER HICKS: (*After a long moment.*) Then look, but just one. I won't have all of you trampling through my house.

(*Hosiah starts.*)

MOTHER HICKS: Not the one with the gun.

(*Alma starts, and Hosiah pulls her back.*)

ALMA: Who then?

MOTHER HICKS: The child.

RICKY: *Mama!*

IZZY: Lord, no. No child of mine…

ALMA: Izzy, please. She can't hurt you, Ricky. Do it for the Girl, Ricky. Dare and double dare.

RICKY: If you ever find that Girl, you gotta swear you'll tell her I did this.

(*Ricky slowly approaches the door. Animal sounds are heard as he enters. Immediately, he comes out.*)

RICKY: I'm dead, I'm killed, I'm killed, I'm dead.

ALMA: No you're not, but you smell like…

HOSIAH, CLOVIS, ALMA: Skunk!!!

RICKY: She ain't there. There's nothing in there but eyes, hundreds of eyes shinin' in the dark.

IZZY: Her incubus! The Devil animals!

MOTHER HICKS: (*This is the last straw.*) That's right! You want a witch? Then witch I'll be! When you look, you see what you want to see.

IZZY: It's a spell!

MOTHER HICKS: (*Every bit a witch.*) Get out of here, before I lock your jaw and turn your blood to poison.

CLOVIS: We don't want any trouble.

MOTHER HICKS: Then get off my property!

(*She lunges at them. Hosiah aims and cocks his gun. She faces him squarely.*)

MOTHER HICKS: And you better have a silver bullet in that gun!

(*There is a moment of tension.*)

ALMA: Hosiah.

(*He puts the gun down.*)

MOTHER HICKS: I'll count to five, and if you're not halfway down the hill by then, I'll spell you all to Sunday! *One!*

IZZY: Come on, Ricky.

(*Izzy and Ricky bolt and exit.*)

MOTHER HICKS: *Two!*

CLOVIS: We don't want any trouble.

MOTHER HICKS: *Three!*

> (*Clovis exits.*)

HOSIAH: Come on, Alma.

MOTHER HICKS: *Four!*

ALMA: I'll be right there.

> (*Hosiah steps aside but remains in shadows.*)

MOTHER HICKS: *Five.*

ALMA: She was ill. She had pneumonia.

MOTHER HICKS: Not anymore.

ALMA: (*Relieved.*) She was here! When did she leave?

MOTHER HICKS: Not long ago.

ALMA: Where...

MOTHER HICKS: I don't know.

ALMA: If she comes back, if you see her...please tell her I want her to come back.

MOTHER HICKS: I know...now, go.

> (*There is a moment of understanding between the two women. Alma turns and walks to Hosiah who takes her hand as they exit together. Tuc steps into a spotlight. A Chorus member interprets.*)

CHORUS: Four days come, and four days gone

> And she ain't here, and she ain't there.
>
> This time the Girl has disappeared
>
> I know, cause I've looked everywhere
>
> And I am used to shadows, but she's not there
>
> Or anywhere.

> (*During the end of Tuc's speech there is a sound of a train whistle and an on-rushing train. Lights come up on shadowy figure of two men warming their hands above an oil drum with a fire in it. Their tattered coats are pulled up around their faces, the glow from the drum casts weird shadows. Girl enters and approaches the men. Tentatively, she pulls on one of the men's coats.*)

GIRL: Excuse me, sir I...

MAN 1: Yeah?

MAN 2: (*Gruffly.*) Whad'da want, kid?

GIRL: Uhhh, never mind...nothing...sorry.

> (*She pulls away from them, and crosses to a group of trash cans, lifts the lid, and rummages through the trash. She finds an apple core, which she devours, and a can of beans. She runs her fingers along the inside of the can to see if there is any left. After a bit, a boy approaches the cans from the opposite side.*)

He does not see Girl. He rifles through the trash, tossing it out, and showering Girl. He comes up with a glass milk bottle.)

GIRL: Hey, watch what you're doing!

(Girl comes up swinging. She gets a good look at him. It is Howie Hammon. He drops the can lid and runs. Girl chases him.)

GIRL: Hey! Hey! Howie!

(They run past a few shanties of a "Hooverville." Girl finally catches him.)

GIRL: I always could outrun you, Howie Hammon!

HOWIE: Girl!

GIRL: Why did you run?

HOWIE: Around here, if someone yells, I always run. What are you doing here?

GIRL: I hopped me a freight train, Howie. It slowed down over to the depot to drop off the mail and I just reached out, grabbed me an armful of wind, and blew right down here to Cairo. I was scared, but I made it.

HOWIE: You come here? On purpose?

GIRL: I been lookin' all over this blamed city for you. Last four days I see things to make you to weep to think of them. People are starving here, Howie.

HOWIE: Why'd you come?

GIRL: I told you. I was lookin' for you. For you, for all your brothers and sisters, for Ella…for Jake.

HOWIE: Come on.

GIRL: What are you doing here?

HOWIE: I live here.

GIRL: Here? All of you?

HOWIE: Come on.

(He leads her a short distance to an odd dwelling that has been fashioned from Jake's truck. All that can be seen is one side of the cab with a canvas roof which extends like a lean-to.)

HOWIE: Hey, Dad?

(A voice comes from inside the cab.)

JAKE: Did you find any?

HOWIE: Dad.

JAKE: I hear they are paying a penny a piece for milk bottles.

HOWIE: Look who's here.

(Jakes emerges from the inside of the cab. He is disheveled; a bottle sticks out of his hip pocket.)

JAKE: Girl!

(Girl runs to him and hugs him hard. He barely responds.)

GIRL: I knew I'd find you. I just knew it!

JAKE: How are you, Girl?

GIRL: I'm fine.

JAKE: It's good to see you, really good. Howie, what have we got to eat?

HOWIE: (*Alarmed.*) Dad you know we don't…

JAKE: (*Ignoring him.*) See what we got to eat. I'm sure we got something to…

HOWIE: Dad…

GIRL: That's okay…

JAKE: (*To Girl.*) You must be tired; you look tired.

GIRL: I'm tired, but I'm here! I thought you'd be living in a big house with two porches, Jake.

JAKE: Howie, see if we got something, some beans or some…

GIRL: (*Sharply.*) I'm not hungry!

(*Jake turns away. There is an uncomfortable pause.*)

GIRL: Where are the others?

JAKE: Gone.

GIRL: Gone? Gone where?

JAKE: Different places.

GIRL: What?

JAKE: Ella and Becca and the baby are over at my sister's. Libby went to my aunt in Memphis. Margaret is working for some folks in Mound City. Frank's joined the CCC and is off in California or some place, and Sarah…God, where is Sarah?

GIRL: You don't remember?

JAKE: I'll remember in a minute. Howie, where is Sarah?

(*Howie takes some bottles out of his coat.*)

HOWIE: St. Louis.

JAKE: That's right. She went with a family. They wanted her to take care of their baby. Sarah was always good with babies. You remember.

GIRL: Sarah was just a baby herself.

JAKE: Anyway, they seemed like nice folks.

HOWIE: Dad, I got ten bottles; that's good, isn't it, Dad?

JAKE: Howie and I…we've just been camping out here in the car until something better comes along, eh, Howie?

HOWIE: Ten bottles is good, isn't it?

GIRL: How could you do it, Jake?

HOWIE: Last night, I only got six. Ten's much better than six.

GIRL: How could you do it?

JAKE: Do what?

GIRL: Let 'em all go like that?

JAKE: I couldn't help it.

GIRL: What about your job?

JAKE: There wasn't any job. (*Jake takes a swig out of the bottle.*)

GIRL: What about the WPA?

JAKE: I wouldn't take a hand out from those crooks in…

GIRL: (*Angry.*) I heard that already, Jake!

JAKE: (*Desperate.*) There wasn't money for food.

GIRL: But there was money for that! (*Points to the bottle.*)

JAKE: (*Defensive.*) Don't judge me. You haven't got the right!

GIRL: You had a family, but you just threw it away!

JAKE: (*Starting to cry.*) I just couldn't hold on to them.

HOWIE: Don't you talk to my Dad like that!

GIRL: You just threw it away.

HOWIE: (*To Jake.*) We're doing okay. Aren't we Dad?

JAKE: There was nothing I could do.

GIRL: You could've held on to them, no matter what. That's what I'd do.

HOWIE: Get out of here.

> (*Girl turns to walk away.*)

JAKE: Where are you going?

GIRL: (*Turns back.*) What the Hell do you *care?*

> (*She walks away without looking back. Howie turns to Jake who is weeping.*)

HOWIE: We're doing okay, aren't we, Dad? We're doing okay.

JAKE: Yeah, *Howie!*

> (*They both exit into the car as lights fade and the sound of the train is heard. Lights come up on Tuc who signs, as a Chorus member speaks.*)

CHORUS: Five days since she ran away
> But I keep looking all around.
> Down to town and back again
> The road gets longer every day.
> It was just before midnight
> I was passing the graveyard
> On my way home.

> (*Lights are dim. The crickets, a distant owl hooting, and the sound of a loon are heard. Tuc crouches in shadow. Girl enters and moves to her hiding place.*)
> (*Mother Hicks enters the graveyard and moves to the same spot she went to before. As she places the baby clothes on the ground, she speaks softly, but her words are audible.*)

MOTHER HICKS: So there you are, and don't you look something all dressed up
    to Sunday. Mind you don't get this pretty little dress dirty; I just washed it.
    (*Girl sits up.*)
MOTHER HICKS: The rabbits is fine and we got ourselves a whole family of
    raccoons.
    (*Girl moves slowly, carefully near her.*)
MOTHER HICKS: Them coons got into rat poison, I reckon; but they're doing
    fine on sour milk and apple peelings…Oh, I wish you could see them.
    (*With great grief and infinite tenderness, Mother Hicks starts to lower herself
    onto the ground. She is suddenly aware of Girl and stops.*)
GIRL: I was afraid you wouldn't be here.
MOTHER HICKS: (*Without looking at her.*) I didn't come looking for you. I had
    other reasons.
GIRL: I'm sorry for what I said to you.
    (*No response from Mother Hicks.*)
GIRL: I just needed it to be true.
    (*No response from Mother Hicks.*)
GIRL: Please, look at me.
    (*Mother Hicks looks at her.*)
GIRL: She's there isn't she? What was her name?
MOTHER HICKS: May-ry.
GIRL: Mary
MOTHER HICKS: It ain't Mary and it ain't Marie. It's May-ry.
GIRL: May-ry. (*There is a pause.*) I'm sorry I ran away.
MOTHER HICKS: They always go when they's healed.
GIRL: But I'm not healed, not yet. But I do know one thing. I know one thing
    for positive sure; someday things are going to belong to me and I'm going
    to belong to them. But there's something I need first and I won't be
    healed until I find it.
MOTHER HICKS: You look all right to me.
GIRL: I'm talkin' about something inside me, like a piece of me left out and
    wanting.
MOTHER HICKS: (*Looks at her evenly.*) You'll never find her. No matter how hard
    you look, you'll never find that poor scared rabbit that gave you birth.
GIRL: I know, that part of me isn't hungry anymore, it's just sad.
MOTHER HICKS: That woman, Alma, she cares. She wants you back.
GIRL: I know, but I can't go back there until I find what I need.
MOTHER HICKS: What?

GIRL: A name. I need a name. So, I wonder, could I have her name? Could I be May-ry?

MOTHER HICKS: That's her name, it ain't yours.

GIRL: But I wish it were.

MOTHER HICKS: (*Simply.*) Well, you can wish in one hand and spit in the other and see which gets full first.

GIRL: Could you help me find my own name?

MOTHER HICKS: (*Looks at Girl.*) I reckon I could.

GIRL: Then I can stay with you 'til we find it, just for a while?

MOTHER HICKS: Creatures come when they need a healing spell, but when it's done, they go.

GIRL: I know.

(*Tuc comes forward and signs. The Chorus enters as a group as at the top of the play. As they speak, Mother Hicks gathers up the baby clothes. Girl carefully folds the quilt piece and places it on top of the grave. She looks to Mother Hicks who nods. Girl pats the quilt piece and leaves it behind.*)

CHORUS: Mother Hicks is a witch, people say

And she lives all alone at the top of Dug Hill

And she works her magic on the town below.

When a child falls sick

And there ain't no cause

And there ain't no cure

Then everybody knows, that it's witched for sure

Mother Hicks is a witch, people say.

(*Mother Hicks extends her hand to Girl who reaches for it just as the Chorus finishes their lines.*)

(*Lights dim to black.*)

END OF PLAY